THE RISE OF
THE ENGLISH PREP SCHOOL

THE RISE OF
THE ENGLISH PREP
SCHOOL

Donald Leinster-Mackay

 The Falmer Press

(A member of the Taylor & Francis Group)
London and Philadelphia

UK   The Falmer Press, Falmer House, Barcombe, Lewes, East Sussex,
            BN8 5DL

USA   The Falmer Press, Taylor & Francis Inc., 242 Cherry Street,
            Philadelphia, PA 19106-1906

First published 1984

Library of Congress Cataloging in Publication Data

Leinster-Mackay, D. P. (Donald P.)
   The rise of the English prep school.

   Bibliography: p.
   Includes index.
   1. Preparatory schools—Great Britain—History.
I. Title.
LC58.6.G7L45   1984   372.942   84-8010
ISBN 0-905273-74-5

Typeset in 10/12 Garamond by
Imago Publishing Ltd, Thame, Oxon

Jacket design by Leonard Williams

Printed in Great Britain by Taylor & Francis (Printers) Ltd, Basingstoke

Contents

To Jewel

Fundamentum totius reipublicae est recta juventutis educatio.
[The right education of youth is the foundation of the whole republic.]

Cicero

Λαμπάδα ἔχουτες ἀλλήλοις μεταδώσομεν

[Having the light we shall share it with others]

IAPS motto

Acknowledgments

This book is the outcome of many years' research, which accounts for the prolixity of my acknowledgments. During this time I have consulted preparatory school headmasters, assistant masters and retired heads to all of whom I am grateful for either information or perceptive comment. Because of the extended period of research, several headmasters have either retired or passed on. Where I am aware of these *post hoc* developments I have indicated them.

I am grateful to: C.L. Adamson (ex-head of Bow School, Durham); the late Gilbert Ashton (former head of Abberley Hall); A.T. Barber (ex-head of Ludgrove); G.W.P. Barber (head of Ludgrove); J.N. Bartlett (head of Stoke-Brunswick); the late A.A.M. Batchelor (ex-head of Temple Grove); the late J.A.D. Bickmore (joint head of Yardley Court); T.H.B. Bowles (head of Bramcote); the late H.F. Chittenden (former head of Newlands); G.W.D. Chittenden (head of Newlands); T.V. Clough (head of Lambrook); J.F. Cornes (head of West Downs); J. Day (head of Wolborough Hill); N. Dunsmore-Rouse (ex-head of Fonthill); D. Evers (head of Lockers Park); B.C. Faulds (ex-head of Bluecoat School, Birmingham); The Hon. R.T. Fisher (head of Bilton Grange); J.V. Gane (ex-head of Marton Hall); A.D.J. Grenfell (head of Mostyn House); G.E.F. Gross (ex-head of St Piran's); R.J. Hackett (head of Hallfield); M.V.D. Haggard (head of Abberley Hall); J.R. Hall (head of Arnold Lodge); J.W. Hornby (ex-head of Clifton P.S. and recently retired Secretary of IAPS); R.N. Hutchinson (head of Dorset House); G.S. Jameson (head of Swanbourne House); D.H. Jordan (joint head of Rosehill, Tunbridge Wells); Mr C.A. and Mrs A. Malden (co-principals of Windlesham House); J.S.L. Marjoribanks (head of Sandle Manor); Klaus Marx (head of Willington); P.C.M. Mills (ex-head of Highfield, Liphook); G.D.L. Milton (head of Seaford Court); N.J. Milner-Gulland (head of Cumnor House); A.R.W. Moore (head of Stubbington House); J.P. Nelson (ex-head of Ardenhurst); M.D.K. Paterson (head of Woodcote); the Rev. D.J. Paxman (ex-Warden of St Michael's, Tenbury); A.E. Perry (head of St Piran's); D.C.S. Phillips (head of Nevill Holt); J.A.H. Porch, (ex-head of Maidwell Hall); S.J. Reynolds (head of Aysgarth); R.C.J. Robertson (ex-head of Heath Mount); the late Commander I.C.M. Sanderson (ex-head of Elstree); J.D. Sewell (head of Old Buckenham

Hall); J.S. Singleton (head of Chafyn Grove); D.W.E. Spencer (head of Amesbury); P.G. Spencer (ex-head of Red House School, Moor Monkton); D.G. Stevens (head of Chelmsford Hall); J.L. Stow (ex-head of Horris Hill); C.G. Syers-Gibson (head of The Downs, Colwall); J.M. Upward (ex-head of Port Regis); P.A. Valder (head of The Elms, Colwall); J.R. Vassar-Smith (head of St Ronan's); R.D. Vickers (head of Scaitcliffe); Peter B. Waterfield (head of The Mall); G.E. Watts (head of Hawtreys); R.N.C. Webster (ex-assistant head of Rottingdean); Michael J.C. Wheeler (head of Cheam); David T. Wickham (ex-head of Twyford); H.C. Witham (head of Widford Lodge); A.D. Wood (head of Taunton Junior School); and Paul Wootton (ex-head of Eagle House). In addition I should like to express gratitude to all other heads who completed my questionnaire(s) (1972, 1977) on their schools.

I gained considerable insights from, and wish to thank, three of the present Vice-Presidents of IAPS: R.J.S. Curtis, OBE: L.H. Hankey, OBE, and the Reverend R.G. Wickham to the last of whom I am most grateful for information about the development of science in the preparatory school curriculum. The late R. Arthur Harrison, another former Vice-President, was also most helpful and hospitable.

My gratitude is extended also to other individuals whom I have either had the pleasure of meeting or had the need to consult by way of correspondence. Among these were Professor H.C. Barnard and Dr T.W. Bamford, historians of education; Mrs Sylvia Belle, wife of the head of Orwell Park; David Cheetham formerly of Abberley Hall and secretary of SATIPS; G.W.L. Courtenay, assistant master of Cargilfield; Roger D.H. Custance, Archivist of Winchester College; Francis Davey, head of Merchant Taylors', Middlesex; Mrs. J.S. Davey, Secretary of AHMPS; Patrick Dudgeon of Dover College; Frank Fisher, Master of Wellington; Mrs Flora Forbes, widow of A.H. Forbes (ex-head of Lambrook); B.C. Harvey, Deputy Secretary of HMC; Trevor Hearl, historian of education; Dr J. Kitching, HMI, formerly of Durham University; Eric Lousada, assistant master at St Wilfrid's, Seaford; Geoffrey Place, assistant master at Mostyn House and local historian to whom I am especially grateful for his interest and enthusiasm; M.P. Rawlins, formerly Assistant Secretary of IAPS; B. Rees, head of Charterhouse; Michael Smith, ex-pupil of Moorland House; M.M. Spencer, secretary for Educational Studies, University of Oxford; Patrick Strong of Eton College; Mrs Erica Thompson, widow of ex-head of Aysgarth, and Edward Upward, author, poet and ex-schoolmaster. I am grateful also to Gabbitas Thring for observations on early preparatory school staffing.

If I have already expatiated long in my gratitude to many individuals there are yet six others to whom my special thanks are due: Professor John R. de S. Honey, who first suggested that I might study the history of the English Preparatory School; Mrs Elizabeth Sarfaty, who has been my committed research assistant for the last seven years; Mrs Marie Coyte, who has borne the main brunt of the typing with unfailing cheerfulness; Jack Dodd, Vice-President of IAPS, whose conscientious and painstaking reading of my manuscript has contributed so much to its improvement and the elimination of many infelicities; Emeritus Professor Harry Armytage, of Sheffield University, who gave me kindly advice and strong encouragement in the final stages of the production of this book and my wife, Jewel Leinster-Mackay, who has read patiently my several drafts and given sound critical advice.

I have visited libraries, record offices and archives and wish to record my gratitude to the staffs of these institutions. My thanks are due, therefore, to the staffs of: the Bodleian Library; the Birmingham Reference Library; the British Library; Cambridge University Library; Durham County Library; the Greenwich Local History Library and the Malvern, Newcastle upon Tyne and Royal Leamington Spa Libraries. I am especially grateful to the staff of the Reid Library of the University of Western Australia for securing for me through the Inter-Library Loans Service, many locally unobtainable items, thus demonstrating that handicaps of distance can be minimized. I have found particularly helpful in Western Australia the *Preparatory Schools Review* on microfilm from the British Library. Mrs Cynthia Hollie (of IAPS) also, by acting as my agent for the transmission and collection of questionnaires, demonstrated the possible minimization of handicap created by distance. In addition, I wish to thank the staffs of Durham County, Northamptonshire, Warwickshire, and Worcestershire Record Offices for ready access to their records.

Three institutions other than libraries and record offices have considerably aided my labours: the former City of Birmingham College of Education (now part of Birmingham Polytechnic) by allowing my sabbatical leave in 1971 to complete my PhD on the English Preparatory School; the Department of Education in the University of Western Australia, by affording me very generous research funding and typing assistance from Miss Ebe Dolzadelli, Mrs Dorothy Atkinson and especially Mrs June Giles, to whom I am grateful for their patience in deciphering my sometimes strange hieroglyphics; and the Australian Research Grants Council (now the Australian Research Grants Scheme) by partly financing my project in 1980.

I publicly acknowledge the help and interest of all the aforegoing individuals and institutions towards any merit in this book; its imperfections I reserve for myself alone.

Abbreviations

The following is a check-list of abbreviations used in the text. Common abbreviations such as HMS, FRS and so forth have been omitted.

AHMPS	Association of Headmistresses of Preparatory Schools	HMC	Headmasters' Conference
AHPS	Association of Headmasters of Preparatory Schools	IAPS	Incorporated Association of Preparatory Schools
AMA	Assistant Masters' Association	ICS	Indian Civil Service
		IEA	Institute of Economic Affairs
APS	Association of Preparatory Schools	ISIS	Independent Schools Information Service
ARP	Air Raid Precautions	ISJC	Independent Schools Joint Council
APSSM	Association of Public School Science Masters	JET	Joint Educational Trust
		JSC	Joint Standing Committee
ASPS	Association of Staffs of Preparatory Schools	LEA	Local Education Authority
BAAS	The British Association for the Advancement of Science	MOSA	Medical Officers of Schools Association
		MMA	Music Masters' Association
CEE	Common Entrance Examination	OPS	Oxford Preparatory School
CEO	County Education Officer	OTC	Officers' Training Corps
DCPS	Dulwich College Preparatory School	PNEU	Parents' National Education Union
DES	Department of Education and Science	PSA	Private Schools' Association
DNB	Dictionary of National Biography	PSR	*Preparatory Schools Review*

PPSYB	Public and Preparatory Schools Year Book	SIC	Schools Inquiry Commission or Taunton Commission
SATIPS	Society of Assistants Teaching in Preparatory Schools		

List of Tables and Figures

Tables

Figure

Introduction

In estimating the value of the various steps in a boy's bringing-up, and their respective influence on his character, the period which he spends at a preparatory school is generally disregarded in a most unaccountable way. (*The Saturday Review*, 7 February 1880)

Strange as it may seem to readers familiar with preparatory schools today, there has hitherto been no published history of the English preparatory school. This gap in English educational historiography is even more surprising when it is recalled that since 1816, when R. Ackermann wrote the *History of the Colleges of Winchester, Eton and Westminster, etc.*, many works have been written on the English public school. Yearly the volumes grow in number; meanwhile the English preparatory school remains virtually ignored. Symptomatic of this neglect is the comment with which Jonathan Gathorne-Hardy begins his book, *The Public School Phenomenon:* 'With this book I *complete* [my italics] a study begun some years ago with *The Rise and Fall of the British Nanny*.' Gathorne-Hardy claimed that his was the most complete history of the English public school because it included girls' and progressive schools; nevertheless, he gave only limited attention to the infrastructure of preparatory schools which serve to feed the public schools. At least half a dozen significant general histories of the English public school, together with other volumes dealing with specific aspects of their history, were published in the 1970s and Dr John Rae's book on *The Public School Revolution* appeared in 1981. This preoccupation with public schools underlines the need to pay similar attention to the preparatory schools which are an integral part of the public school system.

The lack of a comprehensive history of preparatory schools has not gone unnoticed. Professor John R. de S. Honey, in *Tom Brown's Universe* (1977), adumbrated the need for greater knowledge concerning preparatory schools for an understanding of the Victorian public school. The present work aims to make good this gap in educational historiography.

The interpretation of the history of the English preparatory school to be found here is the result of thirteen years' study involving visits to individual preparatory schools and to the headquarters of the Incorporated Association of Preparatory Schools (IAPS) to examine school and Association archives. Institutional and personal links between public and preparatory schools have been established by the examination of the admission registers of certain public schools, whilst a study of *The Times* and the *Preparatory Schools Review* (*PSR*), of school histories, of biography and autobiography has brought to light much valuable information about these underpublicized institutions. Of particular value has been the Report, *Preparatory Schools* [Vol. 6], published in 1900 by the Special Office of Inquiries and Reports of the Board of Education to which volume [Sir] Michael Sadler contributed as editor. This Report examined many facets of preparatory schools at the turn of the century and was an amalgam of contributions from many preparatory school heads and one or two private and public schoolmasters.

Commentary on the English preparatory schools, however, has not been completely absent. In 1966 Mr Philip Masters, a then practising headmaster, attempted in *Preparatory Schools Today* to give a justification of the preparatory schools through a detailed analysis of their contemporary functions and characteristics, but he did not attempt a major historical perspective. More recently the late Mr Arthur Harrison in *How Was That, Sir?* (1975) attempted to provide that historical perspective largely by quoting from the *Preparatory Schools Review*, which yielded several very valuable insights into leaders of the preparatory school world since 1895. Harrison's own rich experience of preparatory schools supplemented the data found in pages of the *PSR*. But this again was not a preparatory schools' history. Even more recently the late Mr A.A.M. Batchelor in *Cradle of Empire* (1981) has alluded to the links between English preparatory and public schools and the British Empire in the nineteenth and early twentieth centuries, but his work was essentially concerned with the history of Temple Grove School. By way of contrast this present work is a more formal history, recognizing the 'mediaeval' and the 'modern' or the difference between the Victorian practice of the earlier schools and the modern pragmatism of preparatory schools today. It considers the origins of preparatory schools going back beyond the nineteenth century. It recognizes that the schools at the beginning and towards the end of that century differed greatly in ethos. The earlier schools were institutions where harsh discipline and Spartan conditions prevailed and contrasted greatly with schools in the last quarter of the century when conditions had improved to such a marked degree that some critics complained of their 'propagating hot-house plants'. The emerging preparatory schools of the early nineteenth century prepared boys for entry to the Royal Navy as well as to public schools; this association with the Royal Navy continued into the twentieth century.

After examining the contributions to the development of boys' preparatory schools of those women, constrained to earn their own living, and of indigent or scholastically-inclined clergy, this book considers other major factors leading in the late nineteenth century, to their consolidation epitomized in the setting up of the Association of Headmasters of Preparatory Schools (AHPS) in 1892. By 1914 this process of consolidation was virtually complete.

After dealing with the institution of the common entrance examination (1903) — intended to alleviate the burdens on the preparatory schools caused by the subject demands of the many public schools — I am concerned to show how the classics were replaced, first by English in the 1920s as the core subject then by science in the 1960s and 1970s. Other areas of the preparatory school curriculum to be highlighted are music and the arts in which the preparatory schools have been pioneers responding to general educational theory of the pre- and post-war periods. Organized games and the emergence of alternative physical activities are seen as reflecting concurrent developments in the public schools.

Preparatory school assistant masters have often shown themselves to be devoted teachers but their pedagogic role and their relationship to their headmasters have changed: like the headmasters, they have now organized themselves into a highly operative association.

Since the 1920s the preparatory schools have experienced in turn 'the economics of hard times' brought on by the depression years and a declining birth rate; they have experienced war-time evacuation and its many exigencies and the feeling of 'post-war euphoria', caused by increasing demands for preparatory and public school education. Since the 1960s, however, their existence has been under some political threat from the Labour Party which seeks their abolition as well as that of the public schools as institutions outside the maintained educational system. The penultimate chapter examines their response (and that of other independent schools) to this threat in the form of ISIS (the Independent Schools Information Service), whilst the last chapter considers the possible impact of vouchers on their existence.

Prologue: Whatever Happened to Mr Wratislaw?

Prologues precede the piece — in mournful verse;
As undertakers — walk before the hearse.
(David Garrick, *Apprentice*)

As the pendulum of educational opinion (if the Plowden Report is anything to go by) swings back to the view that the academic die of boys and girls is cast before the age of eight — indeed if not before the age of five — attention has switched to what happens in school before and after those ages. This is especially so since parents are now so much more interested in what the schools can do that they are having to be promised a much greater say in what schools intend to accomplish for their children — a promise which might well be implemented by the issue of educational 'vouchers' enabling them to choose their own schools.[1] If the opposition from the teachers' unions to such vouchers is to be evaded, there have to be schools in the private sector which would accept those vouchers. These already exist in the shape of preparatory schools. Yet whereas books about 'public schools' are continually exfoliating, those on preparatory schools are singularly rare, and even those which do appear are but pious histories of particular schools.

The purpose of this book is to remedy that gap. Painstakingly compiled from 'customers' opinions' as expressed in autobiographies of pupils and masters, and from biographies of the great and good that have attended them, it eschews high-flying theories and sticks to attested facts. It is neither an apologia for, nor a polemic against, the most neglected institution in the variegated British educational system and the author hopes that those who read it will not hesitate to communicate with him if they have had personal experience of, or think they have information about, any school, mentioned or unmentioned, in the following pages.

But first we must agree on what constitutes a 'preparatory' school. In the nineteenth century the adjective 'preparatory' was often used interchangeably with 'private'. Thus the private school at Ilminster,[2] attended in 1830 by the eight-year-old Edward Thring, the future headmaster of Uppingham, was in later terminology clearly a 'preparatory' or at least a 'quasi-preparatory' school (a term we examine in Chapter 2). But in 1830 it was indistinguishable in name from other private schools which were *not* necessarily preparing young boys for entry into the 'great' or 'public' schools.

'Preparatory' in the nineteenth century covered both its present English and American meanings: the former connoting schools educating young boys before they went to a public school; the latter, schools preparing boys for university. Accepting this two-fold meaning of the term, it is easy to see why historians have hitherto fought shy of attempting a synoptic history of preparatory schools, as they have equally willingly written books on the collectivity of public schools, board schools, grammar schools and, indeed, universities.

Linked to this qualitative problem is one of numbers. It is extremely difficult to uncover any reliable statistical material. In estimating the number of preparatory schools in England at any point in the nineteenth century (as with secondary schools) one is not only hampered by the elasticity of terminology[3] but also because it is difficult to differentiate between an instructional group and a school. Indigent clergymen (like Dr Thomas Arnold with his large family) might have regarded their part-time pedagogical activity as 'taking in a few pupils', or they might have regarded it as 'keeping a rectory school'. Where can the line be drawn? How can acceptable statistics be given about the number of preparatory schools at any one time in the absence of any definition of a school and in the presence of such vagueness in terminology? But one thing we do know. The large rectories of Victorian England were an ideal setting for such activities.

But what about 'dames', those 'surplus women' of the nineteenth century who made a living this way? Indeed they had to, for the surplus grew as men were siphoned off to foreign parts. They actually called their establishments 'preparatory' even though they did not prepare boys for public schools. As many entries in nineteenth century county trades and commercial directories indicate, especially those for counties containing large conurbations such as Birmingham, these were not preparatory schools in the 'classical' sense: they prepared children of tradesmen for a life above that of the 'common' herd who went to the 'National' or the 'British' schools. Since they confound the unwary and sabotage efforts to compile reliable statistics, I have examined only schools[4] known to be 'preparatory', that is, they prepared boys between eight and thirteen for the public schools and the Royal Navy.[5] Working back from statistics of private schools given by [Lord] Bryce in 1895—some 15,000—it is apparent that preparatory schools were many fewer,[6] and also many fewer than the more conservative estimate of 6209 private schools cited by a survey conducted two years later by the Education Department.[7] The latter survey is important in that the AHPS participated in it.[8] Then over 200 strong, the AHPS helped to uncover the existence of some 6209 'private' schools, 1958 of which were boys' schools, 3173 girls' and 1078 were mixed. But boys' preparatory schools — both inside and outside the association — could not have constituted many more than 400 in 1900, according to Mr C.C. Cotterill, the Hon. Secretary of the AHPS. As the return of 1897 itself suggested: 'No clear line can be drawn between the case of a gentleman who takes a number of private pupils into his house, and that of one who teaches a similar number of pupils, but calls his establishment a school.'[9]

Eleven years later in *John Bull and His Schools* (1908) W.R. Lawson expressed himself satisfied with its exhaustive inventory, crediting it with including 'practically every kind of upper class school in England and Wales [*sic*] not receiving State aid. It extends from Eton to the smallest private school of which any record can be obtained.'[10] But the man ultimately responsible for the return, Mr (later Sir) George Kekewich, ruefully confessed that the whole matter was exceedingly obscure.

By the beginning of the twentieth century both public and preparatory schools recognized their mutual inter-independence and the latter were regarded as being a very important part of the public schools' infrastructure. Despite this seemingly natural coalescence the process was by no means inevitable. The divergent origins of the two types of school could have been a major factor militating against such a union as could also have been the preparatory schools' nineteenth (even twentieth) century connections with the Royal Navy. Curricular requirements, for example, by the Royal Navy could even have had a negative influence on the gradual coalescence of preparatory and public schools during the second half of the nineteenth century.

There were, however, several strong reasons for public and preparatory schools becoming one articulated system. The older public schools had long employed dames to look after some of the non-academic aspects of the boys' lives. At Eton, for example, dames even kept boarding houses, the last being 'Evans', owned by a Miss Evans as late as 1906.[11] Moreover, women had long been regarded as being specially suited to looking after young boys. It was therefore very natural for many women, with a need to earn an income, to turn to the teaching of the very young sons of gentlemen in the eighteenth and nineteenth centuries. The schools they ran were known by contemporaries as 'dame-preparatory' schools (see Chapter 7). During the nineteenth century some of these dame-preparatory schools gradually established themselves as feeder-schools of public schools but many of the dames, because of their lack of a classical education, ran schools preparatory to the emerging Classical Preparatory schools. In modern terminology they would be called 'pre-preparatory schools'.

The second propellant of the preparatory school was the indigent clergyman. As early as the eighteenth century they began to absent themselves from their parishes to become full-time private classical schoolmasters,[12] preparing boys for entry to the universities. Now, with the 'revival' of the endowed grammar schools and the growth of public schools in size and numbers, it was increasingly difficult to take in private pupils as did the Reverend William Gilpin,[13] Vicar of Boldre in the New Forest, whose school at Cheam later crystallized into a 'famous' preparatory school. Other private classical schools had grown so large that they demanded the total attention and time of the clergymen[14] if they were to be conducted professionally. This, however, did not prevent other private classical schools being conducted in rectories, preparing a handful of pupils for public schools. Thus Highclere, another eighteenth century school, developed boarding house extensions attached to the rectory, and so would have been rather atypical in the nineteenth century. Other rectories, with their many rooms, were generally large enough for the relatively small number of pupils. The emergence in the early decades of the nineteenth century of the all-age private classical schools such as Twyford and Temple Grove (concentrating on the education of younger boys) set an example to clergymen who began to specialize in a like manner. By the 1830s, therefore, such private classical schools had ceased to be rivals to the public schools. Cheam, on the other hand, did not become fully preparatory until 1855 (see Chapter 10).

A third contributory factor in the emergence of preparatory schools as a recognized avenue to the public school was even simpler: public school assistant masters began, for one reason or another, to set up their own schools, retaining links with their former schools either by naming their school after their public school (as did the Reverend Herbert Bull of Wellington House, Westgate-on-Sea) or by association (as did Mr Alfred Kirk of Arnold House, Leamington) — or in a more concrete way by sending boys in large numbers to their former public schools (as did the Reverend Lancelot Sanderson, former assistant master of Harrow School and headmaster of Elstree from 1869 onwards).

Although the rise of the preparatory schools occurred later than that of the public schools, the one being determined to a larger extent by the other, both rode on the national expansion to empire and industrial hegemony. Ironically the Industrial Revolution was at the heart of this, as with other scholastic booms. The newly prosperous classes of early and mid-nineteenth century England hungered for gentility — or for their sons' acquaintance with the genteel — which the preparatory schools were eager to supply. The *nouveau riche* wanted 'polish'; the lower middle class wished their children to rise in the world. Hence the emergence of day preparatory schools whose ethos was less pretentious than some of the earlier boarding type preparatory schools I have mentioned.

Just as the railways 'made' Rugby, so the spread of lines made it possible for the preparatory schools to flourish in large numbers during the 1860s and 1870s, for those were the years when competitive examinations began to bite deeply into *family* 'connections'. The *new* 'connection' was to go to a school or coach which catered for these life hurdles. Wishing to gain an academic reputation in the light of parental demands for results in public and university examinations, many public schools now began to offer scholarships.[15] Alongside these highly competitive scholarship examinations, the public schools also introduced entrance examinations. As a result the judicious parent who wanted a son to attend a public school would first send him to a preparatory school, in much the same way as his contemporaries sought for their sons' entry to the

Army or the Indian Civil Service (ICS) by sending them to a 'crammer'.[16] Parents soon realized that a preparatory school was the best way of assuring entry, especially in view of the relationship that certain preparatory schools had established with certain public schools.[17]

The rise of the public schools themselves, therefore, constituted a most important factor in the rise of the preparatory schools. Notwithstanding the already ample publication on the subject of public schools, there is still need here for a brief consideration of their growth in the nineteenth century in relation to preparatory schools. In the early years of the century, there were but a handful of 'great' schools, sometimes called 'public schools', which enjoyed national reputations by dint of recruiting boys from all parts of the country. According to Sydney Smith, writing in the *Edinburgh Review* in 1810, a public school was by definition 'an endowed place of education of old standing, to which the sons of gentlemen resort in considerable numbers and where they continue to reside, from eight or nine, to eighteen years of age'.[18] The reference to eight- and nine-year-old boys is of great significance for us since it establishes, early in the century at least, a shared responsibility between public and 'private' schools for the education of very young boys before it became the peculiar responsibility of preparatory schools. Such 'public' schools, according to R. Ackermann, their first historian, were limited in number to nine: Winchester, Eton, Westminster, Charterhouse, St Paul's, Merchant Taylors', Harrow, Rugby and Christ's Hospital. Eight of these nine schools were to be, later in the century (1861–64), the subject of investigation by a Royal Commission, chaired by Lord Clarendon, which was to give them thereafter a permanently high-ranking scholastic status. The exclusion of Christ's Hospital from the Clarendon Commission's investigation and the inclusion of Shrewsbury School reflected both the continuing eleemosynary character of Christ's Hospital in mid-century and the successful opposition of Samuel Butler, headmaster of Shrewsbury (1798–1836), to the earlier omission of his school from being categorized as a 'public school', implicit in Henry Brougham's abortive Bill of 1820.[19]

The public schools had been subject to much criticism from the *Edinburgh Review* in the early years of the nineteenth century and later from *The Westminster Review*, which circumstance no doubt contributed to their institutional instability. The numbers at the public schools during the early years tended to fluctuate quite considerably. The reforms initiated by Samuel Butler at Shrewsbury and by Thomas Arnold at Rugby contributed possibly to the wider acceptance by society of these schools, despite the obloquy in influential journals of keen critics such as Sydney Smith and Henry Brougham.

The Clarendon schools were Anglican and endowed but it was not long before schools, neither Anglican nor endowed, were founded to meet the demands from a socially mobile populace for a classical education. At least two major ways of financing such schools consequently emerged. Some schools, such as Mill Hill, the nonconformist school founded in 1807, were founded on public subscription; others, such as Cheltenham College (1841) and Marlborough College (1843), were founded on a joint-stock basis and became leading proprietary schools.[20] Thus to the nine Clarendon schools were added proprietary schools such as Cheltenham (1841), Marlborough (1843), Rossall (1844), Wellington (1853) and Malvern (1862); revived endowed grammar schools such as Repton (1557), Uppingham(1584) and Sherborne (1550); denominational schools such as Stonyhurst (Roman Catholic), Kingswood (Methodist) and Bootham (Quaker); and private schools such as Bradfield (1850) and Bloxham (1860), owned initially by private individuals. To these generic groupings of nineteenth century public schools must be added two discrete systems of Anglican schools: the Woodard Schools such as Lancing, Hurstpierpoint and Ardingly, inspired by the Reverend Nathaniel Woodard; and the County Schools, such as West Buckland School and Elmham School (now defunct), the creations of the Reverend Joseph Lloyd Brereton.[21] There was, therefore, a great burgeoning of English public schools during the middle decades of the nineteenth century, culminating by the end of the Victorian period in what Honey has described as 'the public schools community'. This 'godly and manly' community was based firmly on the institutions of games,[22] religion and chapel.

This nineteenth century process affected the growth of preparatory schools. Because public schools entered a period of renewed prosperity during Victoria's reign there was a tendency for them to become large institutions. Arising from the size of large institutions there was seen to be a need for preparatory schools to shelter the shorn lamb from the rigours of a senior school.

Thomas Arnold was averse to the presence of very young boys in his school. This was one of the bones of contention between him and Mr W.F. Wratislaw, a Rugby parent and solicitor, which brought them to court.[23] The Wratislaw case exemplified two complementary aspects in the development of public schools in the nineteenth century — the provision of a non-classical education in response to local demand and the education of very young boys — both of which directly affected the development of preparatory schools, although in the case of the former aspect this can be only conjectured.

There had been a tendency for the parents of boys attending locally endowed schools to exert pressure on the schools to vary the classical curriculum to include commercial subjects. The classic example of this was the Leeds Grammar School case of 1805 which had led to Lord Eldon's judgment.[24] This judicial pronouncement safeguarded the classical curriculum of many grammar schools for at least three decades. But the insistent demands of locals for a non-classical education for their sons, based on rights enunciated by the founders' wills, was often deftly avoided by the device of setting up a second school on the foundation to meet these lower middle class aspirations. Three products of this sloughing off process were Alleyn's School (on the same foundation as Dulwich College); the Lawrence Sheriff School (on the same foundation as Rugby); and the John Lyon School (on the same foundation as Harrow). In the case of Tonbridge two schools were formed — the Skinners'

School and the Judde School — to retain the scholastic purity of the old foundation. It can be inferred that at the end of the century these new 'second grade' schools contributed to the eventual demise of many private adventure schools by offering a commercial curriculum on terms of keen financial rivalry. This in turn led to several private schoolmasters becoming purely 'preparatory' schoolmasters. J.V. Milne, for example, kept a private commercial school at Henley House, Kilburn,[25] but later moved to Westgate-on-Sea in Thanet, Kent, where he set up a preparatory school at Streete Court in 1894. After purging his original school of day boys over fourteen, Milne had a nucleus of ten boys with which to start his new school. It prospered and increased to fifty: an average size for a preparatory school in the late nineteenth century. As his more famous son, A.A. Milne, observed, he was 'convinced' that there was no future for his sort of private school. The only privately-owned school which could now succeed was the preparatory school for boys under fourteen.[26]

It was the second aspect of the Wratislaw case, however, which was more closely connected with the early development of preparatory schools. Arnold was one of the first to realize that small boys of eight or nine who had been traditionally taught their early letters in school with senior boys, were probably better off segregated. It is no accident therefore that in the year 1837, when Arnold abolished his Form 1, there opened on the Isle of Wight (where Arnold was born) a school which was later to be recognized as the first English preparatory school.

Notes

1 Cf. A.C.F. Beales, *et al.* (1967) *Education: A Framework for Choice*, Old Woking, Institute of Economic Affairs.
2 G.R. Parkin, *Edward Thring, Headmaster of Uppingham School: Life Diary and Letters*, Macmillan & Co. p. 12.
3 Cf. Admiral Sir William Goodenough, (1943) *A Rough Record*, Hutchinson p. 12. Goodenough not surprisingly hesitates in his description of Temple Grove and other 'preparatory' schools in 1875. He writes: 'Temple Grove, then, with Eagle House and Hawtreys, among the — what shall I call them? — better known *private* schools of the day. . . .' Cf. also the article in *The Saturday Review*, 7 February 1880, 'Private or Preparatory Schools', 49, 87, p. 175. The AHPS on the other hand was angry with the Bryce Commissioners for failing to make the distinction.
4 Cf. Appendix, 'Preparatory Schools Founded in the Nineteenth Century'.
5 Cf. Chapter 3.
6 The Bryce Report figures were based mainly on the estimates of the College of Preceptors and the Private Schools Association which, in turn, based their estimates on trade lists for Longmans and Macmillans, booksellers. These lists are no longer extant.
7 Its full title is: *Return of the Pupils in Public and Private Secondary and Other Schools (Not Being Public, Elementary, or Technical Schools) in England (Excluding Monmouthshire) and of the Teaching Staff in Such Schools on the 1st June 1897.*
8 Although preparatory schools catered largely for boys between the ages of eight and thirteen they were nevertheless regarded as 'secondary' by the Committee of Council on Education. In 1897 the term 'secondary' had class connotations which

were only fully removed by the 1944 Education Act, which reorganized education in England and Wales into three consecutive stages. By this act preparatory schools became independent primary schools.

9 P.P. 1898 Return, p. 564.

10 W.R. LAWSON (1908) *John Bull and his Schools*, Edinburgh, Blackwood and Sons p. 42.

11 J.D.R. McCONNELL, *Eton, How It Works*, Faber & Faber p. 26.

12 NICHOLAS HANS (1951) *New Trends in Education in the Eighteenth Century*, Routledge and Kegan Paul, pp. 117–135.

13 Cf. EDWARD PEEL, *Cheam School from 1645*, Gloucester, Thornhill Press pp. 35–6.

14 Laymen also conducted private classical schools but the majority of private classical schoolmasters were clergymen. (Cf. Appendix 1 of NICHOLAS HANS, *op. cit.*, pp. 221–42.

15 See Chapter 8.

16 Cf. D.P. LEINSTER-MACKAY (1981) 'Competitive examinations in Victorian England: The development and decline of "cramming",' *ANZHES Journal*, 10, 1, Autumn, pp. 24–34.

17 See Chapter 8.

18 Article III Remarks on the System of Education in Public Schools, *Edinburgh Review*, vol. 16, 1810, p. 327.

19 Brougham's Education Bill of 1820 set out to introduce reading, writing and accounts in English endowed grammar schools to remedy deficiencies in the teaching of young boys. Cf. J.W. ADAMSON (1930) *English Education 1789–1902*, 1964 ed., Cambridge University Press pp. 53–5.

20 Cf. D.P. LEINSTER-MACKAY (1981) 'English proprietary schools: A Victorian marriage between commerce and education,' *Education Research and Perspectives*, 8, 1, June, pp. 44–56.

21 Cf. J.R. DE S. HONEY (1977) *Tom Brown's Universe, The Development of the Public School in the 19th century*, Millington pp. 47–103.

22 Cf. J.A. MANGAN (1981) *Athleticism in the Victorian and Edwardian Public School*, Cambridge University Press.

23 Cf. T.W. BAMFORD (1960) *Tomas Arnold*, The Cresset Press pp. 128–42.

24 Cf. R.S. TOMSON (1970) 'The Leeds Grammar School Case of 1805', *Journal of Educational Administration and History*, 3, 1, December, pp. 1–6.

25 J.V. MILNE, father of A.A. MILNE, was an autodidact who took up teaching without any degree. By slow stages he gained a London BA [H.G. WELLS was once a master at MILNE's School in Kilburn] Elected as Hon. Secretary of the Private Schools' Association (PSA) in 1888, MILNE was later twice President of the Association which he had helped to organize initially. It is interesting to see J.V. MILNE dilating on similar topics in the journals of the PSA and the AHPS.

26 A.A. MILNE, (1939) *It's Too Late Now*, Methuen p. 84.

Part 1
Emergence

1   Beginnings

A child that has gone thro' this essay, and been successful in these initial and preparatory studies; that has made himself well acquainted with his Mother Tongue; learnt some general rules of Grammar; and attain'd a Degree of Knowledge above his age; will soon adorn the school he enters.
(From Anonymous (1732) *A Thought Relating to Education Offered to the Examination of Such As Have Noblemen or Gentlemen (from Age of 8–12 aut circiter) under Their Care*, London)

And that God which cause the immense rivers to flow from small spring-heads, vouchsafe to blesse these weak beginnings in tender age, that good learning may proceed hence to its full perfection in riper years.
(Charles Hoole (1660) *A New Discovery of the Old Art of Teaching School*)

Catholic Conception

A strong case has been made that the English preparatory school originated within the structure of seventeenth century Roman Catholic education.[1] For having to operate a private system of education from the time of the passing of the Elizabethan penal laws (1563–93) until their abolition in 1791, wealthy catholics found it both expensive and inconvenient to send their sons to schools like Douai (1568) and St Omer (1592) on the continent and, as the penal laws relaxed, sent them to 'illegal' schools in England.

The first of these 'illegal' schools — Silkstead, close to Winchester — had been opened during the reign of James II, and moved to Twyford[2] in Hampshire in c.1692. It would seem that after the school moved to Twyford it became concerned largely with the education of younger boys. Linking Twyford School with another Catholic school founded in 1749 by Bishop Challoner[3] (at Standon Lordship, Hertfordshire), E.H. Burton, Challoner's biographer, wrote:

> The success of Twyford showed that there were many Catholics of good position who did not wish to send their *younger boys* [my italics] across the seas ... it was desirable that a new school should be established within a convenient distance of London.[4]

Within twenty years the school at Standon Lordship was moved to Old Hall, Ware,[5] to become a harbour of refuge for English boys forced to return to England because of the French revolution. A copy of 'Rules of Standon School' dated 1799 indicates that amongst officials of the school at the end of the eighteenth century was a 'Superior of the Preparatory School'.[6] This suggests that Ware did not entirely lose its original function as soon as the senior boys arrived from the continent. Other early Catholic 'preparatory' schools were to be founded at Sedgeley Park (1763),[7] Bornhem House Academy (1797) at Carshalton[8] and Tudhoe Academy (1797) in County Durham.[9]

The Catholic 'preparatory' schools were the first schools in England to manifest all three principles (see below) of *separation, preparation* and *rustication*, characteristic of later orthodox English preparatory schools. For this reason these Catholic schools must take a prime place in any examination of preparatory schools' antecedents.

Native Roots

Of course there were other precursors. We can identify the basic essentials of preparatory school education — namely (i) the preparation of the young eventually to take their places in institutions largely concerned with the teaching of the classics;[10] (ii) the separation of young from older boys for education in discrete institutions; and (iii) the boarding, mainly in the country, of young boys for this purpose[11] — quite early. These three characteristics of preparatory schools, designated above respectively as the norms of 'preparation', 'separation', and 'rustication',[12] can be seen in early elementary, writing or ABC schools;[13] song schools; and petty schools. Each of these three earlier types of school has something in common with the later preparatory school.

Indeed school was perceived as being mainly *preparatory* before Tudor times, that is, for future study of the classics in a grammar school. And in Tudor and Stuart times both Richard Mulcaster[14] (1530–1611) and John Brinsley[15] (1585–1665) assumed that the elementary school and its curriculum of reading, writing, drawing and music formed a necessary foundation for those going on to study the classics. Thus the mediaeval elementary school paralleled the modern preparatory school in its norm of *preparation*.

The second precursor (of this section) — the mediaeval song school — was, in Foster Watson's words, 'the most important type of elementary school before the Reformation'.[16] Like other elementary schools, the song schools provided a rudimentary education for those who later were to study the classics. The learning of Latin antiphons by rote provided a preparation, of a kind, for future studies in Latin and the classics. After some while there began to emerge in the elementary or song school an 'upper division'[17] which was concerned overtly with those going on to study in a cathedral or grammar school. In such cases the nexus between cathedral or grammar schools and song schools clearly anticipated the later links between public and preparatory schools.

With regard to the third precursor, it is significant that Foster Watson used the terms 'petty' and 'preparatory' synonymously when dealing with Charles Hoole's 'small treatise' on the petty school[18] in *The Old Grammar Schools*.[19] Clearly, Foster Watson, who died in 1929 and lived well into the period of twentieth century institutionalized preparatory school development, was not strictly equating preparatory schools with petty schools. Nevertheless, his synonymous use of the terms suggests that he recognized the similarities between the two institutions. After being initially part of the grammar school set-up in post-Reformation England, the petty school master, by the seventeenth century, was teaching his pupils in a separate school building. It seems likely that one of the main agents of change in this evolution of the petty school was the increasing pressure of the university on the grammar school. There is a familiar twentieth century ring about Foster Watson's point concerning academic pressures from the universities:

> With good and advanced pupils to teach and a small staff ordinarily consisting of a master and an usher for teaching them, the work of preparation for the University of senior pupils became impossible if *there were 'petties' requiring the instruction which preceded the learning of Latin Grammar* [my italics].[20]

Because of such pressures, schools like Alford Grammar School (Lincolnshire) and Merchant Taylors' School (Middlesex), anticipating Arnold in the nineteenth century, refused to admit pupils who had not mastered the rudiments.[21] This rejection of the 'petties' by the endowed grammar schools led to the emergence of private schools catering for them, a development which has close parallels with the emergence of dame/preparatory schools (see pp. 15 and 91–101). It also provides us with a fourth norm — absent before but essential in the eighteenth, nineteenth and twentieth centuries — *the private profit motive*.

So far, apart from the Roman Catholic schools, consideration has been given only to schools which, though sharing characteristics with preparatory schools, had no ontogenic ties. We now turn to three directly-linked antecedents: Christ's Hospital's Hertford division; private classical schools; and dame preparatory schools.

The Example of Christ's Hospital

From its foundation in 1552, Christ's Hospital had two schoolmasters to teach the petties their ABC.[22] It is not known for certain when the school began to use the three Hertfordshire villages or towns of Hoddesdon,[23] Ware[24] and Hertford to cater for the youngest children destined for Christ's Hospital, Newgate Street.[25] But there is evidence to show not only that Christ's Hospital nurses were operating in Hertfordshire at the time of the Great Fire of London (1666)[26] but also that earlier, in the 1650s, pupils had been attending school in Hertford as part of the Christ's Hospital system.[27] It was customary for boys to spend two or three months at Hertford until such time as they became proficient in reading and writing, when they went on to the senior school.[28] This pattern continued up to 1891, with few going straight to the senior school without first spending some time at Hertford.[29]

Between 1680 and 1682 the three provincial branches of Christ's Hospital were merged into the one establishment at Hertford which served both boys and girls. In 1781 the boys at Hertford began to learn the rudiments of the classics with the appointment of a grammar master. Christ's Hospital classical preparatory school can be dated from this appointment.[30] The Governors inspected the school once a year. A few days later, wagon-loads of boys and girls would be taken to London.[31] If Charles Lamb in *Christ's Hospital Five-and-Thirty Years Ago* and Leigh Hunt in his *Autobiography* are to be believed, the three or four months at Hertford helped to shelter the shorn lambs (no pun intended) from the rigours of harsh public school life.

From this brief examination of Christ's Hospital in Hertfordshire it is clear that, as in the Catholic Schools of Twyford and Standon Lordship, all three criteria of preparatory schools, namely *separation, preparation* and *rustication*, can be seen operating from an early date.

The Private Classical School

In his pioneer study, *New Trends in Education in the Eighteenth Century* (1951), Nicholas Hans drew his readers' attention to the existence in the eighteenth century of private classical schools[32] which differed both from the contemporary private academies and from the endowed grammar schools. By contrast with the private academies offering a wide utility-based curriculum, the private classical schools were concerned with a traditional curriculum and with entry to the universities. They differed from the typical local endowed grammar schools in having a more wealthy clientèle and in being generally boarding in character. For those wanting a liberal education in the classics, these private classical schools formed an alternative to the endowed grammar and 'great' or 'public' schools. It is thus irrelevant to consider them in relation to the norms of 'separation' and 'preparation'. However, since most of these private classical schools were boarding schools, they met the third criterion of *rustication*, which has been postulated several times as being one of the essential characteristics of nineteenth century preparatory schools. Moreover, they exemplified the fourth characteristic which became an essential feature of the nineteenth century preparatory school emerging as an identifiable new form of educational provision: they were run for *private profit*.[33] The importance of the classical schools such as Cheam School competing with the public schools rather than providing them with pupils cannot be overestimated in any consideration of the origins of the English preparatory school. Moreover, as we shall see in the next two chapters, they were adaptive products of their age, adjusting to the new circumstances of the early nineteenth century and giving themselves a new preparatory role in a changing educational world.

The Dame Preparatory School

Whereas the surviving private classical schools[34] changed their function roughly in mid-century by preparing younger boys for entry into public schools rather than preparing older boys for entry into university, the dame/preparatory schools upgraded their educational activity to meet a demand for nineteenth century preparatory schools as the century progressed. It is likely, however, that many of the dame/preparatory schools did not cater for the full age-range, their pupils being of an age equivalent to that of the younger boys in preparatory schools or to that of pupils of pre-preparatory schools. In such schools the sons of gentlemen gained a grasp of the rudiments of learning before going on to the classical preparatory school to begin their study of the classics. In these cases the dame/preparatory school can be seen to be performing the function of the petties in the seventeenth century. Although contemporaries were probably happy in their use of the term 'dame' to describe the nature of these quasi-preparatory schools, the educational historian of the English preparatory school, as indicated in the Prologue, is likely to have difficulty in examining the records, since the term was applied to a wide spectrum of schools from unpretentious little back street schools in industrial towns such as Birmingham[35] to modish establishments in spa towns such as Malvern and Leamington and in seaside resorts such as Eastbourne and Brighton. These schools will be examined more closely in Chapter 7 when we come to examine the role of women in the development of preparatory schools. Suffice it to say at this stage that the dame/preparatory schools were an integral part of preparatory schools later in the nineteenth century not only satisfying the criteria of *separation, preparation* and *rustication* but also showing the common characteristic of the *private profit motive*.

The Process of Change

Because the emergent preparatory school of the nineteenth century had precursors in preceding centuries and because some of them such as the private classical school and the dame preparatory school could be regarded as directly lineal forbears, it is very difficult to identify the *first* English preparatory school *per se* if a condition of such identification is that the school should satisfy all the

later assumptions about what constitutes the modern preparatory school. It is
not till late in the nineteenth century, when public schools *per se* ceased to take
boys at an early age;[36] when other schools ceased to include the preparation of
boys for public schools as one of their functions; and when parents[37] began to
seek some protection for their sons of tender years that it becomes possible to
discern clearly what is meant by an English preparatory school. Even though
such a school was still generically referred to as a 'private school', several such
schools had been in existence for some years.

In *Preparatory Schools Today*, Philip Masters records that of the 494
preparatory schools in his survey, 204 claimed foundation before 1900. Of
these

22	(4.5%) were founded before 1800
15	(3.0%) were founded between 1801 and 1850
47	(9.5%) were founded between 1851 and 1875
120	(24.0%) were founded between 1876 and 1900

The figure of twenty-two foundations before 1800 is astonishing: nearly
all such schools were probably cathedral or choir schools.[38] Although founded
in earlier centuries, these schools did not become preparatory schools till the
late nineteenth century, and only two were members of the Association of
Headmasters of Preparatory Schools (AHPS) by the end of the century.[39]
Masters' other statistics for the nineteenth century are more valid and show a
very slow pace of growth in the first half of the century, with a significant
acceleration in the third quarter which developed into a gallop in the last
quarter. It was only in the last twenty-five years of the nineteenth century that
the preparatory school became firmly established and institutionalized.

By mid-century the days of the private classical school, as an all-age
institution in competition with grammar schools, were numbered. Some clergy
in country rectories[40] continued, as they had probably done since the seventeenth century, to prepare boys in classical studies for the universities. But
many were turning also to the preparation of younger boys for public schools.
With the introduction of middle class examinations in the 1850s, such schools
acquired yet another function, so that in the 1860s and 1870s many hybrid
schools existed with a three-fold function of preparation for public school, for
public examinations and for public service. It was from these hybrid schools,
from the country rectories, from private coaching establishments[41] and from
the upper-class dame schools that 'quasi-preparatory' schools emerged in the
decades of the mid-century.

The Importance of Clarendon

The middle years of the century were the watershed of the development of the
preparatory schools. The term 'preparatory' was used then less precisely. The
Rev. J. Pycroft referred in 1843 to the custom of using the term for a finishing

school for young gentlemen.[42] On the other hand, the Rev. William Pound, writing in 1866, did *not* use this term to describe schools preparing young boys for public school: instead he adopted the term 'Intermediate'[43] to indicate schools intermediate between home and public school. This does suggest continuing variation in terminology in the mid-century.

But the *Clarendon Report* (1864) was in no doubt about the nomenclature of the schools from which public schools recruited most of their boys. Not only did it discuss the age of transfer from preparatory to public school but it also considered preparatory schools' deficiencies.[44] Whatever its strictures, the Report recognized the need for the *separate* treatment of young boys. In recommending the separation of the Lower School from the Upper School at Eton, the report declared that: 'the care and instruction of little boys is as important and, in some cases, as difficult as the care and instruction of older boys';[45] but at the same time great incentive was given to the private preparatory school by the fact that the boys in the Lower School at Eton 'should have no preference over the boys from private schools in the admissions to the Upper School.'[46]

The Schools Inquiry Commission, reporting four years later, also recognized that *separate* schools were needed for the teaching of boys going on to first grade schools and that such preparatory schools already existed.[47] For example, in his Report on Surrey and Sussex Mr Giffard gave a profile of fifteen preparatory schools in his area, with valuable details about their sizes, their fees and the subjects they taught.[48]

If the Clarendon and Taunton Commission Reports were clear as to the discrete existence of a *genre* of private school, sometimes called 'preparatory', it would seem the Bryce Commission of 1894/95 enquiring into English Secondary Education was not: they seemed to ignore them.[49]

They were ignored initially, however, not because they were thought not to be a type of private school different from schools whose heads were members of the Private Schools Association,[50] but because there was some doubt as to their 'secondary' nature.[51] As Chapter 11 suggests, the AHPS was constrained to make the claim rather forcefully before it was finally accepted that preparatory schools were 'secondary' schools.

The Profit and the Loss

There was no shortage by the end of the century of individuals willing to take up the venture of preparing boys for the flourishing public schools. But there is some conflict of opinion as to the profitability of such preparatory institutions. Although the will of Mr A.H.A. Morton, a successful preparatory school-master, was executed with a net personalty of £145,473 in 1913,[52] this was no doubt exceptional. According to Mr R.J.S. Curtis,[53] the charge was never high nor the profit large, as 'anyone can discover for himself who cares to look up at Somerset House the estates left by preparatory school proprietors in the last hundred years.'[54] On the other hand the scholastic agency Gabbitas-Thring suggests[55] that as there is no record of such schools closing in large numbers it can be assumed that a private preparatory school was a profitable undertaking, at least for the headmaster. The continuing rise in the supply of preparatory schools up to the First World War seems to confirm this.

From this examination of the origins and development of preparatory schools in the nineteenth century and earlier it can be seen that the educational historian needs to adopt, perhaps, the term 'quasi-preparatory school' to describe schools of a preparatory nature during the first six decades after the end of the Napoleonic Wars. This need is based on the realistic assumption that it is paradoxical to perceive the rise of the English preparatory school *before* there was any significant increase in the size and number of English public schools. As David Ricardo observed in another context: 'a commodity is not supplied merely because it can be produced, but because there is a demand for it.'[56] Thus it was in the development of English preparatory schools.

The Four Stages of Development

To recapitulate, there were four main stages in the development of nineteenth century 'quasi-preparatory' and preparatory schools. Stage 1 was the period up to about 1830, by which date a few private classical schools had abandoned their previous practice of preparing some or all their boys for university and were concentrating largely if not exclusively on preparation for the great schools. Stage 2 was the period up to about 1865 when many other private schools followed suit, causing them to be recognized officially by the Clarendon and Taunton Royal Commissions as 'preparatory' for public schools. Stage 3 was the period ending in 1892, by which time other private schools and schoolmasters had turned to preparatory schooling because of competition from revived endowed grammar schools and higher grade schools following the Endowed Schools Act of 1869 and the Elementary Education Act of 1870.[57] Stage 4 was the period after 1892 when the institutionalizing of preparatory schools as a *genre* of school had been formalized by the setting up of the AHPS. This evolution can perhaps be shown diagrammatically as in Figure 1.

Against such a background of stages of development, it can be seen that some schools satisfied the criteria entitling them to be regarded as preparatory

Figure 1. Evolutionary Stages of the Preparatory School

1800–1830	Private
1830–1865	Quasi-preparatory
1865–1892	Preparatory
1892+	AHPS → (IAPS)

schools in the modern sense long before those norms were themselves generally recognized.

It was calculated at the beginning of the twentieth century[58] that some £1,320,000 was being spent per annum by parents on preparatory school education at more than 200 preparatory schools. By 1899 there were 228 preparatory schools[59] in Great Britain represented in the AHPS and there are grounds for believing that as many again existed which were not members.[60] By the end of the nineteenth century the English preparatory school was firmly established. The rest of this book seeks to examine more closely the shape of that development.

Notes

1 Cf. *The Preparatory Schools Review (PSR)* June 1939, 12, 133, pp. 54–5. Cf. also the thesis of F.C. PRITCHARD (1938) *The History and Development of Boys' Preparatory Schools in England*, MA London, pp. 21–2.

2 The Roman Catholic School at Twyford was attended by ALEXANDER POPE. During the early eighteenth century it declined and was finally closed when the Jacobite rising of 1745 rendered Catholics in England suspect of treason. The Catholic School at Twyford is not linked with the early nineteenth century preparatory school in the same village. Cf. Chapter 2.

3 Cf. E.H. BURTON (1909) *The Life and Times of Bishop Challoner (1691–1781)*, 2 vols, Longmans & Co. Vol. 1, pp. 290–4.

4 BURTON, *ibid.*, Vol. 1, p. 290. H.O. EVENNETT in *The Catholic Schools of England and Wales* (1944) Cambridge University Press cites the foundation as 1753 following the earlier dating by Mgr. BERNARD WARD in *History of St Edmund's College* Kegan Paul (1893).

5 The school, no longer preparatory in character, continues to exist as St Edmund's College, Ware, Hertfordshire.

6 F.C. PRITCHARD, *PSR, op. cit.*, p. 55.

7 Boys at Sedgeley Park were aged between six and fourteen. This school was also founded by BISHOP CHALLONER.

8 Cf. A.S. BARNES, (1926) *The Catholic Schools of England*, Williams and Norgate pp. 93–4.

9 *Ibid.*, p. 113.

10 This was an essential characteristic of preparatory schools until the mid-twentieth century.

11 Preparatory schools have, until recently, been predominantly boarding institutions (cf. Chapter 10).

12 Frequently the rustication took a 'littoral' form, with a preparatory school being set up at the seaside to enable its pupils to benefit from the bracing air (cf. Chapter 10).

13 'Elementary' was a generic term which described those schools which were severally called Reading School, Writing or ABC School. Often those who taught and were taught in such schools were called abcdarians.

14 Cf. RICHARD MULCASTER (1582) *Elementarie* and (1581) *Positions*.

15 Cf. JOHN BRINSLEY, (1612) *Ludus Literarius*.

16 Cf. FOSTER WATSON, (1968) *The English Grammar Schools to 1660*, Frank Cass p. 142., originally published in 1908.

17 Childrey School, founded in 1526 in Berkshire, was an early example. Cf. A.F. LEACH, (1915) *The Schools of Mediaeval England*, Methuen p. 300. NICHOLAS

ORME (1973) in *English Schools in the Middle Ages*, Methuen, refers to the Childrey School as being a chantry school.

18 CHARLES HOOLE, MA (1610–67) educational writer, Master of Rotherham School, later kept a private Grammar School in Lothbury Garden, London and was author of *A New Discovery of the Old Art of Teaching Schoole* (1660) of which 'The Petty-School' formed a part.

19 FOSTER WATSON, *op. cit.*, p. 101.

20 *Ibid.*, p. 155.

21 JOHN BRINSLEY in *Ludus Literarius* (1612) strongly advocated the exclusion of petties from the grammar school. This sentiment of course provided him with a *raison d'être* for his scheme of elementary instruction for petty schools in Chapter 10 of his book.

22 FRANCES M. PAGE, (1953) *Christ's Hospital Hertford*, Bell & Sons p. 15.

23 Hoddesdon Grange, in the same village, became a well-known Victorian preparatory school under the Rev. C.G. CHITTENDEN.

24 It is astonishing that Ware should be a focal point for early preparatory school history in providing school sites not only for pioneer Catholics but also for Christ's Hospital.

25 G.A.T. ALLAN, (1937) *Christ's Hospital*, Blackie & Son p. 19.

26 FRANCES PAGE, *op. cit.*, p. 25.

27 It is known that in 1653 boys, boarding out with nurses, attended the school of Mr AARON PETERS at Hertford. PETERS seems to have been considered the first headmaster at Hertford, where his name is recorded on the school boards in the main hall. Cf. F.M. PAGE, *op. cit.*, p. 29.

28 Cf. THOMAS BALSTON, (1952) *William Balston, Papermaker*, Macmillan p. 2.

29 E.H. PEARCE, (1901) *Annals of Christ's Hospital*, Methuen p. 167. Cf. also GEOFFREY RAWSON, *Sea Prelude* Edinburgh & London Blackwood & Son pp. 3–5. RAWSON was at Hertford for a year between the ages of nine and ten. Cf. also HAROLD E. HAIG BROWN (Ed.), (1908) *William Haig Brown of Charterhouse*, Macmillan p. 2. HAIG BROWN went to Hertford at the age of ten in 1833 before going to Christ's Hospital.

30 F.M. PAGE, *op. cit.*, p. 43.

31 E.H. PEARCE, *op. cit.*, p. 167.

32 Cf. HANS, *op. cit.*, Chapter 6, pp. 117–35.

33 The exceptions to this generalization were the junior schools of public schools which were not typical of most of the nineteenth century preparatory schools.

34 Many of the more famous private classical schools, such as Mr ELWELL's School at Hammersmith, the Rev. BARRON's School at Stanmore and Dr HORNE's at Chiswick, did not adapt sufficiently to survive into the late nineteenth century. Others, such as Cheam, Temple Grove and Twyford Schools, ceased to teach older boys.

35 The nineteenth century commercial and trade directories of, for example, Birmingham, are replete with the names of so-called 'preparatory' schools, run by women, whose pupils were *not* destined for the newly emerging English public schools.

36 Examples from the *DNB* show that, until the mid-nineteenth century and beyond, young boys were accepted by public schools, e.g. ROBERT MOBERLY (1845–1903), theologian and son of GEORGE MOBERLY, went to Winchester aged eleven; the bibliographer, ROBERT PROCTOR (1868–1903), entered Marlborough at the age of ten; ALFRED LYTTELTON (1857–1913), lawyer and statesman, went to Eton in 1868 at the age of eleven; ROBERT BRIDGES (1844–1930), poet laureate, was sent to Eton in 1854 at the age of ten. Eton still receives boys at the age of twelve. Cf. *The Clarendon Report* (1864) Vol. 1, p. 93: 'Hardly any age is considered too early, nor any age (under fourteen) too late, for admission into the Lower School (Eton). Boys

may enter as soon as they are able to read; and they in fact enter, not unfrequently [*sic*], at seven years old.' Cf. also ANTHONY TROLLOPE, (1883) *An Autobiography*, Edinburgh p. 4. He joined Harrow in 1822 at the age of seven. Cf. T.W. BAMFORD (1974) *Public School Data*, University of Hull, p. 33 and Tables 9 and 10, pp. 35–7. BAMFORD's statistics include public school junior school boys and therefore do not invalidate the general point.

37 It was customary for the Victorian middle and upper class mother to regard the early schooling of her children, boys as well as girls, as one of her concerns. Father had more say about the public school his son was to attend.

38 Unfortunately the questionnaire papers upon which the figures of this survey were based were confidential in that code numbers were used by the schools. It must be assumed that those who claimed pre-1800 foundation were not answering *qua* early *preparatory* schools foundations.

39 *Viz.*, Llandaff Cathedral School and St George's, Windsor, Cf. Chapter 10.

40 See Chapter 6 for the role of rectory schools in the evolution of the English preparatory school.

41 The history of private coaching establishments is a much neglected area of educational historiography. Examples of coaches who became preparatory school masters are: The Rev. C.G. CHITTENDEN of The Grange, Hoddesdon (1854), who had been an assistant coach to the Rev. FRANCIS J. FAITHFULL (Cf. Chapter 6); Lt C.R. MALDEN RN of Windlesham House (1837), who had been a coach before setting up his school.

42 J. PYCROFT, (1843) *On School Education* Longmans, p. 37.

43 WILLIAM POUND, (1866) *Remarks upon English Education in the Nineteenth Century*, Rivingtons p. 26 and *passim*.

44 *Clarendon Report*, Vol. 3 p. 122, Minutes 3736–7, Rev. E. COLERIDGE; Vol. 3, p. 182, Minute 5294, Mr E. WARRE.

45 *Ibid.*, Vol. 1, p. 110.

46 *Ibid.*, Vol. 1, p. 109.

47 Schools Inquiry Commission (SIC), Vol. 1, pp. 88–9.

48 *Ibid.*, Vol. 7, p. 172, Table N.

49 See p. 000.

50 The main private schools' organization, 1880–1900. Cf. GORDON B. ROBINSON (1971) *Private Schools and Public Policy*, Loughborough University of Technology, pp. 1–36.

51 'Secondary' status was by no means a clear-cut issue at the end of the nineteenth century. Cf. R.P. SCOTT (1899) *What is Secondary Education?* Rivingtons. The Bryce Commissioners also discussed the meaning of secondary education.

52 Cf. *The Journal of Education*, September 1913, Jottings, p. 626.

53 Formerly Headmaster of Hurst Court Preparatory School, Ore, Sussex, now Vice-President of the IAPS.

54 R.J.S. CURTIS (1957) *The Future of Independent Schools*, University of Sheffield Institute of Education, Occasional Paper No. 3, penultimate page.

55 From correspondence in the author's possession dated 25 August 1970.

56 DAVID RICARDO, (1821:1911) *Principles of Political Economy and Taxation* Dent p. 373.

57 The Elementary Education Act of 1870 led to the development, within a decade, of controversial higher grade schools teaching more than just elementary school subjects. Rate-aided and grant-attracting higher grade schools posed a great threat to endowed grammar schools, to private adventure and commercial schools. The 1902 Education Act was the death knell for many of the latter.

58 SPENCER WILKINSON (Ed.) (undated, c.1902/03), *The Nation's Need*, Archibald Constable & Co. p. 171.

59 As per list published by the *PSR*, 1, 12, pp. 110–12, March 1899. Strictly speaking headmasters and not schools were registered with the AHPS.
60 Women principals were excluded from the Association. The Committee of Council on Education, in its returns of 1897, noted the existence of 6209 private schools including 1958 boys' schools. Commenting on these statistics in its quarterly journal, *The Record*, the National Association for the Promotion of Technical and Secondary Education estimated that there were 589 boys' preparatory schools (Vol. 7, 1898, p. 305).

2   The Question of Precedence

It is a maxim, that those to whom everybody allows the second place, have an undoubted title to the first.
(Jonathan Swift, *A Tale of a Tub*)

Like the claret their customers drank, the age of preparatory schools was not unconnected with their status. Far from age being 'academic', personal contact with headmasters of some of the oldest preparatory schools has indicated great interest in this practical issue. Semantically, however, the question 'Which was the first preparatory school?' is not the same as 'Which is the oldest preparatory school?' For the latter assumes a continued or renewed existence to the present day, whilst the former could include defunct as well as extant schools. So the answer to the second question is a simple one: the school which, irrespective of when it became a preparatory school, has the earliest foundation date. This is the York Minster Song School, founded in 627. Thus Cheam School (1645), founded over a millennium later and the oldest of the more famous preparatory schools, is firmly deprived of a title to which it might otherwise have had some claim.[1] More controversial is the question 'Which was the first known school to possess essential preparatory school characteristics before those characteristics or criteria had been generally accepted in the late Victorian period?'

The difficulty of answering this, in view of the changing nature of so many nineteenth century schools, accounts for the extended debate in both *The Times* and the *Preparatory Schools Review*.[2] And apart from certain schools mentioned in their columns there are others which can support a claim for being the first preparatory school. Twyford and Standon Lordship, the earliest Roman Catholic 'preparatory' schools, and the Hertford Division of Christ's Hospital are in the running, as must also be the quasi-preparatory classical schools and dame schools of the early nineteenth century. Other claims to the distinction of being the first preparatory school have been made on behalf of schools both extant and defunct: Cheam must be again considered as must Hazelwood (1819), Twyford (1809) and Temple Grove (1810); Laleham (1819) and Windlesham House (1837); so must The Elms, Colwall (1614); Woodcote

(1816); Heath Mount (c.1817); Fonthill (c.1820). The foundation dates of at least three other schools are very early if obscure: Dorset House School (? early nineteenth century); Elstree and Cordwalles (? late eighteenth century).[3]

The ensuing examination of these groups will show that either Twyford or Temple Grove has claim on being the first preparatory school.

Group 1

Although the Catholic schools of Twyford (c.1692) and Standon Lordship (1749) share many characteristics in common with later preparatory schools, they seem to be disqualified on several grounds. First, they were not linked with an English 'public' or 'great' school system but with an expatriate one on the continent. Secondly, they were founded as a result of *religious* rather than *private profit* motivation. Thirdly, their aim was *physical* protection against persecution rather than *moral* protection (the separation of smaller from older boys). Despite some similarities these early Catholic quasi-preparatory schools were far less like the 'orthodox' private preparatory school than were the later Catholic preparatory schools of Mr Roper at Ladycross, Seaford (1894) and of Mr Patton at St Anthony's, Eastbourne.[4]

The Hertford Division of Christ's Hospital also seems to be disqualified despite its early foundation date (c.1652) and two entries in the *Dictionary of National Biography* (*DNB*) which refer to the 'preparatory school' at Hertford: it was not 'preparatory' for any other school and it was part of an endowed establishment. On the other hand a claim can easily be sustained that the Hertford Division was the first junior school of a public school. But the junior schools established later in the nineteenth century were not regarded as anything but rivals to the more orthodox private preparatory school. As such, Christ's Hospital's preparatory school must be discounted.

The private classical schools, although antecedents of the late nineteenth century preparatory school, were not all embryonic preparatory schools. Most of them epitomized in education the Darwinian principle of the survival of the fittest, since only those survived which were able to adapt to the changing situation. One of the most famous of these early classical schools not to survive was Dr Nicholas's Academy at Ealing.[5] As J.L. May suggests, 'In the early days of the nineteenth century no private educational establishment enjoyed a higher reputation than did the Academy for Young Gentlemen carried on at Ealing by the Rev. George Nicholas, D.C.L. of Wadham College.'[6] There were several other significant private classical schools which flourished in the early nineteenth century but failed to adapt or to continue into the late Victorian period: Bayford School, Hertfordshire;[7] Dr Dempster's, Dr Everard's and Dr Lee's of Brighton;[8] Dr Horne's of Chiswick; Dr Ruddock's of Fulham; Dr Burney's of Greenwich; Mr Elwell's of Hammersmith;[9] Dr Hooker's of Rottingdean; the Rev. Barron's of Stanmore; Dr Curtis's of Sunbury; and the Rev. Roberts's of Mitcham and later of Brighton. Most, if not all, of these schools, catered partly for the younger boy. Most of them established links with certain public schools. For example, Roberts at Mitcham prepared boys specifically for Eton and had 'a great reputation'. Both Edward Pusey and the 14th Earl of Derby were at Mitcham, and both went to Eton as a natural progression.[10] Despite the fact that several of these schools catered for the English nobility[11] in their early years, their *main* function was to provide a complete classical education. As such, they were rivals rather than feeders of the public schools. For this reason they must also be disqualified as potential 'first preparatory schools'. Only those classical schools which managed to adapt, such as Twyford, Temple Grove, Cheam, and Eagle House, can be considered.

There is no evidence in the *DNB*, or known evidence in biographies or school records, of an early dame/preparatory school which could compete for the distinction of 'the first preparatory school'. There was no Bathsua Makin[12] in the early nineteenth century to compete with schoolmasters in the early education of public school boys. Dame/preparatory schools were likely to cater, in any case, for the youngest boys. For example, Sir Sydney Waterlow,[13] 1st Baronet and Lord Mayor of London, the son of a philanthropist and prosperous member of a City Guild, went first to a dame's school in Worship Street before going to a boarding school at Brighton. It is not until much later in the century that we find women running classical preparatory schools.[14]

Group 2

The second category of candidates (those schools for whom no claim has previously been made) can be considered more expeditiously. All (except perhaps Fonthill) possess an Achilles' heel in that, although they all have an early foundation date, none was an overtly preparatory school till a much later date. The Elms, Colwall[15] in Hereford-Worcestershire, founded in 1614, was recognized during a Board of Education inspection in 1931 as 'one of the oldest preparatory schools in the country', yet its existence as a preparatory school dates back officially only to 1867 when the Rev. R.O. Carter, the then headmaster of the Walwyn Free School, asked permission from the Worshipful Company of Grocers, Walwyn's executors, to build his own private school *in tandem*.[16] Under the Rev. R.O. Carter (1863–76) and his successor the Rev. Charles Black (1876–1910), Colwall, the Walwyn Free School and the Colwall 'Grammar School' co-existed successfully with the one headmaster.[17] There are good grounds for assuming an earlier date for a private preparatory school at Colwall, since the Charity Commissioners inspected Colwall School in May 1855 and found sixty-one boys between the ages of six and fourteen years in a private school run by the resident Master in old buildings attached to the foundation school,[18] but even with this earlier dating it is clear that Colwall cannot be considered as one of the very earliest preparatory schools.

Woodcote School at Windlesham, Surrey, existed as early as c.1816, as a pre-Sandhurst academy.[19] The Rev. Dr James Pears, the headmaster, had been Professor of History at the Military College when it was situated at Great Marlow, but had left in 1809/10 to go into partnership with a certain Mr Knollis, the principal of a quasi-preparatory school in Maidenhead for entrants to the RMC. The Duke of Clarence, later William IV, sent his sons to this school.[20] Pears transferred the Maidenhead School to Woodcote in 1816, building a front block on to an old hostelry called the 'Pelican Inn' to form the new school. By 1823, however, Pears was finding it difficult to sustain a living, possibly because of the school's disadvantageous links with the now obsolescent RMC in the peace following the Napoleonic Wars. Pears closed down Woodcote School and became headmaster of the King Edward Grammar School in Bath. In 1851 his son, the Rev. James Robert Pears, returned to Woodcote House with thirty-four boys and set up a clearly recognizable preparatory school. Such a date, although relatively early, is not early enough for Woodcote School to be regarded amongst the earliest of preparatory schools. Among the boys who came with the Rev. James R. Pears was C.B. Fendall, who married a Miss Pears and later took over the school. It was he, in partnership with C.S. Jerram, who turned Woodcote into a very successful late Victorian preparatory school.

Heath Mount School, Hertfordshire, was originally sited and founded in Hampstead in 1817[21] for the education of young gentlemen. By 1824 this Academy, re-named Heath Mount Academy, was run by a Mr Lawrence to prepare boys for various trades and professions.[22] By the 1860s the school was run as a 'commercial academy' by Mr Alfred Ray even though the curriculum was largely classical and the boys wore Eton suits and silk hats for special occasions. It was not till the school was taken over by the Rev. C.F. Walker in 1882 that Heath Mount could be regarded as a preparatory school.[23] Heath Mount can therefore be discounted from our present consideration.

Fonthill School (1820) probably started in a very modest way when a certain Rev. Dr George Radcliffe opened a coaching establishment in the parish of St Edmund, Salisbury. No records exist to substantiate the date of the school's opening, but 1820 is the foundation date that has always been quoted by the Radcliffe family. The diocesan archives indicate that George Radcliffe held no ecclesiastical office in the diocese before his appointment as chaplain to the Bishop of Salisbury in 1833. It is known, however, that he lived in Sarum from as early as 1808, since the baptismal records show that his children were baptised in the parish of St Edmund from that date onwards.[24] From such circumstantial evidence it can be surmised that from c.1808 the Rev. George Radcliffe ran a coaching establishment. It was not necessarily for boys of preparatory school age, although Sir Charles Lyell, the famous geologist, was a pupil of Radcliffe before leaving at the age of thirteen for Dr Bayley's Classical School at Midhurst. By 1820 Radcliffe's establishment had grown from a handful of pupils to become a recognizable school. No evidence has been unearthed to establish the age-range of the boys at the school in 1820. It is difficult, therefore, either to reject or accept the notion of Fonthill's being a preparatory school in the 1820s. Whilst accepting the 1820 date as being the officially recognized foundation date, it would perhaps be prudent to regard the early 'forties as being the time when Fonthill became a preparatory school *per se*, that is, a little while after George Radcliffe's son, the Rev. William Coxe Radcliffe, was preferred to the living of Fonthill Gifford (1839) and when the son enabled the father to retire by taking his boarders into his newly acquired Fonthill Gifford Rectory. William Coxe Radcliffe and his wife (m.1840) added a new wing to the rectory and filled it with boys. As far as is known, these were boys of preparatory school age, who were to become Etonians, Wykehamists and Marlburians.[25] If, then, Fonthill became a preparatory school sometime between c.1820 and c.1840, it has a high place in seniority amongst preparatory schools.

Cordwalles, called St Piran's since 1919, is possibly one of the oldest preparatory schools, but its origins are shrouded in mystery. Although situated in Maidenhead since 1873, when the Rev. T.J. Nunns re-founded the school, Cordwalles has an existence going as far back possibly as the end of the eighteenth century. The last issue in the nineteenth century of the *Cordwalles Chronicle* (December 1900) claimed that the school had 'existed over a hundred years'. The editorial of this last copy made no extravagant claims as to the school's being a preparatory school for a hundred years: it was merely a private school. It was, however, in the editorial's definition of a private school — 'a school where boys of all ages were to be found whose parents did not care for the then existing roughness of Public School' — that its quasi-preparatory nature can be perceived. Younger boys were more likely to be sent to such schools in larger numbers than older boys, because older boys would have been more able to look after themselves. Hence the practice gradually grew up of sending young boys to private school before public school. Cordwalles was such a school.

The records at St Piran's School are scanty concerning the existence of the original Cordwalles before 1873. But one very significant link emerges. Cordwalles originated in Blackheath,[26] and the claim has been made that it was the school which Benjamin Disraeli attended.[27] This was the school kept by the Rev. John Potticary at the beginning of the nineteenth century, and as such was one of those early private schools in competition with public schools. A consideration of all the available evidence must lead us to the conclusion that Cordwalles was one of those schools of Stage 3 of preparatory schools' development to which I alluded at the end of the last chapter.

Elstree School seems to have some considerable similarity to Cordwalles. Like Cordwalles it was a mid-Victorian re-foundation, having been restored to health and prosperity by the Rev. Lancelot Sanderson.[28] Like Cordwalles, Elstree was probably founded in the eighteenth century. Again, the records are very scanty. Very little is known about Elstree before 1869 except that from 1842 a certain Rev. Rowsell ran a small school at Hill House, Elstree, before it was taken over in 1848 by a far more successful schoolmaster called Dr Leopold Bernays who sent boys from Elstree to Harrow.[29] This suggests that

Elstree was, at least by mid-century, a quasi-preparatory school. There is some evidence, however, for a school at Elstree in the late eighteenth century, since it is claimed that in 1798 the schoolmaster of Elstree, in the absence of the Rector, gave orders for the bells to be rung to celebrate the victory over the French in the Battle of the Nile.[30] Moreover, it has been suggested that the schoolrooms at Elstree, built on to the original mansion, were probably added in 1781.[31] There is an old print of Elstree Hill House (c.1835) with several boys in front of it wearing Eton suits and tam o'shanters, which is evidence for a school at Elstree in the late 1830s. This scanty evidence suggests that there has been a private school at Elstree since the 1780s, and that by the 1840s this school had become preparatory for Harrow.

The last school to be examined in this second category of quasi-preparatory school is Dorset House, Bury Manor, in Sussex, which has had a very chequered career, having moved site several times during its existence. It is linked with Elstree School in some way.[32]

The case for the early existence of Dorset House as a school rests primarily on (a) scanty knowledge about a certain Robert Wilkinson who was Head-master of Totteridge Park and whose family tree is given in Appendix 2 and (b) knowledge gleaned from entries in the *DNB* of the existence of a school at Totteridge Park in the early 1820s and possibly earlier. It is known that in the 1820s the Rev. Abel Lendon, curate of Totteridge, was preparing some boys for Westminster School. The future Cardinal Manning was a pupil of Lendon at Totteridge, as were also the sons of Richard Bagot, the Bishop of Oxford 1829–45.[33]

There are at least seven entries in the *DNB*[34] for boys who attended Totteridge Park in the early years of the nineteenth century. This suggests that it was a very successful school. The evidence from the *DNB*, however, points to Totteridge's being an all-age school as late as 1840. In no case is there a discernible pattern of attendance at quasi-preparatory school followed by public school: Totteridge was either the last school or the only school of all these *DNB* entries except for Sir John Strachey, who left Totteridge at seventeen. In the absence of other evidence it must be judged that Totteridge Park, the familial forbear of Dorset House, became a preparatory school at some unknown time after 1840. It therefore fails to warrant further comment as a candidate for 'the first preparatory school'. But there would seem to have been at least three quasi-preparatory schools at Totteridge: first, the rectory school of the Rev. Abel Lendon (dates unknown); secondly, the preparatory school belonging to Messrs Thorowgood and Wood (1816–1858); and thirdly, the Totteridge Park school belonging to the Wilkinsons and Munros, and the forbear of Dorset House, Bury, Sussex.[35] The very early establishment of a 'preparatory' school by Messrs Thorowgood and Wood, ex-masters of Mill Hill School, in 1816 would seem to establish a good claim for that school to be the first preparatory school especially since it is known that in 1822 the school had fifty-three boys under the age of thirteen.[36] However, although this school began as a feeder to Mill Hill and catered for younger boys it eventually became a serious rival to Mill Hill.[37] Its success in that endeavour, therefore, precludes it from our further consideration.

Group 3

Let us now turn to the quasi-preparatory schools of the third category. The claim of J. Howard Brown[38] is not to be taken seriously that Hazelwood School, Edgbaston, was the first real preparatory school. Apart from the fact that Hazelwood was the successor to Hill Top School founded by Thomas Wright Hill in 1803, it is highly improbable that this 'Chrestomathic' school,[39] established to provide an alternative to the endowed grammar school and supported by the philosophical radicals for that reason, could have functioned as a preparatory school for those very public schools which the Benthamites attacked. Further, the school, although teaching the classics, had a commercial bias which made it more a preparation for the world of business.

The claim of Cheam (1645), with by far the earliest foundation date amongst the more famous preparatory schools, and with its record of distinguished alumni who have gone on to public schools, seems at first sight to be more soundly based. But although it has had a distinguished history[40] with two very famous headmasters — the Rev. William Gilpin (1752–77), alias 'Dr Syntax' and Dr Charles Mayo (1826–46), the Pestalozzian pioneer — it was not a preparatory school till 1855 when the Rev. R.S. Tabor took over. He then 'decided only to have boys from eight to fourteen years old, and weeded out the elder boys, some of whom were twenty years of age.'[41]

For this reason Cheam, despite its antiquity and fame as a preparatory school, has to be discountenanced as being the first.

(i) Another Arnoldian Myth?

Officially designated the first English preparatory school (by C.C. Cotterill[42] in the *Board of Education Special Report*, 1900) is Windlesham House School (1837). This is a surrender to the Arnoldian myth[43] in which Arnold is seen as the architect of the English preparatory school system.[44] Cotterill was in no doubt about Arnold's role in this; he wrote: 'It was Arnold — Arnold almost alone — that brought them to birth.'[45] As headmaster of Rugby School, Arnold discouraged the sending of boys before twelve years old[46] and welcomed the taking over of the school[47] by Lieutenant C.R. Malden, RN, for the education of young boys as an aid to his (Arnold's) programme of reform for Rugby. In one of his early sermons Arnold had admitted that 'the fact is indisputable, Public Schools *are* the very seats and nurseries of vice.'[48] The institution of preparatory schools to look after younger boys seems to have been a necessity in Arnold's view. So it is not surprising that following the publication of the Special Report of 1900 G.H. Wilson,[49] in his official centenary history of

Windlesham House, should declare that 'it was Arnold himself who stood sponsor to the first born of what has now grown into a huge family in Windlesham House.'[50] In the early years most of the boys went to Rugby, but if there was an early link between Rugby and Windlesham this gradually gave way to a much closer link with Harrow and Eton.[51] Cotterill's attribution was accepted by F.C. Pritchard in his recognition of Windlesham House as the first official preparatory school.[52] Its early links with Arnold do not confer upon Windlesham House any claim for precedence over earlier schools which had close links with other public schools, for example, Elstree with Harrow and Temple Grove with Eton. It would seem that if there were schools of an earlier date than 1837 which catered exclusively for young boys, it is among those that the 'first English preparatory school' is to be found.

Arnold's own school at Laleham which he shared with his brother-in-law, the Rev. John Buckland, was of an earlier date, having been founded in 1819. Buckland looked after the younger boys and continued the school after Arnold became headmaster of Rugby. On these grounds Norman Wymer makes the extravagant claim that John Buckland was the 'Father of the English Preparatory School'.[53] This judgment fails to take into account that Buckland's younger boys were the junior section of an all-age school[54] in which Arnold and Buckland were partners until they separated in 1824, with Arnold taking the older pupils. On these grounds the claim for Laleham and Buckland has to be modified, at least until 1824 when Laleham became purely preparatory.

Eagle House (1820), Brook Green, Hammersmith, referred to in W.H.G Kingston's *Three Midshipmen*, has some claim to attention because of its early foundation. But as it was in competition with public schools in the early years and did not become a preparatory school till the time of the Rev. Edward Wickham (1833–47),[55] it cannot be regarded as England's oldest preparatory school, *a fortiori* since there were quasi-preparatory schools before 1820.

(ii)   Twyford or Temple Grove?

As the preparatory school with the longest existence in the same school building, Twyford has an earlier history dating back at least to the eighteenth century.[56] The Georgian house which it occupies today is the one to which the Rev. Liscombe Clark moved the school from Twyford Vicarage in 1809. The Rev. J.G. Bedford purchased the school in c.1815, and it was during the eighteen years of his headmastership that the school took on a preparatory school function. The great-great-grandfather of the headmaster of Twyford in 1982 was an assistant master at the school from about 1818 to 1829 and from 1823[57] onwards there seems to be ample evidence from documents held by the Wickham family[58] that the school was 'preparatory' from an early date. Many of Bedford's boys went to Winchester either before or just after they were thirteen. This is confirmed by a letter dated 29 January 1902 in which Mrs Emma Nelson, the second daughter of Rev. J.G. Bedford, informed the Rev. C.T. Wickham: 'My father's school was distinctly a Preparatory School, chiefly for Winchester College, but boys often went to other schools when too old for Twyford. He never kept them after about twelve or thirteen, and took them as young as eight or nine.'[59] Other witnesses to the early 'preparatory' nature of Twyford School were the Rev. Godfrey Boles Lee (1826–30), who left Twyford between thirteen and fourteen years old and who was quite sure no older boys were at the school when he left; and the Rev. G.W. Paul (1830–33) who, when he left Twyford for Winchester, was of a similar impression that there were no boys in the school at that time above the age of thirteen or fourteen. As the age of entry to public school was gradually raised the age-range of preparatory schools increased, so that even before the headship of the Rev. R. Wickham (1834–47),[60] slightly older boys were to be found in the school. The Rev. Latham Wickham (1862–87), writing of his father's days as assistant master at the school, said that he 'took over all the arrangements from Mr Bedford for boys under fourteen.' He was sure, however, that there were no boys of fifteen or over in the school.[61] From some time after 1815, therefore, it would seem that Twyford was a preparatory school, notwithstanding Thomas Hughes's reference to bullying by the 'biggest' boys in the private school Tom Brown attended in the 1830s.[62]

Twyford's chief rival to the claim of being the oldest preparatory school is Temple Grove, which was founded by the Rev. Dr William Pearson in 1810. Pearson had owned a small school at Parsons Green (near London) since 1802 before he purchased the country house belonging to the Temple family.[63] This small country mansion, in twenty acres at Sheen Grove, near Richmond Park, became a fashionable school first under the Rev. Dr Pearson (1810–17), but more especially under the Rev. Dr Pinckney (1817–35), by which time it was chiefly preparatory for Eton.[64] It is not certain at what stage Temple Grove began to specialize in teaching young boys only, but an engraving[65] dated 1818 suggests that it was a seminary for very young boys, judging by the size of the figures disporting themselves in the grounds by the side of the house. This evidence is of course by no means conclusive.

As in the case of Twyford, however, it is difficult to pin-point any clear change of policy, analogous to that initiated by R.S. Tabor when he went to Cheam in 1855, which might date Temple Grove solely as a preparatory school. So, in the absence of census records before 1841 showing the specific ages of individuals, Twyford and Temple Grove seem to be the oldest preparatory schools in the country, as they became preparatory in character between 1815 and 1835 (in the case of Twyford) and between 1817 and 1835 (in the case of Temple Grove). It would seem, too, that Eagle House and Fonthill could be regarded as among the four oldest English preparatory schools.

Notes

1 Other choir schools, like the Prebendal School, Chichester, are also anterior to Cheam, as is also the Elms, Colwall (1614), unique in its being orginally founded by the Worshipful Company of Grocers.

2 Cf. *The Times* on the following dates: 29 September 1913. Claim was made for Windlesham House at the time of the opening of new school buildings; 6 September 1928. Eagle House history considered; 15 and 25 September 1928. Windlesham and Twyford compared.

In July and August 1939 there was some keen correspondence concerning the oldest preparatory school. Cf. 14, 24, 26, 31 July and 9 August, involving Windlesham House, Eagle House, Twyford and Cheam. Similarly in Volume 5 of the *Preparatory Schools Review* there appeared several histories of older preparatory schools. Cf. also article by F.C. PRITCHARD (1939) 'The earliest preparatory schools,' *PSR*, 12, 133, June, pp. 54–5.

3 Now St Piran's at Maidenhead.

4 Mr PATTON's school is now defunct.

5 Not to be confused with Ealing College of today which was founded in 1820. Cf. I.R. DOWSE (Ed.), (1970) *Ealing College 1820–1970*, Ealing.

6 J. LEWIS MAY, (1929) *Cardinal Newman*, Geoffrey Bles p. 10. It was this school which, ironically, both J.H. NEWMAN (1801–90) and T.H. HUXLEY (1825–95) attended.

7 ARCHIBALD PHILIP PRIMROSE, 5th Earl of Rosebery (1847–1929) was at Bayford then Mr LEE's School at Brighton before going on to Eton. Lord CHARLES BERESFORD (1846–1919) also attended this school before going to Stubbington House. Cf. Chapter 5.

8 Throughout the nineteenth century and into the twentieth century, schools were often called by their principals' names.

9 The musicologist, Sir GEORGE GROVE (1820–1900), and GEORGE GRANVILLE BRADLEY (1821–1903), later Headmaster of Marlborough and Dean of Westminster, attended ELWELL's school at Clapham Common before it moved to Hammersmith.

10 H.P. LIDDON, (1893) *Life of E.B. Pusey*, Longmans Vol. 1, p. 10; Sir STAFFORD NORTHCOTE (1818–87) was also with the Rev. ROBERTS from 1826 to 1831 before going to Eton.

11 Both the fashionable EVERARD's and LEE's were nicknamed the 'little House of Lords' because of the number of peers attending them. The school kept by Mr BRADFORD at Beaconsfield gained a similar soubriquet. Cf. Lord E. FITZMAURICE, (1905) *The Life of Lord Granville*, Longmans Vol. 1, p. 12.

12 The most learned English woman of the seventeenth century; she was tutoress to the daughter of CHARLES I.

13 *DNB* (1822–1906).

14 See Chapter 7.

15 Cf. *PSR*, 16, 10, May 1956 (new series), pp. 16–19. The school was a free school, based on the will of a HUMPHREY WALWYN (d.1612).

16 From letter 21 May 1867 in school archives of The Elms, Colwall.

17 In 1909 the two schools were separated through the Board of Education document, approved by His Majesty in Council, 17 May 1909.

18 From notes on the Minutes of the Court of Assistants of the Grocers' Company, dated 29 May 1855.

19 The discovery of fake drill muskets for children in the school buildings lends some support to this theory of the early nature of the school.

20 Other old boys were H.A. VACHELL, author of *The Hill* and other novels; LEWIS ROSS-MANGLES, the first civilian VC; and E.G. WYNYARD, the test match cricketer.

21 Cf. *The Times*, 6 October 1817 which advertized the Hampstead Heath Academy kept by the Rev. J. DUNCAN.

22 Cf. *The Morning Chronicle*, 25 June 1824, cited by 'J.C.A.', *The Annals of Heath Mount 1817–1934*, p. 9.

23 Cf. *Hampstead and Highgate Express*, January 1887, cited by 'J.C.A.', *The Annals of Heath Mount 1817–1934*, in which an advertisement claimed that 20 per cent of

Heath Mount boys going on to public school from 1882 to 1887 had gained scholarships.

24 M.A.F. COOPER (Ed.), (1970) *Fonthill 1970: 150th Anniversary*, Fonthill.

25 *Ibid.*, p. 5. K.S. STOREY, 'The first hundred years'.

26 The Rev. T.J. NUNNS was a private schoolmaster at 9 Eliot Place, Blackheath from 1864, before going to Maidenhead in 1873. He named his new school at Maidenhead after the house in Blackheath which contained his old school. cf DAVID R. BRIGGS (1983) *The Millstone Race* Exeter, Short Run Press Ltd.

27 From typescript 'Short history of St Piran's' in the school archives. A certain J. DRUITT, one of the candidates for the identity of JACK the RIPPER, taught at this school in Blackheath. DISRAELI was at school at 3 Eliot Place, where the Rev. JOHN POTTICARY was headmaster. POTTICARY passed the school on to his nephew, the Rev. GEORGE B.F. POTTICARY (1796–1883), who kept school there until 1831 when the school moved to 9 Eliot Place. I am grateful to Mr J. WATSON of the Local History Library of Greenwich for this information on Cordwalles' antecedents. All this has been recently documented in *The Millstone Race*.

28 Cf. Chapter 10.

29 According to the late Commander IAN C.M. SANDERSON, ex-headmaster of Elstree School, Dr C.J. VAUGHAN (1816–97) Headmaster of Harrow from 1844 to 1859, used to visit Bernays at Elstree.

30 I am grateful to the late Commander IAN SANDERSON for this information which he gleaned from the Rev. EELES, Vicar of St Alban's, Elstree.

31 From copy of letter in my possession dated 28 March 1964 to Mr SIMS, Headmaster of Dorset House, from Commander I.C.M. SANDERSON.

32 The history of this school is a very muddled one. In 1874 the school was at Hillside, Elstree, when Elstree School was at 'Hill House', Elstree.

33 E.S. PURCELL, (1896) *Life of Cardinal Manning*, Macmillan Vol. 1, pp. 10–13.

34 JAMES WILKINSON (1812–99), Swedenborgian, at Mill Hill and Totteridge; Sir JAMES CHANCE (1814–1902), 1st Baronet, manufacturer and lighthouse engineer, attended Totteridge before going to University College, London; CHRISTOPHER HALL (1816–1902), Congregationalist divine, educated at Rochester and Totteridge; SIR FRANCIS COOK (1817–1901), 1st Baronet, merchant of COOK's of St Paul's, educated at Totteridge and Frankfurt; Sir RICHARD STRACHEY (1817–1908), Lt General of Royal (Bengal) Engineers, Totteridge and Addiscombe; WILLIAM H.R. JONES (1817–85), antiquary, attended Totteridge before going to King's College, London; Sir JOHN STRACHEY (1823–1907), Anglo-Indian administrator, Totteridge and Haileybury in 1840.

35 See NORMAN G. BRETT JAMES (nd.) *The History of Mill Hill School 1807–1907* Andrew Melrose pp. 30, 45, 187, 217.

36 *Ibid.*, p. 58.

37 *Ibid.*

38 J. HOWARD BROWN, (1961) *Schools in England*, Oxford p. 39. Hazelwood had a preparatory class of the youngest boys. Cf. HILL (1825) *Public Education*, p. 95.

39 Cf. JEREMY BENTHAM (1816) *Chrestomathia*, which extolled the virtues of a utilitarian education.

40 Cf. EDWARD PEEL, (1974) *Cheam School from 1645*. Gloucester, Thornhill Press Cf. also MAUD ROBERTS-WEST, 'Early history of Cheam School', *The Genealogists' Magazine*, March and June 1930, Vol. 5, Nos. 5–6; also C.J. MARSHALL (1936) *A History of Cheam and Sutton*, Cheam. Cf. also NICHOLAS HANS, (1951) *New Trends in Education in the Eighteenth Century*, Routledge & Kegan Paul p. 121, where the claim is made for Cheam's being the oldest preparatory school.

41 MARSHALL, *op. cit.*, p. 50. Cf. *The Students' Magazine* (1839 and 1842) or *Cheam School Journal* (1833–6). During these years there were *several* contributions to the magazine by boys of seventeen; *many* of the contributors were aged sixteen. In the

June 1839 issue, reference is made to a boy who stayed at Cheam from eight to eighteen before going to university.

42 COTTERILL was the Honorary Secretary of the Association of Headmasters of Preparatory Schools when he contributed to the (1900) *Special Report on Preparatory Schools.*

43 Cf. T.W. BAMFORD, (1960) *Thomas Arnold,* The Cresset Press pp. 175–90.

44 It fails to take into account that even if ARNOLD's example had been taken up by all public schools — which it was not — such a unilateral action would not determine the preparatory school nature of Windlesham. There is evidence that Windlesham boys were not just of preparatory school age only. For example, Lord MONSON's two boys attended Windlesham, but the elder did not leave till seventeen (1838–46).

45 *Special Report 1900,* p. 4.

46 Cf. BAMFORD, *op. cit.,* pp. 128–42 about the quarrel between ARNOLD and W.F. WRATISLAW. The latter accused ARNOLD of neglecting the younger boys. Nevertheless, in 1847, five years after ARNOLD's death, two nine-year-olds and three ten-year-olds entered Rugby.

47 The school was on the Isle of Wight. MALDEN had retired from the Royal Navy in 1828 on half pay of £90 p.a., and to supplement his income had coached pupils privately for entry to the Royal Navy from 1828 to 1836. In 1837 he took over a school in Newport owned by a Rev. Dr WORSLEY who had conducted the school for four years.

48 T. ARNOLD, (1878) *Christian Life ... School Sermons,* Longmans p. 80, Sermon xii on Galatians, 3:24.

49 WILSON was an assistant master at Windlesham House School.

50 G.H. WILSON and R.S. MALDEN, (1937) *Windlesham House School 1837–1937,* McCorquodale. p. 11.

51 Of 977 ex-pupils of Windlesham House, it is known to what public schools 615 went: *inter alios* 47 to Rugby, 152 to Harrow, 91 to Eton and 48 to Haileybury.

52 F.C. PRITCHARD, *op. cit.,* p. 71.

53 N. WYMER, (1953) *Dr Arnold of Rugby,* Robert Hale p. 55.

54 They ran their 'departments' in separate houses, but it was essentially a combined effort with expenses shared.

55 Former assistant master at Winchester College for ten years.

56 Cf. C.T. WICKHAM (1909) *The Story of Twyford School,* Winchester, Warren & Son pp. 5–7.

57 The (Rev.) ROBERT WICKHAM assisted the Rev. J.G. BEDFORD before going to Oxford. On his return as a graduate in 1823 he became a permanent assistant master.

58 Information from typescript letter dated 1 January 1920 in my possession from the Rev. ROBERT WICKHAM, former headmaster of Twyford. The *PSR,* 5, 42, March 1909, pp. 324–7 cites similar evidence.

59 From manuscript letter in the possession of the Rev. ROBERT WICKHAM.

60 There were three WICKHAM brothers who became noted schoolmasters of preparatory schools: ROBERT WICKHAM — Twyford; EDWARD WICKHAM — Eagle House; FREDERICK WICKHAM — Exmouth.

61 Cf. *PSR,* 5, 42, March 1909, p. 327.

62 Cf. THOMAS HUGHES (1856) *Tom Brown's Schooldays* Nelson edition, p. 64. HUGHES was a pupil at Twyford, and his unflattering remarks about the school which Tom attended for a year are thought to be about Twyford. 'Biggest', though a superlative term, is relative only in meaning.

63 PALMERSTON, as a member of the TEMPLE family, knew the house well. Further, JONATHAN SWIFT, as Secretary to Sir WILLIAM TEMPLE, must have lived there.

64 Cf. Major General SIR ARCHIBALD ANSON, (1920) *About Others and Myself,* John Murray, p. 45. Cf. also H.W. WATERFIELD, 'Temple Grove', *PSR,* 5, 43, July 1909,

pp. 361–4 for the view on this point of the Bishop of Malborough who was a pupil at the school in the 1830s/1840s.

65 This engraving is in the possession of Mr P.B. WATERFIELD, Headmaster of the Mall School, Twickenham, whose forbear was O.C. WATERFIELD.

3   The Famous Five

Parents themselves must be the chief agents of reformation, by refusing to be satisfied with any but first-rate primary schools. That such are to be found, and that the number is already on the increase, we acknowledge with pleasure.
(*The Quarterly Review*, October 1860)

Old, Unhappy, Far-off Days

The harshness of life in pre-Victorian England was true not only for the newly emerging industrial masses but also for the gradually increasing[1] number of boys of middle and upper class families attending England's now increasing number of boarding schools. Symptomatic of this age, school rebellions — sometimes so serious that the militia was called in to quell them — were frequent. The last such major rebellion occurred at Marlborough School in 1851.

The pillory, as Kitson-Clark has reminded us, was not abolished in England until Queen Victoria came to the throne. Public hangings continued till her favourite, Disraeli, became Prime Minister. Offences were punishable by either transportation or capital punishment. A good likeness of Hell on Earth was in Long Chamber at Eton[2] and so it was in the earliest preparatory schools. Though the private or quasi-preparatory school kept by Mr Allen (which Thring attended in Ilminster at the age of eight) was 'much patronised by the country gentlemen of Somerset',[3] it made such a bad impression on him that he became a fervent pioneer of school reform.

Another reformer, Lord Ashley, spent five miserable years at Dr Horne's Manor House School, Chiswick.[4] This was a 'first class school for the sons of Noblemen and Gentlemen': yet living conditions were Spartan there, with 'no bathroom, no washing arrangements[5] nor lavatories, [and] no matron to look after the boys.' He did not begin to enjoy life until he left preparatory school and went to Harrow.

Flogging in these schools was endemic. 'Floggings at Eton were child's play'[6] compared with the ones that were administered at the preparatory school kept by Mr Walton at Hampton. Flogging was considered an inevitable part of school life and formed a necessary part of the duties of those who administered it. Lord Dufferin, for instance, had such respect for Mr Walton that as a distinguished statesman he visited him. The civil servant and financier, Sir Charles Rivers Wilson, who attended Romanoff House preparatory school at Tunbridge Wells kept by Mr Thomas Allfree,[7] confessed that he saw Allfree 'thrash a boy so cruelly that even now it makes me sick to think of it, although he was not really an unkind man, and *I still retain a friendly feeling towards him* [my italics].'[8] Again, Dr Leopold Bernays of Elstree School in the 1840s was an extremely savage headmaster who, it has been alleged, foamed at the mouth when in a rage.[9] Perhaps the reason why the school kept by the Rev. William Montagu Church at Geddington, near Kettering in Northamptonshire, was shortlived was that he was unable to control his temper,[10] despite his school's being patronized by the sons of nobility.

Such cruelty, by twentieth century standards, was widespread. Flogging was administered by the master sitting on the boy's neck, 'and the larger or more restive boys would sometimes lift and carry him across the room in their agonies', according to Guy Kendall who attended in 1837 the Grange School, Stevenage, kept by the Rev. J.O. Seager.[11] A future Governor-General of India was 'flogged every day of [his] life at [a Mr Gough's] school except one, and then [he] was flogged twice.'[12] Terror ever seeps through much of the autobiographies of historians such as J.A. Froude who attended a preparatory school at Buckfastleigh where 'there was plenty of caning'[13] by the Rev. Mr Lowndes, whilst in the 1860s H.O. Arnold Foster attended the school of his kinsman, Mr John Penrose, at Exmouth, where the regime was even more Spartan and severe.[14] The skin of Henry Labouchere, the nephew of the 1st Baron Taunton of Schools Inquiry Commission fame, was in 'a permanent state of discolouration owing to the kind attentions of the master', whose purpose in flogging his boys was allegedly to relieve his lumbago.[15] This was at a quasi-preparatory school in Brighton in 1825.

'It becomes part of the man; it is his sting, his tusk, his horn. It becomes habitual,'[16] wrote the Rev. T. Mozley in an attempt to understand this magisterial penchant for caning. It was he who said that so many private schoolmasters did not like their work because they had to take whatever pupils presented themselves, however stupid. He commented, 'Over these boys they broke their tempers, their strength and often their characters.'

By contrast the food was sparing. Even if the mid-day meal was good, breakfast at the Grange School, Stevenage, consisted generally only of bread and rancid butter. The explorer (Sir) Richard Burton who attended a preparatory school kept by a 'burly savage' called Rev. Charles de la Fosse was both ill-taught and ill-fed.[17] The statesman, Lord Hardinge of Penshurst, was underfed at Cheam School in 1868 under the Rev. R.S. Tabor.[18] It was characteristic of quasi-preparatory schools in the early years to be run on Spartan lines — an educational policy which was consonant with a stringent economic policy, involving poorly paid ushers and the barest victuals sufficient only to sustain the constant flogging. Where the boys were treated luxuriously, as at Dr Everard's fashionable school at Brighton, attended by Frederick Leveson Gower, there was a danger of bankruptcy and loss of livelihood.[19] The fears of such a fate ensured the plainest of food in the majority of schools.[20]

'How I did loathe that preparatory school — preparatory, thank heaven, for a life that was not to be', wrote Herman Merivale, playwright and novelist, about the school he and Anthony Trollope attended.[21] Yet the food was good and there was no flogging. Perhaps Major General Sir Alfred Turner was more just when, commenting on a quasi-preparatory school he attended at Esher in 1851, he wrote:

> I cannot say that the school was a Dotheboys Hall, but it approached nearer to such an establishment than to the luxurious private schools of today [1912]. The discipline was rigorous, the food of the plainest, the application of the rod not infrequent, but the educational training was decidedly good, even in those days.[22]

Lord Lytton, grandson of Edward Bulwer, the 1st Lord Lytton, drew attention in the biography of his grandfather to another problem in the early days, that of bullying. Commenting on his grandfather's experiences of being bumped during a brief stay of two weeks at Dr Ruddock's well-known private classical school at Fulham, he wrote:

> Whatever the alleged cruelties of public schools of that day [1812], I cannot believe that they equalled the atrocity of a genteel preparatory establishment, in which the smallest boy was given up, without any check from the bigger, to the mercies of boys less small.[23]

These quasi-preparatory schools, however, were not all uniformly bad. The small school at Everdon in Northamptonshire owned in the early 1850s by the Rev. William T. Browning (the elder brother of Oscar Browning the Cambridge don and Eton schoolmaster) was run meticulously, with attention being paid not only to sound scholarship but also to good food and sound health. After an astonishing success in gaining first, second and third places in the Eton scholarship examinations in 1853, the Rev. Browning invested further in education and took a large school at Thorpe Mandeville, near Banbury, which gained a high academic record. Another school with a deservedly high reputation was Dr Hooker's school at Rottingdean which Edward Bulwer attended from 1814 to 1818 and which was described by his grandson as 'one of the most celebrated academies in England for the rank of the pupils, the comforts of the school, and the superiority of its training for the great public institutions of Eton or Harrow.'[24] This was the quasi-preparatory school which, in his biography of Bulwer Lytton, T.H.S. Escott described as a school which 'enjoyed, in the days of the Regency, the same fashionable vogue as belonged, in the Victorian era, to "Tabor's" at Cheam.'[25]

The Famous Five

All the schools described so far no longer exist. But others do. Five of them became an élite to which dukes would be pleased to send their sons. These were the famous five: Cheam, Eagle House, Temple Grove, Twyford and Windlesham House. Deferred to by old boys, they became didactic dynasties.[26] Only one of them, Eagle House, has experienced a series of unrelated headmasters, but even this school was kept in the Huntingford family for a while through marriage, A.N. Malan being the Rev. Huntingford's son-in-law. Let us look at them in a little more detail — but for the sake of clarity Table 1 sets out the periods of office of the headmasters (and headmistress) of the five schools in the nineteenth century.

Cheam, in addition to the earlier legendary William Gilpin senior (1754–77), had two headmasters of national repute: Dr Charles Mayo and the Rev. R.S. Tabor. Though the Rt Hon. Hugh Childers, Home Secretary in the third Gladstone Ministry, had mixed feelings about his time there in 1836, it was so good that it sent boys directly to the university, without their passing through a public school. For not only did it practise Pestalozzianism but one of its ushers, Mr Reiner, became tutor to Edward VII when Prince of Wales.[27] It taught science, astronomy, zoology, botany, chemistry and electricity. It was such a hot-house in Childers' time but 'the headmaster was getting old, and saw too much through his wife's [*sic*] spectacles.'[28]

'Sneaking and spying' were encouraged, and schoolboy honour was set at nought in this intensely oppressive evangelical atmosphere.[29] Childers observed that 'the mistrust of the boys shown by the headmaster and his wife increased and was greatly resented.' Dean Fremantle, also a former pupil, concurs with Childers when he writes: 'there was ... a closeness about the system not suited to boys as they grow up. I myself, though leaving at twelve years old, felt glad to find myself in the more liberal atmosphere of Eton.'[30]

The Rev. R.S. Tabor was headmaster of Cheam from 1855 to 1890,[31] during which time he firmly established Cheam as one of the leading preparatory schools. There seems to be little doubt of the efficiency and success of Tabor: both Major Fitzroy Gardner and Lord Hardinge of Penshurst bear witness to this. According to Gardner, Cheam under Tabor was 'the most luxuriously appointed private school in England.' It was equipped with 'the very latest thing in swimming baths; a carpenter's shop fitted with turning lathes; new Eton fives courts, an ideal cricket ground and manservants'[32] to wait on the boys. Many boys attended the school who achieved distinction in later life.

Lord Hardinge had a high opinion of the teaching and the games at the school and noted that there were always one or more Cheam boys in the Eton and Harrow teams at Lords. But both the Rev. and Mrs Tabor were unpopular with the boys. Tabor, described by Hardinge as 'one of the greatest snobs I ever met,' was according to General Sir Ian Hamilton 'sanctimonious', and according to the second Earl Frank Russell[33] 'an unctuous and pious person

Table 1. Headmasters of Leading Early Preparatory Schools

Cheam (1645)	Eagle House (1820)	Temple Grove (1810)	Twyford (1809)	Windlesham House (1837)
1777–1809 Rev. William Gilpin (Junior)	1820–1833 Joseph Railton	1810–1817 Rev. Dr W. Pearson	1809–1815 Rev. L. Clarke	1837–1855 Lt C.R. Malden
1809–1826 Rev. J. Wilding	1833–1847 Rev. E.C. Wickham**	1817–1835 Rev. Dr Pinckney	1815–1833 Rev. J.G. Bedford	1855–1888 H.C. Malden
1826–1846 Dr Charles Mayo	1847–1874 Rev. E. Huntingford	1835–1843 J. Thompson	1834–1847 Rev. R. Wickham**	1888–1896 C.S. Malden
1846–1855 Rev. H. Shepheard	1874–1906 A.N. Malan	1843–1860 Rev. Dr Rowden	1848–1854 Rev. J.C. Roberts	1896–1927 (Mrs C.S. Malden)
1855–1890 Rev. R.S. Tabor	1906–1927 Bruce Lockhart	1860–1880 O.C. Waterfield	1854–1861 Rev. G.W. Kitchin	
1890–1920 Mr A.S. Tabor		1880–1894 Rev. J.H. Edgar	1862–1887 Rev. Latham Wickham	
		1894–1902 Rev. H.B. Allen	1888–1890 Rev. C.T. Wickham	
		1902–1934 H.W. Waterfield*	1890–1897 Rev. C.T. Wickham } H. Strahan	
			1897–1910 Rev. C.T. Wickham	

** brothers
* father of P.B. Waterfield, Headmaster of The Mall School, Twickenham

very soothing to parents.' In a very colourful and lively account of his schooldays, Hamilton relates the effects on him of Tabor's strict, religious regime. At a very impressionable age he was terrified by Tabor's fearsome approach to schoolmastering. One of Tabor's customs, which was common practice at other schools,[34] was to hold court on Monday mornings when the whole school, class by class, was summoned to his study. Writing as a hardened soldier in 1939, General Hamilton declared that 'at twenty to plunge into the most furious battle was as a game of skittles ... when compared with going as a ten-year-old to the study of RST on a Monday morning.'[35] Tabor was not only choleric but in Hamilton's estimation he was also callous, caring little for the sensitivities of small boys. Yet Tabor felt that he was governing the school by divine right, and constantly likened the work of his assistant masters to that of the disciples of Jesus Christ. As Hamilton suggests, 'the whole system of Cheam hung upon the assumption that a bevy of young imps had been handed over by Providence to Mr Tabor so that he might shake them up in a big bag until they had lost their horns and tails.'[36] Hamilton's testimony against Tabor and Cheam is full of invective. He describes his entry to it as 'exactly like a dose of poison'. Even if one discounts the psychological effect the school had on Hamilton the corroborating evidence of Earl Russell and Lord Hardinge confirms that even if R.S. Tabor was a successful teacher, he was also a religious prig and a bully. But not all commentators are so ruthlessly critical as Hamilton. Edward Peel, the official historian of Cheam School, suggests that if boys had no great enthusiasm for the school, parents found less to criticize in view of the 'continuous success and high reputation of Cheam'. Those who enjoyed their stay at Cheam included Lord Aberdeen, Lord Randolph Churchill, Charles Guinness and Lord Burnham.

Like Cheam School, **Eagle House**, Brook Green, Hammersmith, was not a preparatory school in the early years of the nineteenth century. Formerly a ladies' boarding school, it was founded in 1820 by Joseph Railton (1779–1857). It was a rival to, rather than a 'feeder' of, the public schools preparing boys for the universities and business.

The Rev. E.C. Wickham (1833–47), who succeeded Railton as headmaster of Eagle House, was a fine teacher[37] and an excellent cricketer. It was he who restricted boys to those of preparatory school age and through a fairly Spartan regime[38] prepared them for public school. According to Dr Warre, headmaster of Eton (1884–1905), they 'suffered much and learnt a good deal of Latin and Greek'.[39] The school became a veritable nursery for future public school headmasters. During Wickham's time there were seven future headmasters in the school: Dr Blore of Canterbury; Dr Montagu Butler of Harrow and Master of Trinity College, Cambridge; Mr Arthur Butler of Haileybury; Mr Faber of Malvern; Dr Warre of Eton; Mr Wickham of Wellington[40] and Dr Ridding of Winchester.[41] Dr Butler attests that under Mr Wickham the standard of work was high. During his time several preparatory school customs were adopted in the school. On Sundays, for instance, the boys wore tall hats[42] and wended their way in crocodile formation to St Mary's Chapel, Fulham; whilst on half-holidays they played cricket in a field at Shepherd's Bush. Such practices were the antecedents of later preparatory school chapel and inter-school matches.

The school consolidated its position as a preparatory school during the headship of Dr Huntingford,[43] but its numbers declined. The decline brought it down to the level of numbers generally to be found in a nineteenth century preparatory school. Huntingford was succeeded by his son-in-law the Rev. A.N. Malan (1874–1905)[44]. Each of them was responsible for changing the site of the school. In 1860 the school had moved to Wimbledon, where it took over buildings recently vacated by the Rev. J.W. Brackenbury, the army 'crammer'. In the following year a school chapel was built. The school was destined to stay in London for no more than twenty-three years before moving to a more typical late nineteenth century rural site at Sandhurst, Surrey.

The third of the big five, **Temple Grove School**, formerly at East Sheen, Surrey, is perhaps the best documented preparatory school because of the many references in general biography both to the school and to its famous headmaster, Ottiwell Charles Waterfield. By comparison with Waterfield, the school's founder, Dr Pearson,[45] is a shadowy figure. It is known, however, that he invested capital in extra building. After buying the house, he added schoolrooms, erected out-houses, laid down a playground and gravel paths and drained the sodden parts of the grounds, so providing attractive gardens.[46] Little is known about life at Temple Grove under its founder and first headmaster.

This cannot be said of Dr Pinckney's headmastership, aspects of which have been recorded graphically by the Hon. Henry J. Coke in *Tracks of a Rolling Stone* (1905) and by Major General Sir Archibald Anson in *About Others and Myself* (1920). Although describing his school in the 1820s as 'one of the most favoured of preparatory schools', to which the three nephews of the historian Lord Macaulay were sent, Coke likens its asperity to that of Dotheboys Hall. Typical of many private schools of the day, Temple Grove in the 1820s/1830s contrasted strongly with the preparatory schools of the latter part of the century. As Coke suggests in 1905,

> the progress of the last century in many directions is great indeed; but in few is it greater than in the comfort and the cleanliness of our modern schools. The luxury enjoyed by the present boy is a constant source of astonishment to us grandfathers. We were half starved, we were exceedingly dirty, we were systematically bullied, and we were flogged and caned as though the master's pleasure was in inverse ratio to ours.[47]

The food was served with economy in mind. The morning fare consisted of oblong chunks of bread, only one of which was buttered for each boy. The other chunks of dry bread were washed down by an allowance of milk and water.[48] Mid-day dinner began with a rice pudding (to cut down the butcher's bill, according to Coke),[49] followed by roast beef or mutton. Supper was as dull and as frugal as breakfast, so that although, after soldiers, none complain more bitterly about their food than schoolboys, there were nevertheless adequate grounds for such complaints about food at Temple Grove in those early years.[50] Nor did the food improve much under Dr Rowden (1843–60)[51].

If during Pinckney's headship food was not generously given, flogging was. Pinckney had a carefully graded scale of corporal punishment, ranging from the application of the cane on the hand to laying the struggling victim across a table with five boys holding him down, with a Latin grammar put in his mouth to bite upon as pain was inflicted. This punishment generally was given after supper when the boys filed past Dr Pinckney and bade him goodnight. Those due for a thrashing were extracted and hauled off by the five appointed older boys.

Despite this callous practice Pinckney was not altogether an unkind man. He arranged for the very young boys of eight to be placed in a kind of reception centre run by two lady teachers, Miss Fields and Miss Evatt, and provided a special dormitory for them with only twelve beds in it.[52] To raise the spirits of small boys who received no post, Pinckney used to address sham letters to them so that they would not feel too lonely in the cruel world in which they found themselves. Dr Pinckney, then, was somewhat of an enigma: he is described by Eustace Anderson, the author of *History of Mortlake*, as 'a short man with a florid countenance, who enjoyed his glass of port wine after dinner.'[53] This 'wretched Pinckney', as Disraeli once called him, was also wont to give presents of tea and groceries to local almswomen, an action in strong contrast to his other liberality.

Although the Rev. Dr Rowden[54] has gained some of posterity's attention by Disraeli's satirization of him in his novel, *Coningsby* (1844), it is O.C. Waterfield who, with the Temple Grove over which he ruled, has been recorded in more detail for historians of education. This is chiefly because of the fascination with which Waterfield was regarded by A.C. Benson and his brother, E.F. Benson. Though the former was ambivalent[55] about his old headmaster, it might be said that A.C. Benson was to Waterfield what A.P. Stanley was to Arnold — his chief publicist.

A close study of the ample references to Temple Grove in general biography serves to make the reader wary of the testimony of old boys on grounds both of their lack of objectivity and of the inaccuracy of their observations about their *almae matres*. The majestic impression which O.C. Waterfield made on the two Benson boys[56] is brought out in their writings; for it is very evident from their descriptions of him that he bestrode their boy-world like a Colossus. This 'worm's eye view' can be a source of inaccurate information by ill-formed old boys and is likely to mislead the unwary.[57]

Though this chapter is concerned with early preparatory schools, it is justifiable to include in it a study of O.C. Waterfield (1860–80),[58] whose headship overlaps with the later period of preparatory school development because he was a master of the old school. He ruled his establishment from

Olympian heights,[59] striking awe in the hearts of both masters and boys whenever he appeared in the classroom or dormitory. He was a tall, impressive looking man, who always dressed like a gentleman in a frock coat. A.C. Benson described him thus:

> When he was arrayed in a full silk gown he was almost too majestic for words. A faint scent of Havana cigars hung about him. He walked with a slight limp, which gave him a swaying motion, and he had eyes of great brilliance which opened wide, if he was surprised or vexed, and struck terror into our souls.[60]

He had in the 1850s been a master at Eton, where no doubt he had been impressed by the maintenance of order through the liberal application of the cane. He too was a martinet. He ruled by a combination of fear and love and, by a judicious use of his thick ruler, gained both obedience and hero-worship. E.F. Benson in *Our Family Affairs* gives a schoolboy's view of Waterfield's preliminaries before using the stick:

> But the approach of the ruler, like a depression over the Atlantic, was always heralded by storm cones — keys were taken from his trousers' pocket; next the appropriate key was inserted in the lock, then came a short agonizing scene, and the blubbering victim after six smart blows had the handle of the door turned for him by someone else, because his hand was useless through pain.[61]

Waterfield nevertheless hid a kind heart and on occasions, as only Victorian headmasters could do, broke into tears of compassion for discovered wrong punishment or kissed a boy if he felt his fearful harangue had been too traumatic an experience for some sensitive soul.[62]

He was an excellent headmaster who believed in delegation. If he was aloof in his manner, his presence was soon readily felt. E.F. Benson relates how, when he visited a classroom, 'a hush fell as he strode in, and we all cowered like partridge below a kite, while he glared around, selecting the covey on to which he pounced.'[63] A.C. Benson adds to this picture of formidability when he writes:

> I have never in my life been so afraid of a human being as I was of him. I thought of him as wholly indifferent to us boys — that we were just more or less inconvenient adjuncts to his surpassing greatness.[64]

It is clear that Waterfield was a patriarch,[65] exercising patriarchal authority in the patriarchal society of the early preparatory school. The subjective schoolboy views of the academic and literary Benson brothers make this very apparent; but even from a man of the stature of Lord Grey of Fallodon he won great respect. Grey thought that among the teachers he knew Waterfield 'had a personality which gave him without effort a complete ascendancy over masters and boys and was one of the best teachers.'[66]

Temple Grove under Waterfield had many characteristic features of mid-century preparatory school life: it was both austerely Spartan and intellectually demanding. Games at this stage were not assiduously pursued,[67] were not compulsory and therefore played a subsidiary role to the task of acquiring more than the elements of Latin and Greek. The school had its own Latin textbook, *Elementa Latina*, which had to be learnt by heart: Greek, Latin, mathematics and divinity were taught by assistant masters; modern languages by the French and German masters. A little history and geography were taught, but the boys were made to concentrate on winning classical scholarships at the leading public schools, in which activity they achieved considerable success.

Sunday afternoons were periods of rest. As in many preparatory schools of the time, and Crichton House in *Vice Versa*,[68] the boys were given the opportunity of reading specially approved 'Sunday Literature'. Sunday afternoons were the only regular occasions when Waterfield descended from Mount Olympus and read to the senior boys in the fairly relaxed atmosphere of his drawing room. No doubt A.C. Benson had such scenes in mind when he assessed Waterfield maturely as a headmaster:

> If he had seen a little more of the boys and expanded more into his delightful talk; if he could have kept more in control the natural irritability of a highly strung imperious man: if he could have introduced a little more amenity into the life of the place, without sacrificing its simplicity and liberty, it would have been at the head of all private schools.[69]

With Waterfield's retirement in 1880 the school was subjected, under the Rev. J.H. Edgar, to a regime more consonant with the times.

Though fourth in the famous five, **Twyford School** can rightly claim to be one of the two oldest English preparatory schools. Yet its close, if informal, links with Winchester,[70] did not ensure it a really notable number of old boys. Apart from Alexander Pope, who attended the Roman Catholic establishment at Twyford in the seventeenth century,[71] Thomas Hughes of *Tom Brown's Schooldays* fame and [Sir Charles] Hubert Parry, the composer of English sacred music, the school claims few very famous alumni. Apart from Hughes and Parry there are only five ascertained entries (six including Pope) in the *DNB* which indicate early schooling at Twyford.[72] These are Charles B. Mansfield, the chemist and Christian Socialist who abstracted benzole from coal; Evelyn Shirley, archaeologist; Richard Chenevix Trench, Archbishop of Dublin; Evelyn S. Shuckburgh, classical scholar; and Robert C. Moberly, the theologian. A number of army officers attended Twyford, including Major General Sir Henry Hallam Parr, ADC to Queen Victoria; General Arthur Shirley, commander of the cavalry of the Turkish contingent in the Crimea; and Major William Pretyman, who was the first to observe the advance of the Russians at Inkerman.[73] There is little in general biography to supplement, by agreement or refutation, the official history of the school published in 1909. This is unfortunate, since the portrait of the private school which Tom Brown attended before going to Rugby, which is generally regarded as being based on Twyford, is so uncomplimentary.[74]

From the early years of the Rev. J.G. Bedford's headship the school developed modestly, never quite reaching the fashionable heights of schools like Temple Grove, Cheam, Elstree and Hoddesdon Grange, or even some of the fashionable schools in Brighton such as Lee's and Everard's. Like Temple Grove at East Sheen, Twyford had a pleasant exterior and grounds, but living conditions inside the house were Spartan. These were improved in 1841 by the Rev. Robert Wickham, who built a new washing room,[75] and by the Rev. G.W. Kitchin, who provided a dining hall and kitchens together with cloisters connecting them with the main house.

The headmastership of G.W. Kitchin (1854–61) stands out in the history of Twyford School as its nineteenth century heyday. Bedford had started with thirty-seven boys and had increased his numbers: only three times in eighteen years did he have an entry list below double figures. Although the entry figures for the twenty years preceding Kitchin are not recorded, there are grounds for suspecting a decline during the period. In 1854 there were only thirty-four boys in the school, three fewer than in 1815, and this despite the 'Arnoldian renaissance' in the public schools. Kitchin encouraged a widening of the curriculum by the study of mathematics, natural history and the science. Under his liberalizing influence the numbers recovered. When he left in 1861 to become Censor of Christ Church, Oxford, he passed on to his successor, the Rev. Latham Wickham (1862–87), a successful school and a record number of seventy-four boys, exactly double the number in Bedford's original school. Thirty-five boys entered the school in 1860 alone.

The school buildings continued to expand slowly under the Rev. Latham Wickham, who added new sick rooms, masters' rooms, and a chapel (1869). But Kitchin's high rate of recruitment was not maintained. For the first few years the numbers fluctuated, with entries as low as fifteen in 1866, fourteen in 1862 and 1864, twelve in 1867.

It seems that the fault lay with Twyford's reluctance to accommodate itself to a changing situation. The Rev. J.G. Bedford, 'an able and accomplished instructor', had introduced certain educational innovations to the school in 1815 such as the practice of 'Reward Day',[76] 'Standing Up'[77] and 'the Slate',[78] which served as useful extrinsic rewards and punishments to urge on the boys in their classical studies.[79] The conservatism of Twyford ensured the survival of these Bedfordian institutions till quite a late date.[80] This conservative outlook, which followed the successful traditions of J.G. Bedford and G.W. Kitchin, is readily admitted by the Rev. Latham Wickham:

> At first it was quite enough for me to try and carry on everything as nearly as possible in the ways which had already proved so successful. By degrees I found things which seemed to me capable of useful additions, while I was careful to adhere to old traditions.[81]

The last of the five, **Windlesham House**, differed from other early preparatory schools in adopting a novel attitude towards master/pupil relationships. The school's founder, Lieutenant Malden, was not content, as were most early headmasters of preparatory schools of any size, merely to teach the boys himself and leave them for the rest of their time to the care of poorly paid ushers. His constant close contact with the boys in a *family* atmosphere was a necessary part of his school policy. Although this policy at Windlesham during the early decades was not entirely comparable with that of preparatory schools of a later date, it was at least a stage nearer to the close supervision by assistant masters in the late nineteenth and early twentieth centuries. Malden's policy of close supervision by the headmaster, maintained by his son H.C. Malden after 1855, held the seeds of one of the few recorded revolts in preparatory schools. Despite H.C. Malden's being such a devoted schoolmaster he was not well supported by his assistant masters. On one occasion in his absence from school twenty boys staged a two-day revolt in the course of which they squirted ink over masters and maids.

Windlesham House differed from other early preparatory schools, too, in the instability of its early years. Whereas Cheam School did not move site to Headley in Berkshire till 1934; nor Temple Grove to Eastbourne in Sussex till 1907; nor Eagle House to Brackenbury's, Wimbledon, till 1860, Windlesham House (or Malden's as it was called in the early years) experienced a series of locations. It began life at Newport on the Isle of Wight, but at a very early stage Lieutenant Malden, recognizing the premises were insanitary, moved his school first to No. 1 Brunswick Place, Brighton in 1838, and a few months later to 78 Montpelier House. Even this third site did not satisfy Lieutenant Malden, who bought two acres of ground in Brighton and in 1846 built a new school which he named Windlesham House. Windlesham House was, therefore, the first purpose-designed preparatory school.

Notes

1 Cf. F. Musgrove, 'Middle class families and schools, 1780–1880: Interaction and exchange of function between institutions', from P.W. Musgrave (Ed.), (1970) *Sociology, History and Education*, Methuen pp. 117–25.
2 Cf. G.R. Parkin, (1904) *Life of Edward Thring*, Macmillan p. 23. After 8 p.m. young collegers were subjected to all kinds of bullying in the chaos and the 'freedom' of the locked-up dormitory.
3 *Ibid.*, p.12.
4 Cf. Robert Cochrane, (1890) *Beneficent and Useful Lives*, London & Edinburgh, W.R. Chambers pp. 12–13.
   Cf. also *PSR*, 5, 42, March 1909, pp. 338–9 Letter from T.J.F. Haskoll, dated 18 February 1909 re Chiswick House School, alias Manor House School, Chiswick.
5 After breakfast three large tubs were brought into the dining room or schoolroom, filled with water and used to wash some fifty boys.
6 Sir Alfred Lyall, (1905) *The Life of the Marquis of Dufferin and Ava*, John Murray p. 21.
7 He had been a tutor to the Russian royal family: hence he called his school Romanoff House. The school had seventy well-fed and well-taught boys. This school was later called Rose Hill School.

8 From Sir CHARLES RIVERS WILSON, (1916) *Chapters from My Official Life*, Edward Arnold p. 5. RIVERS WILSON used the alternative spelling of 'Allfrey' in describing his old headmaster.

9 MARY E. RICHARDSON, (1919) *The Life of a Great Sportsman*, Vinton & Co. p. 56.

10 Cf. General Sir NEVILLE LYTTELTON, (n.d.) *Eighty Years* Hodder and Stoughton p. 16; also A.C. AINGER, (1917) *Eton Sixty Years Ago*, John Murray pp. 10–14; also GWENDOLEN STEPHENSON, (1936) *Edward S. Talbot 1844–1934* SPCK p. 7.

11 Known as 'Old Jos', which name was used by KENDALL to keep the head and school *incognito*. GUY KENDALL, (1933) *A Headmaster Remembers*, V. Gollancz pp. 28–42.

12 That is, Lord JOHN LAWRENCE (1811–79), the uncle of HENRY HART. G.G. COULTON, (1923) *A Victorian Schoolmaster: Henry Hart of Sedbergh*, Bell & Sons, p. 8.

13 Cf. HERBERT PAUL, *Life of Froude*, Sir Isaac Pitman & Sons p. 9.

14 Cf. MARY A. ARNOLD FORSTER, (1910) *Memoir of H.O. Arnold Forster*, Edward Arnold p. 22.

15 Cf. HESKETH PEARSON, (1936) *Labby — the Life of Henry Labouchere*, Hamish Hamilton pp. 17–18.

16 Rev. T. MOZLEY, (1885) *Reminiscences Chiefly of Towns, Villages and Schools* Longmans, Vol. 1, pp. 286–7.

17 Cf. THOMAS WRIGHT, (1906) *The Life of Sir Richard Burton*, Everett & Co. p. 52.

18 Cf. Lord HARDINGE of PENSHURST, (1947) *Old Diplomacy*, John Murray, p. 4.

19 Dr EVERARD became a bankrupt and had to flee the country.

20 References to uninteresting food, always a point of comment by small boys, are numerous in biography. 'Resurrection pie' was a common description used to identify attempts at domestic economy.

21 HERMAN MERIVALE, (1902), *Bar, Stage and Platform*, Chatto & Windus p. 162. Cf. ANTHONY TROLLOPE, (1883), *An Autobiography*, Edinburgh pp. 4–6 for TROLLOPE's comments on the school at Sunbury kept by ARTHUR DRURY.

22 Major General Sir ALFRED E. TURNER, (1912), *Sixty Years of a Soldier's Life*, Methuen p. 15.

23 Earl of LYTTON, (1913), *The Life of Edward Bulwer, 1st Lord Lytton*, Macmillan & Co p. 40.

24 *Ibid.*, p. 44.

25 T.H.S. ESCOTT, (1910), *Edward Bulwer, 1st Baron Lytton*, George Routledge & Sons p. 23.

26 Cf. Chapter 8, pp. 105–8.

27 EDWARD PEEL, (1974), *Cheam School from 1645*, Gloucester, Thornhill Press p. 125.

28 Cf. Lt Col. SPENCER CHILDERS, (1901) *The Life and Correspondence of the Rt. Hon. Hugh C.E. Childers*, 2 vols, John Murray Vol. 1, p. 8. ELIZABETH MAYO was his sister not his wife.

29 This view of MAYO's Cheam is confirmed by MICHAEL DAVIDSON (1962) in *The World The Flesh and Myself* where he described Cheam as 'an Evangelical counterpart of Eton' — an all-age school where 'sneaking and spying were universal.'

30 W.H. DRAPER (Ed.), (1921), *Recollections of Dean Fremantle*, Cassell & Co. p. 11.

31 Cf. EDWARD PEEL, *op. cit.*, pp. 155–91.

32 Major FITZROY GARDNER, (1921), *Days and Ways of an Old Bohemian*, Hutchinson p. 26.

33 The elder brother of BERTRAND RUSSELL and grandson of Lord JOHN RUSSELL. RUSSELL's private tutor before going to Cheam was a Mr CARDEW, who married the daughter of Dean G.W. KITCHIN, Head of Twyford 1854–61.

34 For example, at LEE's preparatory school at Brighton; St George's Ascot and the Rev. HERBERT BULL's school, Wellington House, Westgate-on-Sea.

35 I.S.M. HAMILTON, (1939), *When I Was a Boy*, Faber & Faber, p. 104.
36 *Ibid.*, p. 93.
37 LONSDALE RAGG, (1911), *A Memoir of Edward Charles Wickham*, Edward Arnold p. 4.
38 Even as late as Dr HUNTINGFORD's time, up to the move in 1860, urination was performed in a leaden trough around the ablutions room which had leaden bowls for washing but no hot water.
39 *PSR*, 5, 41, December 1908, p. 272.
40 He was born at Eagle House.
41 Cf. Lady LAURA RIDDING (1908), *George Ridding, Schoolmaster and Bishop*, Edward Arnold pp. 6–7; also EDWARD GRAHAM, (1920), *The Harrow Life of Henry Montagu Butler*, Longmans, Green & Co. p. 26; also *Eagle House Magazine*, 1906. Letter from the Rev. Dr A. MONTAGU BUTLER referring to the seven future headmasters. The editor added two more: Dr B. POLLOCK of Wellington (1893–1910) and the Rev. L.G.B. FORD of Repton (1901–10). Cf. also PAUL WOOTTON, (1970) *Eagle House 1820–1970*, Thame, p. 5. Of 140 boys under Wickham, seventeen became scholars of Winchester including eleven Scholars and Fellows of New College, Oxford.
42 Cf. *Eagle House Magazine*, 1906. Annals of Eagle House, Part 7 by NEWTON W. APPERLY. In Dr HUNTINGFORD's day the walking-out uniform was long trousers, Eton jackets and top hats.
43 Former scholar of Winchester and Fellow of New College, Oxford. He was related to the TREMENHEERE family by marriage.
44 Came as assistant master in 1870; he became headmaster in 1874. He was a highly skilled craftsman in glass, wood and stone. He was a writer of short stories in 1880s and 1890s. Regular contributor to *Boys' Own Paper* as a serial writer. H.C. BARNARD, the educational historian, liked to read MALAN's stories. Cf. H.C. BARNARD, (1970), *Were Those the Days?* Pergamon, p. 62.
45 He was a friend of the assassinated (1812) Prime Minister, SPENCER PERCEVAL.
46 Cf. W.L. RUTTON, (1906) *Temple Grove in East Sheen, Surrey*, Mitchell & Hughes p. 140. For a description of the grounds and gardens see A.C. BENSON (1915) *Escape and Other Essays*, Smith Elder & Co, pp. 193–4.
47 COKE, *op. cit.*, p. 9.
48 ANSON, *op. cit.*, p. 46.
49 Cf. C.T. WICKHAM (Ed.) (1909) *The Story of Twyford*, Winchester, Warren & Son, p. 10. It was customary in many homes to serve the meat after the pudding because meat was not regarded as a luxury. As prices changed and meat became more of a luxury item the Rev. WICKHAM, Headmaster of Twyford School, decided to put meat before pudding on the menu.
50 The food, according to the Bishop of Marlborough who had been a pupil at Temple Grove, was 'execrable': *PSR*, 5, 43, July 1909.
51 Cf. A.G.C. LIDDELL, (1911), *Notes from the Life of an Ordinary Mortal*, John Murray p. 18.
52 Cf. ANSON, *op. cit.*, p. 46.
53 *PSR*, 5, 43, July 1909, p. 361.
54 Although it is suggested in the Rev. H.W. WATERFIELD's article in the *PSR*, 5, 43, July 1909 that *Coningsby* refers to Dr ROWDEN, it is more likely, in view of *Coningsby*'s publication date (1844), that DISRAELI had in mind Dr PINCKNEY (1817–35) rather than ROWDEN (1843–60).
55 A.C. BENSON's views on O.C. WATERFIELD and Temple Grove are contained mainly in two works: *Escape and Other Essays* (1915) and *Memories and Friends* (1924). In the earlier work his criticism of his preparatory school is reflected in his emotive title. Nine years later he seems to be filled rather with awe than with terror of his school. The fault may have lain with BENSON, who himself admitted that he 'had

little animal spirits, and none of the boisterous rough and tumble ebullience of boyhood'.

56 ARTHUR and EDWARD BENSON, sons of Archbishop E.W. BENSON of Canterbury, had an elder brother, MARTIN BENSON, who died in 1878. He had been at Temple Grove before them. Cf. DAVID NEWSOME, 1961, *Godliness and Good Learning*, John Murray, pp. 142–93.

57 Cf. D.P. LEINSTER-MACKAY, thesis, *op. cit.*, Vol. 2, p. 193, Note 112.

58 WATERFIELD was nicknamed the 'Cow' by the boys because of his initials.

59 In marked contrast to the rest of the school buildings, the library, curtained and carpeted, led to WATERFIELD's study.

60 A.C. BENSON, *Memories*, p. 41.

61 E.F. BENSON, *op. cit.*, p. 78. Cf. also GOODENOUGH, *op. cit.*, p. 14; see also MARSHALL, A (1983) *Whimpering in the Rhododrendrons*, Fontana, pp. 124–5.

62 This behaviour is a good example of the gulf that lies between nineteenth century sentiment and twentieth century realism.

63 E.F. BENSON, *op. cit.*, p.79.

64 A.C. BENSON, 1924, *Memories and Friends*, John Murray, p. 41.

65 WATERFIELD retired in 1880 to become a director of the Ottoman Bank, later dying from a heart attack on a railway station.

66 G.M. TREVELYAN (1937), *Grey of Fallodon*, Longmans p. 7.

67 Cf. A.A.M. BATCHELOR, 'Temple Grove from 1819 to 1880', *Temple Grove School Magazine*, 6. Football was played in knickerbockers and open-necked shirts after ties had been removed.

68 F. ANSTEY, *Vice Versa*, 47th impression 1929, John Murray, p. 174.

69 A.C. BENSON, *Memories op. cit.*, p. 48.

70 Cf. G.W. KITCHIN (1857) *Prayers for the Use of Twyford School*. Some prayers are taken from *Bishop Ken's Manual*, used by Winchester.

71 Cf. C.T. WICKHAM *op. cit.*, pp. 5–7. The two schools were different entities even though a case may be made for continuity through occupation of SEGAR's buildings at different times.

72 This does not mean necessarily that only seven entries in the *DNB* attended Twyford. One of the weaknesses of the *DNB* for the educational historian of preparatory schools is that preparatory school attendance is more often than not omitted. Twyford would be the exception to the generalization about local choice.

73 From a scrapbook of 1855–61 held in school archives.

74 For example, it attacks the system of close supervision to be found in private schools, and the low standing of ushers.

75 At one time boys had to wash themselves at a tap outside.

76 When the school year was divided into two halves, there was an Autumn Reward Day and a June Reward Day. The boys had been graded from *Quam optime* to *Male* on a six-point scale. Those with *Quam optime* were allowed to stay in bed till breakfast-time, after which they prepared themselves for a picnic outing. At the picnic they were joined by the others, who had been up at the usual time doing usual school work.

77 Cf. C.T. WICKHAM *op. cit.*, pp. 20–1. This was basically a mammoth quiz game in which the whole school took part. Twyford also gave prizes for gymnastics. Cf. E.C. MACK and W.H.G. ARMYTAGE, 1952, *Thomas Hughes — The Life of the Author of Tom Brown's Schooldays*, Ernest Benn p. 13.

78 The 'Slate', instituted by BEDFORD, consisted of a record of offenders in two columns: those 'late' and 'other offences'. A daily record of bad marks was kept, but no boy knew how he was faring until perhaps called to expiate his misdemeanours by caning. KITCHIN introduced a more liberal institution, the 'black book', which was examined at the end of each term, when the contents were divulged and those with good records were awarded prizes. Cf. also G.H. WILSON, *Windlesham House*,

Chapter 4 for details regarding the *Classicus* which was the record of marks kept in huge tomes since 1837. The daily marks were awarded on a ten-point scale, with the 'crimes' and punishments logged in the margin.

79 BEDFORD had placed much emphasis on the memory, from which arose prodigious feats of rote learning.

80 For example, Reward Day was not abolished till 1878.

81 C.T. WICKHAM, *op. cit.*, p. 15.

4   National Child Parks?

I thank the goodness and the grace
Which on my birth have smiled,
And made me, in these Christian days,
A happy English child.
(*Hymns for Infant Minds*, 1810)

Snobs are known and recognised throughout an empire on which I am
given to understand the sun never sets.
(William Makepeace Thackeray, *The Book of Snobs*)

Patterns of Prosperity

The period from Wellington's Waterloo (1815) to Disraeli's purchase of the
Suez Canal shares from the Khedive Isma'il (1875) changed gradually from one
of harshness, hardship and repression at home to a state of social and national
'equipoise',[1] followed by a period of intense prosperity which coincided with
what James Morris has called 'the *Pax Britannica*'.[2] This so-called *Pax
Britannica* was in fact based on much British martial activity throughout the
century. According to W.L. Burn, commenting on the period from 1815 to
1855,

> British troops had been in action against Gurkhas, Pindaries, Mahrat-
> tas, Sikhs, Afghans, Burmese, Chinese, Kaffirs, Ashantis and Boers.
> Ships of the Royal Navy had bombarded Algiers, routed the Turks at
> Navarino, operated against Mehemet Ali, underwritten Latin Amer-
> ican independence, blockaded Buenos Aires and the Piraeus, captured
> slavers and waged war on pirates from the Caribbean to the China Sea.
> Assam, Sind and the Punjaub and a great part of Burma had fallen to
> British arms.[3]

This incessant imperialist activity was even more pronounced in the second half
of the century with the unfolding of the ambitions of Cecil Rhodes, leading to
the scramble for Africa in the last two decades, in which Britain took the lion's

share. By 1900 the British Empire — reflected in the writings of Kipling and in the music of Elgar — consisted of some 13,000,000 square miles and contained a population of between 400 and 420 millions. The military and naval activities which acquired this vast empire, of necessity, took the menfolk in large numbers abroad, a fact which, either directly or indirectly, caused many women to seek a living by taking up dame-schooling. Furthermore, the territories taken by conquest or annexation, needed to be administered by men who were recruited from the middle and upper classes. Their absence from the mother country was so prolonged as very often to involve the expatriation also of their spouses. For this cardinal reason there was a need to place children in boarding schools. The need was met by the quasi-preparatory or preparatory schools which can therefore be perceived in one sense as 'national child parks' since their *raison d'être* arose partly from the *national* affair of empire-building. Whilst father and mother were abroad, the preparatory schools became the child parks of their younger progeny.

The development of the 'famous five' from quasi-preparatory to preparatory schools reflected this imperialistic progress. They were, as Meston Batchelor has said of Temple Grove, 'cradles of empire'.[4] This chapter, however, is concerned with other preparatory schools, founded before 1875, some of which still exist today. But before looking briefly at these schools let's first consider the general background to their existence.

Amongst the leading basic factors behind the demand for 'child parks' during the period of Victorian imperialism was the demographic one of a burgeoning population with a steadily increasing birth rate throughout the century as Table 2 indicates.[5] It was from these welling figures that the willing customers came, thus causing preparatory schools to be established in the nineteenth century as fashionable schools for the rising middle classes.

The continuous improvement of National and other denominational elementary schools acted as a spur to the improvement of private schools, the preparatory schools' generic origin. With the increased competition from these church schools and later from higher grade schools where working class sons and daughters enjoyed a widened curriculum which sometimes even included classical studies, the standards of the private or preparatory schools had to improve to continue demonstrating their social superiority. Another spur towards this improvement was the institution of competitive examinations, in which the Victorians had great faith, as a mode of recruitment, by separating the talented from the 'weak' and the 'chaff'. The 1854 reforms of Charles Trevelyan and Stafford Northcote, therefore, though primarily concerned with the reform of the Home and Indian Civil Services indirectly affected the preparatory schools through their repercussions on the public schools.

The standards of living of most social groups improved during the prosperous years of the mid-century and late century. Certainly the English middle classes grew to take prosperity for granted. Examples of this prosperity might be found in the patterns of domestic expenditure, especially on personal

Table 2. Early and Mid-Victorian National Birthrate (in thousands)

Year	Total	Year	Total
1838	464	1857	663
1839	493	1858	655
1840	502	1859	690
1841	512	1860	684
1842	518	1861	696
1843	527	1862	713
1844	541	1863	727
1845	544	1864	740
1846	573	1865	748
1847	540	1866	754
1848	563	1867	768
1849	578	1868	787
1850	593	1869	773
1851	616	1870	793
1852	624	1871	797
1853	612	1872	826
1854	634	1873	830
1855	635	1874	855
1856	657	1875	851

Table 3. Domestic Servants in England and Wales, 1851–71

Females	1851	1861	1871
General servants	575,162	644,271	780,040
Housekeepers	46,648	66,406	140,836
Cooks	44,009	77,822	93,067
Housemaids	49,885	102,462	110,505
Nursemaids	35,937	67,785	75,491
Laundrymaids	—	4,040	4,538
Total	751,641	962,786	1,204,477[6]

servants. Table 3 shows the upward surge of recruitment in domestic servants during the period 1851–71. The sending of sons to English public schools to acquire 'gentlemanly polish' was but another form of consumer spending, based on increasing national prosperity until a recession set in after 1873 when the rate of increase in prosperity did not rise so sharply as before.

Other Quasi-Preparatory Schools

The availability of mansions, the over-production of Oxford and Cambridge graduates in the 1850s, the growing tentacular efficiency of the railways and the example of the 'Famous Five', especially of Windlesham in the wake of Dr Arnold's decision to ban very young boys from Rugby, all combined to help the middle classes, then advancing in Thackeray's phrase to 'manly opulence', to be taken advantage of by preparatory school families such as the unlikely named Allfrees.

Thomas Allfree, with his already preposterously named Romanoff House, bought Rose Hill, Tunbridge Wells, as a second school, appointing his nephew the Rev. Frederick Allfree as resident headmaster. Romanoff House, opened in 1832, had been a preparatory school for universities, public schools and military and naval colleges, and as such could be said to be a 'quasi-preparatory' school. By 1857 Rose Hill was specifically concerned with the preparation of younger boys for public schools. Nor was this all for a third school was started by the Allfrees in addition to Rose Hill and Romanoff House: Romanoff Tower for the very small boys. Rose Hill had the distinction of educating Lord Robert Baden Powell, founder of the Boy Scout movement.[7]

A good example of the links between private coaching in the nineteenth century and the development of preparatory schools is Hoddesdon Grange School, Hertfordshire, founded in 1854 by the Rev. C.G. Chittenden. Both types of institution attracted individuals from the same social group, the classically educated parsons. As an assistant and son-in-law to the Rev. Francis J. Faithfull, Vicar of Hatfield (1811–54),[8] Chittenden took over his private coaching, and, selecting the youngest boys as a nucleus, set up a preparatory school of nine in a gracious Queen Anne house. Here he educated a future prime minister, A.J. Balfour, the Victorian naturalist, F.M. Balfour, a Governor General of Canada and a Tory back-bencher, the Hon. Julian Byng and George Wyndham. Yet despite his success Chittenden kept the school to a small size and did not increase it beyond twenty-five boys.

Going to Hoddesdon Grange at the age of nine in 1866 Lord Frederic Hamilton was impressed by Chittenden's emphasis on concentration and observation and rated Chittenden as 'a remarkable man with a very rare gift . . . a born teacher.'[9] For boys were expected to devote themselves to a topic for no more than a quarter of an hour, and where concentration was not effected, a leather strap was used. Much later when two of these old pupils were staying together in Dublin Castle one of them — George Wyndham — wrote to his old headmaster saying: 'you are the only person who ever taught him [Balfour] anything, and all his other knowledge has been acquired by himself. The result is to me very encouraging for I find myself in precisely the same position.'[10]

Another has written of Chittenden: 'Mr Chittenden was an advanced educationist who never mistook destructive indiscipline for creative self-
expression.'[11]

Yet life at Hoddesdon was, as elsewhere, Spartan: windows were left open
day and night, and there the boys never washed in warm water, and often the
jugs of water were frozen over. It advanced the boys so well that 'the first year
or two at public school seemed like child's play'.[12] But compared with Cheam
or Twyford its athletes were poor. The Rev. C.G. Chittenden[13] was related by
marriage to the Rev. George Renaud of Bath, ex-tutor of Lord Rosebery. Both
priests officiated at the wedding of Mr T.F. Chittenden and Miss E.C. Wheeler
(Chittenden as father and Renaud as uncle of the groom). On this occasion,
which must have been unique, two ex-teachers of two future prime ministers
conducted the wedding ceremony.

Closely connected with Harrow, Orley Farm,[14] like Elstree, did not
achieve great distinction under its first headmaster. Depicted as 'Trollope
House' in Arnold Lunn's novel, *The Harrovians* (1913), its headmaster, Mr
James (*alias* Mr G.B. Innes Hopkins, who was the second headmaster at the
turn of the century), was, says Lunn, 'marked by ferocity towards [his] staff
and pupils, tempered by abject servility towards the parents'.[15] Lunn's vitriol
was probably directed at Mr E.R. Hastings, who was headmaster from 1850 to
1897, as the school after 1897 was more like a happy family. Hopkins, 'who had
a genius for dealing with small boys', kept Orley Farm in the forefront in the
Harrow district, forging even closer links with Harrow School.

One of the earliest purpose-built schools was Hurst Court, Ore, near
Hastings.[16] Founded in 1862 by Dr Pearson, who had earlier kept a school at
Dover, .it later moved to Bournemouth in 1886 and became a Jesuit training
college for two years. Then a Mr Lloyd Griffith moved into it with his school
from Tooting, so that once again it became a preparatory school with three
distinguished headmasters succeeding Lloyd Griffith (1888–1900).[17]

Originally a dame school kept from 1859 by Mrs Worthington, Arnold
Lodge School at 2 Lillington Place, Leamington Spa was, after five years, taken
over by a former assistant master at Leamington College, Mr Alfred Kirk.
Being an admirer of Dr Thomas Arnold of Rugby, he re-named it 'Arnold
Lodge'. Despite his public school orientation Kirk did not confine his
curriculum initially to that of an orthodox preparatory school: he included
science, modern languages and drawing.[18] Nevertheless, several boys went
from Arnold Lodge to Rugby during Kirk's headmastership. Such was the
attraction of his school to parents that he built a new wing. By the time he was
succeeded by the Rev. H.C. Allfree in the early 1880s, the school was an
exclusive establishment catering mainly for boarders.

Another 'feeder' to Rugby was established in a Georgian manor house as
Winton House, by the father of the novelist, E.F. Johns, and a friend of Charles
Kingsley, botanist Mr C.A. Johns,[19] who built into the complex a chapel,
carpentry shop, large gymnasium, indoor swimming baths and two playing
fields. Despite his premature death in 1874 Winton House returned to the

family a quarter of a century later when his son, E.F. Johns, became headmaster in 1897 remaining so for the next forty years. Three years later, in 1940, the school was amalgamated with Dunchurch Hall School, founded by A. Hyde Harrison at Dunchurch Lodge in 1868 before moving to the Hall in 1882/83. He was headmaster for thirty-two years before he retired.[20]

There were other schools which initially offered 'commercial' subjects such as The Mall School, Twickenham, which for the first thirty-seven years of its existence was known as Huntington House School. The first headmaster, Mr George Cumes, taught mainly commercial subjects. So even if his wife also offered preparatory education for young gentlemen, there is some doubt as to whether The Mall School can be regarded as a preparatory school before the time of its third headmaster, Mr Richard Thistlethwaite (1911–37).[21]

The band-wagon was rolling so well that other keepers of private schools got on it quickly. Mostyn House (1852), for example, took boys of all ages until 1890, when A.G. Grenfell became headmaster. As R.S. Tabor had done at Cheam thirty-five years before, Grenfell, as we shall see later, turned Mostyn House into a purely preparatory school, which became a leading school in the late nineteenth and early twentieth centuries.

Stoneygate School at Leicester was opened by Dr Franklin in Leamington in 1844. But it was not 'preparatory' for Leamington College, a now defunct 'quasi-public' school[22] which opened in the same year. Like Mostyn House, Stoneygate was not purely preparatory till 1890, long after it had moved to Leicester. There are no extant records before 1918, but it seems that the school has had no distinguished old boys, but has rather provided an education quietly for the sons of professional men and manufacturers. It has, however, distinguished itself in one respect: taking girls at the school at an early stage. Though they were few in number, it seems likely that Stoneygate was exceeded only by the Dragon School, whose headmaster, C.C. Lynam, displayed considerable sympathy towards the emancipation of women, in the number of girls (excluding daughters of staff) whom it accepted in the days before co-education became fashionable.

Lockers Park, Hemel Hempstead, was in late Victorian times a fairly well established school. It was purpose-designed in 1874, and under its headmaster, H.M. Draper, sent at least twelve boys to Winchester and two to Eton before the turn of the century. Amongst those attending Draper's school was Lascelles Abercrombie, who gained a love of literature at Lockers Park before going to Malvern.[23] Finally, Spondon House (c.1840–1912) is interesting not only because of its early foundation but also because between 1840 and 1900 it had only two heads, both of whom were clerics.[24]

Summary

Most of these schools hovered on the brink of being successful (that is, established) or wanted to be successful like Cheam, Eagle House, Temple

Grove, Twyford and Windlesham House. Generalization is difficult but although the early preparatory schools differed in philosophy, size and success, they had seven features in common differentiating them from preparatory schools after 1875. These seven characteristics were:

1   living conditions were generally Spartan, even by comparison with those of public schools;

2   some masters conducted themselves towards their pupils in a way which in the twentieth century would have led to dismissal and prosecution for cruelty;

3   games were at a very rudimentary stage of development, if played at all;

4   many of the schools were situated in old houses or mansions which were large and draughty;

5   in some schools the boys were given comparative freedom, though others were run on the close surveillance principle of the private school;

6   ushers, where employed, were hacks of the profession who compared unfavourably with assistant masters of a later period;

7   throughout the period great emphasis was placed on the learning of the classics.

In this last respect these preparatory schools did not differ from any other institutions providing middle and upper class education in the nineteenth century. But they were differentiated from other private schools in that they prepared boys for public schools or for entry as future officers in the Royal Navy. This last feature we will now explore.

Notes

1 W.L. BURN (1968) *Age of Equipoise*, Unwin Books.
2 JAMES MORRIS (1975) *Pax Britannica: The Climax of Our Empire*, Faber.
3 W.L. BURN, *op. cit.*, p. 56.
4 A.A.M. BATCHELOR (1982) *Cradle of Empire*, Phillimore.
5 B.R. MITCHELL and P. DEANE (1971) *Abstract of British Historical Statistics*, Cambridge University Press, p. 29.
6 Quoted from J.A. BANKS (1969) *Prosperity and Parenthood*, 3rd impression, Routledge and Kegan Paul, p. 83.
7 Cf. R.M.D. GRANGE, n.d. *History of Rose Hill School*.
8 FAITHFULL had been a very successful classical coach whose establishment was more like a small school. From a Holy Bible presented in 1838 to the Rev. FRANCIS JOSEPH FAITHFULL by the boys of his coaching establishment his clientele can be said to have been very socially distinguished. They included Lord BURGHLEY (the future SALISBURY); Lord BROWNLOW CECIL; Lord GUERNSEY; HON. D. FINCH; Lord ROBERT CECIL; Sir WILLIAM FRASER; and the Hon. BARRINGTON STOPFORD. Lord SALISBURY had spent an unhappy year as a boy with FAITHFULL at Hatfield before being sent at the age of nine to the Rev. HENRY LYTE in Devon. LYTE was the author of the hymn, 'Abide with me'.

9 Lord FREDERIC HAMILTON, 1920, *The Days before Yesterday*, Hodder and Stough-
ton, p. 94. Cf. also J.W. MACKAIL and GUY WYNDHAM, 1925, *Life and Letters of
George Wyndham*, Vol. 1, Hutchinson, p. 23. CF. also K. YOUNG (1963) *Arthur
James Balfour*, G. Bell & Sons p. 12.

10 From Ms. letter from GEORGE WYNDHAM to C.G. CHITTENDEN sent from Dublin
Castle, kept in Newlands School archives.

11 JOHN BIGGS-DAVISON, (1951) *George Wyndham*, Hodder & Stoughton p. 16. One
very different view of this school is given by ANTONY C. DEANE (1945) in *Time
Remembered* Faber & Faber, where he depicts the Rev. CHITTENDEN as somewhat
of an ogre whom the boys called the 'Jowler'. According to DEANE he was subject to
violent tempers, was moody and ought not to have been a schoolmaster.

12 MACKAIL and WYNDHAM, *op. cit.*, p. 23

13 CHITTENDEN retired in 1891.

14 The headmaster of Harrow School, Dr VAUGHAN (1844–59), laid the foundation
stone of Orley Farm School in 1850.

15 A. LUNN, (1913) *The Harrovians*, Methuen, p. 6.

16 This school, which was forced to close in 1961 on the eve of its centenary year, had a
very chequered career. Its early closure in a relatively prosperous period for
preparatory schools was symptomatic of its unfulfilled promise.

17 These were Mr TINDALL (1900–24), who had been an Olympic runner, President of
the Cambridge University Athletic Club, a cricketer for Kent Cricket Club and a
rugby player for Rosslyn Park; Dr VAUGHAN EVANS, his junior partner (1924–33);
and Mr R.J.S. CURTIS OBE (1933–61), one of the four serving Vice-Presidents of the
IAPS. Despite this galactic leadership the school was forced to close a short time
after Mr CURTIS's retirement. I am very grateful to Mr 'DICK' CURTIS for much
information on Hurst Court School. Cf. MAXWELL, G (1965) *The House of Eleig*,
Longmans, pp. 99–120, for account of Hurst Court.

18 Cf. Advertisement KELLY's, *Warwickshire Directory*, 1868.

19 C.A. JOHNS had been second master under the Rev. DERWENT COLERIDGE at
Helston Grammar School where CHARLES KINGSLEY was a pupil (1831–6). JOHNS
was headmaster of Helston Grammar School from 1843 to 1847.

20 He was succeeded by a similarly long serving headmaster, Mr C.G. MALLAM
(1900–24), about whom little is known.

21 Between 1911 and 1937 the school prospered as a preparatory school, having
amongst its pupils the children of Lord STAMP, the economist; the late Professor
FRANCIS CAMPS, the Home Office pathologist; and the late RICHARD DIMBLEBY, the
radio and TV personality. Cf. ANON. (n.d.) *The Mall School 1872–1972*, privately
printed, no pagination, presumed 7.

22 Cf. D.P. LEINSTER-MACKAY (1981) 'English quasi-public schools: A question of
appearance and reality', *BJES*, 29, 1, February.

23 Cf. *Proceedings of the British Academy*, Vol. 25, 1939, p. 394.

24 1840–78 the Rev. T. GASGOINE; 1878–1905 the Rev. E. PRIESTLAND.

5   Servicing the Senior Service

The navy, therefore, must take its boys at the age when they leave the preparatory school; that is, at 12 or 13, at which age the boys should enter the *Britannia*, where they should remain for not less than four years. Whatever the navy requires for entrance to the *Britannia* the preparatory schools will do. There are no schools in the world where boys are better looked after or more carefully taught.
(Spenser Wilkinson (c.1903) *The Nation's Need*)

The Pre-1838 Entry

In the days when Britannia ruled the waves, a naval officer was a gentleman with a passport round the world. To get boys into the navy, therefore, preoccupied many preparatory schools in the nineteenth and early twentieth centuries,[1] especially after 1838 when the Admiralty set an examination for all entrants to the navy.

Until the late eighteenth century it had been customary for future naval officers to enter the navy by way of the 'Captain's Servant Entry'.[2] In 1794 the Admiralty abolished the title of 'Captain's Servant' and replaced it with that of 'First Class Volunteer'.[3] 'Ultimate selection of recruits', wrote Michael Lewis, 'lay not with the Admiralty or any other public body, but with the captains in their private capacity.'[4] So entrenched were the captains in their powers of nomination that 3370 of the 3467 naval officers who entered the navy during the Napoleonic Wars were captains' nominees, with fewer than a hundred being nominated by the Admiralty.[5] The latter had invariably been trained at the Royal Naval Academy at Portsmouth. This academy, founded in 1729, originally confined itself to educating 'the sons of the nobility and gentry',[6] but extended its clientèle in mid-century by recruiting some boys from naval officers' families. The Royal Academy had a very poor reputation. Although its pupils were aged only between thirteen and sixteen, they were renowned for their profligacy.[7]

Many senior naval officers, who set more store by early practical experience within the service, were scornful of the bookish emphasis to be found in the Royal Naval Academy, where the curriculum consisted of navigation, geometry, arithmetic, written English, French, fencing, dancing and drawing. Under the pressure of criticism the Royal Naval Academy was reorganized in 1806 and given a new location and new staff to dispense a more scientifically-based curriculum. Re-named the Royal Naval College, the naval training institution at Portsmouth acquired a new head in James Inman, who became an influential figure in royal naval circles until the late 1830s.[8] His emphasis was on the *theoretical* in seamanship. Over thirty-three years he built up a cadre of élite entrants to the navy. In the early nineteenth century, however, the 'First Class Volunteers' continued to be in the majority. Among such direct entrants were Sir Geoffrey Hornby (1825–95), later Admiral of the Fleet, who in March 1837 joined the Navy at the age of twelve on the *Princess Charlotte*; and [Sir] Francis Cunliffe-Owen (1828–94),[9] another aspiring sailor who entered the navy at the age of twelve. Many of these early direct entries to the navy had gained their early education at 'schools for the sons of gentlemen' or 'quasi-preparatory schools' as did, for example, Admiral John Moresby (1830–1922). T.J.F. Haskoll, headmaster of Peckham House, West Folkestone, writing in the *PSR* in 1909, quoted the case of a pupil from Mr Horne's quasi-preparatory school at Chiswick who joined *HMS Victorious* in 1809 as a 'First Class Volunteer'.[10]

Radical change occurred at Portsmouth Royal Naval College in 1837–38 when the Admiralty, in order to meet the problem of a surplus of junior naval officers, turned the College into a kind of 'in-service training' institution for 'mates' for the next twenty years. *Pari passu*, young recruits to the navy, having been displaced at Portsmouth, went straight to sea following a period in the docks.[11] The Admiralty further reduced the captains' power of nomination in 1838 when it instituted an examination for all entrants to the navy.

The Examination Gets Tougher

At first this examination was relatively easy: the examinees had to demonstrate their ability to write English from dictation and to show knowledge of the first four rules of arithmetic, reduction and the rule of three.[12] But the very fact that an examination for entry was instituted meant that it was now possible to fail to gain entry on intellectual as well as on medical grounds. This possibility of failure had the effect of undermining the force of the captains' power of nomination in favour of competition. The institution of selective examinations had one consequence which was not surprising. Two preparatory schools were opened either before or after the institution of examinations, in order to prepare boys for the Royal Navy: Windlesham House (founded by Lieutenant Charles Robert Malden RN)[13] and Stubbington House, Fareham (founded by the Rev. William Foster). Admiral Lord Charles Beresford (1846–1919), the son of the 4th Marquess of Waterford, was one of those who attended Stubbington House before entering the navy as a naval cadet[14] in 1859. By the time he came to take the naval entrance examination it was still relatively easy, consisting of a little English, less French and Latin (with the aid of a dictionary), scripture, English history, some geography and an elementary knowledge of arithmetic, algebra and Euclid.[15] [Admiral Sir] Cyprian Bridge (1839–1924), who had been nominated in 1852 to a naval cadetship by Admiral Sir Thomas Cochrane (1789–1872), also found his naval entrance examination, held at Portsmouth in 1853, relatively easy. He presented himself for examination with eleven others and all twelve passed.[16] Further naval reforms made it more difficult, from the late 'fifties and early 'sixties onwards, to become a naval officer.[17] This led to an increased use of the naval crammer or the occasional 'quasi-preparatory school' catering for entrants to the navy. One future vice-admiral to be sent to a naval crammer following the Graham reform was H.L. Fleet, who went to Southsea 'to be stuffed with history and geography.'[18]

By the 1880s many preparatory schools were preparing boys for the naval entrance examination. [Admiral Sir] William Fisher (1875–1937), the brother of H.A.L. Fisher, was at the Oxford Preparatory School (or Lynam's) before taking the naval examinations in 1888. Fisher's biographer, Admiral Sir William James, observed that at this time the Civil Service Commissioners responsible for the examination created problems for the preparatory schools. He wrote:

> It was extremely difficult for a boy from a preparatory school to take a high place, as some of the subjects of examination were only taught on the classical side and some only on the modern side, and so parents often denied themselves the good things of life in order to pay the higher fees of a crammer.... Fortunately for the Navy, the crammers did not monopolise all the vacancies and a few boys, educated at good [preparatory] schools, squeezed in each time.[19]

Thirty-two years after Cyprian Bridge had passed into the navy with ease (in 1853), competition had so hardened that, of the hundred candidates who presented themselves for examination on one occasion, only sixty-four passed. One of them was (Admiral Sir) Percy Scott who had been successfully 'crammed' at Eastman's Royal Navy Academy, Portsmouth.[20]

From Britannia to RNC

We return to the 1850s. The major change in mid-century was the reversal of policy implemented in 1837. Instead of being pitch-forked into service at sea at the age of thirteen, the future naval officer was to receive his theoretical and practical training on board the two-decker *HMS Illustrious* under Captain Robert Harris. The new training regime began in Portsmouth Harbour where *HMS Illustrious* was docked, but it soon became clear that a larger ship was required. Two years later, in 1859, the *Illustrious* was replaced by HMS *Britannia*[21] (a three-decker and seventh of that name). The *Britannia* was stationed in Portsmouth Harbour for ten years before it was removed to Dartmouth in 1869.[22] The tradition of 'officer training afloat' lasted until 1903, when the eighth *Britannia* ceased to be a training ship[23] and naval cadets were henceforth trained in land-based royal naval colleges at Osborne and Dartmouth.

During its existence as a training ship from 1859 to 1903, the *Britannia* formed part of the tradition going back to the battle of Trafalgar (1805).[24] Instruction in rigging and sail was still a fundamental part of the naval training as late as the 1880s.[25] Amongst those trained on the *Britannia* were the son of the 2nd Earl of Durham, Admiral Sir H. Meux, who had been educated at Cheam Preparatory School before entry to the *Britannia* in 1870. Admiral Sir Frederick Sturdee joined the ship from RNC New Cross in 1871; Admiral Lord John Jellicoe, of Jutland fame, came from a now defunct preparatory school at Field House, Rottingdean, before he boarded *Britannia* in 1872. David, Earl Beatty also entered the *Britannia* after being 'crammed' at the famous Burney's Naval Academy, Gosport. According to Beatty's biographer, Rear Admiral W.S. Chalmers, the *Britannia* was by the 1880s *two* old ships of the line: the *Hindustan*, a two-decker, and the *Britannia*. They were connected by a bridge and moored in the River Dart. Small craft used to take the cadets to sea and provided 'instruction in sail-drill, marine engines, boat sailing and rowing.'[26]

Naval Schools

So far this chapter has been concerned mainly with the process of recruitment to the navy involving the adoption of examinations at the expense of nominations. Having looked briefly at the history of naval training we can now turn to the institutions which prepared boys for officer-entry to the navy. One of the earliest schools to assume this role was Dr Burney's Academy at Gosport. [Sir] William F.D. Jervois, who was to become a Lieutenant General in the Royal Engineers, was educated at Burney's Academy, as was George C. Musters, who became a Commander in the Royal Navy.[27] Despite the naval orientation of Burney's Academy, at least two other alumni eventually became soldiers: Sir John Cowans, who became a full general after the First World War, and [Sir] Frederick G. Guggisberg, who went on to Sandhurst and later became Governor first of the Gold Coast and then of British Guiana. Burney's of Gosport, however, was not strictly a preparatory school, since it fulfilled only one preparatory school function, and this not its main function. Perhaps, analogously with the private classical schools, it could be described as a 'quasi-preparatory school'.

Another school which was early in the field in the preparation of young boys for the navy was Mr Southwood's school at Devonport attended by

[Admiral Sir] Geoffrey Phipps Hornby, who entered the navy at the age of twelve at the time of the reforms which transformed RNC Portsmouth. Mr Southwood was well patronized for his mathematics teaching.[28] Like Burney's Academy at Gosport, Mr Southwood's, a classical and mathematical school, could possibly be considered also as a 'quasi-preparatory' school since it educated non-military and non-naval pupils such as George R. Prynne, the pioneer of Catholic practices in the Anglican Church.[29]

Eastman's

The greatest rival to the preparatory schools in the second half of the nineteenth century was undoubtedly Eastman's Royal Navy Academy — later to be a member of the Association of Preparatory Schools[30] — situated in turn at Portsmouth and at Northwood Park, Winchester. [Admiral Sir] Albert Hastings Markham was sent to Eastman's after being nominated for the navy, as was also [Admiral Sir] William Henry May who, as naval controller, was responsible for the British Dreadnought policy before the First World War. [Field Marshal Sir] John French also went to Eastman's, having received a nomination for entry to the navy. When he arrived at Eastman's in 1866, Dr Spickernall was the principal. Eastman's success was due very largely to the talents of Dr Spickernall who, for example, when the fleet was in harbour used to organize a small flotilla of boats and take the boys around the ships giving a historical commentary.[31] [Admiral Sir] Percy Scott (1853–1924) entered Eastman's in the same year as Field Marshal French. Eastman's Royal Navy Academy continued to enjoy a high reputation into the twentieth century. In 1898, for example, by which time the school had moved to Winchester, Eastman's put forty-five nominated pupils to compete for naval cadetships under the new regulations introduced that year. Thirty-six of them were successful, with four being among the best ten candidates. The aggregate mark of 3183 gained by Roger Bellairs, who came first equal, was then the highest on record.[32] Another successful naval 'cramming' school was that of Mr Littlejohn at Greenwich attended by [Admiral Sir] Roger Keyes, the first Director of Combined Operations Command in the Second World War. Before his pupil went on to *HMS Britannia* in 1885,[33] he was coached by Mr Littlejohn.

As was to be expected in the nineteenth century, indigent clergymen were at hand in mid-century when pure nomination gave way to a combination of nomination and examination. The Rev. William Rowe Jolley was a good example of such a marriage of the ecclesiastical with the nautical, since he prepared for the navy no less a person than Alfred, Duke of Edinburgh and Duke of Saxe Coburg and Gotha, the second son of Queen Victoria. There were many such clergy who coached boys for the navy in the privacy of their rectories or in their 'rectory' schools.

Gradually, however, preparatory schools came into their own through the preparation of boys for the Royal Navy. In 1896 Heath Mount School,

Hertfordshire, under its new head, Mr John S.G. Grenfell,[34] advertized both in its prospectus and elsewhere its special interest in training boys for the navy. Similarly Farnborough Park School in Hampshire, conducted by Mr Charles Lupton, prepared a limited number of boys for entry to *HMS Britannia*. Following the new regulations in December 1897 Farnborough gained twelve naval cadetships in two years.[35]

Stubbington House

No school had stronger ties with the Royal Navy in the nineteenth century than Stubbington House at Fareham in Hampshire. Founded in 1841 by the Rev. William Foster, then Vicar of Crofton, the school began modestly with about ten boys in an early eighteenth century manor house. William Foster's interest in preparing boys for the navy was probably of a twofold origin. First, the metamorphosis of RNC Portsmouth in 1837 was propitious for other rival educational institutions since displaced boys would need to go elsewhere. Secondly, his marriage to the daughter of Rear Admiral John Hayes gave him links which were made all the stronger by the siting of his school in the nautical county of Hampshire. By the time of his death in 1865, Foster's Academy was *the* recognized school for future naval officers and was prospering in the wake of the recently launched *HMS Britannia*. At one time there were as many as 150 boys in the school.[36]

A development in the 1860s which set Stubbington House apart from other emerging preparatory schools was the establishment of an army department where boys remained beyond the customary age in order to prepare for Woolwich and Sandhurst. When Montagu Foster (Senior) succeeded his father, the Rev. William Foster, as headmaster in 1865, Montagu's brother, the Rev. Courtenay Foster,[37] opened this army department within the grounds of Stubbington House.[38] Courtenay Foster died comparatively early and was succeeded by his nephew, Montagu Foster (Junior), who closed down the army section in 1913 when he succeeded his father as headmaster of Stubbington House. At the time of his accession as headmaster of Stubbington, the school had declined to seventy-seven boys, largely for two reasons. First, it had lost some fifty boys with the closure of the army department. Secondly, after the closure of *Britannia*, boys were going straight to RNC Osborne at a younger age than hitherto. In passing it may be noted that because of its army department Stubbington House gained relatively late recognition as a preparatory school *per se*.[39]

Montagu Foster (Senior) was the chief contributor to Stubbington's pre-eminence in the late nineteenth century. He was responsible for the spacious school buildings which included a dining hall, large library, assembly hall, gymnasium, a well equipped science laboratory and two sanatoria. The future senior naval officers who attended this school are legion.[40] During the time of the Rev. William Foster, [Admiral Lord] Charles Beresford[41] was a pupil and one of the first Stubbingtonians to become an admiral. Amongst the later distinguished old Stubbingtonians were Sir Henry Jackson, a future Admiral of the Fleet and First Sea Lord and pioneer of wireless telegraphy; Captain Robert Falcon Scott of Antarctic fame; Lord Viscount Cunningham of Hyndhope, Admiral of the Fleet and First Sea Lord; Sir John Cunningham, Admiral of the Fleet; Air Chief Marshals Sir John Steel and Sir Arthur Longmore; and Admiral Sir Henry Harwood, torpedo expert and victor of the Battle of the River Plate. At one stage the navy was being run by two old Stubbingtonians: the First and Second Sea Lords Sir Henry Jackson and the Hon. Somerset Gough-Calthorpe.

Although many Stubbingtonians were prepared for the navy and army, many others gained places at public schools, particularly Wellington, Sherborne and Cheltenham, whilst a few others went to Eton. By the turn of the century, however, Stubbington's reputation as a leading preparatory school was still so firmly based on its close links with the navy[42] that it was patronized by royalty.[43] Assuming it had a fairly consistent intake at the turn of the century Stubbington House had a virtual monopoly amongst preparatory schools for entrants to the navy:[44] in December 1894 and in June and December 1895, preparatory schools contributed 42 per cent of all successful candidates for the navy,[45] yet in 1906 the *Report of the Departmental Committee ... on Certain Questions Concerning the Extension of the New Scheme of the Training of Naval Officers* (Cd 2841) showed that Stubbington House had prepared more than 33 per cent of all entrants.

Several biographies and autobiographies have described the school days of old Stubbingtonians. One of the earliest of these was *The Life of Major General Wauchope*,[46] which recorded the life of the officer of the Black Watch killed at the Battle of Magersfontein during the Second Boer War. Wauchope (1846–99) was at school when the Rev. William Foster was alive. During Wauchope's time at Stubbington the school numbered about forty and kept boys until they were eighteen or nineteen — and this was even before the Army department was established. Viscount Cunningham of Hyndhope, in his autobiography *A Sailor's Odyssey*, recorded his years at Stubbington from 1894 to 1897. He enjoyed his time there and admired the efficiency of the masters. He wrote: 'The older masters were wizards at driving knowledge into the heads of the unintelligent.'[47] There is more than a suggestion in Cunningham's autobiography that Stubbington at the end of the century was midway between a naval crammer and a private preparatory school.

After about 1887 changes took place in the Royal Navy which had the effect of converting the senior armed service from a traditionally sail-based navy into a modern steam-orientated one.[48] Reform was accelerated in the wake of the increasing naval rivalry between Germany and Great Britain. The introduction by Great Britain of the Dreadnought policy — basically a policy to retain supremacy at sea — was accompanied by changes in the recruitment of naval officers. The raising of the age of entry for naval cadets in 1898 from thirteen to fifteen temporarily deprived the preparatory schools of their traditional links with the Royal Navy unless individual schools were willing to compromise their essentially 'preparatory for public school' nature by preparing older boys for the navy. The raising of the age for entry of naval cadets seems to have been effected in 1897/98 by those who espoused the virtues of a more advanced general education and a later entry for naval officers. They had gained a temporary advantage over what one commentator called the 'naval school of thought' which favoured an early entry age followed by practical experience.[49] At the Association of Headmasters of Preparatory Schools Sixth Conference the then recent decision by the Admiralty to raise the age of entry was criticized heavily by Mervyn Voules (Windermere House, Barnes Common) and others. A resolution was passed drawing the attention of the First Lord of the Admiralty to the difficulties which the Admiralty's decision was causing.[50]

At its Seventh Annual Conference the Association decided that in view of the new regulations the best policy for the future was to ensure that preparatory schoolboys reached a good standard in Latin, French, mathematics, English and drawing by the age of thirteen and a half when they would be transferred to those public schools which specialized in navy candidates: Marlborough, Clifton, Bradfield and Cheltenham. The object of this policy was to prevent other public schools from eroding the preparatory schools' position still further by offering blandishments to naval cadets in the form of scholarships.[51] This policy, now adopted by the Association as a whole, had been pursued at Elstree School since 1885 with the inauguration of 'a modern side' which allowed boys to pass into the Navy without going to a crammer. Consequently by 1906 there were twenty-five officers serving in the Royal Navy who had been at Elstree School.[52]

Two years later, in 1901, the Association strongly criticized the concession granted by the Civil Service Commissioners to Stubbington House, The Limes, Greenwich, and Eastman's, Portsea, to act as centres for the conduct of the naval entry examination. The Association requested the withdrawal of the privileges accorded to these schools and demanded that all should have an equal chance. The Civil Service Commissioners'[53] assent was one of the early indications of the collective strength of the Association after ten years' existence. But in 1903 the Association gained a more significant victory when the Admiralty decided to revert to an earlier age of entry. From July 1903 all candidates for naval commissions were to be between twelve and thirteen years old.[54] This 'New Scheme', instituted by Lord Fisher, made provision for a return to land-based training in the two royal naval colleges at Osborne and Dartmouth. The successful examinees were to enter one or other of these colleges for two years[55] before joining a training ship.

Schools Raise the Age

The choice of age was seemingly based on a misconception that boys normally moved from preparatory school to public school between twelve and thirteen.

A special conference of the AHPS was convened in March 1903 to discuss the latest development. Mr E.D. Mansfield of Lambrook School presided. It was agreed that 'in the opinion of this conference it would be for the best interests of the boys, and therefore of the Navy and of the Nation, if the age for entry to the Navy were fixed at thirteen to fourteen, instead of twelve to thirteen.'[56] The Admiralty responded positively to this advice and raised the lower age limit by six months 'with the express object of bringing the examination into line with the work of the ordinary preparatory schools'.[57] Meanwhile a regular stream of cadets was entering RNC Osborne from the preparatory schools. The Admiralty was anxious to continue encouraging these traditionally close links, and in a Blue Book entitled *Selection of Candidates for Nomination As Naval Cadets* informed parents of potential recruits that a good preparatory school, without recourse to a naval crammer, was all that was necessary to secure examination success. Certainly this was the view accepted in 1912 at Mostyn House, whose school prospectus declared: 'The Admiralty has very carefully framed the Osborne requirements *to suit the product of the normal preparatory school* [my italics], and sternly discourages anything in the way of special coaching or cramming.' The headmaster, A.G. Grenfell, made it plain to parents that the naval entrance examination was not competitive and that the preparatory school masters' confidential reports were an important part of the selection procedure.[58] Such was the close rapport which had been established between the preparatory schools and the Admiralty by the beginning of the First World War that after the outbreak of war the Association encouraged its members to admit sons of naval officers at a reduced fee.[59]

In 1921 the closing of RNC Osborne confined the training of naval cadets to RNC Dartmouth. The thirteen-year-old Royal Naval Cadet entry was abolished in 1948, and thereafter boys entered at sixteen. At a later date still, the entry age was raised to seventeen/eighteen. The ties between preparatory schools and the Royal Navy were thus finally severed.

Notes

1 As many as 230 IAPS schools and 13 non-IAPS schools prepared boys for the Royal Navy in 1924. Sec C.H. DEANE and A.P.W. DEANE (Eds), (1924) *The Public Schools Year Book 1924*, Deane and Sons, pp. 796–813. Of the thirteen non-IAPS schools twelve were dame/preparatory schools.

2 G.J. MARCUS (1975) *Heart of Oak*, Oxford University Press, Chapter 6, 'The young gentlemen', pp. 87–95. MICHAEL LEWIS (1965) *The Navy in Transition 1814–1864*, Hodder and Stoughton, p. 100.

3 Appointment as 'Captain's Servant' or 'First Class Volunteer' allowed a boy to learn the ropes under the watchful eye of the captain, and was analogous to the apprenticeship system or the nexus, in mediaeval times, between the knight and squire.

4 *Ibid.*, p. 100.

5 *Ibid.*

6 *Ibid.*, p. 103. See also CHRISTOPHER LLOYD and R.C. ANDERSON (Eds) (1959) *A Memoir of James Trevenen*, Navy Records Society, pp. 2–5.

7 EARL ST VINCENT was sufficiently sceptical about the worth of the academy that he steered at least one parent from sending a son to it. LEWIS, *op. cit.*, p. 103.

8 The Rev. JAMES INMAN (1776–1859), Cambridge Senior Wrangler 1800, official astronomer with Flinders in the *Investigator* and *Porpoise* in the Antarctic (1803–4), Professor of Mathematics at RNC Portsmouth (1806–39). INMAN wrote several books on navigation and nautical astronomy. *Inman's Tables* were a *vade mecum* for all naval officers until the early twentieth century.

9 He did not stay in the navy but became Director of the South Kensington Museum.

10 Letter from T.J.F. HASKOLL, dated 18 February, 1909 together with letter from his aunt 'A.T.', dated June 1908. *PSR*, 5, 42, March 1909, pp. 338–9.

11 Exceptions to this practice were those who first attended the Royal Naval College at New Cross like Sir GEORGE NARES (1831–1915), admiral and Arctic explorer, and Admiral Sir FREDERICK RICHARDS (1833–1912), who became a naval cadet in 1848.

12 LEWIS, *op. cit.*, p. 108.

13 MALDEN himself joined the Royal Navy in 1809 at the age of twelve and became a junior midshipman.

14 The term 'naval cadet' replaced 'First Class Volunteer' in 1843.

15 CHARLES BERESFORD (1914) *The Memoirs of Admiral Lord Charles Beresford*, Methuen, Vol. 1 p. 6.

16 Admiral Sir CYPRIAN BRIDGE (1918) *Some Recollections*, John Murray, p. 38.

17 Sir JAMES GRAHAM who instituted them was First Lord of the Admiralty in Lord ABERDEEN's administration, 1852–55, and retained the office when Lord PALMERSTON became Prime Minister.

18 H.L. FLEET (1922) *My Life, and a Few Yarns*, G. Allen and Unwin p. 17.

19 Sir WILLIAM JAMES, (1943), *Admiral Sir William Fisher*, Macmillan pp. 6–7.

20 Sir PERCY SCOTT, (1919) *Fifty Years in the Royal Navy*, John Murray, pp. 3–4.

21 *HMS Britannia* took part in the bombardment of Sevastopol in the Crimean War.

22 In 1869 the seventh *HMS Britannia* was replaced by the *Prince of Wales* which was immediately renamed *HMS Britannia*.

23 Cf. E.P. STATHAM RN, (1904), *The Story of the Britannia*, Cassell and Co. p. 244.

24 Sir PROVO WALLIS, who was at the top of the naval active list in the 1880s when EARL BEATTY joined the navy, had been afloat in 1805.

25 Captain NATHANIEL BOWDEN SMITH, Captain of the *Britannia* in 1884, trained his naval cadets in the old traditions. GEOFFREY RAWSON, *Earl Beatty*, p. 16.

26 W.S. CHALMERS, (1951), *Life and Letters of David, Earl Beatty*, Hodder and Stoughton p. 6.

27 MUSTERS gained the title of 'King of Patagoniz' from his travels in South America, from the Magellan Straits to the Rio Negro, accompanied by Patagonian aborigines (*DNB*).

28 Mrs F. EGERTON (1896) *Admiral Sir Geoffrey Phipps Hornby*, Edinburgh, Blackwood, p. 4.

29 A. CLIFTON KELWAY, (1905), *George Rundle Prynne — a Chapter in the Early History of the Catholic Revival*, Longmans p. 7.

30 By 1924 — and perhaps earlier — Eastman's was a member of the Preparatory Schools' Association.

31 GERALD FRENCH, (1931) *Life of Field Marshal Sir John French*, Cassell and Co. p. 7.

32 J. and J. PATON (1900) *Paton's List of Schools and Tutors*, p. 74.

33 CECIL ASPINALL-OGLANDER (1951) *Roger Keyes*, Hogarth Press p. 11.

34 Son of Admiral SIDNEY GRENFELL.

35 PATON *op. cit.*, p. 75.

36 I am indebted to A.R.W. MOORE, Headmaster of Stubbington House, for much of

the background information about the early history of the school.

37 COURTENAY FOSTER had been well-known in the hunting world and had been an amateur jockey riding his own horses. After a sudden conversion to the Church he became ordained and began coaching boys for the Army examination.

38 The army department was moved from Stubbington to Seafield House (or Park House) in 1886.

39 For example, it does not appear as a listed preparatory school in the *PSR* of March 1899 (2, 12, pp. 110–12).

40 See *The Stubbingtonian*, 18, 2, 1970–71, pp. 48–50.

41 Lord CHARLES BERESFORD (1846–1919) was a friend of the Prince of Wales and left the navy in 1909/10 to enter politics, for the second time, as MP for Portsmouth. He distinguished himself at the bombardment of Alexandria in 1882. He was given a state funeral at St Paul's Cathedral. See *The Stubbingtonian*, 18, 3, 1971–72, pp. 55–8 for a full appreciation of Lord CHARLES BERESFORD.

42 See *PSR*, 3, 20, December 1901, p. 68. Stubbington House was one of the five centres chosen by the Civil Service Commissioners for the holding of the Naval examinations.

43 For example, Prince ALEXANDER ALBERT of Battenburg (grandson of Queen VICTORIA and later MARQUESS of Carisbrooke) was sent to Stubbington House.

44 Its closest rivals in the early twentieth century were EASTMAN's Royal Naval Academy, Northwood Park, Winchester and Mr LITTLEJOHN's 'The Limes', Greenwich.

45 See *PSR*, 2, 2, December 1896, p. 25.

46 Sir GEORGE DOUGLAS (1904) *The Life of Major-General Wauchope*, Hodder and Stoughton.

47 VISCOUNT [A.B.] CUNNINGHAM of Hyndhope (1951) *A Sailor's Odyssey*, Hutchinson p. 14.

48 *The Devastation*, an early prototype steam battleship was built as early as 1870. Cf. MICHAEL LEWIS, *The History of the British Navy*, pp. 227–9.

49 'The entry and training of naval officers', *Blackwood Edinburgh Magazine*, 162, December 1897, p. 742.

50 *PSR*, 2, 9, March 1898, 1. See also article by MERVYN F. VOULES, 'The examination for naval cadetship', *Ibid.*, pp. 20–2.

51 *PSR*, 2, 12, March 1899, p. 84.

52 I am indebted to the late Commander SANDERSON for this information. Letter in my possession dated 22 November 1977.

53 Letters dated 16 January 1902 from the Civil Service Commissioners to F. RITCHIE, the Secretary of the AHPS.

54 The last examination for naval cadets entering *HMS Britannia* between fourteen and a half and fifteen and a half years was held in November 1905. Cf. *PSR*, 4, 24, March 1903, pp. 21–2.

55 P.D. THOMPSON (Ed.), *How to Become a Naval Officer*, Gieves p. 11. The first examination for admission to Osborne was held in July 1903 with seventy-three candidates from thirty-one preparatory schools. *PSR*, 4, 26, December 1903, p. 74.

56 *PSR*, 4, 25, July 1903, p. 52.

57 *Ibid.*, 4, 27, March 1904, pp. 106 and 126–7.

58 *Mostyn House Prospectus*, 1912. Cf. also *Wells House Magazine*, December 1910 which refers to letter from the Admiralty to APS dated 23 November 1910.

59 Cf. letter in *The Times Educational Supplement*, 5 November 1914 under heading 'Preparatory schools and officers' sons'.

Lifelines for Clergymen

And don't let us give way to the vulgar prejudice that clergymen are an overpaid and luxurious body of men ... he must 'look like a gentleman' ... and bring up his six great hungry sons.
(William Makepeace Thackeray, *The Book of Snobs*)

The Clergy and Education

The leading part played by the clergy in private preparatory schools in the nineteenth century can be said to represent the height of clerical activity in English education. Large rectories, small salaries and a plethora of curates necessitated retaining the church's traditional role laid down by the Canons of 1603, at the beginning of the Stuart period, which ensured for the Church a continuing monopoly in schooling when they laid down that: 'no man shall teach either in public school or private house but such as shall be allowed by the bishop or other ordinary.' In such a monopolistic world, individual clergy were given priority in the granting of licences to teach. In song schools, cathedral schools and chantry schools there could in any case be no alternative. But even in other forms of elementary education in mediaeval England, many clergy had dispensed education informally.[1] Moreover in 1529 parish clergy were encouraged by the Canterbury convocation to take up teaching[2] as part of their clerical duty. This ecclesiastical monopoly of schooling went unchallenged until the late seventeenth century when dissenting clergy ran 'illicit' academies. By the eighteenth century this nonconformist practice of private school-keeping had been extended, through laxity and lawsuits,[3] beyond nonconformity. As Nicholas Hans has indicated, new trends were discernible in education in the eighteenth century, trends in which the orthodox clergy were perhaps more assiduously engaged than any other section of the population. In some cases, custom had ordained their schoolmasterly calling; in many others, their inadequate incomes assured it.

Almost invariably the cleric who turned to schoolmastering taught the classics.[4] Some clerics became private tutors preparing boys for entry to university and the great schools alike.[5] On the other hand many clergymen ran private classical schools throughout the eighteenth and early nineteenth centuries. Nicholas Hans divided the private classical schoolmasters of the eighteenth century into two main categories:

1 the professional teacher who had probably taken Holy Orders as tradition demanded but was absent from his parish in the full-time conduct of his school. Such a man was Dr Thomas Horne of Chiswick who was also Vicar of Wilkington in Herefordshire;

2 the resident vicar or rector who for reasons of economy or personal educational philosophy educated his sons at home with other boys of the locality. Often such schools were opened to augment a meagre stipend.

Of the 260 private classical schools mentioned by Hans, as many as 240 were schools run by Anglican clergy. In the early nineteenth century a great many all-age private classical schools or quasi-preparatory schools were run by clergymen in and around London. Some achieved fame in fashionable society.

Private Classical Schools

Autobiography and general biography throw some light on some of these schools through the reminiscences of some of their former pupils and their biographers. According to Canon Liddon, in his biography of Pusey, the Rev. Richard Roberts' school at Mitcham was one concerned with the achievement of accuracy, though this was attained by excessive corporal punishment.[6] Sir Thomas Dyke Acland, probably a contemporary of Pusey at Mitcham, confirmed that the Rev. Roberts was liberal with the cane.[7]

The Rev. Dr Nicholas's school at Ealing, attended by [Cardinal] John Henry Newman and his brother, Francis, enjoyed a very high reputation in the early nineteenth century. In 1817 it was a large school of about 300 boys which the Rev. T. Mozley, in *Reminiscences of Oriel*, later described as being 'considered the best preparatory school in the country'.[8] Dr Nicholas ran his school on Eton lines, ensuring 'sound instruction and an atmosphere of social distinction'.[9]

A school which must have rivalled the Rev. Dr Nicholas's school, if not in size but in reputation, was that of the Rev. John Buckland at Laleham. This school had no fewer than eleven entries in the *DNB* including the future Cambridge don, F.J.A. Hort, who went on to Rugby, and William Spottiswoode, later mathematician, physicist and President of the Royal Society, who went from Laleham to Eton.[10]

The Rev. J.A. Barron's school at Stanmore was another school with a deservedly high reputation.[11] Its foundation went back to 1771 when a certain Dr Samuel Parr left Harrow in disappointment at not being appointed headmaster of that school. In doing so Parr unwittingly anticipated a later trend in the history of nineteenth preparatory schools when assistant masters left public schools to take up preparatory schooling. Barron's school, run on Pestalozzian lines,[12] had about sixty boys looked after by six resident masters. He was a 'progressive' educationist with ideas well in advance of his time, since he had a laboratory built at Stanmore to teach chemistry.[13]

The Rev. Elwell's school at Hammersmith was another clerical private classical or quasi-preparatory school with a high reputation. It was probably recommended by William Wilberforce to the parents of Gathorne Gathorne-Hardy, the first Earl of Cranbrook. The school which produced many distinguished clergymen was nevertheless alleged to be 'a place of narrowness, bigotry, hypocrisy and meanness'.[14]

Clerical Advantages

The private classical schools of Hans's first category — owned by professional schoolmasters who were mainly absentee parsons — were particularly prominent and numerous in the first half of the century. But those of Hans's second category, the rectory schools, were much in evidence throughout the century and were always more numerous than the first category,[15] though by the 1860s many had turned to private coaching. The Anglican clergyman was in a strong position to combine schoolmastering with his clerical duties, for, as Thomas Arnold noted in 1832, 'in schools conducted by the clergy, the parents have this security, that the man to whom they commit their children has been at least regularly educated, and ... he must be a man of decent life'.[16] Some confirmation of Arnold's point had been given during the late Georgian period when the Rev. W. Russell, Rector of Shepperton, received a request from at least one parent to become private tutor to her boy. The letter was sent by the mother of John M. Neale, the writer of *Hymns, Ancient and Modern*, and made the point that Mrs Neale felt Russell was capable of inculcating 'the fear of the Lord which is the beginning of wisdom'.[17] This deferential view of the clergy was confirmed half a century later when *The Saturday Review* pronounced that the clergyman 'can cover his ignorance of all educational matters by the breadth of his broadcloth and the height of his doctrine'.[18] The man of the cloth had a ready-made testimony of his suitability for intellectual instruction and moral guidance. He was able to provide in his country rectory a form of education different from that given in public schools which William Cowper attacked in bitter and vehement terms in his poem 'Tirocinium' or 'A Review of Schools' (1784), based on his bitter experiences at Westminster.

Dislike of Urban Squalor

Certain factors helped to promote increasing clerical participation in middle and upper class education in the nineteenth century. With about half the population (8,410,000) living in towns by the mid-century,[19] many clergy preferred 'the leisurely pace, status and social cohesion of a rural cure'[20] to the jostle and challenge of an urban living. At a time of relative rural depopulation in an increasingly industrialized England, the opportunities for a rural cleric to turn his rectory into a small school increased as his congregation and parochial responsibilities diminished. Another pertinent factor which promoted rectory schools in nineteenth century England was the drive by reforming prelates such as Bishop Blomfield, of Chester (1824) and London (1828), to remove the abuses of pluralism and absenteeism.[21] This caused some clergy to exploit their talents by setting up private coaching establishments or private schools in their ample and roomy rectories.

The Push of Poverty

But the most important factor in this increasing trend towards clerics' taking up schoolmastering — apart from the revival of both universities and endowed grammar schools — was the relative poverty of many of the clergy. Not all clergymen were such fortunate 'Squarsons' as the Rev. Thomas Stevens who was both lord of the manor and rector of Bradfield and founded Bradfield School;[22] or the Rev. Charles Slingsby-Slingsby who owned Red House (Moor Monkton) and Scriven Park (Knaresborough) and who employed Red House preparatory school boys in the early twentieth century as beaters on his many hunting expeditions. Nor were there many clergy so materially blessed as the Rev. the Marquis of Normanby who as Lord Mulgrave (a junior title) inherited 8000 acres in Yorkshire and yet kept a school.[23] Only Canon Newton, later Vicar of Redditch, could compete with such affluence. Having inherited a fortune he found his vicarage in Yorkshire too small and built himself a new one at his own expense; he also built an extensive residence on a loch in Western Scotland where he owned a deer forest.[24]

Many clergymen were moved to open schools because of the desire to educate their own sons at home, while some like Normanby probably did so in order to continue to exercise their intellect in backwaters of rural England. Others were driven to do so through stark poverty. In the unreformed state of the Church at the beginning of the nineteenth century the curates were in an especially parlous state.[25]

The poverty of incumbents was an old problem. According to Geoffrey Best, official recognition of the poverty of some clergy could be traced back to 1704 with the institution of Queen Anne's Bounty.[26] By 1809, 3300 benefices were valued at less than £150 p.a. while some 860 were worth less than £50 p.a. Queen Anne's Bounty provided some relief, augmenting the stipends of about 1000 smaller livings between 1800 and 1820. But as late as 1868 there were still some clergy whose income was £50 p.a. or less.[27] This 'spiritual destitution', as Bishop Blomfield called it during the debate on the ecclesiastical Duties and Revenues Bill in July 1840, was perhaps best epitomized by the existence of the

Society for Clothing Indigent Establishment Clergy.[28] With the appointment of ecclesiastical commissioners in 1836 to spearhead church reform generally, some relief was given annually to the poorer clergy. These augmentations of salary, together with the continuing relief from Queen Anne's Bounty, helped to alleviate some of the poverty of those clergy whose salaries were less than £200 per annum. Those worst off were the parsons whose income depended on the glebe, since they had to rely on harvests gleaned by others. With their incomes so low and with so much time on their hands, many country clergymen in a period of predominantly laissez-faire philosophy converted their rectories into places of education, despite the discouragement of this practice[29] by the reforming zeal of the evangelical and High Church sections of the Church.

The Rectory Schools

Before turning our attention to the rectory schools it is necessary to emphasize again the difficulty of drawing a line between the clergyman *qua* tutor who 'took in pupils' and the clergyman *qua* schoolmaster who kept a school. When does a rectory taking in pupils become a school? It is difficult to say. For instance, the Rev. John Bickersteth (Vicar of Acton from 1812 to 1837) used his vicarage for teaching private pupils. Was this a school? It is impossible for the historian to speak with certainty because of the unknown psychological aspects of the question.

The *DNB* offers very many examples of these small rectory schools throughout the first fifty years of the nineteenth century. By that time the preparatory school *per se* could be said to be emerging as a feeder of public schools through the economic law of supply and demand. Sir James Graham[30] went to the small school kept by the Rev. Walter Fletcher of Dalston [now in Cumbria] before being sent to Westminster in 1807. Richard Durnford, Bishop of Chichester, was sent to the school of the Rev. E.C. James at Epsom from 1810 to 1813 before going on to Eton. General Sir Daniel Lysons went to the school of the Rev. Harvey Marryat of Bath before being sent to Shrewsbury School, whilst the metaphysician, Henry L. Mansel, attended the rectory school of the Rev. John Collins at East Farndon, Northamptonshire, from 1828 to 1830 before going to Merchant Taylors' School at the age of ten. Until he moved on to King Edward's school, Birmingham, the eugenicist Francis Galton attended the small school of about six pupils conducted by the Rev. Mr Attwood at Kenilworth. This was much patronized by such members of the industrial élite of Birmingham as the Watts and Boultons. Samuel Plimsoll, the sailors' friend, was first educated by the curate of Penrith before going to Dr S. Eadon's school in Sheffield. Sir James Fitzjames Stephen, the Victorian judge went to the school of the Rev. Benjamin Guest at Brighton before going to Eton. Sir Robert Herbert, a colonial official, attended the Rev. Daniel's School at Sawston from 1838 to 1840 until he left for Eton. Similarly the poet, A.G.

Swinburne, was prepared for Eton by the Rev. C.F. Fenwick, rector of Brook, near Newport, Isle of Wight. The list could be endless.

General biography, too, gives a number of examples of these rectory schools and naturally throws more light on them than does the *DNB*. Frederick Locker Lampson who became more commonly known as Frederick Locker, the poet, tells in *My Confidences* (1896) how his school days in 1830 were spent with the Rev. Barnett of Yateley in Hampshire, who took in five or six pupils. Locker-Lampson was not happy at this school of 'Orbilius of the birch', whom he hated and feared. After a year's interval in the Rev. Elwell's school in Clapham Common,[31] Locker-Lampson was sent to the rectory school of the Rev. Wight, Vicar of Drearyboro',[32] who advertized school vacancies in *The Record*, a Low Church journal. Locker-Lampson, who stayed only a short while with 'Mr Wight' before going on to Dr Burney's private classical school at Greenwich, was one of two pupils attending the school. Mr Wight's 'school' may have fallen on hard times, but with only two pupils at that stage it was more like a private tutor's establishment.

A rectory school of a slightly earlier date, which achieved much greater success than Mr Wight's small school, was that conducted four miles from Liverpool by the Rev. William Rawson at Seaforth Vicarage, at the mouth of the Mersey. Rawson catered mainly for Cheshire and Lancashire families, but amongst his ex-pupils were William E. Gladstone, the Victorian Liberal statesman; Arthur P. Stanley, Dean of Westminster and biographer of Thomas Arnold; and Archbishop Plunket of Dublin. Another early school, which the future Cardinal Manning attended in 1820, was kept by the Rev. Abel Lendon, curate of Totteridge, who prepared boys for Westminster.[33] A less well known school, contemporary with Totteridge in the early nineteenth century, was that run by a Mr Bowles at Yarmouth. This school was not a rectory school *per se* since Mr Bowles was an ex-actor and Unitarian minister, but it prepared boys for public school in a similar fashion. Sir James Paget, the distinguished surgeon extraordinary to Queen Victoria, attended this school with his three brothers, and all four went from Yarmouth to Charterhouse.

Lord Norton (b.1814), formerly the Rt Hon. Sir Charles Adderley MP, attended both types of private classical school.[34] After three years at a school of thirty to forty boys conducted by the Rev. J. Parsons at Redland, Bristol, the young Adderley was sent to the Rev. F.R. Spragg at Combe St Nicholas where the sons of Wilberforce were his fellow-pupils.[35] Norton, who had decided views on education,[36] referred to his own education at this school as being 'of the most meagre kind in instruction ... though lavish in costliness'.

The rectory schools continued to flourish at least to the mid-century. John Beddoe (b.1826), FRS, the Victorian medical, legal and anthropological expert, attended a school kept by the Rev. Wharton at Mitton, near Stourport in Worcestershire. Wharton gave Beddoe a good grounding in both Latin and Greek, and in a kindly way. This could not be said of the Rev. Francis Kilvert, the antiquary of diary fame, who kept a school at Harnish Rectory attended from 1843 to 1846 by Augustus Hare, the Victorian writer. This school was patronized by boys of the wealthy middle class,[37] but in common with other recipients of this form of education, Hare was critical of the way in which the school was conducted. Though deeply religious, Kilvert, like many of his clerical contemporaries in their war against Augustinian original sin, was not averse to the use of the cane. Hare noted how Kilvert 'was very hot-tempered and slashed our hands with a ruler and our bodies with a cane most unmercifully.'[38] Despite Kilvert's scholarship and the rigour of his regime, Hare felt that he learnt little at this school.

One of the more successful rectory schools was that at Durnford near Salisbury, conducted by the Rev. Canon Parr and attended by two *DNB* entries, Laurence Oliphant, the novelist and mystic, and Sir William Harcourt, of death duties fame. Harcourt's father was averse to the public school system and sent his two sons, William and Edward, to Durnford when it had only five boys. Parr made the boys work hard, with some eleven hours of study each weekday and two hours spent on reading the Greek testament on Sundays. This small school even had its own *Durnford School Magazine*. The school prospered and had grown to twenty-four in number by 1840 when Parr became Vicar of St John's at Preston and transferred his school to Lancashire.

Another excellent rectory school which seemed to foster a tradition for tutoring and schoolmastering was that at Fordington Vicarage, Dorset, run by the Rev. Henry Moule,[39] the father of Handley C.C. Moule.[40] Henry Moule had some fifteen or sixteen boys in his school and educated in his time his eight sons, most of whom gained distinction in later life. Henry Moule (senior) was assisted in his task by a succession of curates. The teaching was very enlightened. Parr did not attempt to force lessons but rather to create an environment conducive to a desire for learning. Handley Moule's biographers record an interesting experiment in the little school with the institution of the Fordington Times Society (1856–9). Its members were the vicar and his wife, their sons and pupils and the parish curate and clerk. Meetings, which were held weekly during term, had the character of a literary and philosophical society, with original prose and verse being read aloud.

A rectory school which gained much kudos for the successful preparation of boys to Rugby was that conducted by the Rev. John Furness, the curate of Newbold on Avon, from 1856. He quickly made a reputation as a coach for boys wishing to enter Rugby at the time when under Dr Temple (1858–69) the demand to enter Rugby grew rapidly. After two years Furness resigned his curacy and bought two houses in Rugby itself. Thus began 'Oakfield', which became a prosperous preparatory school of 130 boys.[41]

The phenomenon of the small private classical school conducted in a country rectory was certainly more common in the first half of the century. Many such schools had prospered because of the parental preference for a close family atmosphere. But with the decline of the ideal of domestic or private education[42] and the gradual growth and improvement of boarding schools, the demand for this type of education dwindled.[43] But the decline was gradual, and small rectory schools continued into the late Victorian period. Both Herbert

Ryle, Bishop of Winchester, and Stewart Headlam, the Fabian and education-ist, attended such a school: that of the Rev. R.H. Wace at Wadhurst, Sussex. Wace was a good example of a clergyman who in the later part of the nineteenth century turned his curcumstances of a large house and family to good effect. He had nine sons who attended the school together with the sons of more wealthy parents. Mrs Wace helped her husband and the school was run like a large family. Another school which had a homely atmosphere was the one conducted by the Rev. Maurice Cowell, Vicar of Ashbocking (seven miles from Ipswich), who looked after twelve boys, including the future Field Marshal Allenby, with the aid of his curate, the Rev. T. Heaviside Peat.

Similar instances abound. Another school of the mid-Victorian period run by a clergyman was that of the Rev. J. Tuck, near Hitchin, which Sir Evelyn Ruggles-Brise, the founder of Borstal, attended in 1866. The Rev. Tuck ran his school of twenty boys without the aid of a curate and ruled it with a rod of iron. The main complaint of the future prison reformer was not the stern discipline but (despite the Rector's surname) the lack of food. Ruggles-Brise, in order to supplement his diet, used to milk cows surreptitiously in the pastures using a barley sugar tin as a cup, and stole peas from the crops of neighbouring farmers. Despite the exigencies of this school, Ruggles-Brise won a scholarship to Eton.

According to the testament of Sir Herbert Maxwell, 7th Baronet of Monreith,[44] a contemporary mid-Victorian rectory school with a much more benign reputation was that of the Rev. James Reynolds Young at Whitnash Rectory, near Leamington Spa. The school seems to have been very fashion-able, with about twelve 'upper class' boys. Amongst Maxwell's school friends were Viscount Adair (4th Earl of Dunraven, 1871) who was a member, like Maxwell, of Lord Salisbury's second ministry in 1886; Arthur S. Barry (created Lord Barrymore in 1902); Henry Butler (14th Viscount Mountgarret in 1900); Salisbury Kynaston Mainwaring, whose family kept a large estate near Ellesmere; Charles C. Coles, later Junior Lord of the Treasury in Gladstone's ministry of 1880; the Hon. Ivo Vesey (4th Viscount de Vesci 1875); Henry H. Drummond, Laird of Blair Drummond; and William Wentworth Watson of Rockingham Castle, Northamptonshire. This aristocratic rectory school en-joyed enlightened educational practice in so far as the boys' experiences were much wider than those available in the average rectory classical school. Emphasis, for example, was placed on the value of natural history and country life, with excursions into the countryside to collect flowers, butterflies, moths and birds' eggs 'in moderation'. There was a private printing press on which the boys practised type-setting, and in winter they attended dancing classes in Leamington.

During the last quarter of the nineteenth century private preparatory schools began to challenge, in increasing numbers, the role of the clergyman and his spacious rectory in preparing young boys for public schools. Through-out the earlier period — a period of great religious fervour — individual clergy had met a demand for a type of boarding education in a quasi-family atmosphere while at the same time supplementing their clerical incomes. For some, private tutoring or private school-keeping was a form of clerical outdoor relief. For others it was a way of supplementing an already adequate income as in the case of the Rev. J.W. Colenso, the future Bishop of Natal, who after marriage in 1846 settled down in Forncett (Norwich diocese) to supplement his relatively large income of £500[45] by private tuition. No doubt the teaching of many clergymen was as excellent as that of the Rev. James Challis (1803–82) who, as rector of Papworth Everard in Cambridgeshire, kept a rectory school before becoming Plumian Professor of Astronomy in 1836. Sometimes, however, the school took second place to the clerical career of individual clergymen. Ambrose de Lisle (1809–78), the Catholic writer, attended the school of the Rev. George Hodson at Maisemore Court, near Gloucester, which was removed to Edgbaston on Hodson's elevation to the archdeaconate of Stafford. Such practices must have been even more frequent later in the century when the impact of church reform against absentee clergy and pluralism was felt.

With preparatory schools *per se* demanding full-time attendance by their owners, many clergy in their rectories had to make a choice between modifying their educational activity (which many did by becoming private tutors preparing more senior pupils for various examinations) or abandoning them to more professional educators who, like the owners of the earlier large private classical schools, had left their livings in favour of the more uncertain career of preparatory school master. A good example of a clerical family faced with this choice was the Storr family. As a young clergyman the Rev. Charles Storr had helped his father teach pupils at Brenchley Vicarage in Kent. By 1878, however, he was able to educate his nephew Vernon F. Storr (b.1869) nearby in Matfield Grange, an authentic preparatory school which had been purpose-designed. It was at this 'feeder school' for Charterhouse that the future Canon Storr received weekly drill and revolver practice from a Sergeant Lee.[46]

Late Century Exemplars

For almost three-quarters of a century the Anglican clergymen in their private classical and rectory schools had been, in an amateur fashion, securing life lines through the early education of the nation's middle and upper classes. For the last quarter, their commitment to education was to be of a more professional nature.

Many of the preparatory schools which began in this heyday period between 1875 and 1900 will be examined in Chapter 10. But seven will be looked at now as exemplifying the continuance of the clergyman at the helm, a characteristic of private preparatory schooling which continued well into the twentieth century. The seven schools in question are: Stoke House (1865); Shrewsbury House (1865); Arden House (1869); Amesbury House (1870); Wells House School (1870); Bilton Grange (1873); and Sunningdale (1874).

Stoke House (1865), Slough,[47] was the creation of the Rev. Edward St John Parry, who had been headmaster of the now defunct Leamington College (1844–1903). Parry's good teaching enabled his pupils to gain many scholarships at public schools, but it was accompanied 'by thumps and ejaculations' expressive of his violent temper. Despite the threatening ethos created by Parry's forceful teaching methods Mark Tellar was able to write years later: 'The three years I spent at Stoke House were the most satisfactory part of my school life'.[48] 'Old Parry', as he was called by the boys, was assisted by his son 'Ted' (E.H.) and both of them were familiar figures at the church of Stoke Poges which the boys attended regularly on Sundays. In such circumstances the 'elegy' written by Gray was regarded almost as a school hymn.

Shrewsbury House School (1865) conducted by the Rev. Henry James Wilson MA and his sister in Claremont Villas, Surbiton, began like so many preparatory schools as a private coaching establishment.[49] Wilson's coaching, conducted on a part-time basis whilst he was senior curate of St Mark's and St Andrew's Churches, prospered so well that in 1880 he moved to larger premises at Surbiton House, No. 11 Claremont Crescent. Further prosperity took the school to even larger premises in nearby Kingston in 1893.[50] At the time of his retirement three years later the school had thirty-six pupils, including eleven boarders. This was the average size of a classical preparatory school at the turn of the century. The Rev. Henry Wilson's brother-in-law, the Rev. Fletcher Woodhouse, succeeded him as headmaster, thus continuing the clerical tradition of the school.

Arden House[51] was founded in 1869 by the Rev. William Nelson in the Manor House at Feckenham, Worcestershire, transferring in 1876 to Henley-in-Arden in Warwickshire. The appearance of Nelson's Arden House preparatory school in 1876 and the closure in the early 1880s of a forty-year-old private commercial school[52] were symptomatic of the changes taking place nationally in educational provision where, as J.V. Milne shrewdly noted,[53] private preparatory school-keeping was the only part of the private school sector that was prospering. Like many other preparatory schoolmasters, Nelson had been a public school assistant master, in his case at King Edward VI School, Birmingham, before taking to preparatory school teaching. A successful headmaster of a school of some thirty boys, Nelson died three years after moving to Henley-in-Arden.

Amesbury School was founded in 1870 by the Rev. Edmund Fowle (1841–99), son of the Vicar of Amesbury, Wiltshire. The school began in a modest way with one pupil at Craven Lodge, Redhill, Surrey. After a year the 'school' moved to Reigate where it remained till 1877, by which time it numbered twenty-six pupils which made the Reigate 'Amesbury House' too small. In 1877 Fowle moved his school to Bickley in Kent, where numbers reached forty-one in 1881. Six years later he sold it to a layman. Fowle achieved some distinction as a schoolmaster by writing textbooks which were favourably reviewed by *The Saturday Review*.[54] As well as being a pioneer in the production of textbooks he was also old-fashioned in his liberal use of the cane. The school remained in Bickley till 1917 when, because of the threat of

Zeppelin attacks, the then headmaster, Mr E.C. Brown, moved it to its present site at Hindhead. There it occupied the Edwin Lutyens purpose-designed buildings[55] of the former Mt Arlington preparatory school which had closed that year because of the decimation of its staff during the war.[56]

Wells House School, Malvern Wells, was founded by the Rev. William Wilberforce Gedge, who moved his Stamford House School from Cheltenham in 1870 and brought a good many of his boys with him.[57] Gedge had a commanding personality and was a great influence in the town. As a schoolmaster 'he gained a great reputation for his ability in coaching scholarships'[58] and many boys came for a short stay, presumably to get their final polish before going to public school. Amongst the 411 boys who passed through his hands between 1870 and his retirement in 1889 was Charles Oman, the future historian. Oman, who was sent in 1871 to Wells House for one year to experience boarding school before going to his public school, confirmed[59] that Gedge had been liberal both with his *exeats* and with the cane, being one of the old school who ruled by a mixture of fear and freedom rather than by the close surveillance which later became normal in preparatory schools. Oman was happy at the school. If the food was simple, it was also good. The dormitories were warm and comfortable and 'the masters good disciplinarians but perfectly just'.[60]

Bilton Grange, another well-known Warwickshire preparatory school, also originated in a different county. It was founded by the Rev. Walter Earle[61] at Yarlet Hall, Staffordshire, in 1873 before moving to Dunchurch, near Rugby, in 1887. The school exemplified the continuing clerical control of classical preparatory schools: the Rev. Walter Earle (1873–1902) was succeeded as headmaster by the Rev. Earnest Earle, (1902–21), who was in turn succeeded by the Rev. Granville Earle (1921–30). The school prospered in its new location. At Yarlet Hall in 1878 it had about fifty boys, but by 1893, only six years after its establishment at Dunchurch, it had as many as 120, which was a large number for the late Victorian period.[62]

The seventh school examplifying a clerical foundation is **Sunningdale School**, which celebrated its centenary in 1974. In 1874 Canon Girdlestone set up school in Sunningdale, Berkshire, where he was joined by his son, Mr Girdlestone, who helped to conduct the school for a quarter of a century. By the year 1900, when the school was sold to the next headmaster, Mr Crabtree (1900–33), the pupils numbered twenty-seven. This suggests that Sunningdale had achieved average success in its clerical foundation. Since 1900 Sunningdale has had a lay headmaster and thus exemplifes the trend away from clerical heads which has been a feature of preparatory schools in the twentieth century.

A Quantitative Measure

So far this chapter has been concerned with the qualitative aspects of the clerical contribution to Victorian preparatory schools. To give it a quantitative

Table 4. Nineteenth Century Lay and Clerical Principals in Worcestershire and Warwickshire

Early Quasi-preparatory school principals

Worcestershire Lay Principals	Clerical Principals	Warwickshire Lay Principals	Clerical Principals
	1836 Rev. Charles Wharton-Stourport		1838 Rev. Charles Badham—Birmingham and Edgbaston Prep. School
			1835 Rev. George Salmon-Coleshil
			Rev. Wm. Field—Leamington
			Rev. R. M'Pherson—Rugby
			Rev. Attwood—Kenilworth
			1850s Rev. Charles Bedford—Allesley, Coventry

Worcestershire Lay Principals	Clerical Principals	Warwickshire Lay Principals	Clerical Principals
1860 Thomas Essex, Gt Malvern	1841 Rev. Edward Meade, Malvern Wells	1864 Mr Alfred Kirk, Arnold Lodge (iii)	1845 Rev. Thos. Bloxam, Rugby
1861 Henry Wilson Rockburn } Holly Mount }	1854 Rev. John Lumb, Eastnor House Malvern	1864) Mr J. William Vecqueray, Rugby (i) 1865)	1854 Rev. J. Congreve, Overslade
1872 E.R.C. Hays, South Lea, Gt Malvern	1864 Rev. Frederick Young, Gt Malvern	1868 Mr David Hanbury, Orwell House, Clifton-on-Dunsmore	1854 Rev. C. Bickmore, Berkswell
1884 William Caldwell, Barbonne	1868 Rev. William Nelson, Feckenham (iii)*	1868 T.B. Eden	1860 Rev. J.M. Furness, Oakfield
1888 William Douglas, Link School College	1870 Rev. W.W. Gedge, Wells House (iii)	1869 Mr Arthur Hammerton, Wolston	1860s Rev. Charles Houghton, Northcote House, Rugby
1888 Alfred E. Tillard, Malvern Wells	1876 Rev. Edward Ford, Hillside, West Malvern	1876 Alfred H. Harrison, The Lodge, Dunchurch (iii)	1860s Rev. George Heaviside, Peat, Coventry
1889 Alfred H. Stable, Wells House (iii)	c1880 Rev. Samuel Latham,	1879 Mr G.P. Nowers and Mr	1868 Rev. F. Clark-Walsh,

1, Waterloo Place, Leamington
1872 Rev. Charles Darnell, Hill Morton (ii)
1876 [Rev.] Thomas Trott, Rugby
1876 Rev. William Nelson, Arden House (iii)
1876 Rev. Samuel Gerrard, Salford Priors
1887 Rev. Walter Earle, Bilton Grange (iii)
1888 Rev. Arthur Jewell, Leamington
Rev. E.J. Bidwell, Uplands (Leamington College Junior School)
1890 Rev. H.G. Allfree (iv) Arnold Lodge (iii)

C.P. Pughe, Hallfield School (iii)
1880 Mr Matthew J.F. Brackenbury, Northcote House
1896 Mr Charles Mallam, Beech Lawn
1896 Mr David Gilmore Leamington

South Lea
1888 Rev. John D. Wallace
1892 Rev. Edward Dew, Fairfield
1892 Rev. Edward Healey, Lickey
1900 Rev. Hugh Fowler, South Lea

1892 Clement W. Roland, Kyrewood Tenbury
1896 Mr Edward Capel-Smith, Fairfield
1896 Dr William Austin, Beechfield
1900 E. L. Jones and E.H.L. Jones, The Priory School

(i) Vecqueray was also Modern Languages Master at Rugby School
(ii) Rev. Charles Darnell became Head of Cargilfield, Edinburgh
(iii) Extant preparatory schools
(iv) No evidence has come to light to link this Allfree with the Allfrees of Rose Hill, Tunbridge Wells
* Now Ardenhurst, Henley-in-Arden

dimension, let's look at Worcestershire and Warwickshire. In these two counties there was a concentration of preparatory schools, with both clerical and lay headmasters, centred principally on Malvern in the one county, on Leamington and Rugby in the other. It will be seen from Table 4 that considering the ratio of clergy to the rest of the male population, their contribution was outstanding. Between about 1845, when the recognizable preparatory school of the Rev. Thomas Bloxam was opened at Rugby, and the end of the century the preparatory schools of Warwickshire had more clerical than lay principals: in Worcestershire the numbers were roughly equal, with the lay principals being in a majority of one.[63] Amongst the clerical preparatory schools in Warwickshire the Rev. Bickmore's school at Berkswell, which claimed to serve the English nobility, probably had the greatest pretensions, though Thomas Essex in Worcestershire prepared boys especially for Eton. The case of the Rev. Thomas Trott is interesting. Originally a commercial schoolmaster in Rugby, he increased his social status first by obtaining a degree and then by being ordained. He then converted his school into a preparatory school.

Another way of obtaining a quantitative assessment of the contribution of clergy to preparatory schools at the end of the nineteenth century is to count the clergy who belonged to the AHPS in 1899.[64] Of the 263 individual members of the association, forty-eight were clergymen (approximately 18 per cent of the membership). The evidence of the Worcestershire and Warwickshire trade and commercial directories would have suggested a larger proportion. Two final comments need to be made. First, the membership figures for the AHPS were those of the penultimate year of the nineteenth century, by which time the clerical preponderance was on the decline both in preparatory and in public schools.[65] Secondly, though the membership list of the AHPS in 1899 shows fewer clergy, some of them occupied powerful positions within the association. Five of them were members of the executive committee of sixteen, including the Rev. Herbert Bull (Chairman), of Wellington House, Westgate-on-Sea and the Rev. Dr C.E. Williams (Vice-Chairman) of Summer Fields. If the clerics represented only 18 per cent of the total membership of the association, they were 31 per cent of the executive committee and occupied 100 per cent of the chief offices.

Notes

1 Cf. Nicholas Orme, *op. cit.*, p. 66.
2 *Ibid.*, p. 67.
3 Cf. J.E.G. de Montmorency, *The Progress of Education in England*, Knight and Co. pp. 48, 51–2.
4 One notable exception was the Rev. Adam Sedgwick, later Professor of Geology, who tutored six boys daily in mathematics whilst a Fellow of Trinity College, Cambridge.
5 Cf. D.P. Leinster-Mackay, PhD Thesis, University of Durham Vol. 1, Chapter 6 for details of this aspect of nineteenth century private education.

6 H.P. LIDDON, (1893) *op. cit.*, Vol. 1, p. 9.

7 A.H.D. ACLAND (Ed.) (1902) *Memoir and Letters of the Rt. Hon. Sir Thomas Dyke Acland*, Privately circulated, London p. 5.

8 Cited by ISABEL GIBERNE SIEVEKING, (1909), *Memoir and Letters of Francis W. Newman*, Kegan Paul and Co. p. 8.

9 J. LEWIS MAY, (1929) *op. cit.*, p. 10. The father of T.H. HUXLEY was the senior assistant master there for some years.

10 SPOTTISWOODE went from Eton to Harrow where he gained a Lyon scholarship in 1842.

11 Rev. ALFRED J. CHURCH, (1908), *Memoirs of Men and Books*, Smith, Elder and Co. pp. 36–41.

12 For example, he took the boys into the fields to learn mensuration.

13 The Rev. JOSHUA GRAY in St Anne's Terrace, Brixton, London and the Rev. JOHN WOOD who kept a school at Hylton Castle, near Sunderland, also pioneered science in the curriculum. Sir JOSEPH SWAN (1828–1914), chemist and electrical inventor, learnt his love of science from the Rev. JOHN WOOD.

14 Hon. A.E. GATHORNE-HARDY, (1910) *Gathorne-Hardy, 1st Earl of Cranbrook*, Longmans p. 14.

15 For example, cf. G.B. WYNNE (1955) *A Study of Education in the English Private Schools of the North East Midlands during the Late Eighteenth and Early Nineteenth Centuries*, MA University of Leeds. WYNNE examined the pages of the *Doncaster Gazette* 1786–1820 and found eight schools of the first category and twenty-five of the second category. As the century progressed the ratio of rectory schools increased as the private classical schools decreased in the face of the rise of the public schools.

16 T. ARNOLD, letter to the *Sheffield Courant, Miscellaneous Works*, p. 228.

17 ELEANOR TOWLE, (1907) *John Mason Neale D.D., A Memoir*, p. 10.

18 *The Saturday Review*, 49, 87, 7 February 1880, p. 174.

19 *Census 1851*, p. 15.

20 R.A. SOLOWAY, (1969), *Prelates and People: Ecclesiastical Social Thought in England 1783–1852*, Routledge and Kegan Paul p. 280.

21 According to R.A. SOLOWAY, pluralism and absenteeism were drastically reduced in the early decades of the nineteenth century, but even in 1850 nearly 2500 ministers were still non-resident.

22 Cf. A.F. LEACH, (1900), *History of Bradfield College*, Henry Frowde p. 4.

23 Lord NORMANBY was a Canon of Windsor the duties of which clashed with keeping a Yorkshire School. He partially solved his problem by moving the school for one term a year to Windsor. Cf. Lt Gen. Sir DOUGLAS BROWNRIGG, (1942), *Unexpected A Book of Memories*, Hutchinson p. 15.

24 EVELYN WAUGH, (1959), *The Life of the Rt. Rev. Ronald Knox*, Chapman and Hall p. 42.

25 HALEVY, (1937), *A History of the English people in 1815*, Vol. 3, Pelican Books p. 19. In his speech in the House of Commons on 25 April 1806, WILBERFORCE referred to the curate turned weaver. (Parl. Debates, Vol. 6, p. 925). HALEVY's general findings for the pre-Waterloo period have been confirmed by (GEOFFREY BEST (1964) in *Temporal Pillars*, Cambridge University Press.)

26 By Act of Parliament in 1704 the Crown's income from first fruits and tenets was to be used to supplement the inadequate income of penurious clergy. By the same Act all arrears to the Crown were to be remitted.

27 BEST, *op. cit.*, p. 204. A skilled tradesman or third-rate clerk could expect an income of c.£150 in the mid-nineteenth century. Cf. also BRIAN HEENEY, (1976) *A Different Kind of Gentleman*, Archon Books pp. 28–9.

28 Archbishop WILLIAM HOWLEY of Canterbury (1766–1848) confirmed the existence of this society to an incredulour Sir ROBERT PEEL in 1835. Cited by BEST, *op. cit.*, pp. 171–2.

29 Cf. B. Simon (Ed.) (1968) *Education in Leicestershire 1540–1940*, Leicester, p. 118.
30 Home Secretary in Sir Robert Peel's second administration.
31 The Rev. Elwell ran this school at Clapham Common before moving to Hammersmith.
32 Locker-Lampson used a pseudonym to conceal the identity of 'Mr Wight'.
33 Cf. E.S. Purcell (1896) *op. cit.*, p. 10. Lendon's rectory school at Totteridge may have been the lineal forbear of Dorset House considered in Chapter 2.
34 William S. Childe-Pemberton, (1909), *Life of Lord Norton*, John Murray pp. 14–15.
35 Cf. also David Newsome, (1967) *The Parting of Friends*, John Murray p. 40. According to Newsome, Samuel and Henry Wilberforce went to F.R. Spragg(e)'s establishment at Little Bounds in Bidborough, near Tonbridge. It would seem that on moving his school, presumably because of the change of clerical living, Spragg took the Wilberforce brothers with him. Spragg was a parson who catered for both younger and older pupils.
35 Cf. Lord Norton (1883) 'Middle class education', *The Nineteenth Century*, 13, January–June, pp. 229–48.
37 For example, William Fowler (1847–1921) the historian, son of a Welsh JP, attended Harnish Rectory from 1858 to 1860 before going to Malborough.
38 A.J.C. Hare, (1896) *The Story of My Life*, George Allen p. 173.
39 Cf. J.B. Harford and F.C. MacDonald (1922) *Handley Carr Glyn Moule*, Hodder and Stoughton p. 2.
40 The eighty-fifth Bishop of Durham.
41 Cf. obituary on the Rev. J.M. Furness in *PSR*, Vol. 3, No. 20, December 1901, p. 70. Furness passed the school on to his assistant master, Mr Reginald S. Lea, in 1880. Ten years later the school moved to Lindley Lodge, Nuneaton.
42 Cf. F. Musgrove, *op. cit., Sociological Review*, New Series, 7, 2, pp. 169–78.
43 Many clergymen turned their rectories into cramming establishments for entry into the army, navy, Indian Civil Service, Home Civil Service and the universities after the reform of examinations at Oxford and Cambridge in the 1850s. A relatively late example of this development was Arreton Vicarage on the Isle of Wight where in 1900 the Rev. J. Black Hyland took in thirteen pupils to be taught by six resident tutors. Other clergymen, like the Rev. J.A.S. Paget Moffatt of Elsted Rectory at Petersfield, confined themselves to preparing boys for public schools.
44 Cf. Sir Herbert Maxwell (1932) *Evening Memories*, pp. 32–40. Glasgow, Alexander Maclenose & Co.
45 Colenso was the author of well-known arithmetic textbooks, the royalties on which must have considerably supplemented his income. He taught private pupils for seven years at Forncett having quarrelled with Dr Wordsworth, headmaster of Harrow, whilst he was an assistant master.
46 G.H. Harris, (1943), *Vernon F. Storr*, SPCK pp. 2–3.
47 Situated at Clifton for the first five years of its existence and now merged with Brunswick House to form Stoke-Brunswick School in Sussex.
48 Mark Tellar, (1952) *A Young Man's Passage*, Home and Van Thal p. 42.
49 *Snrewsbury House Magazine Centenary Supplement* (1965), p. 4.
50 The school moved to its present site at Ditton Hill in 1910.
51 Now called Ardenhurst.
52 Belonging to a certain Thomas Cooper.
53 Cf. page 7.
54 Cf. The educational yearbook of 1879 in which no less than eight of his textbooks were listed.
55 It is believed that this was one of only two preparatory schools which Lutyens designed.

56 I am grateful to Mr D.E.W. SPENCER, headmaster of Amesbury House, for information on this school.

57 *Wells House Magazine*, December 1912.

58 Two Wells House boys gained scholarships to Winchester in 1870. Cf. CHARLES OMAN, (1941), *Memories of Victorian Oxford*, Methuen p. 22.

59 OMAN, *op. cit.*, p. 22.

60 *Ibid.*, 23.

61 He was a member of the AHPS executive committee at an early stage. He is not to be confused with the Rev. WILLIAM EARLE of Harlow College, Essex.

62 Bilton had the facilities to match the large numbers including a gymnasium, carpenter's shop, swimming bath, shooting range, art studio and very large grounds.

63 These calculations are based upon a close examination of county trade and commercial directories for both counties from the 1830s onwards. The dates listed are the years of the directories in which the schools first appear. Cf. also *Rugboeana* by an old Rugbean, pp. 58–9 for a brief account of Rugby preparatory schools.

64 Taken from the *PSR*, 2, 12, March 1899, pp. 110–12.

65 Cf. T.W. BAMFORD, (1967), *The Rise of the Public Schools*, Nelson pp. 54–8. Dr T.W. BAMFORD found a similar decline in the number of clergy amongst the ranks of assistant masters, at least, in public schools in 1893 and a corresponding decline amongst headmasters of public *day* schools.

The most important part of education is entirely trusted to women.
(*Westminster Review*, 1831)

I need only here express my belief that for the elementary teaching of
little boys ... women are better fitted than men.
(H. Giffard (1868) *SIC Report*, Vol. 7)

The Surplus Women

Apart from marriage the only occupational avenues open to a middle class
woman were nursing, teaching or (possibly) writing.[1] In both the eighteenth
and the nineteenth centuries many spinsters and widows found themselves
becoming governesses[2] or setting up school as a means of keeping alive, for
there was a surplus of them with the men abroad.

There seems to be a continuing and prevailing assumption that women are
better suited than men for the task of looking after the very young children.
The governors of Christ's Hospital clearly thought in this way with their
appointment of nurses to look after their petties at Hertford. Some of the early
nineteenth century quasi-preparatory schools also recognized the special
qualities of women. Dr Ruddock, who kept a school at Fulham where Edward
Bulwer received his first lessons, used to pass on to a Mrs Bowen the youngest
of the children sent to him. Similarly, Dr Pinckney at Temple Grove, East
Sheen, as has been noted, used to place boys of eight in the sole charge of two
lady teachers, Miss Field and Miss Evatt. At Temple Grove, which was then
sending boys to Eton in large numbers, the smallest boys slept in small
dormitories with only twelve beds.[3] This would contrast strongly with their
later possible experience of sleeping in Eton's Long Chamber.

Having examined some fifteen preparatory schools in the southern
counties in the 1860s, Mr H.A. Giffard, an assistant commissioner of the
Schools Inquiry Commission, came to the conclusion that women were more
suitable than men for teaching boys between six and eleven years old since [he

thought] they were more patient and painstaking.[4] This opinion is likely to have been strengthened by the prevalence of nannies[5] so that it is not surprising that as well as the thousands of women who ran ladies' seminaries, both day and boarding, there were many who conducted 'preparatory' schools for young boys. Such schools, which provided 'outdoor relief' to many a genteel spinster or widow, may be seen as performing the same function as the petty schools of the seventeenth and eighteenth centuries. An examination of the nineteenth century trade and commercial directories gives ample evidence of the profusion of such schools. Shrewdly styled, these entries in the trades and commercial directories indicate that 'preparatory' schools were distinct from ladies' seminaries or 'boys' boarding' or 'commercial' schools. In Royal Leamington Spa, for example, schools like Bowood House run by the Misses Crane from c.1872 to c.1880, and then by the Penfolds from c.1884 to c.1892, were likely to have been both rivals to, and preparatory for, 'classical' preparatory schools such as Arnold Lodge. It can be said, too, that dame schools covered a wide spectrum below a certain social level, so that probably a large number of them were articulated neither to public schools nor to classical preparatory schools.[6]

At least eighty-three dame preparatory schools are listed in county trade and commercial directories for Worcestershire and Warwickshire in the nineteenth century. Even a rough calculation from these figures would give the reader some approximate idea of the very large number of dame preparatory schools in the country as a whole in the nineteenth century. There were insufficient public schools to be serviced by such a large number.

Qualitative Dimensions

If the trade and commercial directories give only a *quantitative* dimension to dame preparatory schools, the *DNB* and general biography provide a *qualitative* assessment of some of them. It is possible, for instance, to gauge from biography the social level at which some of these dame preparatory schools operated. For example, it is fairly certain that the dame school at Sidmouth attended by Montagu Burrows (1819–1905), later Chichele Professor of Modern History and Fellow of All Souls College, was a socially inferior dame school since the old dame also kept the turnpike gate as well as the school.[7] The dame school at Dulverton in the adjoining county of Somerset, attended by Sir George Williams, the founder of the YMCA, seems to have been at a similar social level as Williams was apprenticed to a draper in Bridgwater. More 'middle class' schools, mid-way as it were on the dame school continuum, prepared boys for entry to less prestigious forms of secondary education. At one such kept by a Mrs Cook at Stanbourne in Essex, Charles Spurgeon, the famous Victorian Baptist preacher, attended before going on to 'a good middle-class classical and commercial school'.[8]

The Thrupp sisters at Moseley prepared Sir (George) William Des Voeux, later Governor of Fiji, Newfoundland and Hong Kong, for Charterhouse, which he entered at the age of seven. The fact that Des Voeux stayed at this school for four years suggests that his parents must have been satisfied with the adequacy of the preparation for a public school. Dame schools prepared James Harris, later 1st Earl of Malmesbury and diplomat, from the age of four before he went to Salisbury Grammar School and later Winchester. Another in Islington educated both John G. Nichols, the printer, antiquary and Fellow of the Royal Society, and Benjamin Disraeli in 1811, just as another dame school in Worship Street, London, as already noted, educated Sir Sydney H. Waterlow, later a Lord Mayor of London, before he was sent off to a classical preparatory school at Brighton.

There were many dame preparatory schools at Brighton. Henry Chaplin, 1st Viscount Chaplin, the politician, whose 'squarson' father sent him at the age of nine to a dame school at Brighton kept by a Mrs Walker, spent two years there before going on to Harrow. Later in the century Brighton became a fashionable town for dame preparatory schools for the upper middle and upper classes. Eastbourne, where Sir Frederick Gowland Hopkins, the biochemist, attended a dame school before going on to the City of London School, was another favourite resort for late Victorian dame preparatory schools.

Joint Spinster Schools

One feature of these dame schools, but more common in 'ladies' schools' or 'ladies' seminaries' was the practice of spinster sisters conducting them jointly. The Victorian novelist Sir Walter Besant attended a dame school at Portsea kept by three sisters, the daughters of a retired naval officer. Similarly William Morris, poet and socialist, before going to Marlborough attended a 'preparatory school for young gentlemen' kept by the Misses Arundale[9] in Walthamstow, from 1844 to 1848. A decade later Francis J. Chavasse (1846–1928), later Bishop of Liverpool, was 'sent away very early to a boarding school for little boys kept by ladies.'[10] W.J. Birkbeck (b.1859), the Russian scholar and antiquarian, went to a dame school at Lowestoft kept by the sisters, the Misses Ringers, who gave a good grounding in English to many Norfolk boys before they went off to their classical preparatory schools.[11] This school later became a leading classical preparatory school.[12]

No fewer than three dame schools kept by spinster sisters were attended by Sir Harry Hamilton Johnston, the celebrated explorer and colonial administrator. The first school (1864–66) was kept by the three Misses Jones and their mother at Brixton, South London; the second was kept by the four Misses Selby at Surbiton where he gained a good knowledge of botany and French[13]. The third, where he was sent at the age of nine, was kept by the Misses Pace in Camberwell Grove which Joseph Chamberlain also attended. Many of these spinsterly sisters, like many fellow private school owners of the nineteenth century, had the spectre of poverty constantly with them. Without any pensions to comfort them, no doubt many of them were in a parlous state in old age. So thin was the shoe-string on which the school was kept by the Misses Crane that G.B. Burgin recalled: 'These three scholastic ladies were painfully poor and fined me a halfpenny every time I forgot to say grace before pudding.'[14]

Dames and the Navy

Nor were dames excluded from preparing boys for that most masculine institution: the Royal Navy. Such a school of about twenty boys kept by a certain Mrs Moore — St Andrew's School, Tenby — was attended by [Admiral] Lord Chatfield from 1883 to 1886. She not only taught mathematics and Latin in preparation for their examinations at Burlington House but also played football and cricket and ran in paper-chases.[15] Another dame preparatory school, Enfield House, from which more than one boy had graduated to *HMS Britannia*, also had Sir Henry Tizard, himself a son of a naval officer, as a pupil.[16]

Coping with the Classics

One of the difficulties which dames encountered in the attempt to offer education to the sons of gentlemen was the lack of a classical training. It would seem that Miss Tyler, in her dame school at Britannia Place, Worcester, attended by the young Edward Elgar (1857–1934), put emphasis on piano instruction by way of compensation;[17] whilst earlier in the century Miss Gartly who kept a dame school in Manchester where Edward Frankland, the Professor of Chemistry at Owen College, Manchester, received his first education, taught chiefly deportment. This school, however, must have been a pre-preparatory school, since Frankland attended it at the age of three. The dame school which the novelist G.A. Henty attended was reputed to have given him the habit of voracious reading.[18] Perhaps the curriculum at Henty's school also placed little emphasis on the classics. This was certainly true at Mrs Philip Myatt's preparatory school for young gentlemen in Evesham, where the curriculum contained French, German, music and dancing, but no classics.[19]

Other non-classically educated dames took definite steps to ensure the teaching of the classics. George Granville Bradley,[20] for example, attended a dame school at Brighton in the early 1830s about which he reminisced fifty years later:[21]

> Our education consisted ... of one process — the imparting of knowledge ... through the appeal to one single faculty, that of memory. Our Latin grammar, indeed, and our arithmetic were taught to us, not by the ladies to whose care we were entrusted, but by a kindly master, who visited us daily.[22]

One well-known dame preparatory school in Cheltenham, kept by the two Misses Hill was attended by the future Oxford historian [Sir] Charles Oman and by Edward Maclagan, the future Lieutenant-Governor of the Punjab. This did not have to rely on visiting masters for the classics as the younger sister, Miss Bessie Hill, was a first-rate Greek and Latin scholar and helped her sister keep about a hundred boys 'in terrific order'.[23] Large as this number would have been for a classical preparatory school in the nineteenth century, it was very large for a dame preparatory school. Another classically orientated dame school was attended in the 1860s by another university don, Sidney Ball at Weston-super-Mare. It was kept by a Miss Manchee, who taught Latin.[24] Similarly, Henry Sanderson Furniss (1868–1939), later principal of Ruskin College and the future Lord Sanderson, attended a dame school in the 1870s kept by a certain Miss Bailey who offered a curriculum of Latin as well as French, arithmetic, English history, English grammar and scripture. Such a curriculum was much wider than that offered by many schools of the time.

Further insights into the standing of good dame preparatory schools can be seen in the esteem in which Mrs Wallace's school at Brighton was held by Christopher Wordsworth, the then headmaster of Harrow, who sent his son John, later Bishop of Salisbury, there in 1853. This was doubly significant as first, Wordsworth began to learn both Latin and Greek at this dame preparatory school and secondly, this choice of school by the Headmaster of Harrow was probably due to its Christian ethos: the Bible and church principles were given an important place in the curriculum, and Bishop Gastrell's *Faith and Duty of a Christian* was a textbook. One is tempted to think that this dame preparatory school was the one cryptically described as 'Mrs W . . .s' by the Rev. the Hon. E. Lyttelton, later headmaster of Eton, in his *Memories and Hopes* (1925):

> It was considered quite one of the best in the country, and I have no evidence to the contrary, except that the well-known Waterfield's at East Sheen and Tabor's at Cheam were well spoken of and certainly were far better than our seminary in teaching.[25]

O.C. Waterfield of Temple Grove, East Sheen, spoke out strongly in 1866 against small preparatory schools opened in an amateurish fashion by indigent clergymen (rectory schools) and orphaned clergymen's daughters (dame schools). His views were natural for these dame schools were very real rivals to early 'professional' preparatory schools, since the gentler sex could become recognized as the more natural teacher of young boys. Indeed, the 'orthodox' preparatory school might well be slowly ground between the upper mill stone of the public school and the lower mill stone of dame school so that little remained for it except the age-range of eleven to thirteen. In the event, the dame schools tended to concentrate on the lower age-range from five to eight and in many cases were pre-preparatory rather than preparatory schools.[26] Such fears were perhaps, therefore, unfounded.

Decline?

The decline in the dame schools was registered by *The Saturday Review* in 1880 when an article on 'Private or preparatory schools' of 7 February noted that dame schools providing preparatory education seemed 'to have fallen into disfavour of late years.' The obituary was premature, for among dame preparatory schools which existed after *The Saturday Review's* 'valediction' was Fir Lodge Preparatory School kept by a Miss Higgins at Crystal Palace, which Ernest Shackleton attended before going to Dulwich College in 1887. The foundation of the nearby Dulwich College Preparatory School in 1885 provides at least one example of the dame preparatory school holding its own against competition from a classical preparatory school.

Survival As the First in a Three-Tier System

Concentrating largely on the younger end of the age-range and overlapping perhaps with the kindergarten and the PNEU movements, dame schools survived. The education of John Rushworth, Earl Jellicoe, is a case in point of the preparatory and pre-preparatory schools, over a period of time, finding their respective roles. In 1866, at the age of seven, the future victor of Jutland attended the dame school kept by the Misses Shapcott at Southampton, staying three to four years before moving at the age of eleven, as already noted, to Field House Preparatory School, Rottingdean, kept by two schoolmasters, J. and W. Hewitt. General Auchinleck attended a dame school at Southsea before going in 1894 to Crowthorne School, the classical preparatory school linked with Wellington. The general pattern of upper class schooling in Victorian England was: attendance at a dame preparatory school, followed by classical preparatory, followed by public school. This was the pattern followed, for example, by the future Major-General Fuller. He attended a dame school in Chichester, then a classical preparatory school in Hampshire, followed by Malvern.[27]

Although neither the dame preparatory school which the poet, Robert Graves, attended at Wimbledon[28] (before eventually going to the classical preparatory school of Mr C.D. Olive at Rokeby, Wimbledon), nor Ashburton House, the school for the sons of gentlemen attended (1891–5) by the educational historian, H.C. Barnard,[29] was a good school, many such dame preparatory schools were very suited to the task of teaching young boys. It was after all the dame preparatory school belonging to Miss Roberts of Bath (10 Landsdowne Crescent), about which its former pupil Arthur Waugh wrote:

> I am inclined to believe that, in spite of all its drawbacks, it was as good and as wise an institution as any that could be contrived by the wit of man. In many respects, indeed, it was better, for very few men understand boys of such tender years, or can manage them as tactfully as women do.[30]

Some of these nineteenth century schools have survived into the twentieth century and now, under headmasters, are members of the IAPS. A dame preparatory school started in 1894 by Mrs Browne, the widow of the Rev. F.H. Browne, headmaster of Ipswich School,[31] has not only survived as St Bede's Eastbourne into the twentieth century but has also incorporated Tyttenhanger Lodge School (formerly of Hertfordshire and later of Seaford, Summer Fields), an early AHPS School once owned by Mr A.R. Trollope.

But perhaps the most famous of dame preparatory schools was that started in Oxford in 1864 by Mrs Archibald Maclaren. When she was succeeded in 1897 by her son-in-law, the Rev. Dr C.E. Williams, it ceased to be a dame preparatory school. Two Bristol preparatory schools, well known in the twentieth century but now defunct, were also started by women. XIV School, which began in 1885 at 14 Apsley Road, Clifton, was kept for two years by two sisters; St Goar School was started by the Misses Lemon and in 1890 (?) was passed to Miss Peake, who in 1906 (?) handed it on to Miss Rose. Old Buckenham School, at Brettenham Park, near Ipswich, was originally owned by the Misses Ringer from 1862 until 1890 when it was taken over by the Rev. W.R. Phillips and ceased to be a dame preparatory school.[32]

Even the young Winston Churchill attended Brunswick House School from 1884 to 1888: a dame preparatory school which began in 1866 at 29 and 30 Brunswick Road, Hove, under the Misses Kate and Charlotte Thomson. Winston's younger brother, John S. Spencer-Churchill, was at Elstree preparatory school. It is likely that Winston's ill health led to the choice of a school near his family doctor's main practice. The Misses Thomson were kind and sympathetic, contrasting strongly with Winston's mentors (or tormentors) at his previous school, and prepared him for entry into Harrow with a curriculum that included French, history, much poetry, riding and swimming. Records show Winston Churchill's account for the first term, 1888 as follows:

Account 1888:   Winston Churchill

	1st term	
School Fees		21. 0. 0
Music Lessons		—
Drawing Lessons		2. 2. 0
German Lessons		—
Dancing Lessons		—
Drilling and Boxing		1.11. 6
Singing Class		10. 6
Laundress		1.11. 6
Seat in Church		10. 6
Books		1. 5. 0
Stationery		5. 6
Music		—
Drawing Materials		—
		28.16. 6

Personal Expenses	c/f	28.16.6
Medical Attendance		10. 6
Chemist		10. 0
Riding Lessons		—
Swimming Tickets		—
Tailor's Account		9. 0
Bootmaker's		—
Hatter's		—
Hosiery		—
Hairdresser		1. 0
Tailoress		—
Pocket-money (cash)		10. 0
Cabs. Carriage of Parcels		—
Travelling Expenses		3. 9. 6
Stamps		10
		34. 7. 4

Winston Churchill's account at end of first term in 1888 rendered by
Brunswick House dame preparatory school.

The school ceased to be a dame preparatory school in 1897 when the Misses
Thomson appointed Llewellyn Thring, nephew of Edward Thring of Uppingham (1821–87), as headmaster.

A school, founded in 1874, which remained a dame preparatory school
well into the twentieth century was Marlborough House School first at
Brighton, then at Hove (now at Hawkhurst, Kent). This school was conducted
by Mrs White and her two daughters, Edith and Gertrude, with help from
Edith's husband, the Rev. T.J. Bullick, from 1894. In 1912 Mrs White passed
the reins to Miss Gertrude, who continued until 1930. It ceased to be a dame
preparatory school when Edith's son, Christopher Bullick, took over and went
into partnership with the late R.A. Harrison, author of *How Was That, Sir?*

Some of today's orthodox preparatory schools began as dame schools long
after *The Saturday Review* had suggested that their days were already
numbered. Amongst these was Westbourne Preparatory School, Sheffield,
whose history began to take shape in 1882 when a Miss Julia Holmes bought an
existing school owned by a Miss Wragg. Moving within a year to 383 Glossop
Road, Sheffield, and taking Miss Sarah Whitfield as partner, Miss Holmes ran
the school successfully for six years before moving yet again to larger premises
in Westbourne Road in 1888. Miss Holmes and Miss S. Whitfield passed over
the school in 1897 to Sarah's two younger sisters, Clare and Louise Whitfield,
who continued the dame preparatory school tradition until 1919 when they
retired and sold the school to Mr Mercer, who soon changed its character by
joining the AHPS and changing its curriculum along the lines of the public

schools' common entrance examination. 'Mercers', as it came to be called, thus became a well established classical preparatory school.[33]

Marton Hall School, Bridlington, another Yorkshire dame preparatory school, had changed location as many as four times by 1912.[34] It began in c.1889 when the two Misses Wilson set up school with two sons of a solicitor and three children of a doctor as first pupils. By the end of the century it had acquired some playing fields and a male partner: boarders were taken in for the first time. Today it is a flourishing IAPS school.

There were several other dame preparatory schools in the 1880s, ten to twenty years after *The Saturday Review* had pronounced their 'valediction'. Miss Mary Mitchell and her sister opened a school in c.1880 at 19 Belmont Park Road, Lea, near Blackheath. This school was taken over in c.1896 by a Cambridge graduate, Mr Arthur Kilby, who called the school 'Lindisfarne'. He developed it successfully, achieving an exceptional reputation for scholarships. In 1916 this former dame preparatory school moved to its present site at Abberley Hall in Worcestershire to avoid the bombing.[35] Willington School was founded in 1885 by Miss Annie Hale and her sister Ada at 3 Dealtry Road, London. Miss Ada was a classical scholar and the school offered Greek and Latin from the start. Under these two ladies the school prospered in what was then an expanding part of London. Tormore School at Upper Deal, Kent, began as a dame preparatory school when it was set up by the Misses Jane and Grace Harrison as Penrhyn Lodge School at Westgate-on-Sea. Its initial aim was to prepare boys who needed special care or individual tuition. Jane Harrison was a typical dame — 'large, formidable with white hair, a lace cap and "jabot" and black silk dress'.[36] The school grew slowly to a total of twenty-nine pupils. But by 1907, when there were probably only fifteen boys, the Misses Harrison sold the school to Mr D.P. MacDonald, who renamed it Tormore School and moved it to Deal in 1913.

Even in the 1890s dame preparatory schools were being created by enterprising women despite the fierce competition from Oxford and Cambridge graduates who were turning to preparatory schooling as being a relatively prosperous form of enterprise. Amongst such schools were Bishop's Court School, Formby, founded in 1982 by Miss Gosford;[37] Quainton Hall, Harrow founded, in 1897, by Mrs Eyden, which remained a dame preparatory school till the 1930s when it was taken over by her son, the Rev. M. Eyden; and King Edward Junior School, Bath, which was a dame school from 1898 to 1921. Perhaps the most interesting of these preparatory schools founded in the 1890s was that of Miss Eva Gilpin, who ran her school at Weybridge in Surrey from 1898 to 1934, when she retired and married the famous educationist, Sir Michael Sadler. At this school Latin was taught by a pictorial method and the school teaching was infused by Herbartian ideas. This school was co-educational, with the girls leaving at thirteen for schools such as St Felix, Southwold, and the Mount School, York, and the boys leaving at eleven for other preparatory schools.

Some day preparatory schools were man-and-wife affairs, like St Faith's,

Cambridge, which was started in 1884 by Mr and Mrs Goodchild and purchased in 1909 by Mr H. Lower. Yet others began as preparatory schools with headmasters at the helm: but because of an early death of the headmaster, the widow found herself in charge, so making the school *pro tempore* a dame preparatory school. There are two good examples of this. The Rev. W. Nelson, who had founded Arden House in 1869, died ten years later. Mrs Nelson carried on the school till she remarried. Then W.L. Bicknell, her second husband, became headmaster. Mrs Nelson's reign as sole head was short compared with that of Mrs Charles Malden who, after her husband's death, was in sole control of Windlesham House School from 1896 to 1927.

As Arthur Waugh has suggested, the dame preparatory schools contributed in no small way to the improvement of preparatory schools in the late nineteenth and early twentieth centuries. They were, however, not fully accepted by the rest of the preparatory schools, which were dominated very largely by male graduates of Oxford, Cambridge and other universities. The reluctance of the orthodox school to accept the preparatory school dames was epitomized by their exclusion from the IAPS till the early 1970s. Faced with both competition and neglect, dame preparatory schools were forced into the backwaters of private educational provision. If the dame schools were ubiquitous their handicaps were indeed great.

Notes

1 It was possible in the case of BRONTË sisters, in early nineteenth century Yorkshire, to attempt to combine two avenues.
2 Cf. J. GATHORNE-HARDY (1974) *The Rise and Fall of the British Nanny* Arrow Books for a career which combined nursing and quasi-educational qualities. According to GATHORNE-HARDY there were many instances of nannies actually choosing the preparatory schools for their charges. *op. cit.*, p. 74.
3 Cf. Maj. Gen. Sir ARCHIBALD ANSON, (1920), *About Others and Myself* John Murray p. 46.
4 *SIC*, Vol. 7, Southern Counties, p. 171.
5 Cf. JONATHAN GATHORNE-HARDY, (1974) *op. cit.*
6 Admission registers in public schools do not throw any light on possible links between dame schools and public schools because no note was made by the public schools of the schools of origin of their new entrants until very late in the century. Cf. Chapter 8.
7 MONTAGU BURROWS, (1908), *Autobiography*, Macmillan p. 2.
8 CHARLES RAY, (1903), *The Life of Charles Haddon Spurgeon*, Isbister & Co. p. 31.
9 J.W. MACKAIL, (1901), *Life of William Morris*, Vol. 1. Longmans and Co. p. 11.
10 J.B. LANCELOT, (1929), *Francis J. Chavasse*, Oxford, Basil Blackwell p. 6.
11 ROSE K. BIRKBECK, (1922), *The Life and Letters of W.J. Birkbeck*, Longmans p. 5.
12 Cf. Old Buckenham Hall School pp. 203.
13 This dame school grew to be a large school. Sir HARRY H. JOHNSTON, (1923), *The Story of My Life*, Chatto and Windus, p. 11.
14 G.B. BURGIN, (1922), *Many Memories*, Hutchinson p. 25. Two of the sisters died in penury from which fate the third escaped through marriage. It is not known if the

CRANE sisters described by BURGIN are the Cranes of Bowood House, Leamington. Cf. p. 92.

15 Admiral Lord CHATFIELD (Alfred Ernle Montacute) (1942), *The Navy and Defence*, William Heinemann Vol. 1, p. 2.

16 RONALD W. CLARK, (1965), *Tizard* Methuen, p. 6. TIZARD did not eventually make the navy his career as intended. Instead he joined the Royal Flying Corps.

17 PERCY YOUNG, (1955), *Elgar O.M.*, Collins p. 34.

18 G. MANVILLE FENN, (1907), *George Alfred Henty*, Blackie and Son p. 3.

19 KELLY's, *Directory for Worcestershire 1880*, p. 140.

20 Was both master at Rugby and Headmaster of Marlborough, later becoming Dean of Westminster.

21 G.G. BRADLEY (1884) 'My schooldays from 1830 to 1840', *The Nineteenth Century*, 15, March, pp. 455–74.

22 *Ibid.*, p. 456.

23 Cf. Sir ARTHUR GRIFFITH BOSCAWEN, (1925), *Memories*, John Murray, p. 3. Cf. also Sir CHARLES OMAN, (1941), *op. cit.*, pp. 12–13. In OMAN's view the school was only sixty strong but this was still a large size for a Victorian dame preparatory school.

24 Cf. O.H. BALL, (1923), *Sidney Ball, Memories and Impressions of an Ideal Don*, Oxford, Basil Blackwell p. 4.

25 E. LYTTELTON, (1925) *Memories and Hopes*, John Murray p. 14. Cf. also EDITH LYTTELTON, (1917), *Alfred Lyttelton*, Vacher and Sons p. 16 is more critical of this school which the three LYTTELTON brothers, EDWARD, ALFRED and BOB, attended. Mrs W's played Windlesham at cricket.

26 Dame schools, which took boys up to ten or eleven, were designated by Gabbitas-Thring as 'pre-preparatory schools' according to a letter in my possession from them dated 25 August 1970.

27 J.F.C. FULLER, (1936), *Memoirs of an Unconventional Soldier*, Nicholson and Watson pp. 1–2.

28 Cf. ROBERT GRAVES, (1973), *Goodbye to All That*, Penguin Books p. 21.

29 Cf. H.C. BARNARD, (1970), *Were Those the Days?* Pergamon pp. 42–50. According to a letter from Professor H.C. BARNARD in my possession, dated 5 May 1969, the headmaster and proprietress of this school was a sister of EDWIN HODDER, the publisher of Hodder and Stoughton.

30 ARTHUR WAUGH (1930) 'A Victorian Dame School', *Fortnightly Review*, 127, January–June, p. 45.

31 V.M. ALLOM, (1967), *Ex Oriente Salus: A Centenary History of Eastbourne College*, Eastbourne pp. 62–4.

32 THE REV. W.R. PHILLIPS was present at the meeting in 1892 which initiated the AHPS. The school was sited originally near Lowestoft and was known as South Lodge before it moved in 1937 to Old Buckenham Hall near Attleborough. Old Buckenham Hall School has suffered from fires twice, once in 1937 after which it moved to the Hall and once in 1952 after which it moved to Brettenham Park, its present location.

33 Cf. J.A.P., *Westbourne Preparatory School — a Short History*, p. 1.

34 I am grateful to Mr JOHN V. GANE, who became headmaster of Marton Hall School in 1937, for this information.

35 I am indebted to the late Mr GILBERT ASHTON, headmaster of Abberley Hall from 1921 to 1961, for this information.

36 From a typescript history of Tormore School 1889–1919 in the school's possession.

37 Miss GOSFORD was succeeded in 1920 by Miss GRACE TREVOR, who ran the school as a dame preparatory school until 1953. It now belongs to the charitable 'Order of Hermit Friars of St Augustine', preparing Catholic boys for Stonyhurst and other Catholic public schools.

Part 2

Giving Early Satisfaction

To gain a scholarship at a private school is the only form of
advertisement open to those who object to figuring in the columns of
the newspapers side by side with oroide gold, cheap sherry, and potent
medicines.
(*The Saturday Review*, 1880)

The more scholarships he can win at Eton, Harrow, Winchester,
Rugby, and the rest, the higher will be the repute of his school; and as
the competition between school and school is fierce and unintermit-
tent, he cannot afford to throw away a single chance.
(Edmond Holmes (1911) *What Is and What Might Be*)

The Family Tie

Though private schools were popularly supposed to be *ephemeral*,[1] opening
and closing their doors with remarkable rapidity, moving sites often and
exhibiting little of the stability of other forms of nineteenth century school
such as National or Board Schools, private preparatory schools have in fact
enjoyed the advantages of being able to move with the times, taking advantage
of improving circumstances. Sometimes private schools were remarkably long
lived, like that belonging to the Belgian Wanostrocht family which existed for
more than three quarters of a century from c.1780 to 1858,[2] whilst an earlier
school of a 'quasi-preparatory' nature lasted for sixty years. This was the
school at Fernyhalgh, Lancashire, kept by Dame Alice Harrison and Mary
Backhouse, who from 1700 to 1760 gave an early education to Catholic boys
before they went across the Channel to their senior schools.[3] This dame
'preparatory' school had about 200 pupils from all over South Lancashire and
from as far afield as London. It might even be argued therefore that *stability*
was a distinguishing feature of the preparatory school compared with other
forms of private school.

Many of the preparatory schools that existed in the early decades of the
nineteenth century (and at least three which may have had their beginnings in

the eighteenth) exist today, several of them being owned by one family over a long period, sometimes stretching back to pre-Victorian times. Though many of these schools have been passed over to boards of governors and have become charitable trusts, the family links are still strong. Thus Fonthill School (1820), founded by the Rev. George Radcliffe, celebrated its sequicentennial year in 1970 under the ownership of Miss Elizabeth Sealy, the great-great-grand-daughter of its founder. The first headmaster who was not a member of the Radcliffe-Sealy family was Mr Nigel Dunsmore-Rouse, appointed in 1975.

The headmaster of Twyford School in 1982, Mr David Wickham, was the great-great-grandson of the Rev. Robert Wickham who took the school over from the Rev. J.C. Bedford in 1834. There have been seven heads of Windlesham House, founded in 1837 by Lieutenant C.R. Malden RN, and all of them (including the present Mr Charles Malden) have been members of the Malden family. Stubbington House (1841) held a similar record up to 1963, with four generations of the Foster family being owners, filling the post of head or principal until 1958. Between 1958 and 1963, when the school was converted into a charitable trust, the headmaster was salaried by the Foster family. The descendants of David Munro, who in 1855 became usher of the quasi-preparatory school at Totteridge in Hertfordshire (which later became Dorset House), continued to own the school some eighty years after David Munro had married Jane Wilkinson, the head's daughter. It was not till 1936 that the Munro family relinquished its ties with the school with the retirement of Malcolm Munro. All five schools have shown a remarkable record of longevity through family ties.

Two schools founded later in the 1850s have continued their family tendencies to the present. Hoddeson Grange, founded in 1854 by the Rev. C.G. Chittenden (1854–91), exemplifies the strength of these dynastic tendencies since despite a lengthy interregnum from 1893 to 1930,[4] the Chittenden family is still today at the helm of the school, although in 1905 it removed to Seaford in Sussex and was re-named (1905) Newlands. The other school founded in the 1850s is Mostyn House in the Wirral, founded as a private school[5] by a Mr E.H. Price in 1852. After eight years the school was purchased by Mr A.S. Grenfell. It has been conducted by a member of the Grenfell family ever since except for a brief six years when a Mr W.F. Barrett was head from 1883 to 1889 (see Chapter 10).

Three other early schools — Stoneygate, Rose Hill, and Woodcote House — are similar examples of a family tradition. Stoneygate, founded in Leicestershire by Dr Franklin in 1844, remained within the family for over a hundred years. Mr G. Rudd (Dr Franklin's son-in-law) took over the school in 1891, passing it on in 1921 to his son, Mr G.B.F. Rudd, who continued as head until 1951. The Allfrees at Rose Hill in Tunbridge Wells did not enjoy such an impressive record of longevity, though T.R. Allfree (1832–67) and F.C. Allfree (1867–80) shared an innings of forty-eight years before the Rev. A.R. Cronk (1890–98) took over. Of these three schools Woodcote House perhaps has the record for persistent dynasticism, even though it was conducted in the nineteenth century by one family and in the twentieth by another. The Rev. James Pears had conducted a quasi-military academy at Woodcote from 1814 to 1823.[6] His son, the Rev. Robert Pears, returned in 1851 to set up a classical preparatory school. Pears the younger passed on the reins to his son-in-law, the Rev. C.B. Fendall, who kept the school within the family until 1892. After an interlude of some thirty-nine years, during which time the school was translated to Folkestone by its headmaster, O.H. Bradnack (1905–31), and re-named Sutherland House, there was a second period of dynastic headmastering with Mr H.D.L. Paterson (1931–58) being succeeded by Mr H.D.L. Paterson Junior (1958–   ).

The custom which led certain preparatory schools by dint of their being private property to remain in the hands of a single family was in evidence throughout the nineteenth century. Three schools, founded (or in one case refounded) in the 1860s, were typical. The school, founded in 1869 by the Rev. W. Nelson at Feckenham in Worcestershire, became Arden House when it moved to Henley-in-Arden in 1876. It was under the continuous control of the Nelson family until 1959 when Mr Jack Nelson relinquished control and it became a charitable trust. Elstree, refounded by the Rev. Lancelot Sanderson in 1869, had a similar almost unbroken run[7] of 100 years of familial rule until the late Commander Ian C.M. Sanderson retired in 1969. The third school, Orwell Park,[8] founded by the Rev. W.G. Wilkinson in 1867, has been linked with the Wilkinson family for over 110 years. During that time the school has been run by either a Wilkinson or a relative through marriage. Two more schools displayed similar characteristics from the 1870s. The Earle family controlled Yarlet Hall and Bilton Grange[9] from 1873 to 1930 when the Rev. Granville Earle passed the school on to a Mr J.F. Fawcus. Rokeby School,[10] founded in 1877 by Mr C.D. Olive, remained in the hands of the Olive family until 1965.

In many cases schools became known by the name of their owner. Victorian England spoke of 'Tabor's' and 'Waterfield's', for example, instead of Cheam and Temple Grove respectively. Sometimes lesser known schools achieved a similar distinction through the longevity of the school's proprietor and his family, or the success of his scholarship training, or both. Horris Hill, opened in 1888, was known at Winchester as 'Evans's' because of A.H. Evans' thirty-one years as headmaster and because of the number of boys he sent to Winchester. Evans was headmaster till 1919 when the school came under the control of the Stow family. Marton Hall School, Bridlington, Yorkshire, although a dame school started by a spinster[11] — and therefore unlikely to be called by the family name — was nevertheless controlled by one family from 1889 to 1970. The foundress, Miss Wilson, passed the school on to her niece, Mrs Gane, who ran it with her husband from 1903 to 1937. Their son kept the school from then until 1970. St Ronan's, Hawkhurst, another school founded in the 1880s, has also experienced preparatory school 'dynasticism'. Started by the Rev. Philip Crick, who conducted it from 1883 to 1909, St Ronan's became the property of Mr Stanley Harris, author of *The Master and His Boys* (1924). He in turn passed the school to W.B. Harris, who continued the Harris line at

Giving Early Satisfaction

St Ronan's for another thirty years. Since 1957 the school has been conducted by the Vassar-Smith family. Scaitcliffe School, Englefield Green, is yet another school founded in the 1880s,[12] keeping family links. Mr Ronald Vickers came to the school as joint headmaster in 1896 and was later effectively sole headmaster from 1902 until his death in 1942. His son, Richard Vickers, the present senior headmaster, assumed his father's mantle in 1946 when he returned from active service. Father and son thus span eighty-five years of almost uninterrupted preparatory schoolmastering.

Extending the evidence from schools opened in the 1880s, of schools opened in the 1890s at least five can demonstrate a continuing family tradition — that of the Cary Fields at West House School, Edgbaston, from 1895 to 1963; the Cruickshanks of Edinburgh House, New Milton, from 1895 to 1947; the Eydens of Quainton Hall School, Harrow, from 1897 to 1969; the Hills of Aldro School, from 1923 to the present. Every head of Yardley Court has been a Bickmore. This record of *longevity* rather than *ephemerality*, as exemplified by the continuing family control of schools, has continued in the twentieth century.[13]

Long Periods of Individual Headship and Public School Ties

Another characteristic contributing to the stability of *some* preparatory schools was the comparatively long periods of individual headship. Nevil Holt and Sunningdale Schools, for example, have each had only six heads in 100 years; New College School has had only four since 1866. Packwood Haugh (War-wickshire) has had only four since 1893, and The Old Ride School (Bradford on Avon) only three between 1885 and 1962.

In view of the ephemeral nature of many other forms of private schooling in the nineteenth century, it is of interest to speculate on the reasons for the different history of many preparatory schools. Was it because one of the characteristics of many of the preparatory schools was their family-like ethos? They endeavoured to provide, at both the conscious and the unconscious levels, the stability to be found in a middle class Victorian home. For such a school to be ephemeral in nature would be out of character. Was it because many of the preparatory school heads were conservative clergy who were not only secure in their rectories but were also, as Arnold suggested, suited for the education of young boys of middle and upper class families and were therefore assured of a continuing additional livelihood? Or did their stability derive from the fact that some of them were Oxford and Cambridge graduates, gentlemen with a vocation rather than a mere venal interest in education? Perhaps, on the other hand, it was their wealthy clientèle which ensured the continuing prosperity of many dame preparatory and rectory schools. It would have been improper for such schools, serving such august clientèle, to be ephemeral. Since in many cases they were not, they continued and became prosperous — prosperous enough for some private commercial schoolmasters to turn instead to this form of private schooling. Another possible reason might be that, having committed themselves to the education of young boys, it was difficult for them to be pedagogically mobile. G.W. Kitchin (1827–1912), who was headmaster of Twyford from 1854 to 1861 and later became both censor of the non-collegiate undergraduates at Oxford and Dean of Durham, was an outstanding exception to pedagogical immobility. Being thus committed, preparatory school headmasters were the more able to achieve stability within their limited sphere. No doubt the proprietary nature of the schools, being passed on from father to son, had a strong influence too. None of these reasons, however, save the last, seems to provide adequate explanation for the stability and longevity which characterized many private preparatory schools. Could it be, then, that the preparatory schools' establishing ties with public schools through the process of scholarships and entrance examinations was the chief cause of their *consolidation* into a complementary system of schooling in the nineteenth century?

How Important *was* Dr Arnold?

When Dr Arnold decided to abolish Form 1 in 1837 and Form 2 in 1838 he theoretically ensured that thereafter no boy under twelve could enter Rugby. This decision may have encouraged some schoolmasters to provide alternative schooling for younger boys destined for English public schools: Lt Malden, for example, opened Windlesham House on the Isle of Wight and Mr T.L. Bloxam started his school in Rugby itself.

But Arnold's action in the 1830s had only a limited effect. More than twenty years later only Harrow amongst the nine schools examined by the Clarendon Commission contained no boys below the age of thirteen. Looking at the average age and the lowest age of the lowest division in each school, the Commissioners concluded that only Winchester and Harrow were endeavouring to accept their boys at a 'post-preparatory' age.[14] Eton appeared to be the worst offender, taking boys at a very tender age. In 1811 forty-one of the new boys were under twelve years old, including William Henry Carter who was only five. In 1821 twenty-five such boys entered Eton, in 1831 thirty-seven, in 1841 fifteen. In 1851 there were sixteen under twelve, including Sampson Hodgkinson (aged seven) and Robert Wellington (aged eight) at a time when thirty-three, aged thirteen, were admitted. As late as 1861, at the time of the Clarendon Commission, twenty-five boys were admitted to Eton under twelve years old, including Arthur H.D. Fraser, George Thurstone and G.W. Douton all aged eight, and Henry Robert Scott who was only four years and one month old.[15]

It is not surprising, therefore, to find the Clarendon Commissioners recommending the separation of the lower school from the upper school in view of the tender years of some of the boys. In recommending this separation, the Commissioners urged, by way of encouragement to emerging private preparatory schools, that 'the boys in it (Eton's lower school) should have no preference over the boys from private schools in the admissions to the Upper School'.[16] By recommending that entry to the Upper School at Eton should be by examination not only for boys in private schools but also for boys in the lower school, the commissioners were virtually suggesting the creation of a preparatory school within Eton. Here, then, were the seeds of Mr J.W. Hawtrey's Aldin House at Slough, which opened in 1869 when Mr Hawtrey left Eton, taking with him all the younger boys.[17]

The Impetus of Clarendon on the 'Scholarship' System

The substantial reform of the age of entry to public schools which followed the Clarendon Report led to an increase in the number of private preparatory schools in the 1860s and 1870s. But if Thomas Baylis (1817–1908) could enter Harrow at the age of seven, Arthur F. Winnington-Ingram could still enter Marlborough, as late as February 1871, at the age of twelve, whilst Eton's practice of admitting boys at twelve continued into the twentieth century. Felix Walter Warre, for example, was only eleven when he entered Eton in 1891. *The Contemporary Review* condemned the continuing practice of admitting boys at an early age to public school, but recognized that the situation had improved considerably since the early years of the century.[18] With the younger boys separated from the older ones for the sake of moral protection and shelter from predatory bullies, it became necessary to link the two types of school to form a coherent system. This was done by the institution of entrance examinations and the award of scholarships. Throughout the nineteenth century public schools instituted scholarships to attract the brighter boys from emergent preparatory schools, and set up entrance examinations to monitor the standard of their ordinary entry.

Eton and Winchester had traditionally awarded a number of foundation scholarships to boys on entry to the school, and the distinction between 'scholar' and 'commoner', or their equivalents, was familiar to both schools. As early as 1840, with the Gregory Scholarships of £100 tenable for four years, Harrow recognized the desirability of attracting able boys. Twenty-five years later the Rev. H. Montagu Butler (1860–85) instituted further entrance scholarships, considerably strengthening Harrow's capacity to achieve this purpose. Montague J. Rendall (1862–1950), later headmaster of Winchester, was the first boy from his preparatory school — Elstree — to win an entrance scholarship to Harrow. Marlborough, too, was early in the field by instituting entrance scholarships in 1854. In 1863 Clifton established two scholarships of £25 per annum for boys already in the school, and these were followed by others in 1864, 1868, 1871, 1880 and 1897. At Charterhouse the Governors were deprived of the patronage of nomination to the Foundation by new statutes in 1868. From 1874 places were thrown open to competition, with junior scholarships being awarded to boys between twelve and fourteen.

Although an attempt by the Rev. F. Heptenstall, headmaster of Sedbergh (1874–80), to establish scholarships in 1874 was thwarted by the Governors who felt that insufficient funds were available, his successor, Mr H.G. Hart (1880–1900), tackled the scholarship problem with more success by remitting house boarding fees for scholars. At Tonbridge New Judd Scholarships of £100 and £80 per annum were instituted in 1880; whilst at Wellington the number of scholarships was raised in 1897 from seven to ten, the values ranging from £30 to £80.

The Importance of Getting into a Good School

It was this institutionalization of stiffly competitive scholarships over a period of decades which H.S. Shelton regarded as the chief cause of the evolution of the late nineteenth century preparatory school.[19]

Some idea of the extent of the growth of entrance scholarships offered by public schools by the end of the century is gained by reference to Table 5, compiled from figures contained in the 1889, 1890 and 1899 issues of the *Public School Year Book*.

Table 5. Growth of Entrance Scholarships to Public Schools, 1889–99.

Schools	1889	1890	1899
	Scholars or exhibitioners*		
Aldenham	—	—	4
Bedford	—	10	—
Bedford Grammar	—	—	1
K.E.S. Birmingham	—	—	1
Blackheath	—	—	2
Blundells	—	—	8
Bradfield	3	7	23
Brighton	1	4	—
King's, Canterbury	—	—	29
Charterhouse	13	10	14
Cheltenham	16	17	9
Chigwell	—	—	4
Clifton	7	17	19
Dulwich	—	2	5
Durham	—	—	5
Epsom	—	—	2
Eton	15	15	10
Felsted	—	—	1
Fettes	4	4	—
Giggleswick	—	—	4

Glenalmond	10	1	—
Haileybury	4	6	7
Harrow	9	7	8
Lancing	2	4	7
Leamington	—	—	11
Malvern	6	15	14
Marlborough	11	23	18
Merchant Taylors'	1	2	—
Mill Hill	—	—	5
Oakham	—	—	3
St Edward's, Oxford	—	—	4
Radley	5	4	6
Ramsgate College	—	—	2
Reading School	—	—	7
Rossall	—	6	9
Rugby	15	12	11
St Paul's	11	13	15
Sherborne	1	—	1
Shrewsbury	20	2	5
Sutton Valence	—	—	1
Tonbridge	—	—	10
University College School	—	—	3
Uppingham	3	7	6
Wellington	10	10	7
Westminster	3	6	11
Weymouth	—	—	5
Winchester	20	19	21
St Peter's York	—	—	5

Note: *These figures excluded many scholarships and exhibitions to boys already in their public schools.

Apart from a few fluctuations the picture is one of intensified ties between public and preparatory schools.

Some preparatory schools gained an early reputation for winning scholarships. News of scholarship achievements was joyously received at the schools of successful scholars, where often a half-holiday was awarded *pour encourager les autres.* Such achievements were invaluable in the enhancing of a school's reputation. Stoke House,[20] for example, achieved a considerable national reputation for its scholarship successes. No year was more dazzling than 1878, when this school of about fifty boys achieved five scholarships at Winchester, six at Eton, one at Wellington and two at Charterhouse.

The Entrance Examination

But only a fraction of the boys going from preparatory school to public school did so through success in scholarships.[21] Most boys did so by way of entrance examinations.[22] These established whether or not a candidate possessed a basic literacy and a classical competency. Decades of examination in the nineteenth century established relationships between particular preparatory schools and public schools which lasted for many years, some continuing to this day. Even in the heyday of athleticism a public school would thus look closely at the quality of its entrants from preparatory schools. For this reason Winchester accepted so many boys from Horris Hill (1888), as the standard of scholarship was known to be high since its founder and first headmaster, A.H. Evans, had been a master at Winchester and J.L. Stow, his junior partner, was himself a Wykehamist. Thirty-five boys from Horris Hill were admitted between 1888 and 1895, far more than the number supplied by many older preparatory schools over a longer period.[23] Harrow's link with Elstree is another example of the founder (or re-founder) of a preparatory school having been a master of that school. In the same year as the Rev. Lance Sanderson took over Elstree, 1869,[24] J.W. Hawtrey left Eton to begin a preparatory school at Aldin House, Slough, which as 'Hawtrey's' established strong links with Eton (see Chapter 10).

Geographical Proximity to Public Schools

If one reason for a close link between a preparatory and a public school was the ownership of the preparatory school by an ex-assistant master of the public school,[25] another was geographical proximity. Some preparatory schools were deliberately sited near public schools. The schools in and around Rugby such as Bilton Grange, Oakfield, Hill Brow and Hill Morton[26] are good examples of this kind of development.

There are many other examples of topographical proximity leading to close educational ties: St Goar (1887) and XIV School (1885)[27] with Clifton; Twyford (1809) and Horris Hill (1888) with Winchester; Elstree (1869) until 1939[28] and Orley Farm (1850) with Harrow; West House School (1895), Edgbaston, with King Edward the Sixth School, Birmingham, Malvern and Bromsgrove; Rose Hill (1832), Tunbridge Wells, and Yardley Court (1898) with Tonbridge; Dorset House with Lancing and Bow School (1885) with Durham School. Yet another example, though not so close spatially, is Mostyn House (1852), Cheshire, with Shrewsbury, to which school as many as 50 per cent of the Mostyn House boys went between 1890 and 1894.[29]

Close relationships existed between some of the London preparatory schools and the London public schools: Durston House (1886), Ealing, sent many boys to St Paul's School; the Hall School, Hampstead (1889), sent its pupils to St Paul's as well as to Westminster. Rokeby School (1877), in Wimbledon, had ties with Westminster from 1883 onwards and with St Paul's from 1886, at the same time establishing links with Charterhouse in 1886 and with King's School, Canterbury, in 1897. Willington School (1885) has enjoyed a strong association with both St Paul's and Westminister Schools, whilst The Mall School, Twickenham, has also had very close links with St Paul's.

The Devon schools of St Peter's (1885), near Exmouth and Wolborough Hill (1877), Newton Abbot, sent many boys to the Royal Naval College, Dartmouth, the causes no doubt being partly proximity, partly county tradition.

The story of the Rev. Walter Earle illustrates the relative influences of the personal and the topographical factors in the formation of ties between preparatory schools and public schools. Earle, who had been second master to Edward Thring at Uppingham, set up a preparatory school at Yarlet Hall in Staffordshire where he remained for fourteen years before moving in 1887 to Bilton Grange, Dunchurch, near Rugby. Whilst his school was at Yarlet Hall its links with Uppingham were very strong. But after Earle moved to Bilton Grange the pattern changed: the early close ties with Uppingham later gave way to similar close ties with Rugby from 1880 onwards. After 1887 the trend of the previous seven years was confirmed, with more boys going to Rugby than to Uppingham each year.

Older School Ties

Some of these links derived from the loyalty of a preparatory school's clientèle to a particular public school. In this category were the schools which sent large numbers of boys to Eton, viz. Summer Fields (1864), Parkside (1879),[30] Sunningdale (1874), Hoddesdon Grange (1854), Stoke House (1867), Fonthill (1820), Cheam (1645). Of the three last-mentioned schools, Stoke House had 765 boys passing through the school between 1867 and 1912: of those, 180 went to Eton, 147 to Charterhouse and seventy-one to Winchester.[31] At Fonthill the number of boys going on to Eton surpassed the number of boys going on to any other public school between 1886 and 1920. Of the boys who entered Fonthill between 1886 and 1900 at least thirty-eight went on to Eton compared with sixteen to Winchester and seven to Rugby.[32] Of the boys entering Fonthill between 1901 and 1910 thirty-one went to Eton compared with ten to Wellington and ten to Marlborough. This trend towards Eton was even more pronounced during the next ten years. At Cheam, under R.S. Tabor (1855–90), most boys went to Eton; 15 per cent went to Harrow; some half dozen went to Rugby and another half dozen were shared by Winchester, Wellington and Marlborough.[33]

The Knoll, Woburn Sands, Bletchley (1892 and now defunct), had links with Harrow, Oundle, Felsted, Charterhouse and Uppingham. St Andrew's School, Eastbourne (1877), had ties with Uppingham and Malvern and, to a lesser extent, with Charterhouse and Rugby. Homefield School, Sutton (1870), had links with Epsom, Dulwich College, Tonbridge and St Paul's. During the space of thirty years[34] boys from Eaton House School, Aldeburgh (now Orwell Park School), went to Eton, Harrow, Winchester, Westminster, Charterhouse, Haileybury, Marlborough, Wellington, Radley, Bradfield, Malvern and Rossall. On the other hand, Liscard Castle Preparatory School (now defunct) in Cheshire,[35] whose head, Mr Grundy, was a profound admirer of William Temple, had closest links with Rugby. Similarly, Cordwalles, under Canon T.J. Nunns, although having some links with Rugby, Charterhouse, Eton and Marlborough, had especially close links with Winchester.[36]

A closer look at the registers of some preparatory schools helps show their ties with certain public schools. For example, the *Register of the Members, Old Bowite Society* (1918) shows that seventy-two Old Bowites went to Durham School after leaving Bow — almost as many as to all other public schools together.[37] The scholarship boards in the school dining hall give a similar picture: the school gained thirteen scholarships at Durham School and only four at Marlborough, two at Rossall and one each at Loretto and Pocklington before 1914.

Another northern school, Aysgarth, near Bedale, established between 1877 and 1906 a similar pattern of close links with several schools. One in particular, Charterhouse, obtained 121; Eton was only a fair second, with 72; and Harrow third with 65.

The first honorary secretary of the AHPS, C.C. Cotterill, had a more evenly spread distribution, with sixty-two boys going to Sedbergh, from his school (now defunct) at Greenbank, Liverpool, fifty-two to Rugby, forty-seven to Shrewsbury, thirty-eight to Loretto and thirty-four to Uppingham between 1888 and 1912. Greenbank's links with the public schools are a good example of a changing pattern of provision. In the late 'eighties and 'nineties, Sedbergh and Rugby were more frequently patronized by old Greenbankians, whilst Loretto and Shrewsbury were patronized more in the second half of this period.

But the preparatory school to send one's sons to, if the aim was to get them to Eton or Harrow, was pre-eminently Summer Fields at Oxford (see Table 6).

Table 6. Summer Fields and Public Schools, 1864–1909: Principal Ties

1864–1879	Eton 56;	Wellington 14;	Charterhouse 11
1880–1889	Eton 51;	Winchester 21;	Harrow 20
1890–1899	Eton 98;	Winchester 46;	Radley 30
1900–1909	Eton 130;	Radley 35;	Wellington 29

Its close relationship with Eton was strengthened with the passing years. It could well be that the writer of the article in *The Contemporary Review* of May 1890 had Summer Fields in mind when he wrote:

> Whether the tendency, which seems to be strengthening in preparatory schools, to associate themselves exclusively with a particular public school is a good one is a question upon which a good deal may be said; for my own part, I regret it as tending to limit the scope and function of preparatory schools[38].

Harrovian orientated preparatory schools were Windlesham House (which between 1837 and 1902 sent 152 boys to Harrow, ninety-one to Eton, forty-eight to Haileybury and forty-seven to Rugby), and Hoddesdon Grange (which between 1854 and 1904 although it sent 154 to Eton, also sent fifty to Harrow, and only eleven went to Charterhouse). But by the time the school moved to Seaford in Sussex and became known as Newlands in 1905, it had lost its special relationship with Eton, but established strong relationships with Wellington and Charterhouse.

Winchester had close links with Twyford but by the late nineteenth century and early twentieth century this preparatory school had lost any particularly close link with Winchester and in some years sent fewer boys there than to other public schools. Eagle House had during the greater part of the nineteenth century maintained close ties with Winchester. During the head-mastership of the Rev. Edward Wickham (1833–48), whilst possibly[39] only five boys went to Rugby and four to Harrow, some fifty-one went to Winchester. Under the Rev. Edward Huntingford (1848–74) forty-three boys went to Harrow and forty-one to Eton, whilst as many as 128 went to Winchester. But during the headmastership of the Rev. A.N. Malan (1874–1905), the school moved in 1886 to Sandhurst. This move (even more than the move between Yarlet Hall and Bilton Grange of the Rev. William Earle) influenced the ties between Eagle House and public schools. Between 1874 and 1886 the figures show forty-four going to Winchester, twenty-four to Cheltenham and eighteen to Charterhouse. From 1886 until 1905 thirty-one attended Wellington (now Eagle House's neighbour), twenty-four went to Harrow and only sixteen to Winchester. The Oxford Preparatory School (or Dragon School, as it is now called) during the period 1882–1913 sent fifty-five boys to Winchester, twenty to Rossal and sixteen to Repton.

Ties of Friendship

Personal friendships between the headmaster of the preparatory school and either the headmaster or a housemaster at the public school were also ties. Thus, when Lashmer Whistler, who was an excellent sportsman, was due to go to Haileybury, in 1912, one of the Harrow housemasters telephoned Mr Vaughan Wilkes of St Cyprian's, Eastbourne, to enquire if he had any promising boys. Wilkes explained that Whistler was going to Haileybury because the fees at Harrow were too high. In the event Whistler went to Harrow on an athletic scholarship.[40] Over the years such relationships waxed and waned as individuals in both institutions passed on. But often the links were long lasting and far outlived their originators. The establishing of ties, such an important factor in the consolidation of preparatory schools in the nineteenth century, derived from these friendships, from the moves of masters from public to preparatory schools, and from geographical proximity. In the twentieth century, the geographical factor has become the most powerful of these influences. The same social forces that have increased the percentage of day boys in the preparatory schools have led parents to give preference to preparatory and public schools within travelling distance of their homes. The process has therefore continued unabated but links between particular preparatory and public schools now derive less from personal contacts than from geographical proximity and this despite the improvements in transport.[41] This does not negate the main point, however, that in the nineteenth century the establishing of ties between the public and preparatory schools was a chief factor in their end-of-the-century success and that this articulation differentiated them profoundly from other private schools.

Notes

1 The Newcastle Commission, in particular, attacked the private adventure schools for this fault.
2 Three generations of the WANOSTROCHT family looked after this school which was at Camberwell Green from c.1780 to 1830 when it was moved to Blackheath. NICHOLAS WANOSTROCHT (1804–76), of the third generation, was a competent cricketer who played at Lords under the pseudonym of N. FELIX. The British Library possesses a prospectus of this school dated 1795.
3 Cf. J. KITCHING (1966) *Roman Catholic Education*, 2 vols, PhD thesis, University of Leeds, Vol. 1, p. 48.
4 When Mr W.A. WHEELER was headmaster.
5 Mr A.G. GRENFELL refounded Mostyn House as a preparatory school in 1890. See Chapter 10.
6 Cf. Chapter 2.
7 Between 1901 and 1904 the Rev. EDGAR STOGDON was headmaster. He was succeeded in 1904 by the Rev. F. DE W. LUSHINGTON (the Rev. LANCELOT SANDERSON's son-in-law), who kept school until 1911 when E.L. SANDERSON took over his father's school.
8 This school started in Lowestoft, Suffolk, then moved to Crespigny House in 1870. It has been known successively as Crespigny House, Eaton House, Aldeburgh Lodge and Orwell Park School when it moved to Nacton in 1937.
9 The EARLES moved from Yarlet Hall to Bilton Grange in 1887.
10 Started at 'Helmsley' on Wimbledon Common. This was the school attended by ROBERT GRAVES and his brother.
11 Cf. Chapter 7.
12 By the Rev. CANON CROSLEGH, probably in 1884, as a tutorial establishment, though it soon became a preparatory school. Cf. letter in my possession dated 11 April 1979 from Mr RICHARD VICKERS, joint head of Scaitcliffe.

13 Earnseat House School (1900–79), Arnside, was associated with the BARNES family from 1900 to 1968; the RICHARDSON family controlled Beaudesert Park School from 1908 to 1970; the SEWELL family have conducted Old Buckenham Hall School since 1923; the STEVENS family, father and son, have controlled Chelmsford Hall, Eastbourne, since its beginning in 1920; and the DODD family, EDGAR and JACK (father and son), were successively headmasters of Downside School, Purley, from 1920 to 1976. Mr JACK DODD became the Secretary of the IAPS in 1976.

14 The figures given are:

	Average age of entry	Lowest age of entry
Eton	10.3	8.0
Winchester	14.9	11.11
Charterhouse	10.4	9.8
St Paul's	11.2	9.9
Merchant Taylors'	10.6	9.1
Harrow	13.11	13.5
Rugby	10.6	10.2
Shrewsbury	11.8	11.8

Cf. Clarendon Report, Vol. 2, pp. 504–5.

15 Figures are derived from admission registers at Eton College.

16 Clarendon Report, Vol. 1, p. 109.

17 Cf. Chapter 10.

18 *Op. cit.*, Vol. 57, May 1890, p. 678.

19 H.S. SHELTON, (1932), *Thoughts of a Schoolmaster*, Hutchinson p. 84.

20 Formerly Tudor House 1867–72. Between 1867 and 1965 Tudor House/Stoke House won as many as 290 scholarships and exhibitions at public schools including at least sixty at Eton.

21 See Appendix 9 for specimen scholarship paper of May 1879 set by Cheltenham College. I am grateful to Mr NIGEL DUNSMORE-ROUSE, ex-headmaster of Fonthill, for this old scholarship paper.

22 No doubt many secured entry through their performance in scholarship examinations even though they failed to secure a scholarship.

23 The Horris Hill records show that in the twentieth century the public schools with the most boys from Horris Hill are Winchester (1946–76 — 240); Eton (1947–76 — 120) and Bradfield (1946–76 — 63).

24 Cf. Chapter 10.

25 The case of J.W.J. VECQUERAY at Hill Brow School, Rugby, shows an even closer link, since VECQUERAY ran his preparatory school whilst still a master at Rugby school.

26 Hill Morton School was owned by the Rev. CHARLES DARNELL, who moved to Edinburgh to become the first head of Cargilfield Preparatory School and third chairman (1894) of AHPS.

27 Originally called St Oswald's from 1885 to 1900.

28 Moved to Woolhampton, near Reading, Berkshire.

29 I am very grateful to Mr GEOFFREY PLACE, local historian and assistant master, and Mr A.D. GRENFELL, headmaster of Mostyn House School, for this information.

30 At Ewell. Moved to East Horsley, Surrey, in 1934, and to Stoke d'Albernon in 1979.

31 Figures have been abstracted from the school prospectus of 1913, when the school moved to Seaford in Sussex. A copy of this prospectus is kept by the Bodleian Library in the John Johnson Collection.

32 These figures have been abstracted from the admission register at Fonthill School, 1886–1926.
33 Cf. Sir IAN HAMILTON, (1939) *When I Was a Boy*, Faber and Faber p. 92.
34 Cf. *Eaton House School Prospectus*, 1892.
35 Cf. G.B. GRUNDY, (1945) *Fifty-Five Years at Oxford*, Methuen p. 13. Liscard was 'a castellated building with turrets and battlements'. The school had about fifty boys of whom about two-thirds were boarders, mainly sons of prominent businessmen in Liverpool and Manchester.
36 Cf. *PSR*, 6, 48, March 1911, p. 105.
37 Marlborough had the next highest with thirteen Old Bowites.
38 *Op. cit.*, p. 678.
39 Figures are taken from the *Eagle House Register 1820–1908* but during the years the records are not complete.
40 Sir JOHN SMYTH VC, MC, (1967), *Bolo Whistler*, Muller p. 32.
41 Boys now expect either to be visited or to go home every two or three weeks instead of once or twice a term. This is a potent factor in causing parents to choose a nearby school. I am grateful to Mr JACK DODD for this information on present day trends.

Outbreaks of even mild epidemics have proved so disastrous to schools
... that the mere suggestion of measles and scarlet fever is sufficient to
instil fear into the hearts of all.
(*The Private Schoolmaster*, November 1887)

The Site's the Thing

Since the consolidation of preparatory schools was due to the development of
close relationships between them and the public schools, they consequently
followed the latter's ethos and learned from their mistakes. Unsuitable sites,
poor sanitation and the slow awareness of hygiene and other prophylactics to
avoid outbreaks of fever and other epidemics that cursed private schools,
constrained their early growth and prosperity.[1] Epidemics of scarlet fever,
diphtheria, whooping cough, and measles were stoically regarded as part of the
natural cycle of school life.

So siting was crucial. Location bore on the school's possible future
reputation as a 'healthy' school, which could and did determine its financial
stability. Such was the connection between healthy site and healthy finances
that in 1900 the Rev. W. Grylls Watson of The Limes School, Croydon,
declared that: 'Croydon is the healthiest town in England, and therefore [*sic*]
probably in the world'.[2] Hence the preponderance of schools in the seaside
resorts of Eastbourne, Brighton[3] and Westgate-on-Sea. But outside the
favoured areas of preparatory school investment in the South East, London and
the Home counties,[4] the greatest concentration of such schools was to be found
at Malvern which, in the nineteenth century, had gained a reputation for its
health-giving spa waters.

But the north of England was not devoid of healthy surroundings. At
Seaforth, the Rev. Mr Rawson kept his school, which enjoyed such a
considerable reputation for preparing boys for public schools that the Liverpool merchant Mr Gladstone sent his son William Ewart there. For Seaforth, as
an ex-Headmaster of Eton has suggested, owed its reputation

Not so much due to its intellectual stamina as to the extreme salubrity
of the situation on the pure dry sands of the Mersey's mouth, with all
the advantages of the strong tidal action and the fresh and frequent
north-west winds.[5]

Nearby at Parkgate on the Wirral, Mostyn House School could similarly
boast much later that it enjoyed a 'dry and bracing' climate where the
north-west winds kept the skies clear and where 'the rainfall is one of the
lowest in the kingdom'. It claimed 'remarkable freedom from the germs of
epidemic or infectious diseases', so that only once in twenty years had there
been any influenza in the school and then it was only a mild visitation.[6] A
similar healthy record at the turn of the century, was claimed by Red House
School at Moor Monkton, escaping all infectious diseases for some twelve
years, largely because of its bracing air in its comparatively remote location in
North Yorkshire.[7] At nearby Bedale the site of the purpose-designed Aysgarth
School (1877) was deliberately chosen by its founder, the Rev. C.T. Hales, for
its healthy aspect.

Health considerations, as an insurance against deaths of pupils, were so
strong amongst preparatory school principals during the nineteenth century
that some private preparatory school owners, realizing the vulnerability of
young boys to infectious diseases, actively specialized in looking after boys in
delicate health. [G.] Lyton Strachey, for example, was sent to the small school
of Mr Henry Forde at Parkstone on Poole Harbour, Dorset, from 1889 to 1893
because of his poor constitution and because Lady Strachey had a great belief in
the beneficial powers of the ozone coming from the sea.[8] Forde's school at
Parkstone was more of a coaching establishment than a school *per se*, but
amongst the more orthodox preparatory schools at the end of the nineteenth
century Eaton House School (now Orwell Park School), Aldeburgh, was
perhaps a good example of a school wishing to capitalize on its healthy
situation when it claimed that the school's climate was 'peculiarly suited to the
requirements of Indian children's constitutions.'[9] Though it was perhaps
difficult to sustain such a claim, it shows the school's keen appreciation of
climate and siting as an attraction to its clientèle.

Drains and the MoH

Gone were the days when schools could sell their night-soil to the gunpowder-
makers, the long years of peace had seen to that, yet general recognition of the
value of good sanitation came only gradually to Victorian England, as the smell
of the Thames testified. Even Chadwick[10] — who found England stinking and
left it sweet — had a long hard struggle to establish a Board of Health in 1848
only to see it abolished six years later. Its successor, the Public Health Board,
was also abolished in 1858 when its functions were assigned to the Home
Office and Privy Council — bodies which were unlikely to place health high on
their priority lists.

Not till 1871 was the country divided into sanitary districts, each with a Medical Officer of Health and an Inspector of Nuisances. Three years later the responsibilities of these sanitary districts were carefully defined[11] so as to include sewerage, drainage, and water supply. As the standards of sanitation rose, so naturally did the standards of health: a marked decline was evident in the incidence of fatal infectious diseases from about 1870 onwards.

So it is not without significance that the first decade from 1870 coincided with the beginning of the rapid increase of preparatory schools in the last quarter of the century. For there were no serious cholera epidemics after 1866, and after 1870 deaths from cholera became few indeed. Furthermore, after 1871 the deaths from smallpox sharply declined. Schools were nevertheless plagued by *minor* infectious diseases throughout the nineteenth century. It was no doubt for this reason that Dr Clement Dukes, physician at Rugby School, contributed to *The Private Schoolmaster* one of a series of articles on school sanitation.[12] Similarly, Dr Tatham, Health Officer of Salford, drew private schoolmasters' attention, through *The Private Schoolmaster*, to Section 126 of the Public Health Act of 1875 which provided heavy penalties for wilful exposure of persons to infectious disease.[13] He suggested to his readers that it was a mistaken policy on the part of schoolmasters to urge, for economic reasons, the punctual return of pupils from vacation if they were recovering from infectious diseases.

The importance of high standards of sanitation in the promotion of good health and the prevention of infections in the closed community of a private boarding school — which the majority of the nineteenth century preparatory schools were — cannot be overemphasized. In such circumstances, when few schools had separate sanatoria, an epidemic of scarlet fever could mean a school's closure for three weeks or a month. This would bring loss of income, and in extreme cases loss of livelihood through the permanent closure of the school. Infectious diseases were regarded by schoolmasters as a scourge from which few expected to escape for very long. In the 1850s Eagle House School was attacked by both scarlet fever and diphtheria. Three boys died. Such a record could be ruinous to a school, and for three years no new boy came to Eagle House. The headmaster, the Rev. Dr Huntingford (1847–74), saw the need for prompt action as 'the calamity of illness had branded the house with ill-repute'[14] and he removed the school completely from Brook Green, Hammersmith, to the vacated buildings of the army 'crammer', the Rev. J.M. Brackenbury.

The Case of Twyford

Though in retrospect Major General Sir Henry Hallam Parr, sometime ADC to Queen Victoria, could record his delight that the school had to close on one occasion before the end of term because of an outbreak of scarlet fever[15] during the headmastership of the Rev. G.W. Kitchin (1854–61), he should have; as a general, appreciated the expense which Kitchin, on another occasion,[16] incurred by moving the school to two hotels for six weeks at Freshwater on the Isle of Wight, when the boys were to visit the house of the Poet Laureate, Lord Tennyson. Well might the Rev. G.W. Kitchin include a prayer in case of dangerous sickness of any member of school, in his *Prayers for the Use of Twyford School* in 1857.

A far more serious outbreak of diphtheria occurred at Twyford in January 1896 when twenty-seven boys out of fifty-seven were ill. In February two boys died within four days of each other, after which the school moved to a recently vacated preparatory school building in Winchester.[17] At the same time the Twyford School buildings were examined by Dr Frederick W. Andrewes, MD (Oxon.), FRCP (London), the Sanitary Officer to St Bartholomew's Hospital. He exonerated the buildings from blame, commending the ventilation and praising the quality of the water supply. He identified the cause of the outbreak as diphtheria poisoning introduced by a boy returning from holiday. When the school buildings had been fumigated and disinfected in May 1896, the boys' parents were invited to send their offspring back to Twyford. Unfortunately, there was a recrudescence of diphtheria and a third boy died in July. After the school assembled for the Michaelmas Term 1896 yet another outbreak of sore throats brought serious disruption which caused the telegraph department of the village post office to be engulfed with enquiries from anxious parents. A lease was obtained on Emsworth House, Copthorne, Sussex,[18] for 1897 so that the uninfected could continue school work whilst the Twyford school building was given over to renewed disinfecting and fumigation. A year of plague was succeeded by a year of exile. Numbers fell to thirty. Of the ten leavers in 1897, five went to other preparatory schools. Only three new boys were recruited in 1898. A change of location was mooted. But in the event a new sanatorium was built, the building was completely overhauled and the water supply and drainage system were, notwithstanding Dr Andrewes' report quoted above, repaired. The overhaul consisted of 'the completed excavation of the soil beneath all floors and round all foundations; the laying of a bed of concrete over the whole of this space; the removal of a large block consisting of very mysterious and unapproachable cupboards and dark places around the boot-room itself.'[19]

If a complete overhaul saved Twyford from further upheaval and from a permanent removal to another location, Hoddesdon Grange was beginning to gain such a reputation for its insanitary conditions that numbers were dwindling. The school moved in 1905 to two rented houses in Seaford. Land was bought cheaply and £10,000 was expended to build a purpose-designed and sanitary preparatory school.[20]

Fears of Fevers

In Victorian times illness was endemic. It was expected that children would experience the childish ailments of whooping cough, measles, chicken pox, mumps and scarlet fever. Some caught the more serious typhoid and a few suffered diphtheria or smallpox. P. Shaw Jeffrey has observed: 'In the 60s, 70s and 80s we knew nothing about vitamins or slimming or diet.... Nobody had ever heard of appendicitis. Typhoid and diphtheria and typhus and smallpox were always epidemic somewhere, and people still talked of and feared the Plague, the Black Death.'[21] It is probably not generally realized that the first operation carried out with anaesthetic was performed as *late* as 1846, that chloroform was used for the first time only in 1850 and that antiseptic surgery was probably not universal until after 1870.[22] Such was the rudimentary knowledge of medical science by mid-century.

The fear which school principals and headmasters had of a scarlet fever or measles visitation is expressed in *The Private Schoolmaster*, which noted that 'outbreaks of even mild epidemics have proved so disastrous to schools — public and private — that the mere suggestion of measles and scarlet fever is sufficient to instil fear into the hearts of all.... Sanitary conditions are now as much desired by principals as examination successes.'[23] The following issue of *The Private Schoolmaster*[24] noted that, in the then current epidemic, fifteen more schools had broken up. A *cri de coeur* went up from the editor: 'How can we keep this monster from assailing us? How can we check the ruinous epidemic when once it obtains admission?' Clement Dukes, the Medical Officer of Rugby School, offered advice in the columns of *The Private Schoolmaster:* instant isolation; perfect quarantine; perfect disinfection; plenty of cubic space;[25] ventilation; efficient drainage; and pure water.[26]

The Summer Fields School Magazine of April 1898 noted a serious influenza epidemic which 'scarcely a boy in the school has escaped': the editor added that nevertheless the school had much to be thankful for since 'nearly every school in England, whether public or preparatory, has been visited by mumps, measles, etc. and sometimes by two or three of these epidemics at the same time.' The editor of *The Draconian*, the school magazine of the Dragon School, Summer Fields' near neighbour, noted gloomily that 'with a measles epidemic on the *tapis*, it is unlikely that there will be much to record in the way of football, hockey or athletic fixtures during the term.'[27] School fixture lists in football and other Spring sports were constantly being wrecked by quarantine. Despite the unhealthy situation of Oxford in the damp-laden atmosphere of the Thames basin, C.C. Lynam, the headmaster of the Dragon School, referred in his speeches at prize days in 1897 and 1904 to the *healthy* situation of the school. This is ironic, especially in view of the outbreaks in June 1890; July 1891; July 1893; April 1895;[28] February 1898; April 1902;[29] December 1903; April 1906 and March 1907. He was merely using the opportunity of prize day, in the presence of many parents in a euphoric mood, to reassure them of the unlikelihood of the school's being attacked by some infectious disease.

It is even more ironic that sickness and disease, which constantly threatened to close schools, should also cause the birth of more than one preparatory school. In September 1903 a small contingent of seven boys went from Summer Fields, Oxford, to St Leonard's-on-Sea and, under the guidance of Mr Maclaren and Mr and Mrs Compton, set up a new Summer Fields by the sea where some time was spent by delicate boys in health-strengthening brine baths.

Such was the persistence of some of the childish diseases in preparatory schools that even as late as 1930 Eagle House School, which had moved from Brackenbury's in 1886 to Sandhurst, Berkshire, was reduced from twenty-nine to five boys by an outburst of chicken pox and measles.[30] But it would be mistaken to infer that infectious disease was attacking *most* schools and *most* schoolboys most of the time. A schoolboy could expect to meet with illness of some kind, yet some boys were fortunate and escaped. F. Anstey (alias T.A. Guthrie) experienced no epidemic whilst at his private school in Surbiton:[31] and Osbert Sitwell could recall very few cases of illness at his preparatory school of Bloodsworth, despite the insanitary conditions of the school where boys bathed once a week 'in the same viscous warm water.'[32]

Early Prophylaxis

What were the early preventive measures in health and hygiene? Preparatory school prospectuses advertised such prophylactic features of their respective schools as plain wholesome diet; no corporal punishment; meat twice daily; separate cubicles; excellent sanitary arrangements as approved by a competent surveyor; and an able and experienced matron.[33] The earliest measure was, of course, the choice of a healthy location: less favoured schools had to resort to physic to retain a healthy record. It was for this reason that at Temple Grove, where A.G. Liddell 'was soon troubled with chilblains'[34] (caused as much by calcium deficiency as by cold), sulphur and treacle were periodically dispensed to the boys;[35] whilst before breakfast at Eagle House the matron brought in a tray carrying wine glasses containing a dose of black senna for those who were unwell.[36] At Arden House in the early years of the twentieth century Dr Ernest Nelson used to dispense 'pink mixture' for the stomach, 'white mixture' for colds and 'black mixture' for the bowels.[37] At Temple Grove the boys' heads were brushed night and morning by the matron, before whom they filed to receive two or three deft strokes of the brush. But they were washed only infrequently. This task was carried out by the lady teachers, who rinsed the boys' heads with a spongeful of rosemary. Feet were washed once a fortnight by the maids.[38]

The Growth of the Sans

Later in the century certain schools saw the advantages of having a sanatorium set apart from the other school buildings. The sickhouse at Mortlake used by Temple Grove in O.C. Waterfield's headmastership must have been one of the earliest preparatory school sanatoria. Stubbington House (1841) was another pioneer in this field: its mid-century building additions included *two* sanatoria.

Yet another early provision of this nature was the sick wing at St Ronan's, Hawkhurst, Kent, which was set up in 1883 when the school first opened. Aysgarth (1877) and Mostyn House (1852) were two other schools to be furnished with sanatoria at an early date, in 1890. Mostyn House gave priority to the establishment of its sanatorium over that of its gymnasium (1892) or its chapel (1897). Similarly The Knoll, Woburn Sands, Bletchley, first provided a sanatorium in 1893, then a chapel in 1897, followed by a gymnasium in 1902.

In a survey of 120 schools which Rev. C.T. Wickham conducted in connection with his *Report on Health and Physical Training in Preparatory Schools* for the *Board of Education Report* 1900, he discovered that of the seventy schools with more than thirty boys, forty-five had a sick room and a sanatorium; thirteen had a sick room and twelve had a sanatorium only. Of the other fifty schools with fewer than thirty boys, twenty-four had a sick room with a sanatorium; twenty-five had a sick room and two had only a sanatorium. Progress, in the larger schools especially, had been quite considerable.

The risk of illness was diminished in later years by the practice of instructing boys to bring a doctor's clearance certificate at the beginning of each term. Generally the school prospectus was very explicit about this important school rule which was enforced strictly by principals.[39] Restrictions in the number of *exeats* also helped to prevent the introduction of diseases from outside.

The Disruptive Impact of Epidemics

During the early years of the twentieth century the AHPS became very conscious of the problems arising from the epidemic diseases which were so disruptive of school routine. From time to time reference was made in the columns of the *PSR* to this aspect of school life.[40]

Letters in the *PSR* demanded action to combat school epidemics. A letter signed 'Maculosis'[41] asked the headmasters of preparatory schools to act against the annual scourge of measles in the Lent term. A few years later Lionel Helbert of West Downs School[42] suggested that the whole subject ought to be brought out into the open so that headmasters, who were usually reticent about admitting to the presence of an epidemic lest anxious parents might remove their boys, could be free to discuss openly possible ways of combating the problem by pooling experiences. In the same edition of the *PSR* appeared a report on the 1907 International Congress on School Hygiene, at which Mr J.T. Ainslie Walker had read a paper on 'Disinfection of schools'. The burden of this paper was that if infectious diseases were to be prevented, dust must be controlled. As if to emphasize the point, there appeared in the same edition an advertisement for 'Florigene' by the Dust Allayer Co. offering to process floors of schools and laboratories during vacations. It was claimed that this service was already being used by the Rev. E.L. Browne of St Andrew's School,

Eastbourne, Mr L.T. Thring of The Wick, Brighton, and Mr O.H. Latter of Charterhouse.

At the tenth Annual Conference of the AHPS in 1901, Dr W. Collier, Hon. Physician to the Radcliffe Infirmary, Oxford, read a paper on 'The preparatory school from a health point of view' which was duly reported in the *PSR* (No. 21, March 1902). Dr Collier observed that during the past twenty-five years more thought had gone into the general health of boys as the number of preparatory schools had increased. More attention was being paid to the sanitary conditions of buildings,[43] to the ventilation of dormitories and classrooms, to the quality of food[44] and to the prevention of zymotic or epidemic diseases.

Concern for the damaging effects of school epidemics led the AHPS to form a sub-committee to inquire into the possibility of taking out insurance against their effects. Mr H. Strahan (Seabrook Lodge School, Sandgate),[45] the chairman of this sub-committee, found that insurance schemes were prohibitively expensive, reflecting the frequency of school epidemics in the nineteenth and early twentieth centuries.

Finding no comfort from this quarter, the Association really got down to the task of considering the problem in December 1911 when a paper entitled 'Infectious diseases' was read at the Annual Conference by H.G. Armstrong, the Medical Officer to Wellington College. Armstrong demonstrated by statistics that preparatory school boys were twice as vulnerable to epidemic diseases as public school boys because some diseases struck only once. His figures were based on five public schools and thirty-one preparatory schools, with a total of 1800 boys. He concluded that amongst preparatory school boys the average incidence of measles was 33 per cent, of whooping cough 19 per cent, of chicken pox 32 per cent, of mumps 11 per cent, of rubella or German measles 17 per cent and of scarlet fever 3 per cent.

Epidemics continued to dog preparatory schools well into the twentieth century, often decimating inter-school sports fixture lists and sometimes closing schools. But since the discovery of penicillin and other antibiotics, infectious diseases in schools are no longer regarded as a scourge. Sanatoria are no longer in such evidence and sometimes inter-school matches are seen as opportunities for introducing childish diseases into schools as a form of inoculation.

Notes

1 Cf. D.P. LEINSTER-MACKAY (1976) 'Out of the valley of the shadow of death via Cader Idris — a study of disease and drains, health, and hygiene in Victorian Public and Preparatory Schools', *Paedagogica Historica*, 16, 2.
2 J. & J. PATON (1900) *op. cit.*, p. 83.
3 The Rev. the Hon. E. LYTTELTON claimed that in Brighton alone there were some 500 preparatory schools, *Memories and Hopes*, p. 15. This incredible figure is either an exaggeration or must have included private schools and tutorial establishments of

every description. But Brighton did have many classical preparatory schools which were well established and definitely not 'ephemeral'.

4 Home counties like Berkshire, Middlesex and Hertfordshire were also thick with preparatory schools reflecting convenience for London and the relatively slow forms of transport compared with those of the twentieth century.

5 E.H. ALLEN and L.P. DEALTRY (Eds) (nd) *The Preparatory Schoolboy and His Education*, Evans Bros. p. viii.

6 From the 1912 Prospectus of Mostyn House School.

7 *The Carterian* (Red House School Magazine), No. 66, April 1914.

8 MICHAEL HOLROYD, (1967) *A Critical Biography, Lytton Strachey*, Heinemann p. 47.

9 Eaton House School Prospectus, 1892.

10 CHADWICK lived in relative obscurity after his resignation from the Board of Health in 1854 till 1889, when he was belatedly honoured by a knighthood for his public services — a year before his death — not unlike P.G. WODEHOUSE!

11 The Public Health Act 1875.

12 *Op. cit.*, 1, 3, 16 January 1888, pp. 45–8. 'School sanitation: The precautions necessary to prevent the occurrence of epidemics in schools'.

13 *Op. cit.*, 1, 6, 16 April 1888, p. 118. 'Schools and infectious disease' and pp. 118–19 'School sanitation: Simple remedies for common casualties'.

14 *PSR*, 5, 41, December 1908, p. 273.

15 Sir CHARLES FORTESCUE-BRICKDALE, (1917), *Major General Sir Henry Hallam Parr*, T. Fisher Unwin p. 48.

16 C.T. WICKHAM, (1909), *op. cit.*, p. 20. No definite date is given for this outbreak.

17 They went to West Fields (now West Downs), formerly run by the Rev. L. LOGIE.

18 The present Copthorne School is an offshoot of Twyford since a nucleus stayed at Copthorne with a separate headmaster after Twyford returned to its Hampshire location.

19 C.T. WICKHAM, *op. cit.*, p. 44.

20 I am grateful to the late Mr H.F. CHITTENDEN, headmaster of Newlands School from 1930 to 1967, for this information. Cf. also G.H.D. BURGESS, (1967) *The Curious World of Frank Buckland*, John Baker p. 16. Laleham School moved to Bexhill-on-Sea for health reasons in 1911.

21 P. SHAW JEFFREY, (1948), *A Schoolmaster's Apologia*, Whitby, privately printed p. 12.

22 G. KITSON CLARK, (1962), *The Making of Victorian England*, Methuen, p. 70.

23 *Op. cit.*, 1, 1, November 1887, p. 1. Cf. also *PSR*, 3, 20, December 1901, p. 82, where a correspondent sought clarification on the question of the return of fees in the event of a school's having to close down through scarlet fever.

24 *The Private Schoolmaster*, 1, 2, December 1887, p. 21.

25 Cf. *Arden House Prospectus 1900*, where reference is made to the dormitories' being so arranged as to allow 800 cubic feet for every boy, as prescribed by Dr CLEMENT DUKES in *Health at School*.

26 *The Private Schoolmaster*, 1, 2, December 1887, *ibid*.

27 *The Draconian*, February 1898.

28 On one day thirty boys were absent: 75 per cent of the school had 'flu.

29 Only thirty-two out of ninety answered names at roll-call for a week.

30 *Eagle House Magazine*, Lent Term, 1930.

31 F. ANSTEY, (1936), *A Long Retrospect*, Oxford University Press p. 52.

32 OSBERT SITWELL, (1946), *The Scarlet Tree*, Macmillan p. 125.

33 'The preparatory school', *Blackwood's Magazine*, Vol. 155, March 1894, pp. 381–2.

34 A.G.C. LIDDELL, (1911), *Notes from the Life of an Ordinary Mortal*, John Murray p. 17.

35 Cf. Hon. HENRY J. COKE, (1905), *Tracks of a Rolling Stone*, Smith, Elder & Co. p. 10. Also *PSR*, 5, 43, July 1909, p. 361.

36 LONSDALE RAGG, (1911), *A Memoir of Edward C. Wickham*, Edward Arnold p. 3.

37 ERIC MASCHWITZ, (1957), *No Chip on My Shoulder*, Jenkins p. 20.

38 H.J. COKE claimed that he never had a bath at Temple Grove during the two years he was there. COKE, *op. cit.*, p. 10.

39 Cf. *Board of Education Report 1900*, Vol. 6, p. 327.

40 For example, *PSR* 3, 16, July 1900, pp. 135–6, report on a case of nasal diphtheria in a school which had to be closed down for three weeks in January 1900 to allow it to be disinfected.

41 *PSR*, 3, 19, July 1901, pp. 60–1.

42 *PSR*, 5, 37, July 1907, p. 137.

43 Cf. CLEMENT DUKES, (1905), *Health at School*, Rivingtons pp. 160–78.

44 The Rev. Hon. E. LYTTELTON noted in an article, 'Feeding of schoolboys', in *The Nineteenth Century* (March 1922) that:

> by 1880 even in low class private school, underfeeding was ... very rare....
> Ever since 1890, not only have boys been encouraged to stuff themselves always to the point of surfeit, but it is very nearly true that, if in any boarding school in England one single case of underfeeding was definitely proved, the Headmaster would have to resign forthwith, for the scandal would inevitably result in a decline in numbers.

45 Formerly joint head with C.T. WICKHAM at Twyford until the crisis of 1896–97.

Part 3
Heyday

10 Prep School Pedigree

It is doubtful whether any part of our national education has been distinguished by a more rapid and comprehensive improvement. In many respects they may be said to be the best schools of their kind in the world.
(Sir Michael Sadler to George kekewich, (1900) *Preparatory Schools*)

The Upward Spread of an Ethic

Largely because of the very good relationship existing between masters and boys in the modern preparatory school, when they went to public school, boys could look on their masters as friends. No more was heard of rebellions in public schools after that at Marlborough in 1851.[1] Most of the barbarity to be found in early public schools had disappeared.[2] Certainly public school masters of the 1890s agreed with Sadler in the light of the different qualities they were now finding in the boys reaching them from preparatory schools, that there was less evidence of boys baiting masters in the public schools. The Rev. the Hon. E. Lyttelton (head of Haileybury and later Eton College) also agreed.

An assistant master at Eton College, Arthur Benson, likewise appreciated the good influence of preparatory schools on public schools. He also gave them credit for the improvement of the status and social position of the 'usher', now an 'assistant master'; for the improved teaching; for their concern with health; and for the decrease in size.[3] Though in his last observation he was only partially correct in that the average number of pupils was found by the Office of Special Inquiries and Reports to be 36.34,[4] life was less rough than it had been in 1850. Food, heating,[5] lighting,[6] and clothing ensured that in Benson's words, there were 'few of the ill-fed, dirty neglected looking boys that existed in most of the large preparatory schools of fifty years ago.'[7] Unobtrusive vigilance, made easy by the adoption of a domestic system, had also grown. The very young boys at Eaton House School were encouraged to seek the help at all times of the ladies of the school, including the matron; whilst the masters 'who spend the greater part of their time with the boys' made a point of 'establishing a high tone and developing a manly spirit.'[8]

Some of the improvement of the preparatory schools was due to the improvement of the status of women in that the relatively emancipated Victorian mother could be instrumental in securing a less harsh regime for the education of her son in his tender years.[9] The tyranny of 'the dormitory' was mitigated also by the cubicle system. Introduced by William Sewell at Radley and by Turning at Uppingham, it was adopted by St George's, Ascot, as it gave to each boy some of the privacy of his home. Similarly Abbey School, Beckenham, Kent, had divided its two dormitories into seventy-one cubicles. In other schools such as Eaton House all the school bedrooms were close to staff bedrooms and were 'visited late and early, and watched and guarded, as those of children at home.'[10] Indeed an anonymous contributor to *Blackwood's Edinburgh Magazine* (1894) suggested that 'a preparatory school should be a nursery for hardening young cuttings, not a hot-house to force exotic plants'.[11] His picture of the preparatory school boy of the 1890s was that of a 'Jaeger-clad wearer of night socks' whose pampered existence contrasted strongly with the lot of earlier preparatory school boys whose experience had included 'long night-journeys on mail coaches, and ... the chilly atmosphere of the big school room'.

A pupil at Hill Brow in the 1890s, whose proximity to Rugby School benefited it, has left us a clear picture of this school as 'representative of its class', with fewer than fifty boys taught by the headmaster and four or five assistants.[12] This school's strong respect for boys destined for the navy or army gave the drill sergeant instructor especial esteem. Like most preparatory schools of the 1890s, it was a boarding school preparing boys for public school and *HMS Britannia*. Achievement in academic work and games was at a premium, with a curriculum based largely on a study of Latin, Greek, mathematics and French. The boys at this school were usually dressed non-uniformly in tweed knickerbocker suits, but on Sundays they wore their 'Etons' to attend matins at the parish church. Yet this old boy recognized that, even in the 1890s, a preparatory school was still an institution whose regime aimed at toughening up the boys and encouraging that Victorian public school virtue, 'manliness'.

Although the reasons for the existence and role of preparatory schools had been recognised in the Taunton Report,[13] in that it was beneficial for small boys to be separated from their older fellows, this was by no means generally accepted. On the contrary, H.M. Rankilor, an assistant master at Blundells School published *Suggestions on the Preparation of Young Boys for Public School Life* (1897), in which he confessed 'no hesitation ... in strongly advising parents to send their boys to a Public School at as early an age as the authorities [would] let them — provided always that a school is selected where proper arrangements are made for small boys.' This recognition and advocacy of junior schools attached to public schools led him to endorse 'the principle of admitting small boys to a Great School [as being] one which can be strongly advocated.'[14]

Cream for Cheam and Others

In January 1891, Arthur Tabor succeeded his father at Cheam and increased the number of boys from eighty-nine in 1890 to 111 in 1897. In his father's day Cheam School had numbered amongst its pupils Prince Emich of Leiningen, Count Gleichen, a cousin of Queen Victoria and several of the sons of the Duke of Westminster[15] and now during Arthur's headship a few Indian princes and Prince Louis of Battenburg attended Cheam. But after 1890 the clientèle was, by and large, less aristocratic, as the prospect of getting into Eton (to which Cheam boys went in large numbers) attracted many. Hence when the inception of the AHPS was mooted Arthur Tabor was invited to chair the first meeting in 1892, even though he had been a headmaster for less than two years. Cheam retained a pre-eminence throughout the twentieth century.

The other aptly named school for high-flyers was Eagle House, which was moved in 1886 from Wimbledon to its present site at Sandhurst by the Rev. Dr A.N. Malan, headmaster from 1874 to 1906.[16] This kindly man's versatile talents and sporting prowess[17] endeared him to pupils such as Lionel Ford (later headmaster of Harrow from 1910 to 1925) whose biography quoted another of Malan's pupils as acknowledging 'we owed an immense debt to that rich and interesting personality: he taught classics, mathematics, science, drawing and religion, cricket, fives and football, all these with a brilliance and liveliness.'[18]

The third sacral school was Temple Grove, which after O.C. Waterfield's retirement in 1880 continued to prepare boys mainly for Eton and Harrow. Although Waterfield's successor, the Rev. J.H. Edgar, lacked his breadth of personality, he was in some ways a more beneficial influence in the school. He caused to be published a booklet entitled *General Rules for the Conduct of Temple Grove School.* This guide to assistant masters[19] set out rules about punishment, hygiene and other school matters which clearly defined areas of jurisdiction and determined the rights of others. During this period the school prospered and the number of boys rose to 140. The school physically expanded with the additions of a swimming pool and a chapel. Temple Grove also moved with the times in the field of sports, which it took seriously and with some success: for instance, the school cricket group of 1887 included five future university blues.

Yet conditions of living at Temple Grove were still Spartan. 'In the dormitories snow frequently piled upon the blankets and ice formed on the water jugs: the lavatories ... would have been condemned in a slum tenement.'[20] In 1907, under the pressure of medical advice which advocated a seaside location, the school moved to Eastbourne, where it took over the buildings of New College, a defunct quasi-public school run by Frederick Schreiner which had been a rival to Eastbourne College. The school did not finally move to its present very pleasant location at Uckfield, Sussex, till 1935. But Twyford, the fifth of 'the famous five', experienced a steady decline in numbers, aggravated in the 1890s by outbreaks of serious illness. The last two and a half decades were the years of the headship of the Rev. Latham Wickham

(1862–87) and the Rev. C.T. Wickham (1888–90), who was joined by Mr H. Strahan from 1890 to 1897 as joint head before he resumed the reins alone in 1897 for another thirteen years.

The Necessity of Alternatives

The institution at Twyford in 1889 of the band of purity,[21] whose members were encouraged to abjure impure thoughts and keep themselves pure in mind and body by signing a pledge, reflected new concern of many boarding schools with masturbation, publicized by Clement Dukes, the medical officer for Rugby School, when he claimed that 'from 90 to 95 per cent of all boys at boarding school masturbate'.[22] The Rev. J.M. Wilson, headmaster of Clifton College, pre-empted the views of Dr Clement Dukes to a certain extent when he gave the Presidential address to the Education Society in November 1881, about the need for schools to give 'that self-restraint of the body, that purity of moral tone' on which the nation depended. He was reticent in defining clearly to what he alluded but he was convinced that it 'has been of late increasing among the upper classes in England' in such a way that 'the nation may be on the eve of an age of voluptuousness and reckless immorality'. 'Immorality of manhood [was] often a direct consequence of earlier immorality' according to Wilson and as such he felt it was 'the business of schools to prepare boys to face this evil'.[23] So to occupy the boys' hands in more acceptable ways at Twyford a carpentry class was formed just before Mr Strahan left in 1897 to become headmaster of Seabrook Lodge near Folkestone. The Hampshire County Council Technical Education Instructor was aptly enough employed in the gymnasium (which had already been tried as a 'purifier') to teach ten boys the skills of the carpenter. This was the precursor of many craft activities conducted in preparatory schools in the twentieth century. Three years later the Rev. C.T. Wickham initiated another experiment in which he encouraged parents to contribute to the financing of a programme of visiting lecturers on subjects like natural history, modern inventions, travel and exploration.[24] The appeal to parents was formally justified on grounds of the increasingly sophisticated nature of the emerging modern world which, Wickham thought, surpassed the competence of his staff. More probably it was to divert them from giving way to their 'animal propensities'.

With middle class parents increasingly worried about their children's future (and having fewer of them in consequence) they clamoured for better tuition to meet the demand to enable their children to get to a public school. Some small coaching establishments were indistinguishable from the small rectory schools which ostensibly prepared boys for entry into public schools, and in the course of time they had become preparatory schools. Thus Hoddesdon Grange, under the Rev. C.G. Chittenden (1854–91) (as was noted in Chapter 6), became a small but leading preparatory school, and when found to be unsuitable on health grounds land was purchased cheaply at Seaford where a new purpose-designed school was built.[25] It has flourished ever since under its new name, 'Newlands'.

Another private schoolmaster who recognized that the only profitable form of private school was the private preparatory school was J.V. Milne, father of A.A. Milne of *Winnie the Pooh* fame. Abandoning his private commercial school at Henley House, Kilburn (as already noted), he set up a preparatory school, Streete Court, in 1894. J.V. Milne became a preparatory school master by moving to Westgate-on-Sea. Here he was in competition with other prosperous and fashionable Thanet schools headmasters from Oxford and Cambridge. (although not necessarily with Blues or Firsts).[26]

The Example of Mostyn House

Just before this Mostyn House also changed from an all-age private school to a genuinely private preparatory school.[27] For when A.G. Grenfell[28] assumed control of Mostyn House in 1890 he was the fourth headmaster of a school of only twenty-eight boys. Within six years he had increased the number of pupils to 103. This transformation of Mostyn House into a preparatory school can be pin-pointed. The 1889 school prospectus had announced that, from the time when A.G. Grenfell became headmaster in the following year, school vacations would be arranged to coincide with those of Shrewsbury School for the convenience of families with boys at both schools. It is clear that this policy was justified since, of the 115 boys who went to public schools from Mostyn House between 1890 and 1899, forty-four went to Shrewsbury, with the next highest number of only nine going to Clifton. Grenfell quickly transformed the school into one of the country's largest preparatory schools. He launched a massive building programme and almost re-built the school at a cost of more than £20,000 giving it at least three times the original floor area.[29]

By 1891 new ablutions had been provided and a gymnasium built. Two years later a large swimming bath, filled from an artesian well sunk for the purpose, had been added to the new amenities of the school. 1893 saw the formation of a cadet force[30] and the organization of air-rifle shooting, a preparatory school activity pioneered by Mostyn House which led to the Preparatory Schools Air Rifle Association in 1905.[31] A school chapel,[32] completed and visited by W.E. Gladstone in 1897 was blessed by the Bishop of Chester in 1898.

As a believer in the sturdy preparation of boys for public school Grenfell was anxious 'to ensure that every boy who leaves it shall enter a public school creditably and do well once there, than that a few of the best should be crammed for special results.' So his school timetable was thoughtfully arranged to allow for an hour's break in mid-morning. There was no school before breakfast (unlike in many early preparatory schools) or after tea; only the upper classes were to do preparation, and then only twice a week.

The evenings were devoted to other activities. Each boy in the school was expected to spend two evenings a week at drill, two at drawing and two for preparation on 'general information'. The drill for cadets was thirty minutes' military drill and thirty minutes of dumb-bell exercises to music: for those not in the cadet corps, gymnastics were substituted for military drill.

Much attention was paid to health, which was greatly improved in 1894 by the installation of electric light to replace gas jets. In 1897 the drainage was reorganized, the whole system being thenceforth flushed periodically by 22,000 gallons of water from the swimming bath. Special attention was paid to the spacing of beds in the dormitories, and partitions, three feet high, were placed between the beds to allow 600 cubic feet of air for each boy. The school had a large sanatorium 200 yards along the sea-shore, under the care of a trained hospital matron. Being very health-conscious, Grenfell made it quite plain to parents that he did not expect boys to go home during term time. He earnestly begged 'that parents will *never* [Grenfell's italics] ask to have their boys home during term time without some really urgent reason', for he feared the risk of infection from railway carriages.

A.G. Grenfell introduced innovations at Mostyn House which later found widespread acceptance amongst other preparatory schools. For example, after his 'stars and stripes' system of extrinsic rewards in school was publicized in 1905, more than 100 schools introduced this method of discipline.[33] He later became interested in the teaching of spelling and handwriting and instituted inter-school competitions to promote these skills. He even designed his own school desks with ingenious sliding tops, some of which were still being used in 1977. A.G. Grenfell's success arose partly from his headmasterly qualities and partly from his entrepreneurial gifts.[34] By 1914 Mostyn House was firmly established as a leading preparatory school whose reputation owed much to the headmaster who had so quickly converted what had in 1890 still been partly a private school into a purely private preparatory school.

Purpose-Built Schools

Such was the market for preparatory schools that purpose-built premises were constructed, following the example of Windlesham House at Brighton, which was from 1846 onwards the first to enjoy a purpose-designed building. After removals from Newport, Isle of Wight, to 1 Brunswick Place, Brighton, and then to 78 Montpelier Road, Brighton, the school's founder, Lt Charles Malden (1837–55), bought Windlesham House[35] and two acres of adjoining land in Brighton on which to build his purpose-designed school. The new building, which was ready for occupation early in 1846, was but the nucleus of this school which expanded slowly throughout the century. Charles's son, Henry C. Malden (1855–88), added a new west wing to the House in 1864. Five years later the Yard was converted into the Big Schoolroom. In 1883 he built a further wing, known as 'the Cottage', which was originally intended as the infirmary.[36]

At the jubilee celebrations at Windlesham House in 1887 Mr 'Harry' Malden publicly observed that it was not given to every private school to exist long enough to celebrate a jubilee, but that his establishment was older than seven public schools in England.[37] It is very probable that the purpose-designed nature of Windlesham House was an important contributory factor in its successful fifty years.

Another purpose-built school was Horris Hill, which made some considerable impact on the late Victorian preparatory school world because of its sporting and academic achievements. Founded in 1888 by A.H. Evans (who remained as headmaster until 1919), this built up academic links with Winchester. Amongst its old boys was D.R. Jardine, Captain of the MCC team which toured Australia in 1932. Such was the success of this school that it had grown from twenty-five boys in 1888 to eighty boys in 1898.

A third purpose-designed school, was West Downs School. The buildings were erected in 1880 to provide a grammar school originally to meet the needs of the lower middle classes in Winchester.[38] But this Winchester Modern School collapsed within six or seven years, and a preparatory school was established in the vacated buildings, which were re-named Westfields. As Westfields it did not survive in the purpose-designed buildings, which were meant for more numerous and older boys.

In 1895 the school closed, leaving the buildings empty. Two years later, Lionel Helbert, who had been a clerk in the House of Commons, took over the school, re-named it West Downs and turned what had hitherto been a double failure into a great success. Helped financially by Lord Northbrook and Lord Rothschild, a co-religionist, Helbert soon attracted eighty or ninety boys at the school, and established close links with Eton and Winchester. Old boys included Duncan Sandys, Christopher Soames, the naturalist Peter Scott, Roger Makins (Lord Sherfield) and Terence O'Neill (Lord O'Neill). An early feature of the school was its association with the Boy Scout movement, since Lionel Helbert was a personal friend of William Phillips, one of Baden Powell's lieutenants. Never one for half measures, Helbert caused the whole school to join the Boy Scouts. He died prematurely in 1920 at the age of forty-nine.[39]

Telescoping Villas

Narrow staircases, small classrooms, limited grounds allowing no room for playing fields or swimming bath — these were, then as now, the characteristics of the villa-type preparatory school. Schools like the Bow School, Durham, the Hall School, Hampstead, in its early days,[40] and possibly The Mall School, Twickenham, in its earlier location[41] shared some of these limiting characteristics. Willington School, founded in 1885, is perhaps one of the most typical of such villa day preparatory schools.

Opened in 1885 by the Scottish Annie Hale and her younger sister Ada, Willington School has experienced four villa-type locations in the Richmond district of London. Recent evidence[42] shows that the school began at 3 Dealtry

Road but moved in 1889 to Willington House, 313 Upper Richmond Road, where it remained until 1912. Lawrence R.G. Oates, of Antarctic fame, attended the school in Upper Richmond Road from 1890 to 1892, because (it is claimed) his father was impressed with the stentorian voice of the drill sergeant instructor. [Captain] Basil [Liddell] Hart[43] and [Sir] Maurice Bowra (1905–09) were at the Upper Richmond Road School together, though probably both had left when the son of A.F. Pollard, the historian, arrived at the school in 1909. The school, described by Maurice Bowra as his 'first and best school',[44] was excellent in character: it had 'rewards but no punishments'.[45] It is indicative of the facilities of the school that at least until 1910, when it acquired a sports field,[46] there were no compulsory games. During the winter, dancing lessons were held in the big schoolroom. In 1912 the school moved to 14 Colinette Road, where it remained for four years before moving in 1916 to its present site, 5 Colinette Road. Before 1914 Willington sent boys to a wide range of forty schools, with St Paul's receiving the most — seventeen. Again it is indicative of the location of the school, and possibly of its restricted site, that as many as fifteen other boys between 1891 and 1914 left the school for health reasons to go to other preparatory schools on the south coast where the air was bracing and more beneficial.

Often the preparatory school was affected by the kind of leadership it enjoyed. The non-classically educated dame, for example, or the indigent, but parish-bound, clergyman might be the cause of a less than successful education for a boy whose parents' choice of school had not been discerning. There was no problem, however, at Willington which has had a lady principal for sixty-two of its ninety-eight years' existence. Like many a dame/preparatory school of the late Victorian period, Willington employed a man (Mr Wolf) to teach Latin, and this was despite the proficiency of the Principal, Miss Ada Hale (1885–1909), in the classics. Moreover, the future distinguished Oxford classicist, C.M. Bowra, was taught Latin during his last year by Mr Cecil Botting, a master of St Paul's School.[47]

The Remarkable Woman of Windlesham

Although other well-known preparatory schools had lady principals, such as Mrs Maclaren at Summer Fields, no lady principal was perhaps so impressive as Mrs Grace Scott Malden, widow of Henry Charles Scott Malden. This remarkable woman fought against Dr Welldon of Harrow's public condemnation of women principals of boys' preparatory schools.[48]

A woman of impulse, self-willed and determined,[49] she was also an excellent organizer[50] who kept her school well to the fore in efficiency and reputation. She did not find her sex a handicap even in the male world of the private classical preparatory school: Mr H.M.S. Malden deputised for her at AHPS, so that Windlesham was not excluded from it by virtue of its having a woman principal.

Her reforms and experiments were manifold. Windlesham was one of the five preparatory schools to be inspected by the Board of Education before 1914 (in 1903 and 1913). She started the first English company of the Church Lads' Brigade for 'the sons of gentlemen', though in 1907 the Scouts superseded the Church Lads' Brigade at Windlesham. Both units were formed to make the smaller boys self-reliant. Another of her experiments was the dropping of the monitorial system in favour of the 'progressive' idea of a School Council based on Red Indian law, with a head chief and medicine man. Yet she could be pragmatically autocratic when she chose. Her 'progressive' experiment in self-government ended after a year, when she decided it was not working. When the Scouts were grumbling at their lot, she disbanded the whole troop and began again carefully building up a more contented group. Both the boys and masters went in awe of her, but during her long term of office from 1896 to 1927 she ensured that Windlesham House moved with the times.

Clerical Entrepreneurs

In 1869 the Rev. Cowley Powles, a well-known schoolmaster and great friend of Charles Kingsley, Rector of Eversley, moved his school from Blackheath[51] to be near his friend, who often visited Wixenford School and gave the boys an interest in natural history. Kingsley sent his son, Maurice, to the school as a pupil. A number of Scottish boys attended this school, but amongst the others were Nugent Hicks, the future sixty-fourth Bishop of Lincoln; the future Marquess Curzon of Kedleston; Sir Thomas Carmichael, colonial administrator and art connoisseur; [Field Marshal Sir] Archibald Montgomery-Massingberd; Robert Trevelyan, poet and brother of Charles Trevelyan, the politician and George Trevelyan, the historian; Major General Lord Sackville (Charles Sackville West); Fritz Bramwell (later Clerk in the House of Commons); F.W. Pethwick-Lawrence MP; Sidney Clive (later General Sir S. Clive); and a German princelet, Prince Friedrich Von Wied, for a short time King of Albania before the reign of King Zog.[52] Clearly the Rev. Cowley Powles' school, Wixenford, was successful and fashionable.

Another very successful school which exemplified the cleric's very significant contribution to preparatory school development in the late Victorian period was the school at Thorpe Mandeville, near Banbury, conducted by the Rev. William Browning. Browning won a distinguished reputation for his success in turning out scholarship winners. Oscar Browning, the Cambridge don, his younger brother who was himself taught by the Rev. William Browning,[53] wrote of him: 'I doubt whether any preparatory school in England of the same size has turned out so many distinguished scholars as the school which he conducted for so many years at Thorpe Mandeville'.[54] This brilliant reputation as a successful preparatory schoolmaster was cut short by his premature death at the age of sixty.

A third 'clerical' school, Highfield School, Liphook, originated in 1887 in

Southampton where a layman, Mr E.A. Wells, conducted a private[55] school successfully until his enforced retirement in 1904, when the school numbered thirty-eight pupils. He was succeeded by the Rev. W.R. Mills, who after two years as a salaried headmaster bought the school from Mr Wells. The Rev. Mills decided to make what was a largely day preparatory school into a more orthodox boarding school in the country, and reconnoitred surrounding Hampshire on his bicycle to choose a suitable site. He settled on the village of Liphook where he built his new school. In September 1907 Highfield moved to Liphook where it has since remained. The main addition to the original buildings was the very handsome chapel, dedicated in 1912, which epitomized the corporate spiritual life of the school under the Rev. Mills, who later became an honorary Canon of Portsmouth Cathedral. Under his guidance the school flourished and gained many scholarships to leading public schools. The buildings increased in size by way of extensions, and the boys increased in numbers from sixty-two in 1914 to eighty in 1918. By the time of Canon Mills' death in 1953 the school had increased to 130 boys and had become one of the more typically traditional preparatory schools of the IAPS, with a strongly Christian ethos.

Public School-Linked Preparatory Schools

Since the day in 1837 when Lieutenant Malden opened his preparatory school on the Isle of Wight in response to Thomas Arnold's public declaration that he would no longer have very young boys at Rugby, there have been (as indicated in Chapter 9) close links between certain public schools and certain preparatory schools. Such links were quite often forged by an assistant master in a public school leaving the school to become a private or preparatory schoolmaster. In 1869 a decision was made which represented a landmark in the improvement of the English preparatory school. It was made by an assistant master at Eton, the Rev. John Hawtrey, who had himself been to Eton at seven. On 5 June 1869, following the celebrations of the Fourth,[56] a notice appeared in *The Times* announcing that the Rev. John Hawtrey intended to continue his work of looking after young boys, but *outside* Eton.[57] The school began at Aldin House, Slough, in September, when most of the fifty boys who formed the nucleus of the new school had been the youngest boys at Eton. From that time Aldin House, or Hawtrey's as it was generally called, was *the* preparatory school for Eton. Hawtrey's boys were prepared psychologically for Eton which was only two miles away, though occasionally, as in the case of Stanley Baldwin who went to Harrow in 1881, some of Hawtrey's boys went to other schools. From the beginning it was renowned for its special care of young boys; for its small teaching groups (ranging from two to ten); and for its compulsory games.[58] In 1871 Aldin House began to play other schools like Waterfield's (Temple Grove) of East Sheen and Tabor's of Cheam: Hawtrey's boys were made to dress formally for their games, for which they were intensely coached, and many old boys played in public schools' XIs. It distinguished itself also by having the owners and riders of three future Derby winners in the school between 1869 and 1883.[59]

Arthur Sebright, who was originally at Eton as a small boy and was one of Hawtrey's original pupils at Slough, was full of praise for his early *alma mater*. This aristocrat, sportsman and man of the world, wrote:

> I do not suppose that there ever was, or ever will be, a school where the boys were so well cared for, so well fed, or received in every respect so much individual attention as they did at Aldin House. No school ever possessed a better tone, or took more pains to bring up the boys to be gentlemen in every sense of the word.[60]

Despite this encomium, Hawtrey's provides an excellent example of conflicting views about the merits and defects of a nineteenth century preparatory school, which suggests that all evidence from general biography about such schools should be tempered by a recognition of its subjective quality. If Sebright was very happy at Hawtrey's, Douglas Ainslie was very unhappy. In his *Adventures, Social and Literary* he writes:

> What a monstrous and foolish tradition this is of the private school! Boys would be better taught at home until they go to Eton. A private school like Aldin House of my day might be described as 'Dotheboys and Parents Hall'.[61]

Ainslie was particularly hostile to Mrs Hawtrey, whom he describes as 'pompous' and as much in touch with the boys as Queen Victoria. Even on simple questions of fact there appears conflicting evidence when Ainslie's comments are compared with those of W. Somerset Maugham. Maugham refers to the small classes, but Ainslie avers that 'the classes were far too large to be managed efficiently, and boys followed more or less their own desires.' To Sebright the food seemed plentiful: but Ainslie[62] referred to it as being poor, consisting some days of 'dry bread and tasteless stodge'. The Hawtreys shared the boys' food only once a week.[63]

This conflict in evidence about the worth of Hawtrey's is partly resolved by the independent witness of R.H. Quick. Himself a former preparatory schoolmaster,[64] Quick was interested in Hawtrey's, which he visited in his recently adopted role of educationist. Unfortunately, most of his comments are concerned less with the conditions of living than with the standards of the school's scholarship. Quick was worried by the ruthlessness of Hawtrey's methods and of his treatment of his well-paid masters[65] if they failed to produce scholarship winners. But he noted *en passant* that the food at Hawtreys was good and that everyone there was sumptuously fed.

The school moved to Westgate-on-Sea in 1883 into what has been described by one old boy, Lord Grantley, as 'a hideous collection of red brick villas' on both sides of the Margate-Westgate road, connected by a gas-lit subterranean tunnel.[66] The Rev. John Hawtrey retired in 1889 and passed the school on to his son, Edward Hawtrey, an ex-Cambridge Blue, who ran the school successfully with the aid of his very personable wife who looked after the youngest boys. During his headship from 1889 to 1916 Edward Hawtrey, known to all his boys as 'The Beetle', ran a school which lived up to its reputation as a chief nursery for Eton. Colonel Sir Mike Ansell remembered his school days at Hawtrey's, Westgate-on-Sea, where the head porter's dark blue suit and blue cap embroidered with 'St Michael's'[67] were matched in splendour only by the Eton suits and top hats which the boys wore on Sundays. Symptomatic of the acceptance by parents of the school's reputation as a nursery for Eton was an incident described by Colonel Ansell when he was due for corporal punishment:

> The Head Porter arrived in Mr Hawtrey's study with what looked like a birch broom: the noise it made was worse than the pain, blood drawn in a few places, but worst of all my mother found among extras on the bill: one birch, ten shillings. A very expensive besom.[68]

The Other Sanderson

1869 was a significant year in the history of another preparatory school refounded by the Rev. Lancelot Sanderson at Elstree. This school, according to Walter Headlam, was 'one of the pioneers ... of the modern luxurious and efficient private preparatory schools'.[69] Sanderson took over a school which, after the days of the notorious Dr Bernays, had declined since 1861 under the Rev. Thompson Podmore. Lance Sanderson, an assistant master at Harrow, had been encouraged by his headmaster, the Rev. H. Montagu Butler, to take over the school at Elstree and revive it as a classical preparatory school with continuing close links with Harrow.[70] Sanderson put Elstree once again on the preparatory school map between 1869 and 1901.[71] During the late Victorian period Lance Sanderson employed a group of masters who were not only good classicists but also fine cricketers and the school gained fame for its cricketing prowess. Archibald Campbell Maclaren distinguished himself as a pupil both at Elstree and at Harrow before going on to make an international reputation in cricket. Many of Lance Sanderson's Elstree pupils later made their mark. Among them were the ornithologist John Whitehead; W.G. Headlam the HM Inspector of Schools; M.J. Rendall, headmaster of Winchester; and H.H. Joachim, the Oxford logician and philosopher. Six of Sanderson's assistant masters became headmasters of preparatory schools: A.J. Richardson of St Peter's Court, Broadstairs; Arthur Dunn of Ludgrove School, Wokingham; W. Hornby and C.P. Wilson of Sandroyd, near Salisbury; Ernest Smith of Folkestone; and the Rev. Vernon Royle of Stanmore Park, Middlesex.

Hawtrey's and Elstree were not the only late nineteenth century bright stars in the preparatory school firmament, made prosperous by close institutional links with public schools. The fortunes of Lambrook School, founded by

Mr R.J. Burnside in 1860, rose when it was attended by many children of the court at Windsor, including two of Queen Victoria's grandchildren. From 1884 to 1904 the headmaster was Mr E.D. Mansfield, a former assistant master at Clifton. The author of the Latin primer, *Initia Latina*, and co-author of the well-known Abbot and Mansfield Greek grammar, he was a schoolmaster guided by a clear educational philosophy of *active* learning. A first-rate teacher, he caused Lambrook boys to do well in public school examinations. His admiration of Clifton School led him to enforce the playing of Rugby rather than Association football. During his headship, the ties with Clifton were relatively strong. As indicated in Chapter 11 Mansfield was a leader amongst the leaders of the AHPS. Though W.F. Bushell[72] agreed that Lambrook enjoyed 'a considerable reputation' he suggests that Mansfield was aloof with the boys. This conflicts with the personality projected by Mansfield as a leading AHPS man with a fund of sympathy for schoolboys.

Public Schools Establish Their Own Preparatory Departments

The junior school or preparatory department attached to a public school was a phenomenon largely of the second half of the nineteenth century. It arose, like all other educational institutions of a private nature, as a matter of *supply* meeting *demand*. At a time when some public schools were experiencing difficulties in recruitment, the institution of junior cadres would create a ready-made supply. Such an arrangement had several advantages. The boys imbibed the traditions of the senior school at an early stage; they had no examination pressures as those in private preparatory schools; and they acquired a more balanced view of their own relative prowess by their proximity to older boys. For the schools, there was a constant supply of young pupils and the masters had a better chance of knowing their boys over a longer period. The preparatory school of St Paul's, Colet Court, which Compton Mackenzie attended,[73] was founded in 1881 at 33 Edith Road, and is a good example of this type of preparatory school. Its creation had been suggested by the High Master of St Paul's, Dr F.W. Walker, to stimulate recruitment. Samuel Bewsher, an assistant master of St Paul's, became headmaster. It began with six pupils, but within three years it had 200. By 1890, when it moved to new premises in Hammersmith Road, it had more than 300.[74] There were several reasons for this phenomenal growth: the great increase in the population in that part of London; the accessibility from other parts of London because of new developments in bus and train services; the sound organization and teaching at Colet Court; and the growing reputation of St Paul's as a public school. The success of Dr Walker was the touchstone for the creation of the preparatory (junior) school.[75] The school gained stability under James Bewsher, an ex-Balliol scholar who succeeded his brother, Samuel, in 1887 as headmaster and remained till 1929.

Dulwich College Preparatory School (DCPS) was another London public school 'junior school' which reached very high figures in a short space of time. Founded as a private preparatory school in 1885 in Alleyn Park, Dulwich, with J.H. Mason as head (1885–7), it began with ten boys. But by 1914 it had approximately 400, largely because of the success of its two succeeding heads, the Rev. J.H. Mallinson (1887–1909) and the Rev. W.R.M. Leake (1909–34). Although the *raison d'être* of DCPS, which JEC Weldon, Headmaster of Dulwich College (1883–1885) helped to create, was to prepare boys for both entrance and scholarship examinations for the senior school, it remained a private school, despite very close association, until 1957. As early as 1880 *The Saturday Review* had passed comment on the large size of the forms in preparatory schools attached to the public schools. It denounced the slackness to be found there and recommended that such schools should have no more than fifty boys so that the headmaster might get to know them all.[76] Clearly such schools lacked the family-like intimacy of some of the private preparatory schools but the success of such junior schools and quasi-junior schools as St Paul's and DCPS offered evidence to undermine *The Saturday Review's* earlier assumptions.

The Result of Allowing Dons to Marry

Of the preparatory schools with strong geographical or topographical characteristics, those located in university towns form a small group where excellence has been a corollary of the likely intelligence level of their clientèle.

The two Oxford preparatory schools excelled well before the end of the century. Not only did Summer Fields and the Oxford Preparatory School (OPS or Dragon School) exemplify the successful late nineteenth century preparatory school, but also they showed the possible contrasts to be found within this relatively small sample of schools. The wife of Archibald Maclaren,[77] the founder of Oxford University's gymnasium, began her school in 1864 in a very modest way when in her back drawing-room she taught the two sons of Shirley Brooks, the Editor of *Punch*, and the son of Thomas Hughes of *Tom Brown's Schooldays* fame.[78] These were soon joined by the son and nephews of the publisher, Alexander Macmillan.[79] From the beginning the school had two characteristics which it shared with other preparatory schools but developed with particular intensity. It was firstly a *family* school: each of the two sons-in-law of Mrs Maclaren became headmaster after Mrs Maclaren's death — the Rev. Dr Charles E. Williams in 1897 and the Rev. Hugh (Bear)[80] Alington in 1917. This continuity in the family, which lay behind the success of Summer Fields, seemed also to be characteristic of the assistant masters, some of whom stayed for many years. The continuity was reflected also in the school doctors, of whom there were only four from 1884 to 1964; in the school matron; and in the school groundsman, Charlie Fathers, who held the record of sixty-three years' continuous service.

The other Summer Fields characteristic was the emphasis that it put on classical scholarship, especially under the headmastership of Dr Williams, who was a fine classical scholar and excellent forecaster of examination questions.[81] Reference has already been made to the close links with Eton, and Summer Fields[82] was always well represented on the Eton lists. It was a veritable hot-house of classical scholarship, in which Ronald Knox[83] flourished and in which encouragement was sometimes given by a generous use of the cane.

With the school's reputation for scholarship, it is not surprising that it was patronized by those who prized such achievements. Christopher Hollis, who was at Summer Fields from 1911 to 1914, noted in *Along the Road to Frome* (1958) that the sons of Liberal Cabinet ministers tended to patronize it, since two sons (1912 and 1913) and a nephew of Runciman, the McKenna boys (1918 and 1920) and Anthony Asquith (1913)[84] were all at the school. Other old boys of Summer Fields have been Harold Macmillan; Lord Wavell; Julian Amery, the Tory politician; John Lehmann, the editor of the *London Magazine*; Victor Pasmore, the artist; Julian Slade, the author and composer; Bernard Darwin, the golfer and author of *The English Public School* (1929); and Sir Harold Caccia, diplomat and Provost of Eton (1965–77). Many rival scholarship seekers amongst the preparatory schools regarded Dr Williams as 'a crammer', but as Ronald Knox pointed out in *The Times* on 15 March 1941, the 'Doctor' was simply 'an amazingly successful educationist.'

There are several points of comparison between Summer Fields and the Dragon School. Both were, and still are, famous Oxford preparatory schools; both had strong family links,[85] and both Dr Williams and C.C. Lynam were senior officers of the executive council of the AHPS. The points of contrast, however, were much greater. Summer Fields was an orthodox school, whereas the headmaster of the Dragon School aimed at producing individuals and avoided any manipulative moulding.[86] The contrast basically lay in the differing characters of the two headmasters, the Rev. Dr Williams (1897–1917) and C.C. Lynam (1886–1920): the one an austere scholar with the traditional preparatory school clerical background, the other an easy-going yachtsman with distinct ideas on freedom, character and religion. The one was a 'hot-house expert' in the rearing of scholarship holders at Eton, who strode in his school in majesty and authority; the other was a man with ideas on co-education, who liked to be called 'Skip' rather than 'Sir' by his boys and who took them to the British Museum and Madame Tussauds. It would be an error to suppose, however, that OPS did not gain academic success. For example, Charles D. Fisher, the younger brother of H.A.L. Fisher, gained first place in the Westminster Challenge scholarship examination in 1891.[87]

The sudden liberation of the university society from a mediaeval celibacy 'had led to inevitable and instant results.'[88] So 'at that time [when] perambulators began to appear in North Oxford', the Oxford Preparatory school was founded to supply a natural want.[89] Established by thirty resident graduates, including four college heads and seven professors as well as the Rev. G.W. Kitchin, former headmaster of Twyford Preparatory School and then an Oxford don, its early pupils were mostly sons of the founders.

The first headmaster, Mr (later Rev.) A.E. Clarke, who had been on the staff of Dr Walker's Manchester Grammar School, was of the old school: a strict disciplinarian who was not reticent in using the cane. It was during the headmastership of Clarke that C.C. Lynam came to the school as an assistant master. When Clarke died of pneumonia in 1886 Lynam borrowed £2000, bought the school from Clarke's widow[90] and became headmaster. Lynam was to become one of the most *avant garde* preparatory school headmasters. He established shorter hours for school and longer holidays and since he thought the prefect system among little boys was quite unsuitable he gave them independence, allowing them to go almost anywhere on their bicycles, much to the envy of the Summer Fields boys who were kept on a tighter rein. Lynam even allowed them to see their parents during the term, unlike other preparatory school heads, who did their best to discourage the practice. One old Draconian suggested that 'he gave to England a totally new idea of what a preparatory school' could be.[91] Lynam developed a faith in giving his boys freedom and complete trust. At the prize day on 14 July 1900 he declared to the parents:

> I think there are few preparatory schools where the boys have so much liberty as they have here. The elder boys are greatly trusted, they can go into town by just asking leave, they can go on the river, they can spend what they like and as they like, they can read what they like, and I hope and believe that this trust is not at all abused.[92]

He exhibited further enlightened ideas by introducing girls into his school before the Bryce Report had proclaimed the desirability of education of boys and girls together between six and nine.[93] Though the girls never formed more than a very small fraction of the total in the school (on average one girl pupil being admitted per term), by 1914 the 'Head Boy' was a Norah Joliffe. Lynam's other innovations were the institution of a Shakespearean play which he produced annually and to which all parents were cordially invited; the holiday diary task;[94] and a school magazine, *The Draconian*, which started in 1889. After its early puerile executives had gone bankrupt (1893), Lynam himself became editor. This school magazine is thought to be one of the oldest magazines amongst preparatory schools.[95] Many of its pages were devoted to descriptions of the headmaster's Scottish sailing holidays in his yacht the 'Blue Dragon', which he harboured in Oban Bay. Like Arnold, who made for Fox How in the Lake District as soon as he could get away from Rugby, C.C. Lynam was sure to be on his way northwards as soon as his duties had ceased to claim him. The headmaster became the mariner as the train sped from Oxford to Oban. Cynics said 'the Skipper used to make out the boys' accounts in the train on the way to Scotland ... with few data beyond his impression of the wealth or otherwise of the parents.'[96]

The memorial volume to Lynam, entitled *The Skipper*, is an unusual document about an unusual headmaster. Apart from the *Memorials of Lionel Helbert*, it is — as far as I am aware — the only tribute to a preparatory school head of its kind. In it, an O.D. who left in 1915 wrote:

What would he [Arnold] have thought of a Headmaster who arranged strawberry feasts for his pupils at the Trout Inn; who played cards with them out of school hours; who encouraged them to write English verse rather than Latin verses; who laid bets with them in the classroom; who kept livestock in his study, and who did not wear a neck-tie?[97]

This was the man who in the later nineteenth and early twentieth centuries controlled the Dragon School and shaped its character — a character very different from that of its early predecessors and that of fellow preparatory schools in university towns. For only in Oxford or Cambridge could such unconventional ideas flourish.

The South Coast Belt

But the most representative kind of preparatory school was that found on the south coast, especially in Kent, Sussex and Hampshire. Of these St Andrew's School, Eastbourne, under the Rev. E.L. Browne, was one of the most successful. Founded in 1877 by a not very successful Warden of Bradfield School, the Rev. Francis Souper, it had a poor start, the number of boys falling from thirty in 1880 to twenty in 1886 and twelve in 1890. Then Souper sold the school to the Rev. E.L. Browne, a bluff Yorkshireman who quickly raised numbers to fifteen in 1890; thirty-three in 1891; fifty-one in 1892. By 1896 there were 109 boys. To cater for this increase in the school's prosperity it became necessary to provide a dining room, five more classrooms, a sanatorium, a gymnasium and three open fives courts. All this had been achieved by 1895. In the same year a chapel was provided as a gift from one of the parents. By the turn of the century St Andrew's School was virtually complete as far as buildings were concerned.[98] The Rev. Browne clearly demonstrated first the importance of a strong personality in a school's head and secondly the possibilities of success in a school on the south coast. He ran St Andrew's like a benevolent dictator from 1890 to 1925 when he went into part-retirement. During these years he showed himself to be both a convinced 'muscular Christian' with a deep love of games[99] and a traditionalist in much school work. Such a success did he make of St Andrew's that his younger brother, Harold, who had been a master there, also 'set up his own school called Aldro — the first of many offshoots of St. Andrew's'.[100]

Pride of the North

Of the few schools north of the Mersey/Humber line, Ghyll Royd School, Ilkley; Marton Hall School, Bridlington; Oatlands School[101] (now defunct); Carteret House, Harrogate (later Red House School, near Monkton); Moorlands School, Foxhill, Leeds; 'The School' at Aysgarth (now defunct); Bramcote School, Scarborough; Orleton School (now defunct); Southcliffe School (now defunct) at Filey; the Bow School, Durham; and Westbourne School, Sheffield were all small. By the late 1880s the north-east was without a large preparatory school to match those in the south. This deficiency was remedied by the Rev. C.T. Hales in 1890 who built a large school for about 100 boys just outside the Yorkshire village of Bedale, so providing the first *great* preparatory school of the north.

Hales, a Cambridge graduate, had for a brief period been private tutor to Lord Verulam before taking a post as assistant master at Richmond Grammar School, Yorkshire. Here within five years he had persuaded the headmaster to let him form a preparatory department to boost the declining numbers.[102] This was a great success and by 1876 had 138 boys. After a quarrel with Snowden, the headmaster, Hales, a very forceful character, left the school in 1877 taking forty-five boys with him and set up a school first at the Zetland Hotel, Saltburn by the Sea, but moved in the same year to the Palmer Flatts Hotel at Aysgarth in Wensleydale. He stayed there for thirteen years before finally setting up a purpose-designed school on a carefully chosen site[103] near Bedale village and Newton-le-Willows. It is not known from where Hales secured the £27,000 for the building of Aysgarth School, but there is no doubt that it was an astonishing and impressive provision at the end of the nineteenth century. It remains today in much the same form as in 1890. The architects' drawings (by Clarke and Moscrop) and plans (reproduced here) give some indication of the magnificence of the provision.

Sited in forty acres of grounds with gardens, greenhouses and stables to promote self-sufficiency, the main complex of buildings contained detached classrooms; dining hall; gymnasium; concrete playground; fives and racquets courts on both the Eton and Harrow plans; dormitories for six to eight boys; a water and clock tower (which gives the school great character); a fine chapel (opened by the Lord Bishop of Ripon in June 1891); and a magnificent organ. Within the grounds there was, and still is today, a swimming bath with water pumped by a pulsometer, at temperature from 45°F to 70°F; a dynamo for electric lighting[104] installed by Mr Massey, the electric light engineer to Queen Victoria, and a sanatorium with two large and four small wards.[105] In addition to this a separate, well-proportioned house was built for the comfort and privacy of the assistant masters, of which many contemporary public school-masters would have been envious, so complete was the provision and so thoughtful had been the Rev. C.T. Hales. The most astonishing factor in this was that it had been provided all in one fell swoop. In a letter dated 8 March 1900 to R.W. Charles, editor of *The Cantuarian*, the Rev. J. Mitchinson, headmaster of King's School, Canterbury, said of Hales that: 'the creation and development of Aysgarth, one of the very best preparatory schools ... of the latest decades of the nineteenth century, was the great achievement of his life. He devoted himself body and soul to it.'

Hales, a monocled and fanatical Jacobite, was a very succcessful schoolmaster:[106] for though he was against any special preparation for scho-

New · Aysgarth · School · Newton-le-Willows · Yorkshire

Ground Plan

Block Plan of Property

Clark & Moscrop · Architects ·

· for the Rev. C. T. Hales : M.A.

larships, (since such practice might lead to the neglect of the ordinary boy), yet twelve Aysgarth boys in ten years gained places at Eton, three of them becoming Newcastle Scholars.[107] The ornithologist, Colonel R. Meinert-zhagen, who was a boy at the school, judged that 'the school was no doubt one of the best in Britain and, though severe and hard, had many good features'.[108] Meinertzhagen's autobiography, *Diary of a Black Sheep*, gives a fairly good idea of life in this northern school in the late nineteenth century. Life was still rough and harsh compared with home comforts,[109] but he had pleasant memories of a school with no overdue strain in the work and little harsh discipline. The boys enjoyed a large measure of freedom and, as at Lynam's, were allowed on half holidays to go out (in pairs) wherever and whenever they wished.[110]

The history of Aysgarth School after Hales' death in 1900 is significant in two further details. First, after the resignation of George Brooksbank[111] in 1908, the school was taken over by the Rev. W.H. Chitty, but not without some acrimony between him and Mary Hales, the founder's daughter. This acrimony arose because Chitty, who was a good businessman,[112] declined to take on the school till he had received a satisfactory sanitary report. Such was the importance attached to this aspect of school administration by an experienced headmaster. Chitty was another successful headmaster responsible for several improvements.

Secondly, Aysgarth School is an excellent example, especially in view of the magnificence of the provision, of the paramount importance of the headmaster to the success of the school. At the time of Hales' death in 1900 the numbers in the school were eighty-five; during Brooksbank's headship the decline in numbers to fifty-five, which left the school almost half empty, was economically disastrous. After Brooksbank's departure and under the positive leadership of the Rev. Chitty the numbers gradually rose again to ninety-eight.

Schools with Religious Ties

Thus far in this survey of variations amongst late Victorian and Edwardian preparatory schools we have been concerned solely with schools which, with the exception of junior schools of public schools, owed their original existence to the private profit motive of the school proprietor. This was not so with Catholic schools and choir schools.

Some Catholic preparatory schools have been privately owned. Despite the earlier contribution in the eighteenth century of the Catholic Church to the development of preparatory schools;[113] and despite the relatively early date of two milestones in the re-establishment of the Catholic church in England — Catholic emancipation in 1829 and the restoration of the Catholic hierarchy in 1850 — the development of Catholic preparatory schools was relatively late. Nearly all Catholic public schools now have a junior school or preparatory department run by religious orders. But there have been lay-run Catholic preparatory schools since at least the 1890s. In the tradition of the dame, Mary Ward of Fernyhalgh, Lancashire,[114] the Misses Gosforth opened in 1892 a Catholic preparatory school in Formby, near Liverpool, largely for boys going to Stonyhurst. This preparatory school, which at one time had the Rev. Martin D'Arcy SJ as a pupil and is now run by the Order of Hermit Friars of St Augustine, was not only a typical Victorian dame preparatory school[115] but was also the prototype of other lay Catholic preparatory schools founded at the end of the nineteenth and beginning of the twentieth centuries. Like many dame preparatory schools it began in a modest private house in 1892 before moving a year later to Vaughan House, Freshfield, Formby, where it remained until it moved to its present location at Bishop's Court, Formby, in 1924. Its links with Stonyhurst continue to be strong.

The majority of the thirty-four English choir schools[116] in the Association are preparatory schools. Preparatory choir schools *qua* preparatory schools are of comparatively recent date. By 1899 only two choir schools — Llandaff School and St George's School, Windsor — were members of the AHPS (and one of those was a Welsh rather than an English school). Llandaff School was refounded in 1880 by Dean C.J. Vaughan, ex-headmaster of Harrow School, as a preparatory school for twenty choristers. In 1888 the Rev. Ernest Owen was appointed headmaster of Llandaff School. He was described at the time of his death as 'one of the most remarkable of modern heads of preparatory schools in England'.[117] Having been an assistant master at Wells House in Malvern, Owen, with the active cooperation of Dr Vaughan, 'evolved one of the best schools of its type in England'.[118] He was a strict disciplinarian who laid great stress on honour, which was the main criterion in the choice of his head-boy. According to his obituary in *The Times*, 'he perfected, even if he did not invent, the idea that a preparatory school should possess the continuity of a public school.' His boys never 'left' the school and were always welcomed back. In pursuit of his ideals Owen conducted a world-wide correspondence with his old boys. He later founded a preparatory school at Stancliffe Hall at Matlock in Derbyshire. Even making allowance for the excessive panegyric common to obituary writing, Owen clearly made an impact on the world of the preparatory choir school.

St George's, Windsor (not to be confused with St George's, Ascot, where Sneyd-Kynnersley was headmaster), founded in 1352, became a preparatory school in 1892 when it appointed Ashley Bickersteth as headmaster (1892–4). This preparatory school has throughout its history been owned and run by the Church of England.

Old Blues Stand By

Other schools concentrated on 'letting off steam' on the playing field, and appointed staff who had shown their manliness on the sports field. Thus Ludgrove School at Cockfosters in Hertfordshire was founded by Arthur

Dunn, an ex-master of Elstree School and a sportsman, and quickly gained an outstanding reputation for its cricket and football. When Dunn died prematurely in 1902 he was succeeded by the England footballer and university cricketer, G.O. Smith, in partnership with W.J. Oakley, the great-uncle of the present head. Smith had gained a 'Soccer Blue' at Oxford and played twenty times for England between 1893 and 1901. He had scored a century for Oxford in the inter-varsity match of Lords in 1896. With such an outstanding record Smith was a worthy successor to Arthur Dunn as head of Ludgrove School. Sir Alec Douglas-Home, like many of his family was at Ludgrove at Cockfosters before going on, as did eighty to ninety of the boys in the years preceding the first war, to Eton. According to Kenneth Young, Sir Alec's biographer, Ludgrove used to keep its best batsmen for as long as it could.[119] In 1937 Ludgrove moved from Cockfosters to buildings in Wokingham vacated by Wixenford School, which had become defunct in 1934 through lack of clientèle.[120] The sporting traditions at Ludgrove continued at Wokingham. When A.T. Barber joined the staff at Ludgrove in 1930 there were three international sportsmen on the staff. Barber, who became a joint head of the school in 1937, was himself an ex-captain of Oxford's cricket team and had played for Yorkshire. With such a continued galaxy of sporting talent on the staff Ludgrove gained a great reputation as a 'sports' school.

The last quarter of the nineteenth century saw a great boom in preparatory schools to prepare boys for public schools and service in the largest empire in the history of the world, containing almost a quarter of the land surface and a quarter of its population. But there were other reasons for the boom. Since the 1860s the lower middle classes, sharing in the general prosperity of Britain, were upwardly mobile and thus the demand for more preparatory schools in the 1870s was a repetition of that for 'gentlemanly polish' by the *nouveaux riches* earlier in the century. This, old Blues were only too willing to supply. Many of the day preparatory schools of this period were created in response to this lower middle class demand. The decline in domestic education[121] and the improved tone and management of preparatory schools had contributed to the increased demand for them in the late nineteenth century. The fact that fewer public schools were now accepting boys under twelve served to magnify the effect of these other factors.[122]

Were the Whimperers Right?

Were these hearty old Blues responsible for some pupils whimpering and wingeing? Pupils who, like Stephen Spender, claimed that they were unhappy at preparatory school because of the constant ragging and the penchant of the headmaster for using the cane[123] were, as men of letters, prone to exaggeration. True the regime in many schools had to be a combination of kindness and rigour. Just such a school was St Aubyn's at Rottingdean where Mr Stanford, in the 1890s, eschewed corporal punishment and administered his discipline through a good conduct marks system. He appealed to corporate responsibility and honour (as had Thring at Uppingham). But he was a bad teacher; he not only had favourites but, worse still, he also had an uncontrollable temper.[124] When he was succeeded by Mr R.C.V. Lang, who had been an assistant master under Mr Stanford, the tone of the school improved immeasurably, since Lang was better able to put into practice the theories of his predecessor.

Sir Harold Nicholson's school at Folkestone (also attended by A.L. Irvine) was run by the Rev. A.L. Hussey, 'a bachelor with grizzled beard, red veined nose and rather bloodshot eyes' who believed in corporal punishment providing it was administered swiftly and on the spot. Of him Irvine observed: 'It cannot be said that his manner was winning, and his furies were formidable. But parents trusted him, he had a good school and I am grateful for having been there.'[125] Sir Osbert Sitwell described his school, Bloodsworth (now defunct), where Cecil Sharp was a music master, as a 'fashionable private school [which] ... bore the reputation of being a very good school, among the best of the period'[126] but he nevertheless averred that 'beating and bullying were almost as much a part of the order as morning and evening prayers.'[127]

H.A.L. Fisher also looked back on unhappy days at Cordwalles School, at that time conducted by the Rev. T.J. Nunns. To be fair to Nunns, Fisher made no specific charge: he was merely as unhappy as many other small boys who have to leave home (where they would prefer to be) for school. He throws some light on contemporary strict observance of the Sabbath when he writes that on Sundays the boys at Cordwalles were not allowed to read books unless they had been approved by Nunns, who particularly encouraged them to read Keble's *Christian Year* at the rate of one poem a week. Fisher's plight was probably typical of many of his age at preparatory school in the 1870s when he wrote: 'I cannot say that I was ever really happy at my preparatory school. Indeed I vividly remember thinking during my first term that all joys were at an end and that I should never know what happiness was again.'[128] Maurice Collis was at the same school in the 1890s when the Rev. C.W. Hunt was headmaster.[129]

The writer, Norman Douglas, attended Yarlet Hall[130] whose head, the Rev. Walter Earle, whom he once described as 'a pious hog ... a worm in human form ... a reptile' kept the boys herded together in common subjection through fear of punishment.[131] Viscount Buckmaster, who was sent to a preparatory school in Kent in 1899, appears to have had an even worse headmaster, a Mr Edwardson, who behaved like 'a burly bully'. Shooting skylarks was one of his favourite sports: he was just as inclined to give frequent beatings to his pupils, who numbered ten.[132]

At Winston Churchill's preparatory school, St George's, Ascot, the Rev. Herbert Sneyd-Kynnersley, with his red Dundreary whiskers, was a cruel headmaster. The young Churchill and Sneyd-Kynnersley were in constant conflict and although, as Randolph Churchill suggested, 'schoolmasters who preside over fashionable establishments tend to mitigate the severity of their reports to influential parents lest these should encourage the parents to believe that it is a bad school and take their children away',[133] it was a harsh school. It was run by a fanatical Tory who burned Mr Gladstone in effigy on Guy Fawkes night. As a boy, Roger Fry had to assist in holding down boys whilst Sneyd-Kynnersley caned them, on some occasions drawing blood. Little wonder Sneyd-Kynnersley died of heart failure at the age of thirty-eight.[134] Yet another pupil of Sneyd-Kynnersley testified to the headmaster's genuine interest in his boys and to his enthusiasm for natural history (which motivated him to take them on expeditions into the countryside) and to his high standard of teaching.[135]

Even Mr Gambril of Elmley preparatory school (which in the 1890s was considered by some 'to be one of the best preparatory schools of the day'),[136] was criticized by Sir Gerald Tyrwhitt-Wilson, the 14th Baron Berners, musician, artist and author, who described Gambril as 'making one of his victims go down on his hands and knees and lick a straight line on the floor in front of the assembled school.'[137] To Tyrwhitt-Wilson, Gambril's

> terrifying personality seemed to hover over the school like some obscene vulture over a flock of lambs. The rustling of his wings was forever in the air. At any moment he might pounce. He was like the Angel of Death stalking through a plague-stricken city. No-one was immune from that dreadful summons.[138]

Such a deep impression on the psyche of the future Lord Berners did Gambril make that he could not help feeling that a man so obviously afflicted with blood lust, coupled with an uncontrollable temper, ought not to have been a schoolmaster.[139]

Sent from Aysgarth to Fonthill in 1889 against his wishes as a boy, Colonel R. Meinertzhagen, the naturalist, did not take to the joint owners Walter and Ashton Radcliffe.[140] Both of them, according to Meinertzhagen, had sadistic tendencies, for he quickly became the *bête noire* of the first and was beaten three or four times a week. Since letters to parents were censored and his parents had no inkling of the beatings, Meinertzhagen turned on his tormentor and slashed his head open with his own cane.

The 'ungovernable' temper of the ominously named Mr Grill of the now defunct St Asaph's in Eastbourne prompted Robert Hartman to dismiss him as 'thoroughly unsuited to be in charge of small boys'.[141] Beatings took place regularly and ceremoniously on Wednesdays after lunch, when the whole school and the kitchen staff were made to watch the weekly manifestation of Mr Grill's sadism. Again strict censorship of letters prevented an early disclosure of such activities. But once they came to light and became common knowledge only two boys were presented at St Asaph's for the following term.

But the school which has excited a positive choir of *literati* was St Cyprian's (The Kippers) at Eastbourne.[142] Cecil Beaton, Lashmer Gordon Whistler, Gavin Maxwell, Cyril Connolly and Eric Blair (George Orwell), all criticized it, the last two being careful, in their separate denunciations of the school in *Enemies of Promise* and *Such, Such Were the Joys*, to describe it under the pseudonym 'St Wulfric's' (in the case of Connolly) or Crossgates (as in the case of Orwell when published in America); and the headmaster Mr Vaughan Wilkes and his wife as 'Sambo' and 'Flip'. Connolly was perhaps less bitter than Orwell about St Cyprian's, admitting that the school probably did him some good. His attack was directed less against the school than against the general principle of very young boys' being separated from their parents at the age of eight. According to Connolly 'it is one of the few tortures confined to the ruling classes and from which the workers are free.'[143] Connolly sarcastically observed of the school that 'though Spartan, the death rate was low', but he had to admit that 'it was well run', adding that it was 'based on that stoicism which characterised the English governing class.'[144] Orwell, not being in the same Social Category as Connolly, was not in sympathy with its aims. In an expensive and snobbish school Orwell was there by the grace and favour of his headmaster (and of his wife, who more than equally ruled the school) who had reduced his fees to admit him. Orwell commented on this practice of taking in a few scholarship boys when he wrote: 'Over a period of two or three years the scholarship boys were crammed with learning as cynically as a goose is crammed for Christmas.'[145] They were a kind of investment whose successes could be advertized in future school prospectuses. Orwell's criticisms were levelled at the teaching of history in the school. The snobbery of the school was such, though near to Eastbourne College, few boys went there as Vaughan Wilkes aspired to send his boys to Eton and Harrow.[146]

Yet in preparatory schools where the headmaster was lax, bullying prevailed. That attended by Hugh Walpole before he went to King's School, Canterbury, was just such a school since it was run by Canon Graves at Marlow with such a loose rein, that when Walpole was sent back to school three weeks late he found that no-one had missed him. In *The Crystal Box* Walpole described the bullying which arose from this lax rule.

> There was a period from 8.30 to 9.30 in the evening, when small boys were dismissed to bed but, instead spread themselves to an empty classroom.... The bigger boys held during that hour what they called 'the circus'. This consisted of small boys [being] made to stand on their heads; hang on to the gas bracket; fight one another with hair brushes; jump from tops of lockers; roasted into the front of the fire; being forced to strip naked and have pins stuck in the anatomy.[147]

Conclusion

This chapter has attempted to give the reader some extended insight into the late Victorian and Edwardian preparatory school. Such a necessarily lengthy treatment of these schools has sought to emphasize the effusion of schools of this last quarter of the nineteenth century, leading to the establishment of the association of preparatory schools in 1892. Some idea of their nature will have been gleaned from details of individual schools, but some quantitative aspects of such an examination are still missing. This gap can be filled by turning to the 1900 Board of Education Report on preparatory schools, which conveniently took the form of a national survey of AHPS schools.[148]

Eighty-two per cent of preparatory school boys were boarders and of the fifty-four schools where day boys were received, only seventeen were predominantly 'day' in character; the average late Victorian preparatory school was therefore boarding in character. By 1900 the age of entry to and leaving from preparatory school was established at nine and thirteen years respectively. The schools themselves varied in size. Of 120 schools, twenty-two had fewer than twenty boys; twenty-nine had between twenty and twenty-nine boys; thirteen between fifty and fifty-nine; eight between sixty and sixty-nine. Only thirteen between fifty and fiifty-nine; eight between sixty and sixty-nine. Only six had over seventy boys.[149] Of 421 graduate teachers, 375 came from either Oxford or Cambridge. Their forms were of between eight or nine pupils, with between four or five forms in each school.

The range of facilities varied, as a glance at Table 7 shows.[150]

Table 7.   Accessory Buildings of AHPS Schools, 1900

Amenity	Out of 120 Schools	Percentage
Museum	33	27.5
Chapel	26	21.7
Covered gymnasium	70	58.3
Uncovered gymnasium	13	10.8
Sanatorium detached	51	42.5
Sanatorium Attached	17	14.7
Swimming pool	22	18.3
Carpenter's shop	91	75.8
Fives courts	45	37.5
Tennis courts	44	36.7
Gardens	53	44.2

Several inferences can be drawn from these figures: (1) considering the very significant contribution of clergymen to the development of preparatory schools few of them provided chapels; (2) the importance of attention to health in the continuing prosperity of the schools is evidenced by the numbers who provided detached sanatoria; (3) the percentage having carpenter's shops reflected their belief in the value of woodwork in the curriculum — for at least two reasons![151]

Given the task of inquiring into dame preparatory schools as part of the Board of Education Report of 1900, C.D. Olive, the head of Rokeby School, Wimbledon, was of the opinion that their numbers had declined over the previous generations; lady principals seemingly saw their role as guardians of the youngest boys and specializing in the education of boys between seven and ten. Thus the school 'for the sons of gentlemen' attended by H.C. Barnard in north-west London was itself preparatory for Henderson's, a more conventional preparatory school for older boys to which he transferred in 1895.[152] The Hoe Preparatory School for the sons of gentlemen in Plymouth that was taken over by the Rev. Dr Alfred Chennells from the Misses Lane was an example of Olive's views on the decreasing number of lady principals, for when L.A.G. Strong attended this school in 1906/7, Dr Chennells was in full control, although he still employed three ladies amongst his teaching staff.[153]

The Rev. the Hon. E. Lyttelton, then headmaster of Haileybury, surveying the schools for the English upper classes towards the end of the century, recorded the satisfaction of the upper ranks in society[154] when he wrote: 'It is undeniable that civilisation has made enormous strides of late in all schools. There is far less roughness, less coarseness, less bullying: there is better teaching, better feeding and a much better relation between man and boy.' More importantly he went on to observe: 'More especially is this true of the preparatory schools, in which ... the improvement is most striking.'[155]

Notes

1 Cf. E. LOCKWOOD, (1893) *Early Days of Marlborough College* Simpkin and Marshall for an account of the revolt. Monkton Combe did experience a minor rebellion in 1900.
2 CYRIL NORWOOD, (1929), *The English Tradition of Education*, John Murray p. 71.
3 Board of Education (1900) *Preparatory Schools*, p. 476, from article 'The preparatory school product'.
4 *Ibid.*, p. 29.
5 For example, the whole school building of Abbey School, Beckenham, in Kent, was warmed by hot water.
6 St George's, Ascot, was fitted with electric lighting in 1884, and must have been one of the earliest examples of this kind of illumination in schools. Aysgarth in its purpose-designed building of 1890 was lit by electricity supplied by its own generator.
7 Board of Education, *op. cit.*, p. 478.
8 Cf. 1892 Prospectus of Eaton House School (now Orwell Park School).
9 For a contemporary discussion of the pre-preparatory stage see Mrs ENNIS RICHMOND (1898) *Boyhood — A Plan for Continuity in Education* Longmans. See also E.D. MANSFIELD, 'Preparation for the preparatory school', in Board of Education (1900) *Preparatory Schools*, Vol. 6, p. 422.
10 Eaton House School Prospectus, 1892.
11 *Op. cit.*, March 1894, p. 387.
12 The sub-title of his book is 'Some findings of fifty years 1894–1944'. J.H. SIMPSON was headmaster of Rendcomb School and later Principal of a Church of England Training College and one of His Majesty's Inspector of Schools.
13 *SIC*, Vol. 1, pp. 88–92.
14 H.M. RANKILOR, *op. cit.*, pp. 6–7.

15 ARTHUR INKERSLEY (1893) 'An English preparatory school', *Education* (Boston), November, p. 138.

16 Son-in-law of Rev. EDWARD HUNTINGFORD (1820–1905), headmaster of Eagle House from 1848 to 1874.

17 Captain of the Sherborne XI in 1865. Cf. [P. Wootton] *Eagle House 1820–1970*, pp. 8–9.

18 CYRIL ALINGTON (1934) *Lionel Ford* S.P.C.K. p. 4.

19 During WATERFIELD's headship ARTHUR SULLIVAN, the musician, had taught at the school. From 1885 to 1886 ROBERT MORANT, the future distinguished educationist, was an assistant master before he went to Siam as tutor to the nephews of KING CHULALONGKORN.

20 A.A.M. BATCHELOR (1968) 'Temple Grove from 1880', *Temple Grove Magazine*, p. 4. Similar hardy conditions prevailed at Aysgarth in the 1890s. RONALD C. JASPER, in his biography of GEORGE BELL, Bishop of Chichester (b.1883) (Oxford University Press, 1967), does not allude to these conditions when dealing with his subject's preparatory schooldays at Temple Grove, where he joined his future brother-in-law, [Sir] RICHARD LIVINGSTONE.

21 See pledge document including prayer for purity, Summer Term, School Archives, 1889.

22 CLEMENT DUKES (1884) *Preservation of Health*, p. 150, cited by HAVELOCK ELLIS, (1897) *Studies in the Psychology of Sex*, Vol. 1, Wilson and Macmillan p. 236.

23 Rev. J.M. WILSON, 'Morality in public schools, and its relation to religion', *Journal of Education*, 1881/82, p. 253.

24 See circular letter to parents from Rev. C.T. WICKHAM, 2 November 1899, school archives, 1899.

25 One of the original boys at Newlands was the future Major-General H.D. WILMOT SITWELL, who on retirement from the army was appointed Keeper of the Crown Jewels.

26 A.A. MILNE, (1939) *It's Too Late Now*, Methuen p. 85.

27 I am most grateful to Mr GEOFFREY PLACE, assistant master at Mostyn House School and local historian, for much of my information on this unusual school. Its founder, the Rev. EDWARD H. PRICE, had been a man of great energy who fathered thirteen children of whom three became headmasters of preparatory schools. EDWARD M. PRICE and HERBERT PRICE were joint heads of the Philberds School, Maidenhead; the Rev. FREDERICK W.S. PRICE was headmaster of Ovingdean Hall Preparatory School. Through his marriage to ANNIE PRICE (née PRICE) he was brother-in-law to BONAMY PRICE (1807–88), Professor of Political Economy at Oxford. He himself founded *two* preparatory schools. Having opened a preparatory school at Tarvin, Cheshire, in 1852, PRICE transferred the school to its present location at Mostyn House in 1855. The buildings had been the Mostyn Arms Hotel until the decease of licensee, Mrs BRISCOE in 1855. It was bought for £1580 by THOMAS BRASSEY the railway pioneer, who leased the building to the Rev. PRICE. He conducted the school of about sixty boys as an all-age private school rather than a preparatory school. JAMES WARD, for example, the future philosopher and psychologist, entered Mostyn House at the age of eleven during PRICE's headship but did *not* subsequently go to a public school. After seven years the Rev. PRICE sold the goodwill of the school to his nephew, the Rev. ALGERNON S. GRENFELL, in order to go south to Maidenhead where in 1862 he founded the well-known but now defunct Victorian preparatory school, 'The Philberds', in a house which had once been presented by CHARLES II to NELL GWYN. The Rev. A.S. GRENFELL, who had been an assistant master at Repton under S.A. PEARS, began gradually to change the character of the school to become more consonant with that of other emerging preparatory schools. GRENFELL bought the school buildings from THOMAS BRAS-

SEY in 1875 for £2750, but it seemed like a bad investment. ALGERNON G. GRENFELL, son of A.S. GRENFELL and later re-founder of Mostyn House, described the condition of the buildings in retrospect as 'ruinous and decrepit', with damp walls, a leaky roof and very primitive ablutions. With the school going downhill, the Rev. A.S. GRENFELL was forced to retire, leaving the school in the hands of an old boy, a Rev. W.F. BARRETT, who was unable to make a success of the venture and declined to take up a further option on the expiry of his seven-year lease.

28 ALGERNON G. GRENFELL, brother of Sir WILFRED T. GRENFELL (1865–1940), medical missionary of Labrador fame, had been a pupil at Clifton College and after four years as a scholar of Queen's College, Oxford, had been an assistant master at Westminster School before becoming head of Mostyn House for forty-three years (1890–1933).

29 Cf. *School Prospectus*, 1897.

30 During the early days of E.H. PRICE there had been a rifle corps in which the boys wore red coats and black trousers and used wooden rifles for drill. This corps had been one of the earliest in the country after those of Rossall and Eton. The institution of such school corps arose from growing fears of the ambitions of Napoleon III of France.

31 See article by G. PLACE in *News and Views* (Summer Term, 1970) — magazine of the Society of Assistants Teaching in Preparatory Schools (SATIPS).

32 CANON J.M. WILSON, headmaster of Clifton College, laid the foundation stone in 1895 and sent his son, [Sir] ARNOLD WILSON to Mostyn House as a pupil.

33 Cf. MAURICE RICHARDSON (1968) *Little Victims*, Andre Deutsch pp. 66–7.

34 The school is filled with evidence of this. The headmaster's study is lined with Spanish tiles which A.G. GRENFELL bought as a job lot. In 1920 he was in Normandy and snatched the opportunity of buying sixty-two carved wardrobes for the school, many of which are still in use. He invented an inexpensive way of building with corrugated iron and concrete which he later improved on by another system of building with pre-cast concrete 'Cyclops' blocks.

35 The photograph of the first Windlesham House shows clearly the economies made by previous owners arising from the notorious window tax. It is a good example of adaptation, modification and extension (see page 166).

36 Wick Villa nearby was used as the school sanatorium from 1888 onwards.

37 G.H. WILSON and R.S. MALDEN, *op. cit.*, p. 48.

38 The Bishop of Winchester was Visitor. Lord NORTHBROOK, who had just returned from India as Viceroy of India, was Chairman and Dr RIDDING of Winchester College was also on the Governing Body. 'Baron Corvo' was an assistant master at the school.

39 I am indebted to Mr J.F. CORNES, silver medallist at the 1932 Los Angeles Olympic games and headmaster of West Downs since 1954, for much of the information on LIONEL HELBERT. Cf. also PAMELA GLENCONNER, (1919), *Edward Wyndham Tennant*, London and New York, John Lane pp. 77–8.

40 From 1889 to 1891 it was situated at 41 Belsize Park Gardens.

41 Huntington House, Hampton Road, Teddington.

42 Cf. *Willington School Magazine*, November 1966, notes by Brigadier General R.N. DICK.

43 LIDDELL was made to drop the first part of his surname whilst at Willington to please Miss ANNIE HALE, who had rooted objections to hyphenated names. The late General MOSHE DAYAN once described LIDDELL-HART as 'the Captain who teaches the Generals'.

44 From letter, dated 7 January 1971, to the present headmaster, Mr KLAUS MARX, from MAURICE BOWRA shortly before he died.

45 C.M. BOWRA, (1966), *Memories*, Weidenfeld and Nicoeson p. 14.

46 C.P.B. HODGSON, *The First Eighty Years at Willington School*, pp. 3–5.
47 Mr BOTTING was the co-author of Latin textbooks with his High Master, HILLARD. Cf. BOWRA, *op. cit.*, p. 14.
48 Having begun as a critic of Mrs MALDEN's sex, WELLDON became a most loyal ally to Windlesham.
49 On one occasion she went to the Admiralty and made their Lordships change their minds about the merits of a Windlesham boy who had been turned down by the Naval Selection Board. Cf. WILSON and MALDEN, *op. cit.*, pp. 50–60.
50 For example, in February 1901 she took the school to Southsea, hiring an empty house for the day to allow her boys to watch the funeral ceremonials of Queen VICTORIA.
51 FREDERICK MYERS, the poet and essayist, attended the day preparatory school belonging to the Rev. R. COWLEY POWLES at Blackheath from 1851 to 1854, as also did ARNOLD TOYNBEE, the social philosopher and economist. PAGET TOYNBEE, the Dante Scholar, also attended. Cf. DAVID R. BRIGGS *The Millstone Race* Privately printed 1983, pp. 25–39.
52 MAURICE HEADLAM, (1944), *Bishop and Friend, Nugent Hicks*, Lincoln, MacDonald & Co. p. 17.
53 At Everdon in Northamptonshire where he was curate before going to Thorpe Mandeville to devote more of his energy to teaching.
54 OSCAR BROWNING, (1910), *Memories of Sixty Years*, London and New York, John Lane p. 12. Cf. also *St Neots Magazine*, (1934) 1, 1, March.
55 In 1892 Mr WELLS moved his school to a house in Highfield Lane in Southampton and decided that it should become a purely preparatory school.
56 GEORGE III's birthday has been traditionally celebrated by Eton in view of the interest taken in the college by its former neighbour.
57 W. SOMERSET MAUGHAM (Ed.), (1924), *The Truth at Last from Charles Hawtrey*, Boston, Little, Brown and Co. p. 26.
58 MAUGHAM thought HAWTREY's was possibly the first school to have compulsory games.
59 Viz., GEORGE A. BAIRD on 'Merry Hampton' in 1887, Sir JAMES MILLER on 'Sain Foin' in 1890; and Major EUSTACE LODER on 'Spearmint' in 1906.
60 A. SEBRIGHT, (1922), *A Glance into the Past*, Nash and Grayson pp. 14–15.
61 DOUGLAS AINSLIE, (1922), *Adventures Social and Literary*, T. Fisher Unwin p. 42.
62 AINSLIE left HAWTREY's and went to Woodcote School near Reading, where he felt Mr NINDE ran a better school.
63 R.S. TABOR and his wife also had food different from that served to the boys. This does not make for general acceptance of food provided generally. It might even be seen as a source for discontent.
64 After being an assistant master at Cranleigh and Harrow, Quick himself bought a preparatory school in Orme Square, Bayswater, which had belonged a few years previously to a Mr MEIKLEJOHN, later Professor of Education at St Andrew's University. He gave up this day preparatory school and opened a boarding school at Guildford before turning to write on education.
65 HAWTREY paid his masters £200 per annum plus board and lodging, which was a good salary for assistants at this time. If they failed to produce scholarship winners they were liable to be dismissed at the end of the term without notice. The whole school was drilled by a syntax master. Cf. F. STORR (Ed.), *Life and Remains of Rev. R.H. Quick*, Cambridge University Press, p. 189.
66 MARY and ALAN WOOD (Eds) (1954) *Silver Spoon*, Hutchinson, pp. 27–28.
67 Its name changed on its removal from Slough. It has been called HAWTREYS since 1916, when EDWARD HAWTREY died and was succeeded by his son-in-law, FRANK CAUTLEY.
68 Sir MICHAEL ANSELL, (1973), *Soldier on*, P. Davies p. 8.

69 CECIL HEADLAM, (1910), *Walter Headlam: His Letters and Poems*, Duckworth & Co. p. 16.

70 Cf. W.F. BUSHELL, (1962), *School Memories*, Liverpool, Philip, (George) Son & Nephew pp. 20–1. SANDERSON had only a second class honours degree and although it was the best second class of his year he was excluded from being a housemaster at Harrow under the Rev. MONTAGU BUTLER's rule. BUTLER encouraged SANDERSON and kept his rule intact.

71 It was taken over by the Rev. EDGAR STOGDON on behalf of SANDERSON's son, E.L. SANDERSON, who was on active service in the South Africa War.

72 Cf. W.F. BUSHELL, *op. cit.*, p. 28.

73 COMPTON MACKENZIE (1963), *My Life and Times*, Octave Two 1891–1900, Chatto and Windus pp. 11–43. LEONARD WOOLF, was also a pupil at the school which he hated. Cf. LEONARD WOOLF, *Sowing*, Hogarth Press p. 59.

74 JAMES BEWSHER *et al.*, (1963), *The Story of Colet Court*, Eastbourne, Strange the Printer p. 4.

75 *Ibid.*, p. 5.

76 Cf. *The Saturday Review*, 49, 87, 7 February, 1880, p. 175.

77 Cf. R. USBORNE (Ed.), (1964), *A Century of Summer Fields*, Methuen p. 80.

78 Cf. *Summer Fields Register* 1864–1929, p. 7.

79 The portrait of another MACMILLAN and old boy, the ex-Prime Minister HAROLD MACMILLAN, hangs in the Summer Fields Library.

80 Called this by the boys because he was so fierce.

81 JOHN CONNELL, (1964), *Archibald P. Wavell, Scholar and Soldier*, Collins p. 24.

82 See Chapter 8.

83 It had been the custom at Summer Fields to admit boys between the ages of eight and ten only. There was some difficulty over the entry of DILLWYN KNOX who was over ten years old, but Dr WILLIAMS waived the custom when he learnt that RONALD KNOX, DILLWYN's younger brother of six, was already reading Virgil. He had a 'nose' for a future distinguished scholar. One of KNOX's objections to Summer Fields was 'a loutish little boy called HUGH DALTON' — Chancellor of the Exchequer in 1945. EVELYN WAUGH, (1959) *The Life of the Rt. Rev. Ronald Knox*, Chapman and Hall, p. 42.

84 The Hon. CYRIL ASQUITH was also at the school. *Register*, p. 60

85 C.C. LYNAM's father, CHARLES LYNAM, was the architect who designed the new school buildings at Bardwell Road. His brother, ROBERT O. LYNAM, was the school doctor for thirty-two years; two sons were masters and later headmasters at the school. A son and a daughter were educated there as were three grandsons. See *The Skipper — A Memoir*, Dragon School, Oxford, p. 1.

86 On one occasion C.C. LYNAM was explaining to a clerical father the *unconventional* character of an O.P.S. Sunday: he concluded by saying, 'Now there's a very good school up the road called Summer Fields, which is more orthodox, and will, I think, be just what you want.' *Ibid.*, pp. 106–7.

87 CHARLES TENNYSON, (1953), *Life's all a Fragment*, Cassell and Co. p. 4.

88 E.B. POULTON, (1919), *The Life of Ronald Poulton*, Sidgwick and Jackson p. 45.

89 *The Draconian*, August 1904.

90 He purchased the school with the approval of the Oxford dons, Dr PERCIVAL *et al.*, who had set up the school.

91 *The Skipper*, p. 12.

92 *The Draconian*, August 1900.

93 *The Draconian*, 1895, quoted from *The Skipper*, 32.

94 LYNAM tried to help boys to be creative by keeping holiday diaries. In 1899 seven of them were sent by him to the educational exhibition held at the Imperial Institute, South Kensington.

95 The earliest preparatory school magazine would seem to be that instituted at Stoke

House, Stoke Poges, founded by the Rev. EDWARD St J. PARRY.

96 *The Skipper*, 16.

97 *Ibid.*, 166. On the other hand even ARNOLD had been capable of being carefree with his boys at Laleham.

98 PAUL SPILLANE, (1971), *St Andrew's School*, Southampton, Hobbis the printers, p. 17.

99 His sermons were frequently illustrated by cricketing similes.

100 *Ibid.*, 22.

101 Oatland School, Harrogate, was founded in 1856. It closed in 1961 on account of the illness of the co-principals Mr G.W. and Mr E.F. BOYERS.

102 LESLIE P. WENHAM, *The History of Richmond School*, Yorkshire, p. 109.

103 A healthy spot near a railway station.

104 It was one of the first buildings in Yorkshire to be lit by electricity.

105 See article on Aysgarth in *St James's Budget*, 21 September 1894.

106 Cf. JOHN LORD, (1920) *Duty, Honour and Empire — The Life and Times of Colonel Richard Meinertzhagen*, Hutchinson p. 50. Every year on 29 May HALES celebrated Royal Oak Day by causing his boys to sport a sprig of oak in their jackets and by toasting the King over the water.

107 *PSR*, Vol. 2, No. 15, March 1900, pp. 79–80. Cf. also obituary in *The Times*, February 12th 1900.

108 Colonel R. MEINERTZHAGEN, (1964) *Diary of a Black Sheep*, Oliver and Boyd, p. 132.

109 The windows were kept perpetually open, which meant that sometimes during really inclement weather the boys would rise in the mornings to find the bare boards covered by mini-snow drifts. Cf. LORD, *op. cit.*, 51.

110 MEINERTZHAGEN, *op. cit.*, p. 132. In this respect HALES' School was like earlier quasi-preparatory schools where less close supervision was evident.

111 BROOKSBANK was a recluse who had none of the *savoir faire* of HALES. A good mathematician and ornithologist, he was a poor businessman.

112 He bought the school from MARY HALES for £14,000 in 1909 although it had cost £27,000 to build in 1890.

113 Cf. Chapter 1.

114 Cf. p. 105.

115 It continued to be a dame preparatory school until 1953 when Mr MICHAEL TREVOR took over the school from Miss GRACE TREVOR, principal from 1920 to 1953.

116 See Choir Schools' Directory, latest edition.

117 *The Times*, 30 October 1926. Obituary on the Rev. ERNEST OWEN.

118 *Ibid.*, notwithstanding its *Welsh* location. It is now a school on the Woodard Foundation.

119 KENNETH YOUNG, (1970), *Sir Alec Douglas Home*, Dent p. 14.

120 Mr GREGG who was the last head of Wixenford had eight boys at the time of closure.

121 According to HORACE MANN, who analyzed the educational aspects of the 1851 General Census, there were more than 50,000 children in the country who were educated at home either by tutors of parents.

122 Cf. *Blackwood's Magazine*, March 1894, p. 380.

123 GRAHAM GREENE (Ed.), (1934) *The Old School*, Jonathan Cape p. 185.

124 JAMES S. BARNES, (1933), *Half a Life*, Eyre and Spottiswoode p. 24.

125 A.L. IRVINE, (1958), *Sixty Years at School*, Winchester, Wykeham Press p. 7.

126 OSBERT SITWELL, (1946) *The Scarlet Tree*, Macmillan Vol. 2, p. 124.

127 *Ibid.*, p. 126.

128 H.A.L. FISHER, (1941), *An Unfinished Autobiography*, Oxford University Press p. 35.

129 MAURICE COLLIS, (1952), *The Journey Outward*, Faber and Faber p. 28.

130 EARLE kept school at Yarlet Hall from 1873 to 1887 before moving to Bilton Grange (see Chapter 8).

131 MARK HOLLOWAY, (1976), *Norman Douglas*, Secker and Warburg p. 28.

132 VISCOUNT BUCKMASTER, (1970), *Roundabout*, Witherby p. 25.

133 RANDOLPH S. CHURCHILL, (1966), *Winston S. Churchill*, Vol. 1, Heinemann p. 49.

134 *Ibid.*, p. 54. Cf. also JOHN LORD, (1920), *Duty, Honour, Empire, The Life and Times of Colonel Richard Meinertzhagen*, Hutchinson, p. 68.

135 HUGH TREVOR-ROPER, (1977), *A Hidden Life — The Enigma of Sir Edmund Backhouse*, Macmillan p. 17.

136 Lord BERNERS, (1934), *First Childhood*, Constable p. 115.

137 *Ibid.*, p. 133.

138 *Ibid.*, p. 174.

139 *Ibid.*, p. 134.

140 Cf. R. MEINERTZHAGEN, *op. cit.*, pp. 158–74. Cf. also JOHN LORD, *op. cit.*, pp. 67–73.

141 Cf. ROBERT HARTMAN, 1964 *The Remainder Biscuit*, Andre Deutsch p. 43.

142 Eastbourne seems to have been unfortunate in some of its schoolmasters. Besides St Asaph's and St Cyprian's there was in the 1850s a private school in Eastbourne run by a THOMAS HOPLEY, who in 1860 was sentenced to four years penal servitude for the manslaughter of one of his pupils, REGINALD CANCELLOR. Cf. D.P. LEINSTER-MACKAY (1977) 'Regina V. Hopley: Some historical reflections on corporal punishment', *Journal of Educational Administration and History*, 9, 1, January, pp. 1–6.

143 CYRIL CONNOLLY, (1938), *Enemies of Promise*, Routledge and Kegan Paul, p. 206.

144 *Ibid.*, p. 207.

145 ORWELL, S. and ANGUS, I., (1971), *The Collected Essays, Journalism and Letters of George Orwell*, Vol. 4, Penguin Books, p. 385.

146 Both CYRIL CONNOLLY and Eric Blair went to Eton. St Cyprian's was incorporated into Summer Fields, Oxford, in 1942.

147 RUPERT HART DAVIS, (1952), *Hugh Walpole*, Macmillan p. 17.

148 The statistical data on these schools are based on a questionnaire sent to 252 schools, of which 120 replied.

149 1900 Board of Education Report, p. 29.

150 *Ibid.*, p. 33.

151 One school had six hours of woodwork per week on the timetable. This was unusual.

152 BARNARD, *op. cit.*, pp. 58–62.

153 L.A.G. STRONG, (1961), *Green Memory*, Methuen p. 53.

154 The late Victorian preparatory schools had their critics. Cf. *The Saturday Review — 1880*, also *The Blackwood Magazine*, March 1894, also ERIC PARKER, 'Private schools: Ancient and modern', *Longman's Magazine*, 29, November 1896 and April 1897.

155 The Rev. the Hon. E. LYTTELTON, (1892) *Mothers and Sons or Problems in the home training of boys*, Macmillan p. 91.

Windlesham House, Brighton

11 Did Bowling Bring Them Together?

This meeting is of the opinion that it is not advisable for boys under fifteen to use a full-sized ball with the wickets pitched at twenty-two yards.
(Resolution passed unanimously on 30 March 1892 at the first meeting of the AHPS)

Big Brothers or Cricket Balls?

To ensure that small boys should not be intimidated by full-sized cricket balls and be a credit to their older brothers in public schools, the Rev. A.S. Tabor of Cheam convened a meeting of preparatory school headmasters on 30 March 1892. At this Herbert Bull suggested a second meeting to discuss other topics. The analogy between their colloquy and that of their senior colleagues in public schools was striking, for the public school heads had discussed preparatory schools at their twentieth conference at Oxford, two years earlier. Like their senior colleagues in the Headmasters' Conference, the Association of Headmasters of Preparatory Schools was formalized only after a second meeting. For just as Mitchinson of King's School, Canterbury, was responsible for the first calling together of heads of some leading endowed grammar schools — after which Thring took over the helm and suggested an annual meeting — so Herbert Bull (Wellington House School, Westgate-on-Sea) seized the initiative amongst preparatory school headmasters by suggesting a second meeting following the initial one called in March 1892 by A.S. Tabor.

The second meeting was virtually inevitable since their senior colleagues of the HMC had, two years earlier, agreed with a motion put forward by J.E.C. Welldon of Harrow that it was desirable 'to make the relation between preparatory and public schools somewhat closer and more systematic'. Describing the rise of large preparatory schools as 'one of the most remarkable developments of modern education', Welldon had cited, as evidence of public school interest in preparatory schools, the institution of junior school departments. Of the 134 different preparatory schools providing boys for his school he detected a small minority as quite capable of passing on boys of poor quality. For this and other reasons[1] Welldon, seconded by the Rev. W. Furneaux of Repton, put forward his motion. A rider to the resolution was proposed by the headmaster of King's School, Canterbury, that 'the Committee be asked to associate with themselves a number of the preparatory schoolmasters to discuss in what manner Mr Welldon's resolution might best take effect.' But the implication — close links between public and preparatory schools — led to the motion being withdrawn after the Rev. E.C. Wickham of Wellington College alluded to the successful cooperation between public and private schools in the Church of England Purity Society, and proposed instead: 'that the Committee be requested to bring this resolution to the notice of preparatory schoolmasters, and to invite them to consider whether by some representative organization they can put themselves into fuller communication with schools represented in this Conference.' This motion was seconded by Dr Moss of Shrewsbury. For one headmaster on the conference, however, a special relationship between preparatory and public schools would lead to dull uniformity, a view later voiced in the AHPS itself.[2] Denying that preparatory schools had the sole prerogative of feeding public schools (since endowed grammar schools and other private schools did so too),[3] Eve of University College School spoke from personal experience since he had stayed at Mill Hill School till he was over fourteen before going on to Rugby. But despite this dissentient voice there was a general feeling that the time was ripe for the institution of an organization amongst preparatory schools, analogous to the HMC, with which the latter could confer.

Bryce Brings Matters to a Head

It was at the second meeting on 23 December 1892,[4] initiated by the Rev. Bull, that it was decided to form the AHPS. A committee of fifteen was chosen whose first task was to organize the 1893 conference. It was at these early meetings, as in any society's formative period, that leaders emerged and important policies were formulated.

The need for such an association was now urgent for in 1894 the Bryce Commission, charged with examining secondary education, not only failed to offer representation to the newly formed AHPS but actually asked preparatory schools whether or not they wished to be considered with private schools. This was enough to warrant a special conference hurriedly called for September, chaired by the Rev. Charles Darnell of Cargilfield. This drew up and transmitted a paper to the Bryce Commission drawing attention

> to the difference between preparatory schools, in the proper sense of the word, and private schools in general, upon the ground that preparatory schools confine themselves to boys at an age earlier than that at which they enter public schools, and therefore provide an

organization of which private schools, taking older boys, are in no sense the equivalent.[5]

This greatly clarified the issue for, as their then chief ally in the Civil Service, Michael E. Sadler, averred, preparatory schools were to be regarded as the first stage of a public school education.[6] This policy was endorsed at the third annual conference in December 1894, over which Rev. C. Darnell again presided. In a *Memorandum of the Objectives of the Association*, it was stressed that they were:

1   to draw more closely together headmasters of preparatory schools and organize their opinion;
2   to advance the interests of education as affecting those schools; and
3   to provide a recognized channel of communication with the public schools and other educational bodies.

The Politics of 'Preparation'

Those who, like Eve of University College School, feared that the AHPS would facilitate uniformity amongst preparatory schools were quite wrong, for no sooner was it formed than members began to discuss the very *raison d'être* of their schools — the entrance scholarship examinations to the public schools. Those whose schools were already gaining a large number of such scholarships resigned from the *all hoc* Scholarships committee rather than pursue what they construed as a policy of dilution.[7] These — as might have been expected — were H.B. Allen (Temple Grove), Walter Earle (Bilton Grange), and E.H. Party (Stoke House). A referendum was held on the subject and the dissidents led by H.M. Draper (Lockers Park), Lancelot Sanderson (Elstree), A.S. Tabor (Cheam) and C.E. Williams (Summer Fields) lost heavily.[8] The rift demonstrated that the Association had 'traditionalist' and 'progressive' elements which occasionally revealed their extreme positions. The lowering of the standard of Greek was to continue to be a bone of contention within the Association. The dissidents had lost the day on this occasion. But in 1908, when the Association had well over 300 members, 114 members representing 101 schools tried to influence the deliberations of the HMC on the future of Greek by expressing satisfaction with the *status quo* in a letter dated February 1908. Though this letter and the number of its signatories[9] showed the strength of the traditionalists, the views of 'progressives' like E.D. Mansfield, C.C. Lynam and Lionel Helbert finally prevailed.

Cramming was a most contentious issue. The editor of *PSR*, C.C. Lynam, wrote an article about the possible dangers to health of cramming. Two years later he suggested in his 'Notes and Comments' that the constitution of the Association be changed and that all members of the Committee, instead of being three years in office, should re-apply each year. As an attempt to break the bureaucratic style it failed and Lynam offered his resignation, partly on the ground that he had been criticized for showing partiality as editor,[10] and partly because some members had resigned from the Association. His suggestion was not taken up and his resignation was not accepted. Meanwhile in 1900 the Rev. E.L. Browne (St Andrew's School, Eastbourne) suggested a different kind of alteration to the constitution: regional representation on the Executive Committee to allow centres of scholastic concentration like Brighton, Hastings and Eastbourne to be fully represented. However, he withdrew the motion which anticipated Lionel Helbert's scheme by nine years on the advice that it would raise organizational difficulties.

If the Association was not ready for regional representation in 1900, two years later it felt sufficiently well-established to accept the offer (again at the suggestion of the Rev. E.L. Browne) of a well-known firm of accountants in the City to act as honorary auditors.[11] This was followed in 1906 by the appointment of Mr H. Hughes Onslow as solicitor to the Association. This appointment marked yet another stage in the Association's consolidation and developing strength.[12] However, the rank and file appeared to be resisting the bureaucratization of the AHPS when it rejected a proposal for a permanent home for the Association.[13] Once again the majority of members had shown a sturdy independence of mind.

Pellatt's Pellets

One of the Association's sternest critics was Thomas Pellatt.[14] As one who sent something like 75 per cent of his boys to Eton from Durnford Preparatory School, he attacked the way in which the Association was developing, and in an article for the *PSR* in 1903 entitled 'A word in time' he drew attention to the absence of many preparatory schools, including some of the leading ones, from meetings of AHPS[15] and suggested that the Association was tending to take up too much power for itself and that its 'clique-ism' would lead to uniformity. He went on to accuse the editor of the 1900 Blue Book of filling it with 'Germanolatry' and cuttingly suggested that as 'public schoolmasters manqué' preparatory schoolmasters should not criticize those who had succeeded. Pressure on the HMC by the 'progressive' members of the AHPS, virtually producing a new curriculum, seemed to Pellatt 'a strange medley of ill-digested Froebelism'. His *Public Schools and Public Opinion* (1904) further tried to rectify some false impressions given by some other preparatory schoolmasters in the Blue Book.[16] Attacking both the 'cram for exam' techniques of some preparatory schools and the diluted and varied curriculum of the progressives, Pellatt was quite satisfied with the entrance examination, and at one meeting with public school headmasters, which he attended as a preparatory school representative, he commented:

> We all felt as we listened to the arguments on the other side that it was no use fighting any more; the entrance examination provided a most convenient means for regulating the public schools' entrance list . . . so

there was the end of it. As we broke up, I seemed to see the shade of Thring looking down upon these public school headmasters in their splendid struggle after the ideals they preached in their school chapels.[17]

To Pellatt the movement to unify the preparatory schools was 'a most pitiable tragedy', and though not critical of Herbert Bull (the nephew of the Marlborough Senior Master, C.M. Bull, whom he knew well)[18] he attacked 'the axe-grinders, the faddists, the Johnny head-in-the-airs who collared the machine'.[19] Of these he declared:

> They cared nothing whatever about the welfare of little boys: if they had they would never have joined hands with a certain type of public school headmaster and invented an entrance examination of twelve or fifteen papers which is condemned root and branch by ... Dr Cyril Norwood.[20]

Pellatt was here attacking 'progressives' like E.D. Mansfield and F. Ritchie who played such an important part in the setting up of the Common Entrance examination in 1904. His loyalty to his old colleague, C.M. Bull at Marlborough, where he had been an assistant master for four years, made him blind to the fact that the Rev. Herbert Bull sat on the first Board of the Common Entrance with E.D. Mansfield and three public school heads.

For a year Pellatt allowed himself to be a member of the AHPS Executive Committee, but found himself out of step with the rest of his committee colleagues. He did not agree with the main aim of the Association, which seemed to him to be to interfere and to dictate to headmasters. Pellatt asserted that he had 'in vain tried to catch Mr Boots devoting his morning to the furtherance of Mr Timothy White's prosperity.'[21] Why should the AHPS, he asked, arrogate to itself this privilege?

Pellatt was a voice in the wilderness. Although from time to time other critics, like Mervyn Voules (Middleton School, Bognor, and later Windermere House, Barnes Common) and Oliver Wyatt of Maidwell Hall voiced their opposition to 'progressive' tendencies in the 'Tom Pellatt tradition', Pellatt himself was for the most part a one-man ginger group. Not so Lionel Helbert (West Downs, Winchester), who was responsible for the major change in the constitution of the Association in 1909. Joining the AHPS in 1898, he was elected to the Committee in 1907 but a year later criticized it for allowing itself to fall into the hands of a clique whose schools were centred on London, a development against which Pellatt had given warning. Helbert proposed to give the Executive Committee a local representative character by dividing the Association into local branches, each of which should elect representatives to serve on the Executive Committee. The then recent letter to the public school headmasters concerning Greek, signed by 114 members, had shown the need for this committee to become representative. Exploratory letters were sent out by Helbert, and the replies showed strong support for his proposals. Helbert's motion 'that this Conference approves of the principle of local representation'[22] was carried after two amendments had been rejected. His scheme was finally accepted, after some considerable opposition in some quarters, at a special conference on 2 October 1909.[23] Despite Helbert's own misgivings about the strength of his opponents and despite early setbacks, his scheme of local representation still largely holds good today, with thirteen local representatives and nine general representatives making up the IAPS Council.[24]

Knowing What Was Wanted

Because many of the members had been public schools assistant masters before they took up preparing young boys for entry to them, they knew what was wanted. Edward Stone,[25] before opening a school at Stonehouse, North Foreland near Broadstairs, had been an Eton master for twenty-seven years from 1857 to 1884, so his school prepared for Eton. At Clifton, E.P. Arnold (d.1917) had been the chief modern languages master from 1874 to 1878 under Dr Percival and E.D. Mansfield, too, was an ex-Clifton master; Frank Ritchie had been a master at Westminster; Arthur M. Curteis, a Fellow of Trinity College, Oxford, had been an assistant master at Leamington College and Sherborne, where he helped Harper build up the school, before taking over Hillside preparatory school, Godalming, in 1876: here he was joined in 1888 by Mr Gidley Robinson (third editor of *PSR*), an assistant master from Charterhouse. Herbert Bull began his teaching as an assistant master at Wellington College; whilst C.C. Cotterill was a master at Haileybury under A.G. Butler and at Fettes (1870–90), having been invited to be second master by Dr Potts, the headmaster.

Some were very influenced by their previous headmasters: E.P. Frederick (Wells House, Malvern) was by Almond of Loretto; the Rev. Walter Earle (Bilton Grange, Rugby) by Edward Thring. So at both his schools, Yarlet Hall and Bilton Grange, there was a wide range of activities including the visit of professional musicians to the school. The Rev. Charles Darnell, 'venerated' Arnold,[26] and started a preparatory school at Hill Morton, near Rugby. Six years later he was invited by Dr Potts to begin a preparatory school in Edinburgh. This was the origin of Cargilfield, perhaps the most famous of Scottish preparatory schools.[27] It would seem that Darnell, who was Chairman of the AHPS in 1894 and played a leading role in the formation of the Association in 1892, had something in common with C.C. Cotterill, who was also an 'Arnoldian' summoned to Edinburgh by Dr Potts. After Haileybury, Cotterill had been salaried headmaster at Hill Brow School for its owner, J.W. Vecqueray,[28] who was also modern languages master at Rugby. After spending twenty years at Fettes, during which time he became a friend of H.H. Almond, Cotterill was the second headmaster of Greenbank School[29] outside Liverpool, but had to retire in 1898 through ill health. From 1898 to 1901 he was the Honorary Secretary to the AHPS in succession to Rev. H. Bull, the Association's first Secretary. From 1903 to 1906 he was headmaster of Combe Field Preparatory School, Godalming. Cotterill was a man with an active social conscience who spent his last years championing the cause of the poor by writing books on the subject.[30]

Cotterill in his day had been a powerful figure in the AHPS. But perhaps F. Ritchie, who at one time held three posts in the Association,[31] was even more influential. After his spell at Westminster School, Ritchie had served as an assistant master at Oakfield Preparatory School under the Rev. W. Furness.[32] His career took him to Plymouth, where he helped to found a secondary school (later Plymouth College) before founding his own preparatory school at Sevenoaks in 1881.[33] In 1899 he too retired from schoolmastering in order to write books. His retirement allowed him to play a full part in the Association, and he was responsible for setting up the machinery for Common Entrance examinations. In C.C. Lynam's memoir, *The Skipper*, some recognition is given to colleagues who helped to mould the AHPS in the early years. He wrote: 'Darnell, Herbert Bull, Arnold, Mansfield, E.L. Browne, Gidley Robinson, (and) Black all did noble work, and I was proud to be associated with them. They were the first to get into intimate touch with the Headmasters of the Public Schools and to get our Schools recognised as the Junior Departments of the Public Schools.'[34] To these names should be added those of 'Clem' Cotterill and Frank Ritchie, each of whom contributed as much as Lynam himself, if not more[35] to the stability of the Association in the early days.

The Achievements of AHPS

How effective was the AHPS in the pursuance of its aims? Most of the features of the IAPS today were either established or at least had been mooted before 1914.

First discussed at the instigation of the AHPS in 1895,[36] agreement on the curriculum of preparatory schools was not reached till 1903 about a common entrance examination for some public schools. Throughout those eight years the majority of preparatory school headmasters, believing that the curriculum was overcrowded, pressed this view on public school headmasters, of whom some were more receptive than others.

Despite internal dissensions the Association gave the private preparatory schools a solidarity that enabled them to achieve in the course of a few years what it would have taken decades to achieve had they remained unorganized. As the Blue Book reported, it gave them a sense of a common public spirit.

> Before the existence of the Association, each man was usually pursuing his own work in his own way and devoting himself to his own school, ignorant of the work, aims, difficulties, mistakes, successes of others, giving nothing to them, receiving nothing from them. All this is now changed.[37]

Not only were they now in communication with one another but they had also established a precedent for official discussion with public schools by the creation of a joint sub-committee of heads of public and preparatory schools. The prolix discussion of the curriculum and examinations had been beneficial in more ways than one.

Success in other fields followed. Very early, largely because of the initiative of E.D. Mansfield and the Rev. C. Darnell, an Oxford University scheme was instituted for the training of preparatory schoolmasters: Mr M.W. Keatinge, the Tutor and Lecturer in Education at Oxford, ran a one-month Diploma Course in the Theory and History of Education in 1897 and in succeeding years. Another measure was the institution of a Benevolent Fund,[38] the nucleus of which was formed from funds obtained through the Common Entrance Examinations. A measure to assist headmasters was the Guarantee Fund set up in 1902/03 to assist those who found themselves involved in costly litigation.[39]

The AHPS was also able to persuade the Admiralty that 13 years was a better age than twelve to thirteen[40] for entry to the navy, if it were to fit in with the preparatory schools' other function of feeding the public schools.

The AHPS was not quite so successful with another government department. Preparatory schools were liable to pay the Inhabited House Duty tax, introduced in the late 1890s. A.G. Grenfell (Mostyn House) and E.L. Browne (St Andrew's School, Eastbourne) led a vigorous campaign to cut the tax by 33 per cent as far as preparatory schools were concerned.[41] A fighting fund of £360 was set up in December 1899 to fight a preparatory school case in the courts. The test case was conducted before Justice Phillimore on 20 June 1902 to determine whether or not the Rev. E.L. Browne's School at Eastbourne had been properly assessed at £750. Browne's victory was duly reported in the *Preparatory Schools Review* (No. 22 of July 1902). But his triumph was short lived. The Crown appealed against the decision and the Court of Appeal reversed it.

But 1914 brought another victory. Since the institution of the Secondary Schools Code of 1904 the preparatory schools, straddling the boundary between the age ranges of elementary and secondary schools, had been denied the right to receive free inspections, to which secondary schools were entitled.[42] Because of this exclusion, the preparatory schools had been charged the full amount for the cost of any inspection, which had been prohibitive: consequently up to 1913 only five preparatory schools had been inspected.[43] A combined deputation from the HMC and APS[44] sought recognition of the preparatory schools as an integral part of the public school system, as had been advocated by Michael Sadler for some time. In the event the Board of Education compromised and gained sanction from the Treasury to inspect up to twenty preparatory schools per year free of charge.[45] It would seem that the preparatory schools were, to quote the words of C.C. Cotterill, 'at last recognised to be not an aimless aggregate of private commercial establishments, but an integral and quite indispensable portion of the national system of Secondary Education.'[46]

Bull and Mansfield

The Association undoubtedly owed most[47] to the Rev. Herbert Bull and Edward D. Mansfield. Bull's physical disabilities did not affect his capacity for beating little boys when he felt it necessary. Having been at Rugby as a boy and served as an assistant master at Wellington 1880–6, Bull launched out with his brother[48] on a school at Westgate-on-Sea which he named Wellington House School after Wellington College. One old boy of the school and ex-pupil of Bull[49] has described him in a short memoir as 'completely honest and always trying to do his best for us'. By 1896 some considerable new building had been carried out and Bull had a prosperous school of fifty boys. The old boy went on, 'I doubt if he really knew us. His own outlook was "play up, play up and play the man." He felt simply and deeply himself, and expected us to do the same.' There is a suggestion in this memoir that Bull was out of touch with the sentiment of his boys, who showed not the slightest patriotism and did not share their headmaster's interest in the Second Boer War. But he was devoted to his school and to education. As first honorary secretary (1892–97) and twice chairman of the AHPS, he was 'one of the first to realise the importance of a properly constituted body to act as a liaison between the Public and Preparatory Schools.'[50] He was always an enthusiast, a man with definite views, who looked upon the Association as a band of brothers of which he was one of the natural leaders. A deeply religious man, he waged a campaign in his later years against the public sale of 'obnoxious' literature[51] and, at his last appearance at the AHPS Conference in 1917, spoke strongly in favour of the retention of the Scripture paper in the Common Entrance Examination. Outside the Association he was a member of Westgate Council for many years and worked tirelessly for the Canterbury Diocese[52] to whose care he left his school.[53]

Edward Mansfield was more 'progressive' in outlook that Herbert Bull. Becoming headmaster of Lambrook School in 1884 'to test his own carefully thought out ideas about the education of young boys'[54] he took a leading part in the formation of the AHPS and had the distinction, unique before the First World War, of thrice being its Chairman (1893, 1895, and 1903). For nine years he was the honorary treasurer and 'it is not too much to say that, as long as he remained in the profession, no voice carried so much weight as his in Committee and at the Annual Conference.'[55] Mansfield was the champion of reform; Bull was to be found amongst the conservative moderates. Mansfield was a leader in the reform of the curriculum and in the provision of teacher training courses for preparatory schoolmasters, and he played a leading role in the establishment of the Common Entrance examination. It has been said of him that 'if Frank Ritchie devised the machinery of the examination, Mansfield's was the guiding spirit.'[56]

In 1904 Mansfield retired from Lambrook but continued to give public service: he became an alderman on the Berkshire County Council and was on the governing bodies of several secondary schools, on the Berkshire Education Committee and on the Council of the University of Reading. The view of Mansfield given by W.F. Bushell[57] is not a flattering one. By contrast the *PSR* obiuary on Mansfield[58] states that he was a schoolmaster of the highest quality with a belief in his mission to boys. With leaders like Mansfield, the Association achieved much in these early years. By the beginning of the First World War it was well and truly established, ready to face the rest of the twentieth century.

Notes

1 For example:
    1 the need to arrive collectively at some agreement between preparatory and public schools concerning the age of transfer;
    2 the need to defer Greek till possibly the public school stage;
    3 the need to defer boys for confirmation till public school stage;
    4 the need for close liaison between preparatory schools and public schools on boys' being transferred. See *Report of HMC at Oxford*, 1890.

2 See pp. 170–172 and view of Mr T. PELLATT.
3 SIC was against this practice. See Volume I, pp. 190–2.
4 The first official Annual Conference at which fifty-four were present.
5 BRYCE, Volume V, p. 333.
6 M.E. SADLER (1904) *Report on Secondary Education in Birkenhead*, p. 37.

> Yet to say that a school which gives the first half of such a graded course is not a secondary school because the boy leaves it at thirteen or fourteen in order to go on to another and closely related school where he will receive the residue of his secondary education, could be like saying that a passenger who has taken a through ticket from Birkenhead to Crewe is not, in respect of the first part of his journey, a through passenger at all, if the convenience of the railway company obliged him to change trains at Chester. The English preparatory schools provide a curriculum which, though it ends so far as they are concerned at thirteen and a half or fourteen years of age, is if anything far too closely dove-tailed into and assimilated with the curriculum of the great public schools in which their pupils usually complete their long course of secondary education. To call the preparatory schools anything but secondary schools would obviously be to fix upon them a misnomer, and to deny the existence of educational continuity where such continuity is the very essence of the relationship.
> See also *Board of Education Report 1900*. Sadler, 'The place for the preparatory school for boys in secondary education in England.'

7 That is the lowering of the standard of Greek, the total abolition of Latin verse and the lowering of the standard of mathematics.
8 106 to 14, 8 'don't knows' and 18 did not reply.
9 Amongst the other signatories were: J. BEWSHER (Colet Court); H.C. BRODRICK (Orley Farm); F.D. BROWNE (Lambrook); F.M. BUCKLAND (Laleham); P.S. DEALTRY (The Leas, Hoylake); G.S. CHITTENDEN (Street Courte, partner of J.V. MILNE); E.H. DOUGLAS (The Link School, Malvern); S.S. HARRIS (St Ronan's Worthing); W.S. MACLAREN (Summer Fields); D.H. MARSHALL (The Hall, Crossfield; OSWALD NELSON (Arden House); C.D. OLIVE (Rokeby); T. PELLATT (Durnford House); R. FRAMPTON STALLARD (Heddon Court, Cockfosters); MERVYN VOULES (Middleton School, Bognor); H.W. WATERFIELD (Temple Grove); and A.J. DE WINTON (Gore Court).

H.W. WATERFIELD (Temple Grove); C.E. WILLIAMS (Summer Fields); and A.J. DE WINTON (Gore Court).

10 Mr GIDLEY ROBINSON, Editor of *PSR*, at a later stage was also attacked for showing partiality on the Greek question. See *PSR*, 5, 42, March 1909, pp. 314–15.

11 *PSR*, 3, 21, March 1902, p. 98.

12 *PSR*, 5, 33, March 1906, p. 1.

13 *Ibid.*

14 Educated at Lancing from eight to eighteen, PELLATT had been Professor of History and Literature at the Royal College, Lahore, India.

15 It was not apparent to which 'leading preparatory schools' he referred since all the older preparatory schools such as Twyford, Temple Grove, Cheam and Windlesham House were members.

16 Largely a set of essays by leading members of the Association on varying aspects of preparatory schools, together with other essays by outside contributors like MICHAEL SADLER and J.H. BADLEY.

17 T. PELLATT, (1936), *Boys in the Making*, Methuen p. 178.

18 *Ibid.*, pp. 121–3.

19 *Ibid.*, p. 180.

20 *Ibid.* He cited Dr CYRIL NORWOOD, headmaster of Harrow, as one of the country's leading educationists.

21 PELLATT, *Boys in the Making*, p. 179.

22 *PSR*, 5, 42, March 1909, p. 312.

23 ANON (1926), *Memorials of Lionel Helbert*, Humphrey Milford p. 77. See also *PSR*, 5, 44, December 1909, pp. 393–8 for full account.

24 See *PSR*, 6, 45, March 1910, pp. 19–20. The first election of twelve members from twelve districts was almost abortive: eight elected; three elections void; no convener; therefore no election. Four members had to be co-opted to fill vacancies in Districts 1, 8, 9, 10. In the following year six had to be co-opted.

25 The father of CHRISTOPHER STONE of gramophone/radio fame. Cf. HERBERT BUCKMASTER, (1933), *Buck's Book*, Grayson and Grayson pp. 14–17.

26 *PSR*, 4, 24, March 1903, pp. 35–6. Obituary notice on Rev. CHARLES DARNELL.

27 Cargilfield under DARNELL was a very famous preparatory school which achieved 'parity of esteem' with Scottish public schools. DARNELL was not only a very successful teacher of Latin prose but also a headmaster of considerable stature. He was a skilful manager of men and boys and created an elaborate organization within the school. During his headship (1873–98) Cargilfield gained a reputation for athletic prowess.

28 See 113 and footnote 25 on p. 118.

29 HERBERT G. SPEARING (Herbert Green in FOSTER's *Alumni Oxonienses*) was the founder of the school which opened in 1888 at 'The Hollies', Greenbank Road, Wavertree. SPEARING announced his retirement and the closure of the school in 1890. Parents with boys at the school refused to allow this and formed a company to allow it to continue. So the school of which C.C. COTTERILL became headmaster in 1890 was a proprietary school. COTTERILL persuaded the businessmen of Liverpool to support it and in 1892 it moved to new Greenbank buildings costing £30,000.

30 Viz. 1907 — *Human Justice for Those at the Bottom: An Appeal to Those at the Top*; 1910 — *The Victory of Love*; 1912 — *A Living Wage a National Necessity*.

31 He was Honorary Secretary of AHPS; Editor of *PSR*; Secretary of the Board of Management of the Common Entrance Examination.

32 See p. 79.

33 RITCHIE went into partnership with J.S. NORMAN, who was later Chairman of the Eighteenth Annual Conference.

34 LYNAM, *op. cit.*, p. 34.

35 Sometimes LYNAM's rash if generous nature got the better of him. In 1899 HERBERT MILLINGTON, headmaster of Bromsgrove, wrote a letter to the editor of the *Spectator* in which he attacked preparatory school magazines. LYNAM, as editor of *PSR*, took exception. He replied that Bromsgrove was a school that 'no respectable Preparatory School Head' would send his boys to. LYNAM had to apologize on behalf of the AHPS for this calumny. Although in the apology it was represented that the editor had mistakenly interpreted MILLINGTON's remarks as a slur on the *PSR* it is tempting to see in his outburst as editor of that journal a defence of his own school magazine, *The Draconian*. LYNAM's savage attack on MILLINGTON cost the Association £40 legal costs despite the public apology. On this occasion LYNAM offered his resignation, but it was not accepted. He resigned soon after, however, when he quarrelled with some executive committee colleagues on another matter.

36 In seconding the motion at the 1895 HMC meeting, Mr G.C. BELL, of Marlborough read an extract of letter sent by Rev. H. BULL as Hon. Secretary of the AHPS.

37 *Board of Education Report, 1900*, p. 11.

38 *PSR*, 5, 42, March 1909, p. 310.

39 *PSR*, 4, 24, March, 1903, p. 2.

40 See SPENSER WILKINSON, (n.d.) *The Nation's Needs*, Archibald and Constable pp. 280–1. Although WILKINSON supported the view that boys should be at preparatory school before going into the navy he made the same mistake as the Admiralty in believing that boys left preparatory school between twelve and thirteen.

41 The point at issue was whether school buildings such as chapel, gymnasium, classrooms and carpenter's shop could be counted as 'inhabited' and should therefore be taxable. GRENFELL and BROWNE aimed at cutting the duty from ninepence to sixpence in the pound for preparatory schools.

42 This simultaneous separation and association was epitomized in the book on educational law by A.H.H. McLEAN (1909) entitled *The Law Concerning Secondary and Preparatory Schools*, Jordan and Sons.

43 Inspections in the nineteenth century were conducted by individuals, sometimes on behalf of the University. They could be thorough, or no more than a formality, as when on one occasion the inspector turned up unexpectedly when the school was engrossed in cricket. Of this occasion Mr J.P. NELSON relates: 'Eventually he [the inspector] accepted a whisky and soda, departed with mutual regards on both sides, and later wrote an excellent report.' From an unpublished history entitled *1869–1966 Feckenham, Arden House, Hurst House and Ardenhurst*, p. 13.

44 The Association was called the Association of Preparatory Schools (APS) from 1905.

45 *Board of Education Report, 1913–1914*, p. 31, Paragraph 70.

46 *Board of Education Special Report, 1900*, p. 21.

47 Among other leaders of the early Association were C. DARNELL (Cargilfield); C.C. LYNAM (Dragon School), who became first editor of the *PSR*; CLEMENT C. COTTERILL (ex-Greenbank, Liverpool), who from 1898 to 1901 was the Honorary Secretary of the Association and who in conjunction with MICHAEL E. SADLER produced the 1900 Board of Education Special Report on Preparatory Schools; E.H. PARRY (Stoke House), an early committee member and Chairman; E.P. ARNOLD (Wixenford), Chairman of the Sixth Conference and early committee member; the Rev. WALTER EARLE (Bilton Grange), committee member and early contributor to *PSR*; the Rev. J.H. WILKINSON (Waynflete, Woodcote near Reading), a representative of AHPS in 1896 when the first meeting with HMC members discussed reform of the curriculum; the Rev. C.T. WICKHAM (Twyford) and Dr C.E. WILLIAMS (Summer Fields), both Vice-Chairmen before 1900; Mr FRANK RITCHIE (ex-Sevenoaks Preparatory School), who succeeded both COTTERILL and LYNAM, as Secretary (1901) and Editor of the *PSR* (1900) respectively, and who also became Secretary of the Board of Management of the Common Entrance examination

(1904); C.D. OLIVE (Rokeby) and the Rev. C.W. HUNT (Cordwalles), were committee members. In the early years the preparatory schools of Malvern were well represented by the Rev. C. BLACK (Colwall), chairman of the eleventh conference, and W. DOUGLAS (The Link School). E.P. FREDERICK of Wells House later played some part. At the beginning of the twentieth century, new leaders came forward in the shape of G. GIDLEY ROBINSON (Hillside, Godalming), third editor of *PSR*; LIONEL HELBERT, who introduced lasting constitutional reform; E.L. BROWNE (St Andrew's School, Eastbourne), who seemed to play the role of gadfly until elected to the committee; A.G. GRENFELL (Mostyn House); and H. STRAHAN (Hythe).

48 Rev. R.A. BULL migrated and set up his own school of St Andrew's, Southborough, Kent.

49 PREBENDARY C.W. TREVELYAN of Bath, who wrote a short memorial for PATRICK DUDGEON, of Dover College to whom I am grateful for information on BULL.

50 *PSR*, 9, 101, December 1928, p. 501.

51 *PSR*, 5, 42, March 1909, p. 316.

52 He was Rural Dean of West Bere.

53 He left his school in the hands of the Canterbury Diocesan Board on the understanding that they would rent it only to a man of Christian principles.

54 He believed in extrinsic rewards and allowed boys who had done particularly well to go to the races at nearby Ascot. *PSR*, 11, 91, June 1925. The obituary on Mansfield in the *PSR* wrongly claims he founded Lambrook. He was in fact second headmaster from 1884 in 1904.

55 *Ibid.*

56 *Ibid.*

57 See p. 145.

58 *PSR*, 9, 91, June 1925, p. 142.

12   Bull at the Common Entrance Gate

In the interests of education a definite and uniform curriculum for all boys who are prepared for entrance to the Public Schools is desirable. (The Rev. H. Bull (1895) *PSR*, 1, 1, p. 3)

Getting at Greek

At its first annual general meeting in December 1892, the AHPS had considered one aspect of the curriculum which had been a bone of contention with the public schools — the study of Greek. It agreed that not all preparatory schoolboys should have to take Greek for entry into public school and that the latter should be encouraged to facilitate the entry of boys without an early grounding in Greek.[1] The Rev. Herbert Bull's remarks were made at the annual conference in the following year, and were coupled with the suggestion that English (including history and geography), French, Latin and mathematics should be compulsory subjects, with Greek and German being options for cleverer boys. The question reappeared in 1895 at the fourth annual conference, which came to two conclusions: that the curriculum was overloaded, and that it needed to be fairly uniform up to the age of fourteen.[2] This vote of no confidence in early specialization,[3] was inspired by educational, economic, organizational and commonsense reasons.[4] So if the public schools agreed to the postponement of Greek to fourteen, this would have the overall effect of providing a uniform curriculum.

They were not charging a locked gate, for the Headmasters' Conference had in the same year discussed the topic, the headmaster of Winchester, Dr W.A. Fearon, presenting the view of the preparatory schools, and securing a seconder in the person of the headmaster of Marlborough, G.C. Bell, that 'with a view to relieve the crowded state of the curriculum for young boys it [was] desirable to define the range of subjects for entrance exams at Public Schools.'

For the preparatory schools were torn in two directions; the navy demanded modern subjects and the public school held to classical examinations. To cope with this they had to divide their schools. This was a costly business for many private preparatory headmasters, unless the optimum size of a school (sixty to seventy boys) was raised to 150 to allow such fragmentation into special classes. The wide variety of demands from individual public schools within the subject areas additionally aggravated the cost.

Unfortunately, public school headmasters could not all appreciate this. Retention of the early study of Greek was supported by Mr T.W. Dunn of Bath College, the Rev. Dr H.A. James (Rugby School) and the Rev. R.S. de C. Laffan (Cheltenham) but they could not prevent their colleagues from agreeing that the question should be discussed with the two bodies. This was duly done on 24 March 1896. Significantly, the Rev. Dr Warre of Eton took the chair. The representatives from the preparatory schools[5] forcibly advocated the abolition of Latin verse and the lowering of the standard of Greek in the entrance examination. Although *not* unanimous about these topics the representatives of the preparatory schools had been briefed by the Association to ask the public schools to agree that due credit would be given in all scholarship elections for good work in *all* subjects of the preparatory school curriculum.[6] The preparatory schools were thus not only concerned with uniformity in the curriculum but were also set against undue specialization. This could affect the outcome of scholarship as well as of entrance examinations. The public schools responded to this request. In particular, Eton and Marlborough agreed to examine scholarship candidates in French; Repton was prepared to give credit for 'all round' performance and Haileybury made similar modifications to its scholarship examinations.[7] But although Eton and Marlborough now regarded French as a subject for scholarship award, other public schools still clung to the idea that scholarships should be awarded for proficiency only in the classics and mathematics. This feeling was still overwhelmingly strong in 1899.[8] So in July 1899 the AHPS executive worked out a policy to present to senior colleagues in the HMC. Their recommended curriculum for young boys was to be based on the following principles:

1 (a) It should be *wide* rather than *special*, and should aim at developing all faculties in due proportion;
   (b) the course of education should be adapted to the *average* rather than to the *exceptional* boy.
2 The following subjects should be included in all entrance examinations:
   (a) Latin — Translation, Grammar, Prose (obligatory);
   (b) French — Translation, Grammar, Sentences (obligatory);
   (c) Greek — Translation, Grammar (optional);
   (d) Mathematics — Arithmetic (obligatory); Algebra and Euclid (optional);
   (e) English — Divinity, English, Geography, History (obligatory); and
   (f) Drawing — optional.
3 Entrance Scholarship Examinations should be the same papers together with papers on *Latin Verses* and *Greek Sentences*.

4 Due credit should be given to all subjects and all scholarships should be awarded on aggregate marks obtained.[9]

The Common Entrance Examination

This continuous debate on the scholarship and entrance examinations, generated in the 1890s, involved the institution of a common entrance examination so that instead of preparatory schoolboys' travelling to several public schools to sit for individual public school entrance and scholarship examinations, chaperoned by a staff member, they took one examination for all schools. In 1900 the Chairman of the ninth annual conference, Frank Ritchie of Sevenoaks, suggested as an alternative the establishment of examination centres at places like Malvern, Brighton, Westgate-on-Sea and Eastbourne,[10] adding the significant rider that

> There seems to be no very good reason why the various Public Schools should not set identical papers, at all events in the ordinary subjects, and an imaginative person might even dream of a time when such papers would be set by a board on which preparatory schools would be represented.[11]

But AHPS could not agree among themselves, and only two years later in December 1902 the Rev. Herbert Bull (Wellington House School) and the Rev. C.T. Wickham (Twyford) — two major figures in the AHPS — were at daggers drawn. On this occasion, as on so many others, the wisdom of Mr E.D. Mansfield prevailed. When the protracted proceedings of the eleventh annual conference seemed to be leading to an *impasse* he moved formally:

(1) That no settlement of the curriculum will be satisfactory to this Association which imposes on young boys the rudiments of three languages besides their own.
(2) That this conference is in favour of one single leaving examination for preparatory schools in place of the present widely differing examinations of the different public schools.[12]

With the passing of these resolutions the preparatory school representatives — Messrs E.D. Mansfield, C.C. Lynam, H. Bull, E.H. Parry and F. Ritchie — were able to negotiate[13] with Canon E. Lyttelton (Haileybury), Dr Warre (Eton) and Dr H.A. James (Rugby) as representatives of the Headmasters' Conference. They proposed a common entrance examination based on a common curriculum. The examination would assume a preparatory school timetable, which excluded Greek, of thirty-two hours a week. Warre and James were resistant to the AHPS recommendations for the dropping of Greek but agreed to take all their proposals to the HMC for further discussion. There it was agreed in 1903 to institute the common entrance examination with a board of five managers: the Rev. Canon Bell (ex-Marlborough Head); the Rev. Dr

James (Rugby); the Rev. H.A. Dalton (Felsted); Mr E.D. Mansfield (Lambrook) and the Rev. Herbert Bull (Wellington House).

Was It a Cram-Orgy?

Described by Tom Pellatt (Durnford) as 'the wildest cram-orgy ever contrived in the whole history of education',[14] initial implementation of the common entrance 28/29 June 1904 by thirty public schools was certainly an improvement on existing practice. 329 entries, mostly for Bradfield, Charterhouse, Cheltenham, Clifton, Felsted, Haileybury, Marlborough, Radley, Repton, Rugby and Tonbridge, were registered from 190 preparatory schools, including 133 whose heads belonged to the Association.[15]

In the second common entrance examinations held on 22/23 November 1904, there were 181 candidates, with papers being sent to 147 schools, of which ninety-seven belonged to the Association. In March 1905 there were 303 candidates, and in July 1905 more than 400. The common entrance examination scheme was well and truly launched.

This development brought uniformity and even closer ties with the public schools. It also met the difficulty which had faced preparatory schools since at least the mid-nineteenth century of having to cater for the several Latin grammars used by different public schools.[16]

The Displacement of Greek

The question of the place of Greek in the preparatory school curriculum was still unresolved. It took another six years of heated debate before Greek was made to concede ground to other subjects in the curriculum. The most often quoted authority on the English preparatory school's curriculum at the beginning of the twentieth century is the Blue Book, issued by the Board of Education (1900) *Special Reports on Educational Subjects*, Vol. 6.[17] The excessive time devoted to the classics and mathematics in all types of preparatory schools, and the relative neglect of English language and grammar, geography and history and especially of science (totally ignored in 72.5 per cent of the schools surveyed), was revealed by H. Frampton Stallard (Heddon Court)[18] who noted that though French was taught in all the schools surveyed only in 41 per cent of them was German taught. And though 65 per cent of the schools had drawing, little time was given to it. Singing, instrumental music and carpentry, not being subjects in which the public schools were interested, were treated in variable fashion by the individual schools, but it was a most exceptional school which gave six hours a week to woodwork.[19] Stallard's plea for more time for English subjects concluded with the observation that the importance of the classics was 'exaggerated' and so he proposed 'to use time taken from these subjects, say three or four hours a week, to give a proper grounding in Geography, embracing elementary Science and the literature and language of our own country.'[20] Similar sentiments were expressed even more cogently by Michael Sadler[21] who, although a great supporter of the preparatory schools, regarded them as 'unduly neglectful of the mother tongue, of English composition and of English literature; it is too heavily loaded with Latin; *too soon encumbered with Greek* [my italics] . . .' and providing 'far too little drawing . . . and manual training generally'. Sadler went on to suggest that 'it might do more to interest boys in natural history and to train them in a scientific way of looking at things' and lamented that they were 'prevented from doing all this chiefly by the dead weight of habit and by the rules for the entrance examinations at the public schools.'[22] As a great consumer of curriculum time, Greek evoked other criticisms too. A writer using the pseudonym of 'Classicus' in *The Journal of Education* recalled Matthew Arnold's satirical comment in *Friendship's Garland* through the mouth of Teufelsdrockh: 'Innumerable dead vocables they crammed into us, and called it fostering the growth of the mind,'[23] and lamented that 'the boy in one of our expensive preparatory schools who should be receiving the all-round training suitable to his age which is attempted in the public elementary schools, instead of this is being crammed with *Greek* and Latin.'[24]

Further Changes

The introduction of the common entrance examination broke down the gate and the AHPS began to look at other changes in the curriculum made possible by the displacement of Greek from its hegemony of the timetable. 'Progressive' and 'traditional' factions emerged in the Association. The Rev. C.T. Wickham (Twyford) and Mr E.D. Mansfield (Lambrook), the protagonists of reform, argued for a revision of the curriculum 'on scientific principles'; Wickham even favoured the idea of a Royal Commission of Inquiry into Secondary Education.[25] Mr Mervyn Voules (Bognor) opposed this proposal and suggested, not without grounds, that such a move would be inviting state control of preparatory schools.[26]

Notwithstanding the overcautious attitude of Mervyn Voules towards curriculum reform and possible government intervention, some change was recommended both inside and outside the Association. At the December 1904 annual conference the teaching of science was debated. This discussion was complemented in the following year by a report of the sub-committee of the Association of Public School Science Masters, emphasizing the value of nature study in preparatory schools.

As early as July 1887[27] Greek had been singled out as the sop to the Cerberus of curriculum reform when in a letter to client preparatory schools[28] the HMC suggested that an introduction to Greek should be postponed until boys were twelve so as to allow more time for the study of history, geography and English literature. It was therefore not surprising to find the early study of Greek taking the brunt of the attack whilst Latin still held its own.

Now twenty years later *PSR* in December 1906 was bemoaning the fact that public schools, especially Rugby and Eton, were reluctant to abandon the demand for Greek from preparatory school boys. But in the same month the 'Greek bastion' began to crumble when the HMC voted that Greek should *not* be required in entrance and scholarship examinations.[29]

Ironically the decision was not applauded by *all* in the Association. Dr C.E. Williams (Summer Fields), who had been devoting twenty-five hours in classics per week to his top form, indicated his distrust and disapproval of the 'dreadful tangle in which preparatory schools now find themselves owing to their frantic rush after everything modern, such as Nature study, the New Mathematics. . . .' In his opinion 'the so-called Natural Science which these unhappy children are supposed to learn' was 'pronounced by Public Schools specialists to be worse than useless.'[30]

In contrast to Dr Williams' deep distrust of contemporary trends, the APS donated ten guineas in 1907 to the Art for Schools Association (ASA), and shortly afterwards the Editor of the *PSR* gave enthusiastic support to *Sloyd*[31] and Manual Training which had been recently recommended by the report of The Curriculum Committee of the British Association. These 'reformist' straws showed the direction in which the wind was blowing, for in November 1907 the Association held a poll on Dr Upcott's resolution of December 1906 which showed support for it in a ratio of almost 2:1 (180 in favour: 96 against).[32] Nor, too, were the public school headmasters unanimous at their conference at Oxford in 1907. A motion calling for the lowering of the standard of Greek in preparatory schools was put by Dr H. Burge (Winchester), and seconded by the Rev. the Hon. E. Lyttelton, who took occasion to compliment preparatory schoolmasters by reminding the HMC 'how great a debt Public schoolmasters owe to these men.'[33] Yet the motion was lost, with the arch-traditionalist Dr James of Rugby leading the opposition. This division amongst public school headmasters was a signal for the 114 traditionalists in the APS, including Tom Pellatt, Mervyn Voules and C.E. Williams, to frame a letter[34] supporting the *status quo* and giving encouragement to Dr James to remain firm. According to the 114 there was much exaggeration in the notion of a congested curriculum in preparatory schools. Their averred aim in writing was 'to strengthen the hands of those who are bent on maintaining the standards of Greek in schools of England.'[35]

In the same month as the letter was sent to the HMC, Mr Gidley Robinson (Hillside, Godalming) affirmed that Dr Upcott's motion of December 1906 was the policy of the Association's executive committee. It mattered not that he was later rebuked for bipartisan editorship.[36] Gidley Robinson's views on the postponement of Greek were endorsed two months later by Dr W.H.D. Rouse of the Perse School, Cambridge who, in a letter to the Association, opined that there was insufficient room for both Latin and Greek in the preparatory school curriculum and suggested that the learning of Greek should begin in the public school.[37]

In December 1908 the HMC passed resolutions which led to the displacement of Greek from the preparatory school curriculum. This led Dr James to make a gloomy forecast about the future of Greek in public schools. The eventual displacement of the language caused much satisfaction amongst the many preparatory school headmasters who had regarded the comparatively high standard of Greek required by public schools as the chief time-consumer and the chief stumbling block to a more 'liberal' education. Looking back at these complex negotiations with the HMC from a distance of more than seventy years, we see how the majority in the APS eventually impressed public school heads with the reality of *their* situation. By 1908 the hope which Thomas Arnold expressed to Lord Denbigh in 1829 that the preparatory school curriculum would be widened was much nearer to fulfilment.[38]

The End of an Era

Jeremiahs might well point to the decision of HMC in December 1908 as the beginning of the end of classical studies in English schools, even though Greek was not banished immediately. A committee was set up by the HMC to confer with the APS on a scheme for the future studies of boys between the ages of nine and sixteen. It was not surprising that the 'reformists', Mr E.D. Mansfield and the Rev. C.T. Wickham, were chosen to act as assessors by the APS. The curriculum reformers of the early twentieth century were the harbingers of pragmatism amongst English preparatory schools. Their achievements in the establishment of the Common Entrance Examination and disestablishment of Greek from the preparatory school curriculum foreshadowed greater changes in the later twentieth century.

Notes

1 *PSR*, 1, 1, July 1895, p. 2. See also *ibid.*, pp. 7–9. It has been argued by the present headmaster of Cheam School, Mr MICHAEL WHEELER, that this early attack on the teaching of Greek was the main reason for Mr ARTHUR TABOR, a keen Greek scholar, stepping down from the leadership of the new Association.
2 This opinion was based on a survey of forty-three preparatory schools conducted by the Rev. the HON. E. LYTTELTON. The survey demonstrated the chaotic nature of the curriculum through *ad hoc* development. *PSR*, 1, 1, July 1895, pp. 4–5.
3 *PSR*, 1, 3, March 1896, p. 53.
4 It was argued that (a) boys who came to Greek at fifteen were no worse off three years later than boys who had been reared on it from the age of eight or nine; (b) it was a mistake to teach two dead languages simultaneously; (c) many boys went to the modern side of public schools where Greek was not necessary; (d) the exclusion of Greek released six or seven periods a week for other studies; and (e) boys going into the navy did not require Greek.
5 Rev. J.H. WILKINSON (Wayneflete, Clifton); E.D. MANSFIELD (Lambrook, Bracknell); the Rev. C.W. DARNELL (Cargilfield, Edinburgh); the Rev. HERBERT BULL (Wellington House, Westgate-on-Sea); and E.H. PARRY (Stoke House, Stoke Poges).

6 Cf. *PSR*, 2, 8, December 1897, p. 92.

7 *PSR*, 2, 9, March 1898, p. 2.

8 *PSR*, 2, 12, March 1899, p. 82.

9 *PSR*, 2, 13, July 1899, p. 1.

10 Several public schools such as Bradfield, Malvern, Marlborough, Radley, Uppingham and Wellington conceded the preparatory schools' demand to allow their examinations to be conducted at individual schools. Harrow was similarly concessionary until it was discovered that a preparatory school (outside the Association) was giving aid to examinees. Cf. *PSR*, 3, 22, July 1902, p. 131.

11 *PSR*, 3, 18, March 1901, p. 24.

12 *PSR*, 4, 24, March 1903, pp. 9–10.

13 Mr C.T. WICKHAM (Twyford) recommended this in November 1902. Cf. *PSR*, 4, 28, July 1904, p. 147.

14 T. PELLATT (1936) *Boys in the Making*, Methuen, p. 170.

15 *PSR*, 4, 28, July 1904, p. 149.

16 Cf. SIC Report, Vol. 7, p. 172. One preparatory school had to use as many as four different Latin grammars in one form.

17 Cf. Mr H. FRAMPTON STALLARD, 'The time-table of work in a preparatory school'; Mr G.G. ROBINSON, 'The preparatory school curriculum'; Rev. C.E. WILLIAMS, 'The teaching of Latin and Greek in preparatory schools'.

18 Cf. *Board of Education Report 1900*, Vol. 6, p. 43. Mr STALLARD divided preparatory schools into four categories:

   1 those that made a special point of competing for scholarships;
   2 those that did not;
   3 those that prepared boys for a particular public school;
   4 those that prepared for the Royal Navy.

19 *Ibid.*, p. 55.

20 *Ibid.*, p. 59.

21 Sadler was the editor of the volume and the Director of the Office of Special Inquiries and Reports from which the reports emanated.

22 *Ibid.*, p. 90.

23 *The Journal of Education*, December 1903, p. 861.

24 *Ibid*. This article, entitled 'The real failure of our preparatory and public schools', was strongly supported by C. SIMMONS in 'The preparatory day school of the future', in *The Contemporary Review*, Vol. 90, September 1906, pp. 344–58.

25 *PSR*, 4, 28, July 1904, p. 154; *PSR*, 4, 29, Dec. 1904, pp. 176–7; *PSR*, 4, 30, March 1905, p. 219. WICKHAM was supported by MANSFIELD in his notion for a national inquiry into the secondary schools' curricula. MANSFIELD later persuaded the Federal Council of Secondary Schools Associations to adopt the idea. Cf. *PSR*, 5, 36, March 1907, p. 87.

26 *PSR*, 4, 30, March 1905, p. 219.

27 *Board of Education Report 1900*. G. GIDLEY ROBINSON 'The preparatory school curriculum', p. 76.

28 This was before the foundation of the AHPS.

29 See *Report of HMC at Malvern December 1906*. The motion was put by Dr UPCOTT of Christ's Hospital and passed by twenty-six votes to four.

30 *PSR*, 5, 36, March 1907, pp. 113–14. Cf. also Rev. C.E. WILLIAMS, 'Entrance scholarships and cram' in ANON (1906) *The Public Schools from Within*, Sampson, Low Marston and Co., pp. 265–72 in which Dr WILLIAMS defends the classics in preparatory schools.

31 The Scandinavian educational emphasis on the training of the hand and eye through wood and metal work. Cf. T.G. ROOPER (n.d.) *School and Home Life*, A Brown and Sons pp. 465–79.

32 *PSR*, 5, 38, December 1907, p. 167.
33 Cf. The Report of the thirty-fifth Headmasters' Conference.
34 Cf. p. 000.
35 *PSR*, 5, 40, July 1908, pp. 237–8.
36 *PSR*, 5, 42, March 1909, p. 314.
37 *PSR*, 5, 40, July 1908, p. 240.
38 Lord DENBIGH sought ARNOLD's educational advice on one occasion. Cf. photostat of MS letter held by the Warwickshire Record Office from THOMAS ARNOLD to Lord DENBIGH, dated 21 September 1829.

13   Athletes and Aesthetes

The real truth is that the ultimate objects of athletics have been lost
sight of in the wave of fashionable enthusiasm which has engulfed
them.
(S.S. Harris (1925) *The Master and His Boys*)

It is likely that the greatest cultural achievements of man rest upon
predilections acquired between the ages of five and thirteen.
(Anthony Stow, 'The Meaning of Music', *The Times Literary
Supplement*, 20 November 1970)

Manliness

The ethos of the English preparatory school changed during the nineteenth
century as did that of the English public school: from 'godliness and good
learning' to 'manliness and godliness'.[1] If the Duke of Wellington ever really
said that the battle of Waterloo was won on the playing fields of Eton he could
only have had in mind the disorganized but aggressive activities of schoolboys
in meadows near Eton College. Organized games were a much later feature of
schoolboy life. Harrow was one of the first schools to develop cricket and
football, the first Eton vs. Harrow match dating back to 1821.[2] The first
inter-school Rugby football match was played in 1864, and then between the
two Victorian foundations of Clifton and Marlborough.[3] It was long after
Waterloo, therefore, that organized games entered into public schools, and
then rather by fortuitous accident than by cool design. According to Cyril
Norwood:

> As cricket and football spread among the schools it did not take long
> for the discerning among the school-masters to see what they had
> elaborated by accident was not merely an excellent method of letting
> off physical energy, and occupying spare time, but also a fine
> educational instrument. What, indeed, they had discovered by accident
> was the team-spirit, which alone builds character: ... team-spirit is a

commonplace to us, but it is a recent arrival in the field of educational thought, and is indeed one of the present English contributions to methods of true education.[4]

If in 1860 organized games in public schools were fairly commonplace, by the end of the century they were compulsory for all boys unless excused on medical grounds. Naturally, preparatory schools reflected these changes. Thomas Hughes, for example, enjoyed sport at Twyford School.[5] But the distance between schools, their generally small size and their extended family[6] role made this more difficult. In a school with a total complement of twenty to twenty-five boys it was difficult to organize games on either a 'house' basis or an inter-school basis. With such small schools, the value of games as a creator of *esprit de corps* and discipline was in any case very low. Only by the late Victorian period could preparatory schools be seen as being arenas of muscular Christianity.

Even in well established preparatory schools organized games were a relatively late phenomenon. At Twyford, 'Tom Brown's' prep school and perhaps England's oldest existing preparatory school, the Rev. Latham Wickham (1862–87) was the first headmaster who attempted to put cricket on a regular footing by providing a proper cricket field to replace a much-used playground[7] for the 'pitching of the leather against the willow'. Temple Grove in the 1860s was similarly lacking in well-established organized athletics, although cricket, football and fives were played.[8] Enthusiasm for cricket of the new headmaster of Cheam, Robert S. Tabor (1855–90), led to its taking on teams from Hawtrey's, Elstree and Temple Grove,[9] though during the 1860s and 1870s very little of the cricket played at Cheam was of an inter-school nature, often with masters taking part. During the early development of school sports generally, this was fairly typical. If cricket developed slowly at Cheam, winter games were even slower off the mark. It is a matter of record that under Robert Tabor there were no football, fives or athletics matches against other schools.[10]

Even at Elstree School whose cricketing record is particularly good,[11] the game did not begin to flourish until the 1870s. The new headmaster, the Rev. Lancelot Sanderson (1869–1900), quickly enlarged the existing cricket field, enlisted cricket and football blues on his staff and employed two bowling professionals from Lords to help with the coaching.[12] Elstree played its first inter-school match with Aldin House (now Hawtrey's) in 1874 and played Cheam in 1881 for the first time. Elstree enjoyed a well-deserved reputation as a cricketing school from the mid-1870s. Although Association football got off to an even later start than cricket — there is no record of a football match until 1875 — Elstree quickly won a high reputation in this sport through the outstanding coaching of two assistant masters, C.P. Wilson (1883–98) and Arthur Dunn (1885–91),[13] both of whom were England soccer internationals.

Thomas Hughes and Charles Kingsley inspired for some sixty years schoolmasters and schoolboys first in public and, later, in preparatory schools such as Twyford, Temple Grove, Cheam and Elstree. Two of the four headmasters concerned in these improvements at these schools were clergymen. Preparatory schools began to take an increasing interest in the value of the sports field[14] — perhaps sometimes an excessive interest: for instance, at Gresson's School, Worthing, in the 1880s [General Sir] Charles Harrington's foot was pegged down in the nets so that he could not run away.[15] Eaton House School took its game seriously too: one of the assistant masters, the Rev. E.B.H. Benwick, a county football player, supervised the football and all boys were expected to play.[16] But the epitome of 'Muscular Christianity' was the Rev. E.L. Browne, headmaster of St Andrew's Eastbourne (1890–1933), whose school magazine was given over almost completely to reports on matches and his sermons were frequently illustrated by similes drawn from cricket. He is reputed to have preached a sermon which explained the difficult concept of the Trinity by the splendid analogy: 'three stumps, one wicket'.[17] No fewer than four professionals — twice as many as at Elstree — looked after the cricket coaching and these were assisted by assistant masters, many of whom were Blues.[18] Stubbington House, the naval preparatory school, was in the 1880s equally devoted to both football and cricket. The editor of *The Stubbingtonian* even claimed in the 1885 issue that they had introduced soccer into the navy:

> We think we can take credit for introducing this excellent game into Her Majesty's Navy. Association Football is, we hear, very successfully carried on by *HMS Britannia* — chiefly, we have good reason to believe, through the influx of Old Stubbington boys.[19]

Cricket was pursued equally seriously. In 1885 fourteen matches were played but, significantly, not against other preparatory schools.[20] Commenting on his old preparatory school, Sir Gerald Tyrwhitt-Wilson, 14th Baron Berners, wrote: 'At Elmley you were made to feel ... that organised games were the touchstone of character [because of] the eternal obsession of games. [For Elmley] games were the criterion of ultimate failure or success.'[21] Certainly such 'cult devotion' was evidence of the preparatory schools' pursuit of excellence; Tom Pellatt declared that this was even stronger than in the public schools.[22] The Rev. Herbert Bull (Wellington House, Westgate-on-Sea) epitomized this pursuit of the best. At school football and hockey matches he was constantly on the touch-line, giving advice, encouragement and criticism. Bull left the younger boys in the charge of his non-cricketing music master whilst he tended to the cricket coaching of his senior boys, using a mechanical bowling device to enable him to do so. This was partly because he was lame. But lameness did not deter him from his pursuit of excellence in his boys' performance. He rewarded his 1st XI football team with round gold-braid caps and his 1st XI cricket team with large deep-red silk squares.[23] In similar recognition of sporting prowess, the three best Rugby players at St George's, Ascot, were allowed to wear a light blue velvet cap with a silver Maltese cross and a tassle on it.[24] This cult of athleticism, as rampant eventually in the preparatory as in the public schools, filled school magazines with reports of matches and critical comment,[25] and was responsible for the recruitment of internationals, Blues, or at least county players as staff members. Thus at Dunchurch Hall Preparatory School the headmaster was a former Oxford cricket Blue, and of six assistant masters, two had played Rugby for England, one had captained Kent at cricket, one was a famous Corinthian and soccer international, and one had played hockey for England.[26]

Mr E.P. Frederick of Wells House School, Malvern (1903–28), was perhaps the chief exemplar of athletic enthusiasm though the school he took over from Mr A.H. Stable was not noted for its devotion to games. Frederick had taught mathematics at Loretto from 1882 to 1892[27] under H.H. Almond — whom he greatly admired — placing his portrait in 'Big School'. One of his first reforms was to replace Association by Rugby football because he thought it a better preparation for games at public school.[28] One of the first inter-school rugby fixtures was with the Oxford Preparatory (Dragon) School. Under Frederick's Almond-inspired leadership the rugby reputation of Wells House grew rapidly. In the 1908–9 season the first XV actually scored 252 pts — 0 against all its opponents.

As joint headmaster of Routenburn School before coming to Wells House Frederick had adopted Almond's then unconventional mode of dress for boys consisting of flannel trousers and open necks, and he introduced similar dress for Wells House boys in 1903.[29] In 1907 he appointed Mr A.M. Paterson from Loretto as assistant. Paterson eventually succeeded him as headmaster. Two years later he strengthened links with Loretto by appointing Sergeant Beeden as instructor in drill, gymnastics, fencing and boxing.

For something like sixty years football and cricket were treated by many preparatory schools as if they were religious exercises. But there were others growing slowly: fitness and scouting. Table 8 indicates the number of articles appearing in the *PSR* during the decades between 1895 and 1965 on physical activities in preparatory schools. From this table it can be seen that over the years the *PSR* was preoccupied with two activities which lay apart from the cult of athleticism and reflected a philosophy of individualism rather than of team-spirit: physical training and Boy-Scouting. Amongst schools there were of course exceptions such as Aysgarth[30] overwhelmingly interested in golf, or Parkside in hockey.

Alternatives Develop

This cult of athleticism had its critics, including Edward Thring. Later, in the 1890s, when 'Muscular Christianity' was at its zenith, *Blackwood's Magazine* wondered whether games 'taught as sedulously as Latin or Greek', and cricket in particular, were any better despite the 'billiard table' pitches and excessive coaching by professionals.[31] Eric Parker, writing in *Longman's Magazine* three years later, was doubtful of the efficacy of games when they excluded all other extra-curricular activities.[32]

Table 8. PSR Articles on Physical Activities in Preparatory Schools, 1895–1965

1895		1905		1915		1925		1935		1945 (Jan–May)	1955		1965	
PT	2	Swedish Drill	2	Boy Scouts	5	PT	5	Scouting	1	N	Games	1	'Sport'	1
Cricket	1	Rifle	2	Boxing	1	Scouting	3	PE	1	O	Cricket	6	Cricket	1
Rifle	1	Hockey	1	PT	2	PE	1	Archery	1		Scouts	1	Swimming	1
		PT	2			Rugby	2			P	Tennis	1	Athletics	1
		Boy Scouts	4			Tennis	1			S	Swimming	1	Scouting	1
						Swimming	1			R	Dancing	1	Archery	1
											PE	2		

By the 1920s such critical sentiments were gaining strength. Stanley S. Harris, headmaster of St Ronan's, Hawkhurst, and Chairman of the Association in 1924, established the 'true' place of games in his book, *The Master and His Boys*. Whilst recognizing their great importance, he referred to the 'false value' that had been put on them. He suggested to his readers that the objectives of athletics were fourfold: (1) recreation for mind and body; (2) physical development; (3) training of character; and (4) promotion of *healthy* [Harris's emphasis] competition and ambition.[33] If (1) to (3) were emphasized more, then a distorted and pernicious view of (4) would be less likely. Certainly by 1925 it was possible to write critically of athleticism. Commenting on the evolution of the preparatory school, C. Sankey wrote: 'the worship of athleticism, though powerful, had not yet degenerated into a craze, nor was its gossip the sole topic of a junior's conversation.'[34] By the 1930s the *Journal of Education* could claim with some justification that the worship of the àthlete was much more irrational and exaggerated in the national esteem than in the public (and preparatory) schools.[35]

The cult of athleticism was being brought to an end in the 1930s by educational philosophy's new emphasis on *individual* development. At the London University Institute of Education Sir Percy Nunn was expounding his philosophy of individualism while Kurt Hahn, first in Germany and later at Gordonstoun (1934), was pioneering an alternative tradition.[36] Closer to the experience of preparatory schools, Baden-Powell had extolled the virtues of Scouting, the development of which will be examined shortly.

Reasons for the continued hegemony of organized games and athleticism in English preparatory schools are not difficult to discern. As Mr E.S. Dudding, headmaster of Wolborough Hill School (1892–8), once observed: 'The boy who learns to play for his side at school will do good work for his country as a man.'[37] If patriotism was one factor in the development of the cult of athleticism, another was less high-minded. Some headmasters saw sporting activity as an insurance against ill-health. A well-exercised boy would hopefully be less prone to maladies and epidemics which could close down schools and cause financial loss or even personal ruin. Having thus recognized the value of good health through games, the committed headmaster needed to secure the right staff for the successful playing of games. Football and cricket having been established as vital activities, the preparatory school headmaster was forced into a position of his school excelling at these games or facing possible decline — rather like twentieth century academics faced by the 'publish or perish' syndrome. As Eric Parker observed: 'Get a Blue, and you will see your money back again.'[38] So the university class lists were annually searched for the young graduate with a Blue. These were the men who coached cricket and football, each in its season, every Wednesday and Saturday afternoon, either in the form of school practice or a school match. Competition was very keen.

So Thring's principle of 'every boy being good at something' began to prevail, for boys who were not good at ball games had to be given an activity in which they could find satisfaction. Whether or not such activities benefited the community at large, they were introduced in order to benefit the individual who undertook them.

By the autumn of 1898 a letter appeared in *The Times*, signed by 'M.D.'[39] which further accelerated such changes. The author — presumably the medical adviser of a public school — severely criticized the physical and muscular development of boys entering public schools. This letter may be interpreted as a direct criticism of the physical training preparatory schools gave their boys. As such it may seem a little unfair in view of the interest that preparatory schools took in physical training. It was commonplace for schools to employ an ex-drill sergeant to take charge of physical training. At Scaitcliffe School in 1898 Sergeant Lanning of Coopers Hill drilled the whole school once a week, and in the spring term of 1899 the gymnastic instructor from Windsor Barracks was to take over this duty.[40] At Matfield Grange in the 'seventies a Sergeant Lee came weekly to the school to drill the boys.[41] J.H. Simpson in *Schoolmaster's Harvest* describes how the drill sergeant at Hill Brow School, Eastbourne, emphasized Swedish drill. The drill sergeant was known as the Director of Physical Training at this school and

> it is certain that he was no mean all-round performer with the horizontal and parallel bars, Indian clubs, dumb-bells, ropes, rings, foils and boxing gloves ... it is equally certain that he sincerely believed that in introducing us to these he was improving both our bodies and our minds.[42]

As Table 8 has shown, the *PSR* took a keen interest in the development of physical training in preparatory schools. Wallace Maclaren, the son of Archibald Maclaren of Oxford University gymnasium and Summer Fields fame, contributed an article in the *PSR's* first issue on the subject of 'Physical training in preparatory schools'.[43] He distinguished between the objectives of mere games and those of physical training, concluding that the latter promoted health more effectively since it exercised more than just the lower limbs. In contrast to the board schools (and later the local authority schools), where Swedish and military drill were adopted at different stages in the development of physical training, both kinds of drill were used concurrently by many preparatory schools. Mr W.P. Herringham, a physician of St Bartholomew's Hospital, made a speech in 1906 to the Medical Officers of Schools Association (MOSA) in which he recognized the four chief methods of physical education: (1) Games; (2) Athletic Sports and Swimming: (3) Physical Drill and Gymnastics; and (4) Military Drill and Rifle Practice.[44]

By the early 1930s there were differing emphases emerging. In an article in the *PSR* G.H. Bickmore (Yardley Court) threw some doubt on the 'old fashioned' military-type of exercises which he thought were more suited to men than to boys.[45] Meanwhile it was becoming fashionable to refer to 'physical education', as opposed to 'physical training', which was thought to be the proper responsibility of a teacher rather than of a drill sergeant.[46] Despite the concern of the *PSR* and of individual headmasters about the subject in preparatory schools, at least one critic in the 'thirties felt that: 'the standard of Physical Training in our Preparatory schools is appreciably lower than that which pertains to the secondary schools.'[47] Whether or not he was justified in this view it is difficult to determine. But sixteen years and one World War later, an official publication of the IAPS[48] took great care to give a balanced and authoritative account of the physical side of preparatory school education.

The excitement stirred up by the Second Boer War and the burgeoning interest in the Officer Training Corps (OTC), established by Haldane, prompted the APS to take up rifle-shooting. Proposals for a rifle-shooting association were put forward and interested schools were put in touch with each other. An article entitled 'Rifle-shooting' appeared in the *PSR* in 1904.[49] The Rev. E.L. Browne (St Andrew's, Eastbourne), the Rev. Herbert Bull (Wellington, Westgate-on-Sea) and Mr Robert Vickers (Scaitcliffe) showed an early interest.

Captain Soltau-Symons, the Adjutant of Eton College Corps, offered in 1905 to organize an annual shooting competition amongst preparatory school VIIIs. For this purpose the War Office offered to lend carbines and to provide fifty rounds of ammunition per head free of charge to any school cadet corps.[50] Later that year Captain Soltau-Symons chaired a meeting of preparatory schoolmasters in London at which a committee, consisting of the Rev. E.L. Browne, the Rev. H. Bull and the Rev. A.J. de Winton (Gore Court), was formed to draw up a constitution for an association. The Preparatory Schools Rifle Association was duly formed in 1906 with Earl Roberts, KG, as President, and Mr A.G. Grenfell (Mostyn House) as Hon. Secretary. Grenfell had set up the Preparatory Schools Air Rifle Association the previous year and was happy to associate with the newly formed society. The Association started with fifty-five schools, of which twenty had previously taken part in rifle-shooting competitions. Within six months 120 schools had joined. Four years later the 'Lord Roberts Cup' was instituted. The introduction of rifle-shooting was expensive, involving not only a capital outlay on the provision of a range and the purchase of rifles, but also the recurring cost of ammunition. A satisfactory solution was found by one school: Aysgarth opened up a school tuck shop and used its profits to pay for the rifle club and shooting shed.[51]

Another venture with military origins was the Scout Movement. It was established by an old Carthusian, Robert Baden-Powell, the hero of Mafeking, who had been educated at a private preparatory school, Rose Hill. In 1908, towards the end of his distinguished military career, he had published his *Scouting for Boys*. This led to the nationwide formation of Boy Scout troops. Baden-Powell's original idea had been stimulated by the Japanese and his book launched a new movement with an egalitarian ethic — reflected in the scout uniform — and a new moral code.

The Scout Movement got off to a very slow start in the preparatory schools. There is some uncertainty as to which school first formed a scout troop. In an article in the *PSR*[52] A.H. Trelawney Ross (Sherborne) adjudicated in favour of Sandroyd School in Surrey. Then Miss Joy Malden claimed that

Windlesham House formed a scout patrol in 1908 soon after the publication of Baden-Powell's handbook.[53] Colonel Ulick de Burgh, the Deputy Chief Commissioner of the Scout Movement, played a considerable part in the creation of troops in the preparatory schools. Invited by the APS to a dinner in December 1909, de Burgh emphasized the high code of honour to which scouts bound themselves and the powers of initiative that scouting developed in growing boys. It was not until December 1911, however, that the APS held an *ad hoc* meeting to discuss the future of the Scout Movement in preparatory schools. At this meeting it was acknowledged that public schools were already concerned with the Scout Movement, Clifton being the first to have set up a troop.[54] Undoubtedly there were difficulties in running a scout troop in a preparatory school, as Windlesham had found. Scouting was intended to break down class barriers (cf. the fourth Scout Law), yet school hours, school regulations and school precautions against infection kept the boys safely away from the community outside.[55] The visit by Baden-Powell to Brighton in 1910 to inspect Sussex Scouts no doubt encouraged the Windlesham scouts to persevere in their early days. There were many problems. Only one hour a week could be given over to scouting; furthermore, there was the difficulty of finding suitable personnel to lead the scout patrols.[56] To train leaders a camp was held for potential school scout masters in Cheshire during August 1912.

After the First World War an attempt was made to strengthen the Scout Movement within the preparatory school world by the appointment of a liaison officer between the APS and the Boy Scouts Association. The headmaster of Sandroyd School, Mr F.V. Selfe, was one of two appointed.[57] But such was the extent of unawareness by the preparatory schools of the international and educational nature of the Scout Movement that a conference held in April 1919 on scouting in preparatory schools was very poorly attended. This poor support continued right into the 1930s. A survey in 1936 showed that out of 180 public schools 121 had a scout troop, whilst only 127 out of some 500 IAPS schools had scout troops or cub packs.[58] The strength of the Scout Movement had increased considerably by 1951 if the very supportive comments by the IAPS publication on *The Preparatory Schoolboy and His Education* are any gauge.[59] By 1960 there were 131 preparatory schools with cub packs and 142 with scout troops, making a total percentage of 55.5 having one or the other or both.[60] One school, however, paid more than lipservice to the Boy Scout Movement. This was the Downs, Colwall, which Geoffrey Hoyland (1920–40) reorganized on scout lines in the first year of his headmastership. His purpose was to solve three educational problems:

1 how to capture the cooperative team spirit for school work;
2 how to secure a healthy public opinion on matters like punctuality, cleanliness and good manners; and
3 how to extend the valuable educational experiences of responsibility and leadership to more boys.[61]

Recognizing, like Mrs Charles Malden earlier at Windlesham House, that the ethos of scouting was beneficial to a preparatory school regime, Hoyland went even further than she had done by designating the school as a 'Tribe', and dividing the seventy-odd boys into six packs of eight boys and two packs of 'pups' — the younger boys. Tribe leaders formed, with a few members of staff, a Tribe Council which became the hub around which the school revolved. Hoyland was still conducting the experiment eight years after its introduction.[62]

The Advance of Aesthetics

Thring's Uppingham saw the advent of manual and aesthetic subjects being not only the first English public school to have a gymnasium (1859) and the first to offer boys music, drawing and carpentry. Though preparatory schools had to distinguish their boys by preparing them for entry into public schools — which meant facility in the classical languages — even these afforded the good teacher an opportunity for comment and digression.

Moreover, some preparatory schools actually fostered aesthetics, as Lascelles Abercrombie (1881–1938), poet and critic, testified: his taste for music and literature was fostered at a preparatory school before he went on to Malvern College.[63] Richard G. Verney, Lord Willoughby de Broke, too, when he joined Winton House School in 1879 was under that 'most versatile of men', Mr Willingham F. Rawnsley, who, strong in outdoor pursuits, could also draw and paint and was interested in drama. (It is no wonder that Rawnsley and Geoffrey Hoyland, to be considered later, both wrote educational biographies of Edward Thring of Uppingham.)[64] Verney wrote of his preparatory school days: 'if education has indeed been properly described as "the equipment for a full life" we certainly got something very like education at Winton House.'[65] Winton House continued its aesthetic tradition when C.A. Johns, the novelist and man of letters, became its headmaster. In his youth C.A. Johns had been influenced by the aesthetic movement of the 1880s and 'got as much of the aesthete's pleasure out of running his own school as a younger man might have done from carrying a lily down Bond Street.'[66] Johns, who also played the 'cello, probably had greater depth in his teaching than many of his less able and less colourful fellow schoolmasters. Indeed Winton House was an exception amongst preparatory schools in its enjoyment of an aesthetic ethos. Manual craft, on the other hand, in the form of carpentry, was fairly well established amongst preparatory schools by the turn of the century. In a survey of 120 preparatory schools in 1900, ninety-one were equipped with a carpenter's shop.[67] Sixty-five per cent of schools surveyed had drawing on the timetable, but little time was allowed for its enjoyment. Some schools (Scaitcliffe, for example) had singing and instrumental music by which they were able to provide musical *divertissements* in the form of chamber music and well modulated singing in the school chapel on Sundays.[68] At Scaitcliffe, too, as with some other preparatory schools, dancing formed part of the extra-curricular activities.[69]

At the beginning of the twentieth century it was difficult to determine exactly what place the subject held in the average — if such there were — preparatory school. Wakeling Dry described it as probably lying

> somewhere between a harmless past-time politely conceded to an imaginative parent, proud in the possession of a budding Budoni or a possible Paderewski, (and) the desire of the prospectus-compiling pedagogue, who scents an increase in the alluring list of extras.[70]

Not quite so cynical but equally perceptive was the admission by G. Gidley Robinson (Hillside) in the Board of Education Report that preparatory schoolboys needed 'a richer curriculum ... discovering and developing attitudes which now languish for want of opportunity; less bookwork, [but the] teaching of how to use eyes and hands.'[71] Gidley Robinson advocated a greater allocation of time to art, music and handicrafts in preparatory schools in order to cultivate a love of beauty and give a healthy occupation in leisure hours.[72]

Keeping Up with Educational Strategies

But so imperative was the demand for efficiency in the classics that little time could be afforded for aesthetic appreciation. So *PSR* and IAPS may take some credit over the years for these changes in emphasis by the publication of articles which have reflected an educational milieu beyond the preparatory schools' world and thus kept them in the mainstream of educational development. The articles and correspondence on the subject of drawing and manual training at the turn of the century are a case in point. They kept preparatory schoolmasters abreast of the latest ideas of *Sloyd*, the Scandinavian educational concept of the training of the hand and eye.[73] The *PSR* published articles by leading contemporary educationists like Professor H.E. Armstrong and Dr William James of Harvard[74] and reports on conferences such as the Third International Drawing Congress.[75]

Belief in the great moral benefit arising from manual training[76] gave way by the later 'twenties and early 'thirties to the aesthetic considerations of art education. Amongst the protagonists of this 'new' school of thought was J.P. Nelson (Arden House) who advocated what he called 'creative education', based on the ideas of J.H. Whitehouse, in *Creative Education at an English School* (1928) in which art was seen as cross-disciplinary medium with the aim of fostering 'interest'.[77] When Nelson advocated the introduction of one public schoolmaster — Whitehouse — into preparatory schools he was criticized by another. — R. Gleadowe of Winchester —, for putting insufficient emphasis on the importance of form in aesthetic education.[78] Art as a preparatory school subject received a much needed impetus in 1938 with the founding of the

Society of Art Teachers, and another in the 1950s with the creation of the Society of Assistants Teaching in Preparatory Schools (SATIPS), which from its inception supported an increase in the influence of art in education and sought to arrange for an art exhibition at its 1957 conference.[79]

Music

Music was regarded in many public schools in the nineteenth century as a study inappropriate for boys. The ability to play an instrument or to sing was regarded as an accomplishment suitable only for girls. This masculine view of music was challenged when Thring introduced singing and instrumental music as compulsory subjects of the curriculum at Uppingham and invited musicians like Sterndale Bennett, Herr Joachim and Villiers Stanford to Uppingham.[80] But public schools at large displayed such little interest in the subject that music in the preparatory schools (except of course in choir schools) was no more than an *extra-curricular* activity for many years into the twentieth century.

An early contribution to the theory of preparatory school music was made by Professor Stewart Macpherson in 1912 when he suggested that the development of musical discrimination through the cultivation of aural perception was gaining ground over the old minority emphasis on acquiring a musical accomplishment. He saw music lessons for the many not as a means by which they might acquire musical techniques but as a means by which they might learn to appreciate music *per se*.[81] In the mid-1930s music in preparatory schools was still a peripheral subject with music teachers still mostly employed part-time. Their position in the teaching profession was strengthened in 1936 by the formation of the Music Masters Association (MMA). Preparatory school musicians were invited to join the MMA.[82] Through Dr Thatcher of Harrow overtures were made by the public schools for a closer rapport between public and preparatory school music teachers, and the IAPS was invited to elect two representatives to the MMA Council.

By the 1950s there were some schools like Arden House and The Downs where the curriculum was strongly orientated towards the arts. In such schools music formed more than a minimal part of the curriculum. Part-singing was not confined to the choir schools, and a Bach choir in a conventional preparatory school was capable of singing many of the major oratorios. Though such musically orientated schools concentrated, *inter alia*, on the building of gramophone record libraries to enhance musical appreciation, it was in the playing of musical instruments that the greatest strides were made.

By 1951, 75 per cent of boys in some schools were learning an instrument,[83] and this sometimes caused difficulties in both accommodation and staffing. Some schools have even made the playing of the violin in the second year compulsory.[84] In 1966 some 267 preparatory schools, 54 per cent of the total, had a specialist music room whilst 106 schools, some 21 per cent, had an orchestra.[85] The IAPS, in its customary supportive way, has encouraged the musical efforts of its schools. In 1972 it held its first IAPS orchestral course when seventy-seven players from thirty-one schools met to enjoy a musical experience. Both Benjamin Britten and Imogen Holst, who composed for the first concert, strongly supported this venture.[86] In 1979 the numbers had increased to 115 players from fifty-five schools who came together to practise and play Wagner, Britten, Sibelius, Dvorak, Fauré and Ravel.[87] If there is a centre of excellence in the preparatory school music world it must be in Suffolk where (i) each year the IAPS holds its orchestral course at Brandeston Hall and its concert at the Maltings, Snape; (ii) where Old Buckenham Hall School's alumni included Benjamin Britten and (iii) whose Governors included (until his death in 1980) Arthur Harrison who had so much to do with building up the traditions of the Maltings. Old Buckenham Hall School, run by the Sewell family,[88] has a strong music department. Apart from class music lessons, formal lessons in the piano, violin, 'cello, clarinet, flute, and brass instruments are given by visiting teachers. The school runs an orchestra, recorder groups, a percussion band and a choir.[89]

Notes

1 DAVID NEWSOME (1961) *Godliness and Good Learning*, John Murray. Cf. Chapters 1 and 4.
2 The first Oxford vs. Cambridge cricket match was played in 1827; the first inter-varsity boating match was rowed in 1829.
3 NORWOOD, *op. cit.*, p. 100. See also A.G. BRADLEY, *et al.* (1893) *A History of Marlborough College*, John Murray, p. 275.
4 *Ibid.*, p. 101.
5 NEWSOME, *op. cit.*, p. 212.
6 Cf. MAURICE FITZGERALD (1928) *Herbert Edward Ryle, Bishop of Winchester*, Macmillan, p. 17. In the 1860s RYLE attended Hill House School, Wadhurst, run by the Rev. R.H. WACE, with nine or ten boys in the school. This was typical in early days. Cf. p. 80.
7 C.T. WICKHAM (1909) *op. cit.*, p. 15.
8 A.C. BENSON (1924) *Memories and Friends*, John Murray p. 33.
9 EDWARD PEEL (1974) *Cheam School from 1645*, Gloucester, Thornhill Press, p. 280.
10 *Ibid.*, p. 282.
11 I.C.M. SANDERSON (1979) *A History of Elstree School*, privately printed p. 23. Between 1874 and 1900 Elstree boys made seventy-seven appearances at the Lords Eton vs. Harrow match. In 1885 seven out of eleven Harrow palayers were ex-Elstree. ARCHIE MACLAREN, Captain of Lancashire and England in five Test series against Australia was also from Elstree.
12 *Ibid.*, p. 22.
13 ARTHUR DUNN left Elstree to found Ludgrove, another leading football school.
14 Board of Education (1900) *Special Report No. 6*, Cf. A.J.C. DOWDING, 'Games in preparatory schools'.
15 C. HARRINGTON (1940) *Tim Harrington Looks Back*, John Murray.
16 Cf. 1892 Prospectus of Eaton House (now Orwell Park). I am grateful to Mrs SYLVIA BELLE, wife of the headmaster of Orwell Park, for this information.
17 I am indebted to Mr JACK DODD for this reference to the Rev. E.L. BROWNE.

18 Paul Spillane, (1977) *St Andrew's School 1877–1977,* Southampton, Hobbis the printers pp. 25–7.
19 From a typescript history of Stubbington House given to me by the headmaster, Mr A.R.W. Moore, to whom I am very grateful.
20 Amongst their opponents were regimental teams from the Norfolks and North Lancashires, the Royal Marine Light Infantry and Portsmouth Grammar School.
21 Lord Berners (1934) *First Childhood,* Constable, pp. 143–4.
22 T. Pellatt (1904) *Public Schools and Public Opinion,* Longmans, p. 59.
23 Prebendary C.W. Trevelyan (1970) 'Memoirs of Herbert Bull', typescript.
24 Maurice Baring (1922) *The Puppet Show of Memory,* Heinemann, p. 97.
25 *Ibid.,* p. 100.
26 Desmond Young (1963) *Try Anything Twice,* Hamish Hamilton, p. 18.
27 He left Loretto to become joint headmaster of Routenberg Preparatory School, Largs, Scotland. With Norman Maclachlan he built this into a thriving school before going south to Malvern. Cf. F.L. Robertson and N. Maclachlan (1903) *Routenburn Preparatory School Directory,* 2nd ed., Glasgow, pp. 7–9. I am grateful to Mr Trevor Hearl for drawing my attention to this school and for generously giving me his copy of the school's directory.
28 *Wells House Magazine,* December 1903. A.G. Grenfell in *Custodibus Custos* took a different view. He felt that association football for young boys was a good preparation for rugby football later, p. 67.
29 In 1909 the Dragon School adopted flannels, copying this Lorettonian custom from Wells House School through their mutual rugby fixtures.
30 Cf. *Aysgarth School Magazine,* 1, 3, December 1909 which refers to the then current popularity of golf and to its eight greens.
31 *Blackwood's Magazine,* 155, March 1894, p. 391.
32 Eric Parker, 'Private schools: Ancient and modern', *Longman's Magazine,* 29 November 1896–April 1897, p. 448.
33 S.S. Harris (1925) *The Master and His Boys,* Winchester, Warren and Son, pp. 69–70.
34 C. Sankey (1925) 'The evolution of the preparatory school', *PSR,* 9, 91, June, p. 144.
35 *The Journal of Education,* 63, March 1931, p. 180.
36 Cf. D.P. Leinster-Mackay (1976) 'The other tradition: An appreciation of Kurt Hahn', *Unicorn,* 2, 1, March, pp. 47–9.
37 Richard Watts (1977) *A History of Wolborough Hill School 1877–1977,* Newton Abbot, p. 8.
38 Eric Parker, *Longman's Magazine, op. cit.,* p. 449.
39 *The Times,* 24 October 1898, p. 14f.
40 *Scaitcliffe Notes,* December 1898, p. 5.
41 G.H. Harris (1943) *Vernon F. Storr,* SPCK, p. 3.
42 J.H. Simpson (1954) *Schoolmaster's Harvest,* Faber and Faber, p. 23.
43 *PSR,* 1, 1, July 1895, pp. 10–12.
44 *PSR,* 5, 34, July 1906, pp. 36–9.
45 *PSR,* 10, 103, July 1929, pp. 39–40.
46 Cf. *PSR,* 10, 111, March 1932, p. 289. Also *PSR,* 10, 113, November 1932, pp. 339–40.
47 R.J. Halcomb (1935) *The Vital Years,* Winchester, p. 14.
48 E.H. Allen and L.P. Dealtry (Eds) (nd) *The Preparatory Schoolboy and His Education,* Evans Brothers, pp. 43–7.
49 *PSR,* 4, 29, December 1904, p. 174.
50 *PSR,* 4, 30, March 1905, pp. 233–4.
51 *Aysgarth School Magazine,* 1, 1, December 1908.
52 *PSR,* 6, 49, July 1911, pp. 147–8.

53 G.H. WILSON and R.S. MALDEN, *op. cit.*, p. 101. There is some confusion over the date since Miss MALDEN claimed her troop was formed in 1907 which was *before* the publication of Baden-Powell's book.
54 *PSR*, 6, 51, March 1912, pp.236–7.
55 G.H. WILSON and R.S. MALDEN, *op. cit.*, p. 102.
56 *Ibid.*, pp. 102–3.
57 *PSR*, 8, 72, March 1919, p. 15.
58 *PSR*, 11, 123, March 1936. p. 221.
59 ALLEN and DEALTRY, *op. cit.*, p. 46.
60 PHILIP L. MASTERS, (1966), *Preparatory Schools Today*, A. and C. Black, p. 123.
61 GEOFFREY HOYLAND (1929) 'An experiment in preparatory school organization', *The Journal of Education and School World*, April, pp. 226–7.
62 *Ibid.*, p. 227.
63 *DNB.*
64 W.F. RAWNSLEY (1926) *Edward Thring, Maker of Uppingham School*, Kegan Paul, French, Trubner and Co., and GEOFFREY HOYLAND (1945) *The Man Who Made a School*, SCM Press.
65 RICHARD G. VERNEY (1924) *The Passing Years*, Constable, p. 118.
66 GERALD BRENAN (1962) *A Life of One's Own*, Hamish Hamilton, p. 57.
67 Board of Education (1900) *Special Report*, p. 33.
68 *Scaitcliffe Notes*, December 1902, pp. 6–7.
69 *Scaitcliffe Notes*, December 1901, p. 3.
70 WAKELING DRY (1900) 'The teaching of music in the private school', *Educational Review*, Vol. 2, p. 467.
71 Board of Education (1900) *Special Report*, p. 67.
72 M.E. SADLER (Ed.) (1908) *Moral Instruction and Training in Schools*, 2 vols, Longmans, Vol. 1, p. 160.
73 Cf. *PSR*, 1, 1, July 1895, p. 18; *PSR*, 1, 2, December 1895, p. 50; *PSR*, 9, March 1898, pp. 9–14; *PSR*, 5, 38, December 1907, p. 150; *PSR*, 5, 39, March 1908, pp. 191–2.
74 *PSR*, 5, 41, December 1908, p. 262.
75 *Ibid.*, pp. 266–9.
76 Cf. *PSR*, 5, 44, December 1909, pp. 390–1. Sir HARRY MICHAEL, 'Handwork in preparatory schools'.
77 *PSR*, 10, 106, June 1930, pp. 132–3. J.P.N., 'Creative education at a preparatory school'.
78 *PSR*, 10, 107, November 1930, p. 172.
79 *PSR*, 17, 2, October 1957, p. 64; *PSR*, 17, 3, February 1958, p. 70.
80 G.R. PARKIN, *op. cit.*, p. 227.
81 *PSR*, 6, 53, December 1912, pp. 306–9.
82 *PSR*, 10, 125, November 1936, p. 266..
83 E.H. ALLEN and L.P. DEALTRY, *op. cit.*, p. 27.
84 *Ibid.*, p. 28.
85 P.L. MASTERS, *op. cit.*, p. 121.
86 *PSR*, 26, 1, February 1977, p. 10.
87 *Conference*, 16, 3, October 1979, p. 23.
88 Linked with WILLIAM SEWELL, the founder of Radley.
89 Old Buckenham Hall School prospectus 1973, pp. 6–7.

14   Assistants

To many an unknown genius postmen bring
Typed notices from Rabbitarse and String.
(W.H. Auden, 1938)

Agenda for Assistants

The very first issue of the *PSR* in 1895 carried an article on 'The assistant master, past, present and future' which distinguished between the graduate usually to be found teaching in preparatory schools and those in public schools or quasi-public schools. The latter followed their college tutor's advice: 'never have anything to do with a preparatory school if you want to get on.' But for a graduate with a third class honours or pass degree who refused to emigrate there was little else to do, 'with the nip of poverty ... at his heels he perforce entered the door which [bade] him leave all hope behind.' The *PSR* article went on to make suggestions some of which were later to be taken up by the APS: an insurance scheme for assistant masters; a register of assistants; lower salaries initially to allow for increments; responsible and well-paid posts without supervision duties for successful preparatory schoolmasters over thirty; a system of student masterships for pre-university men wishing to take up schoolmastering after gaining their degrees. The fifth proposal conformed to the nineteenth century idea of teacher training, embodied in Dr Kay-Shuttleworth's pupil-teacher system of 1846: the future teacher would learn by a process of apprenticeship. The idea that certification should follow pupil-teachership and subsequent teacher training was a natural development. For the preparatory school assistant this was to take the form of a short teaching diploma course at Oxford University.[1]

The immediate cause of this diploma course was prodding by the Royal Commission on Secondary Education (1894–5), which asked the Association's view on professional training.[2] The Association replied with a memorandum which affirmed its strong belief in the need for such provision.[3]

The Oxford diploma course introduced in 1897 consisted of four weeks of lectures and extensive reading. The course was modest, being attended by seven teachers not all of whom were from preparatory schools. Some headmasters opposed the course, fearing that trained assistant masters would entertain ideas, contrary to their own, on how *their* schools should be run.[4] It seems that this early gesture towards professional training was inadequate. The Committee of Council on Education's 'Report of the Joint Committee on the Training of Teachers', published the following year, recommended that a graduate should not be permitted to teach until he had undergone a whole year's training — a measure which was not implemented till 1974. Such a scheme would have excluded 'birds of passage' who took posts in preparatory schools in order to pay off college debts and give themselves time to 'look around' for other employment — thus devaluing the status of the dedicated long-serving assistant master. Possibly because of the seeming inadequacy of the new Oxford Diploma course, Mr E.D. Mansfield (Lambrook) attempted to secure the adoption of the 1895 *PSR* proposal for a student-mastership scheme. But the Association gave him little support and the scheme was temporarily put to rest at the eighth annual conference in 1899.

With many joining the Colours the glut of schoolmasters between 1870 and 1890 that Baron discerned had been, by 1914, converted into a severe shortage.[5] Thus the matter of the professional training of assistant masters was not resurrected until the 1920s following a period of short supply because of the ravages of the First World War. The staffing shortage was made worse by recognition of the need for a three years' apprenticeship scheme to ensure the entry into the profession of a body of ex-public school boys as trained assistant masters.[6] Charles Mansfield of Wixenford School, in correspondence with the *PSR*, called for united action and pressed for the desirability of employing *trained* assistant masters in the preparatory schools.[7] A similar plea was made in 1926 by F.J.R. Hendy, Director in the Training of Teachers, Oxford. He emphasized the importance of both practical experience under close supervision and the acquisition of educational theory.[8]

This renewed interest in teacher training by the Association led to the development of IAPS refresher courses. The first of these, held in April 1930, was in mathematics. Following the success of this course it was decided to set up machinery in the form of a Refresher Courses Committee to organize such courses annually.[9] The Association's initiative in mathematics was followed by a similar course in geography, through the auspices of the Geographical Association. A three-day refresher course was held at Harrow from 22 to 24 April 1931, attended by forty-seven preparatory and public school masters.[10] Refresher courses were held in mathematics in 1932; in geography at Harrow in 1933; in French at Dieppe in 1933; and in physical training at Loughborough in the same year. A second French refresher course was held again at Dieppe in 1934, whilst in 1935 Hertford College, Oxford, played host to similar courses in Latin, English, divinity and music. These refresher courses had the effect of making preparatory schools aware of current educational Deweyan philosophy (which stressed the cooperation between the teacher and the taught), and of the bi-polar theory of Sir John Adams (who made the point that a good teacher was not so much teaching a subject as teaching his pupils'. The courses laid emphasis on the teaching of the whole man and recognized the importance of affective subjects such as handicrafts, art and music.[11] These ideas received reinforcement at an educational conference at Oxford in April 1936 on New Ideals in Education.[12] Once having gained momentum these refresher courses became a regular feature of the IAPS calendar, with a physical training course at Loughborough in 1938, and English, Latin, French, mathematics and educational teaching-theory and practice courses being held in Oxford just after the outbreak of war. Whereas the numbers attending these conferences in the early years had been in the thirties and forties, the post-war refresher courses were attracting more than 100 members.

An assessment of the refresher courses scheme was made by M.L. Jacks, Director of the Oxford Department of Education, just before the outbreak of war.[13] He confirmed that generally the preparatory schoolmaster was averse to taking a year off for postgraduate training in education. He therefore recommended refresher courses as the best method of training masters with some experience, although he had to admit that such courses were too short and gave insufficient emphasis to the study of pedagogy.

Steps were taken after the war to remedy the defects of the situation noted by M.L. Jacks. After much deliberation an eighteen month IAPS training scheme for non-graduate assistant staff[14] — of whom there was an increasing number — was instituted in September 1951. The first course, of which the first session took place at Worcester College, Oxford, began modestly with twenty-five members under the directorship of Mr G.W. Paget, a retired senior staff inspector from the Ministry of Education. In many years, therefore, the IAPS was committed to the concept of teacher training in a manner somewhat different from the national post-war emergency training scheme, but also it was continuing to run refresher courses for its graduate or certificated teachers. As if to set a seal on its commitment to teacher training, the Association was asked by the Oxford Institute of Education to nominate an IAPS representative on the Institute's advisory committee.[15]

The Registration of Assistant Masters

Closely linked with the professional training of assistant masters was the question of their registration. From the date of its foundation in 1873 the scholastic agency, Gabbitas-Thring, kept records of assistant preparatory schoolmasters for whom it had found posts.[16] But this register was by its nature incomplete, and it was not accessible because it was held in *private* custody. More significant developments took place outside the preparatory school world in the form of a *national* Register of Teachers. The Bryce Commissioners asked for the views of the Association on the registration of teachers as proposed by the Select Committee of the House of Commons of 1891.[17] The Association was in favour of registration in principle, and in favour also of registered teachers' being qualified both academically and professionally.[18] Thus committed to the principle of registration, the Association began to debate in earnest the formation of such a register for preparatory schoolmasters. There was likely to be general support from assistant masters, who would see their registration, along with public school masters, as establishing a bridge between the two types of school; thus a preparatory schoolmaster could entertain the possibility of his elevation to a teaching appointment in a public school. Moreover registration, with its attendant emphasis on qualifications, might perhaps lead to a better deal for the qualified assistant master.[19] To bring these ambitions closer to fruition a Joint Agency for assistant masters and tutors was set up in 1904. This was recognized by ten teachers' associations, including the Association of Headmasters of Preparatory Schools and the Headmasters' Conference. Meanwhile a national Teachers' Registration Council had been set up by Order-in-Council in 1902[20] to complement the Joint Agency. The two had differing functions. The Teachers' Registration Council was concerned with the recognition of teachers as qualified professional individuals, whilst the Joint Agency was concerned with placement, and to that extent complemented the private scholastic agency, Gabbitas-Thring.

The history of the Teachers' Registration Council is intensely complicated, stretching over a decade from 1902 to 1912[21] and beyond. Interminable wrangling between elementary and secondary school teachers led by turns to its abandonment and resuscitation. The original register contained separate columns for elementary and secondary teachers. This arbitrary classification gave cause for such indignation among elementary teachers that the first register was quickly abandoned. The reconstitution of the Teachers' Registration Council in 1912, again by Order-in-Council, had its origin in the Education (Administrative Provisions) Act of 1907 which got rid of the divisive two-column entry. This development made it more likely that a qualified preparatory school assistant would be regarded as an acceptable candidate for a public school's teaching post. The permanent establishment of a Teachers' Registration Council had one constitutional effect on the APS in 1916 when the Annual Conference resolved to equate 'registration' with 'qualification' in future applications for membership of the Association.[22] At the assistant master level such registration had already for several years been a *sine qua non* for an appointment to a good school.[23]

The institution of a universal teachers' registration council had several implications, which were beneficial. More than professional recognition was involved. As early as 1898, when the problem of 'birds of passage' was still in evidence, Eric Parker had raised the matter of salary differentials.[24] Clearly there was a need, argued Parker, for a salary scale which would recognize long service. Teacher shortages and the need to offer more attractive salaries and a career structure had in 1919 led to the introduction of the Burnham Salary

Scales[25] in LEA maintained schools. The preparatory school assistant master now had a yardstick by which he could judge his own position. In 1920 the salary scales being considered by the LEAs for their graduate masters were £240–£500, and for non-graduates £190–£400. The recession of the following five years brought salary cuts for all teachers. But Oxford and Cambridge graduates earning £120–£150 in preparatory schools in 1925 could take little comfort from this, even if many of them were also provided with board and lodging,[26] when they saw their colleagues in elementary schools earning as much as £180–£360,[27] with *initial* salaries in some well-known public schools ranging from £300 to £400 and climbing to a maximum of between £700 and £800.[28] It is not surprising that well-qualified Oxford and Cambridge graduates felt that preparatory schoolmastering was only second best. A committee set up in 1919 under the chairmanship of the Marquess of Crewe to inquire into the position of the classics readily recognized the depressed status of the poorly paid preparatory schoolmaster.[29]

A.L. Maycock of the University of Cambridge Appointments Board tried to resolve the continuing problem in 1938 when he suggested that masters should be required to serve in preparatory schools before applying for posts in public schools. He felt that provided prospects were improved, a salary of £160–£180, plus board and lodging, might be a satisfactory initial salary. After seven or eight years a preparatory schoolmaster might expect to receive £300 per annum plus board and lodging. A school of a reasonable size might finally pay £600 per annum to a master who had both drive and experience, or might offer him a junior partnership.[30] This practice of partnerships is today much less characteristic of preparatory school administration.

Invoking State Endorsement

The March 1900 issue of the *PSR* made a forecast that 'Registration — Inspection — Training — the whole organization of Secondary Education — possibly even State competition' could be expected in the next ten years to become accomplished fact. Contrary to possible prejudiced belief, the preparatory schools eagerly sought this outside intervention.

The whole question of inspection of schools was tied up closely with those of registration and recognition. With the establishment of a two-column teachers' register in 1902 — no matter how ephemerally — it became imperative for assistant masters to achieve status as secondary schoolmasters if they were not to be submerged in the mass of elementary schoolteachers. To achieve this status, they must have worked in a 'recognized' school, a 'recognized' school being one that was recognized as efficient by the Board of Education after inspection by Her Majesty's Inspectorate of Schools. It became very desirable, therefore, that a school be 'recognized' if it were to continue to enjoy satisfactory staffing. Under Section 3 of the 1899 Board of Education Act the Board was willing to inspect in a limited number of schools annually their administration, the condition of the school buildings (including sanitation, boarding houses and recreational facilities) and the curriculum. Unfortunately this first scheme of free inspection did not apply to preparatory schools, which were expected to pay prohibitive costs for their inspections. By 1908 several requests by preparatory school headmasters for their schools to be inspected had been virtually 'turned down'[31] on grounds of cost. So great was the cost that by 1913 only five preparatory schools had been inspected and recognized. It therefore became a matter of urgency for preparatory schools to be recognized as part of the integral structure of public schools. They would then, like them, qualify for free inspection. As we have seen, this status was achieved in 1914, despite internal suspicions,[32] and the Board of Education undertook to inspect without charge, an annual quota of twenty preparatory schools, all of which must have at least thirty boys. Despite these limitations, the principle had been established through co-operation between preparatory and public schools.

H.A.L. Fisher's Education Act of 1918 introduced a new measure of central control when it stipulated[33] that unless a preparatory school were already recognized as efficient, the headmaster was to send to the Board of Education the name, the address and a short description of the school, under penalty of £10 for non-compliance. Additional pressure was applied when the Association itself encouraged preparatory schools to apply for inspection. The Chairman of the IAPS in 1929, A.S. Grant (Hillside, Reigate), advised his fellow members to seek inspection if they had not already done so. He reminded them that under Section 147 of the 1921 Consolidating Education Act the Board had the right to demand entry to inspect any school. He noted that up to March 1928 some seventy to eighty IAPS schools had been inspected and given 'recognized' status.[34] By March 1931 the number of recognized schools had risen to 142 out of a total of 528 schools. In that year the Association decided to refuse election to the headmaster of an unrecognized school unless he gave an undertaking to have his school inspected. This decision was quite crucial for the institutional health of the Association. The IAPS was now using 'recognition' as its own entrance examination. Its merits were that it was (a) free; (b) impartial; and (c) the more credible because it was conducted by inspectors who were appointed by the Board of Education and owed no allegiance to the independent schools. A huge number of preparatory schools would probably not have bothered to seek recognition unless its possession had been a condition of IAPS membership. Parents seeking schools looked only at IAPS schools because they knew all IAPS schools were 'recognized as efficient'. 'Recognized' schools joined IAPS because they knew parents would respect the IAPS label. One valuable product of the system of inspections was the beneficial advice that HMIs were able to offer the schools as an outcome of their inspections. In 1934, for example, an informal meeting was held at the Board of Education between certain Council members and four HMIs who had inspected some 150 IAPS schools.[35] The inspectors' criticisms were constructive.

Though the inspectorate made no attempt to control or interfere in the running of the schools, many headmasters remained suspicious of inspection. One such was A.E. Lynam of the Dragon School. On the occasion of the school's first inspection in 1930 he wrote: 'We have held back through a disinclination to invite an interference which we felt in some way might militate against our freedom of action and opportunities for experiment.'[36] He had to admit, however, that the inspectors were helpful and that they had not sought to imply that their suggestions were mandatory.

By February 1939 approximately 300 IAPS schools had been inspected and 'recognized as efficient' by the Board of Education. The process of inspection received a fillip after the Second World War with the creation in 1948 of an IAPS panel of inspectors, the main purpose of which was to remove suspicion about inspection.

Coming to Terms with the Twentieth Century

In 1912 'Custos', a fierce critic of 'Our Gentlemen's Schools', wrote:

> One of the first reforms is the matter of the masters. It is time that more should be expected from the masters than a healthy aptitude for games. And the reforms, beginning with the 'preps', should cut right through the public schools. It is time to end the preferential treatment of the cloth, with its wooden, feudal outlook. In these democratic days, what is wanted is initiative, adaptability, courage, world common-sense, not the tutorial pedantry of sacerdotalism.[37]

In some respects this attack on the preparatory school cleric was misplaced. Undoubtedly the more conservative preparatory schools remained devotees of a highly classical and intellectual curriculum in which books and blackboards were the only visual aids. The reputation for coaching scholarship winners of the Rev. Dr C.E. Williams and the Rev. E.H. Alington at Summer Fields would be a case in point. There were other schools where masters were less steeped in the scholarly (and clerical) tradition. Such men were perhaps more likely to avail themselves of mechanical aids to teaching. Some of these, such as Pathescope — the new portable cinema — were coming on to the market at roughly the time when 'Custos' was fulminating against the preparatory school cleric.[38] Some did not readily admit the value of the cinematograph as a teaching aid. It was one thing to use a cinematograph to amuse boys on a wet Saturday afternoon; it was quite another to make use of it in the classroom. Yet as H.C. King observed in 1926,

> In a sense all preparatory schoolmasters are faddists, and it is well they should be. Fads are merely experiments and without experiments there will be no progress in education.[39]

If there were some who deprecated the use of the cinematograph as a teaching aid, there were others who did not. Major W.R. Creighton, in an article in the *PSR* entitled 'The Use of the Cinema in Schools' was very optimistic about the cinematograph's potential and claimed that the educational film could be a supplement to the text book.[40] One anonymous contributor to the *PSR*, who had installed a cinematograph in his school as early as 1920, was enthusiastic about its educational value. He advised his colleagues to be clear about their objectives when showing a film, and suggested ways in which the film could be integrated with classroom work.[41] The pioneering spirit of this preparatory schoolmaster can be gauged by a *Times* report of 1930 that only 230 schools of any kind had a cinema.[42] The willingness of preparatory schools to experiment was shown when several of them took up an offer by the Western Electric Company to exhibit films to their pupils.[43] The IAPS supported the use of films in school. In 1933 Mr B.D. Robinson, the Assistant Secretary to the Commission on Educational and Cultural Films, contributed an article to the *PSR* in which he made extravagant claims for the visual image which were seemingly innocent of the relative merits of 'visile' learning and 'audile' learning.[44]

It is difficult to gauge the extent of commitment of the preparatory schools to the use of educational film: although the response of schools generally to film and cinema was very limited,[45] it is very likely that preparatory schools were in the van in this area of educational technology. Certainly a boarding school which saw in the cinematograph a solution to the problem of weekend leisure hours would be early in the market. Machines bought for that more pressing need now could be used later for more formal educational purposes.

The use of the radio in preparatory schools made very slow progress in the early days. School broadcasting was instituted in 1926 yet three years later, at the time of the first meeting of the Central Council for School Broadcasting, the IAPS representative on the Council was unable to raise any interest amongst his colleagues in the use of school broadcasting as a teaching aid.[46] This lack of interest by the preparatory schools may have reflected the divergences between them and the maintained elementary schools for whom the programmes were largely geared. As late as 1952, only 18 per cent of the IAPS were using school broadcasts in their teaching compared with the national figure of 50 per cent.[47] It probably also reflects discrimination or discernment on the part of preparatory schools that they did not allow the developments of modern science to dispossess the teacher, to any appreciable extent, of the function of teaching, in the traditional sense of the word. How often do third rate teachers utilize first rate programmes to assist in their flagging efforts in an overcrowded classroom? Similarly with the advent of television, although the IAPS had a senior representative on the Schools Broadcasting Council in the person of L.P. Dealtry, the future secretary of the Association, the schools themselves made only limited use of television as a teaching aid. The report of a survey conducted in 1957 on the use of television in schools showed that because of their wider vocabulary preparatory school-boys were able to overcome difficulties involving language and concentration more quickly than their peers in maintained schools. It was possible, for instance, for preparatory school boys of eleven to thirteen to take benefit from scientific and mathematical programmes designed for secondary modern children from fifteen to sixteen.[48] It can be argued that the reluctance of preparatory schools to use school broadcasts extensively was not caused by a lack of innovatory spirit. A more positive reason would be that with small classes in preparatory schools there was less need for radio and television, whose main virtue is their ability to deal with large numbers.

Prebends for Poets

A beneficial by-product of the preparatory schools was the opportunity it gave to men of literary talents, to novelists and poets, to earn a living in relatively pleasant surroundings. When W.H. Auden was at The Downs, Colwall, Stephen Spender, Christopher Isherwood and Nevil Coghill used to visit him. T.S. Eliot's time as assistant master at Highgate Junior School in 1916 has been captured by John Betjeman in *Summoned by Bells*:

> The American master, Mr Eliot
> That dear good man, with Prufrock in his head[49]

If Eliot's stay at Highgate was short, L.A.G. Strong's at Summer Fields, Oxford, from 1915 lasted for fifteen years. Engaged as a general subjects master by the Rev. Dr C.E. Williams, teaching Latin, French, English and arithmetic for £120 a year, Strong was given a more specialized responsibility of teaching the boys creative essay writing and paid £150 by way of reward. Readers of his *Green Memory* will remember his picture of the successful, if mechanical, teaching methods of Dr Williams and the Rev. Alington at Summer Fields.[50] To one of Strong's ex-pupils, the High Court Judge, Sir Denys Buckley, his arrival at Summer Fields marked a 'decrease in institutionalised formality which has so much ameliorated preparatory school life in the last forty years.'[51]

L.A.G. Strong recruited another young man of parts: C. Day Lewis. Day Lewis, who had got a Fourth in Greats, was persuaded by Strong to apply for a vacancy at Summer Fields, and was much impressed with his fellow staff at the 'Eton Nursery'. But he too winced at the teaching of classics as not leaving 'much room for individual method. Over the years a system had been worked out which was, from the scholarship-winning angle, as near foolproof as any system can be'.[52]

After leaving Summer Fields Day Lewis went to Larchfield School, Glasgow, and then to Cheltenham Junior School, a post obtained for him by Maurice Bowra, then a governor of Cheltenham College. But Day Lewis was not temperamentally suited to be a preparatory schoolmaster. Reprimanded by the Junior School headmaster for publishing lyrics, he adopted the pseudonym of Nicholas Blake and published a detective story about a preparatory school like Summer Fields or Cheltenham Junior School. After further scrapes with authority, he resigned his post to become a freelance writer. Yet another poet and writer who became a preparatory schoolmaster before becoming a member like Day Lewis of the Communist Party and joining the staff of Alleyn's School, Dulwich, was Edward Upward who taught the author of this book. Upward's brother, J.M. Upward, ran Port Regis Preparatory School, Shaftesbury.

These and other young men of parts were epitomized by Cecil Day Lewis paying tribute in his address at Strong's funeral:

> That is why a generation of boys at Summer Fields have remembered him affectionately as the man who gave them their first feeling for literature; and why so many other students will be grateful to him all their lives for the insights he gave them into poetry....[53]

SATIPS

Though a few preparatory schoolmasters belonged to the Assistant Masters' Association (AMA),[54] a body of 5000 strong, it was not until after the First World War that they formed their own Association of Staffs of Preparatory Schools (ASPS). From 1920 onwards, this body, more like a trade union than an association of professionals, had as its immediate objectives 'to get in touch with the council of the APS on all matters affecting the interest of their staffs such as pensions, salaries, etc.'[55] Its ineffectiveness can be gauged by the fact that at the end of thirty years only 50 per cent of the assistants had the right to pension. Despite its self-serving nature the ASPS did not survive long in a period of economic hard times followed by total war. Assistants in preparatory schools had to wait until 1953 before achieving a thriving association. Then the Rev. John Williams, senior master at The Hawthorns, Redhill, started the Society of Assistants Teaching in Preparatory Schools (SATIPS). In a letter to the Editor of the *PSR* he suggested that 'staffs of IAPS schools ought to be able to contribute as a body to the welfare of the association and its boys'.[56] He suggested that with the provision of training schemes and opportunities to meet, a highly skilled body of men and women could add to the strengths of the IAPS. The main objectives of the new Society were agreed upon at its first annual general meeting in April 1953. They were as follows:

1. to draw more closely together assistant teachers in preparatory schools and to provide a channel for the expression of their opinion;
2. to advance the interests of education, especially those affecting preparatory schools;
3. to protect and improve the status of persons engaged in teaching in preparatory schools;
4. to procure relevant information and circulate it amongst members;
5. to take part in or send delegates to meetings and conferences; and
6. to provide facilities for intercourse and the exchange of ideas between headmasters and assistants.[57]

From the beginning the SATIPS, unlike the IAPS, admitted both men and women to membership. Concerned from the beginning with standards in the curriculum and with teaching methods, the Society has assiduously tried to improve them. For example, SATIPS decided in 1954 to arrange for the pooling of ideas in English subjects, classics, French and mathematics.[58] Since the 1950s, SATIPS membership has gradually gained strength, as Table 9 shows.

Table 9. Membership of SATIPS, 1954–78

1954	100
1955	100+
1956	198 in 117 schools
1958	200
1959	320 in 200 schools
1960	500 (more than half from IAPS schools)
1963	c.700
1978	c.1300

Although SATIPS has developed into a society concerned with the improvement of the preparatory school curriculum and with raising the standard of teaching through an exchange of ideas, one of its earlier ventures was a survey into preparatory school salaries in 1954 which indicated a wide discrepancy between schools. The average salary in the survey was £430 per annum, the highest salary £650 and the lowest £165 with board and lodging provided.[59] It is not surprising, therefore, that during the early years the prevention of injustice to assistants was one of the major concerns of the Society. From the beginning though, it has been one of the basic assumptions that salaries are a matter of private determination between assistant and head. It is significant that this matter of salaries and conditions of service did not come to a head until 1962/63 when the IAPS and SATIPS came together in a spirit of amity and a search for understanding. A conference, arranged in London in January 1963 on the theme of 'Conditions of Service', was attended by three senior members of the IAPS — L.P. Dealtry, R.A. Harrison and R.J.S. Curtis. This conference brought about healthy mutual understanding.[60] In the 1950s SATIPS gave much attention to the Common Entrance Examination. A committee was set up in 1954 to report on the CEE and developed into the SATIPS Education Committee. Having achieved a more satisfactory *modus vivendi* on salaries and conditions of employment SATIPS members turned their minds with renewed vigour to the curriculum and to the IAPS Report, *Foundations*. The curriculum was debated in the columns of the SATIPS journal. This information debate led to the creation of Subject Groups and to the production of Subject Broadsheets for English and physical education and sports. To promote reform of the curriculum and the CEE, SATIPS decided to invite public schoolmasters to share in their deliberations. This led to further cooperation between assistant masters at the two levels,[61] complementing the work of the Joint Standing Committee of the HMC and IAPS and enhancing the chances of satisfactory solutions to the problems of the curriculum and the CEE. In the 1960s some attempts were made by SATIPS to establish links with teachers in the maintained schools. A two-day conference took place in September 1963 during which thirty-two SATIPS members visited London primary and secondary schools and seven preparatory schools were visited by LCC teachers.

The continuing strength of the Society has rested upon the meetings and conferences which have been held since 1953. The one-day meetings in London on general topics began in 1954, whilst the three-day residential conferences date from 1957.[62] By 1961 members in the North of England felt the need for their own Northern Conferences, the first of which was held in St John's College, York, in January 1962. This development coincided with the setting up of district branches of SATIPS. In 1966 full-time staff serving in schools belonging to the Association of Head Mistresses of Preparatory Schools were admitted to full membership of SATIPS.[63]

During all these developments of the Society there has been a 'Newsletter' which first appeared in November 1954. By the end of 1962 this 'Newsletter' had developed into a twenty-four-page publication and has subsequently been replaced by the Society's journal, *News and Views*. In the late twentieth century the assistant teachers have achieved through their Society, with its district branches, its subject groups, its group broadsheets, its annual meetings and its journal, a cohesion such as the IAPS achieved at the beginning of the twentieth century. The development of both the Association and the Society has worked for the benefit of the schools themselves. Preparatory school assistants have progressed far since their early reliance for employment on educational agencies such as Gabbitas-Thring.

Notes

1 This course had been made possible by the creation, in 1890, of university day training colleges for the professional training of secondary school graduate teachers following the recommendations of the CROSS Commission Minority Report (1888). Mr M.W. KEATINGE was the first director of studies in 1897. See LEILA TOMLINSON (1968) 'Oxford University and the training of teachers: The early years (1892–1921),' *British Journal of Educational Studies*, 16, October, p. 299.
2 BRYCE Commission Report 1895, Vol. 5, pp. 330–1. Letter dated 20 June 1894 from WILLIAM N. BRUCE to the Rev. HERBERT BULL.
3 *Ibid.*, pp. 331–3.
4 *PSR*, 2, 8, December 1897, p. 97.
5 *PSR*, 7, 59, December 1914, p. 69. Cf. G. BARON (1952) 'The Secondary Schoolmaster 1895–1914', PhD, University of London, pp. 50–3.
6 *PSR*, 8, 80, December 1921, p. 271.
7 *PSR*, 8, 84, March 1923, p. 417.
8 *PSR*, 9, 95, December 1926, p. 287.

9 *PSR*, 10, 108, March 1931, p. 196.
10 *PSR*, 10, 109, June 1931, p. 223.
11 *PSR*, 11, 121, June 1935, pp. 118–19.
12 *PSR*, 11, 123, March 1936, p. 201.
13 *PSR*, 12, 132, March 1939, pp. 18–19.
14 The eighteen-month course for non-graduates began with a conference at Oxford after which students studied at home, coming together formally again in April and September. There was no formal examination but a certificate was issued after satisfactory completion of the course. This consisted of reading selected books, visits to independent schools and maintained schools and a considerable number of essays and reports. Cf. MICHAEL P. RAWLINS (1957). 'The IAPS Training Course', *PSR*, 16, 12, February, pp. 12–14. The scheme came to an end in 1979.
15 *PSR*, 17, 10, (New Series) May 1952, p. 42.
16 When GABBITAS-THRING moved offices in 1938 all pre-1914 records were destroyed. Information from letter in my possession, dated 25 August 1970, from GABBITAS-THRING.
17 BRYCE, *op. cit.*, p. 331. The question of a teachers' registration council had a longer history, going back to 1879 when a Bill to set up such a body was instigated by the College of Preceptors.
18 *Ibid.*, p. 332.
19 *PSR*, 2, 15, March 1900, pp. 91–4.
20 The original Order-in-Council of 6 March 1902 was modified by a second of 11 August 1902.
21 Cf. ASHER TROPP (1957) *The School Teacher*, Heinemann, pp. 195–8. Cf. also G. BARON (1954) 'The teachers' registration movement', *British Journal of Educational Studies*, 2, 2, May.
22 *PSR*, 7, 66, March 1917, p. 265.
23 *PSR*, 7, 61, July 1915, pp. 125–6.
24 ERIC PARKER (1898) 'Preparatory school assistant masters,' *Longmans Magazine*, No. 184, February, p. 337.
25 Lord BURNHAM was the first chairman of the Standing Joint Committee concerned with establishing national salary scales for teachers.
26 *The Times Educational Supplement*, 7 February 1925, Special Article.
27 ASHER TROPP, *op. cit.*, p. 275, Appendix III.
28 *The Times Educational Supplement, op. cit.*
29 *The Classics in Education*, 1921, Report of Committee appointed by the Prime Minister, p. 129.
30 *PSR*, 11, 130, June 1938, p. 456.
31 Cf. (ooo) pp. 174.
32 The day preparatory schools did not like the idea of a copy of the HM Inspectors' report being sent to the LEA office, fearing that their autonomy might thereby be weakened.
33 Section 28: Collection of information respecting schools.
34 *PSR*, 10, 103, July 1929, p. 46.
35 *PSR*, 11, 119, November 1934, p. 36.
36 C.H. JAQUES (1977) *A Dragon Century*, Blackwell, p. 130.
37 *The English Review*, September 1912, p. 310.
38 *PSR*, 6, 55, July 1913, Advertisements.
39 H.C. KING (1926) 'Private and preparatory schools', *The Journal of Education and School World*, April, p. 253.
40 *PSR*, 10, 102, March 1929 Major W.R. CREIGHTON 'The use of cinema in schools', pp. 15–19.
41 *PSR*, 10, 104, November 1929, pp. 67–9.
42 *PSR*, 10, 107, November 1930, p. 158.

43 *PSR*, 10, 108, March 1931. This was an attempt to develop talking pictures in education.
44 *PSR*, 10, 115, June 1933, pp. 401–2. The limitations of television for educational purposes are more readily recognized today.
45 *PSR*, 14, 3 (New Series), February 1946, pp. 17–20. Article by J. MACKAY-MURE, 'The film in education', which indicates that despite advances in film technology which caused a boom in the commercial world, in schools it was of only limited interest.
46 *PSR*, 10, 102, March 1929, p. 1.
47 *PSR*, 17, 9 (New Series), February 1952, pp. 4–5.
48 *PSR*, 17, 2, October 1957, p. 19.
49 JOHN BETJEMAN (1960) *Summoned by Bells*, John Murray, p. 29.
50 L.A.G. STRONG (1961) *Green Memory*, Methuen, pp. 199–200.
51 RICHARD USBORNE (Ed.) (1964) *A Century of Summer Fields*, Methuen, p. 131.
52 C. DAY LEWIS (1969) *The Buried Day*, Chatto and Windus, p. 184.
53 R. USBORNE (Ed.), *op. cit.*, pp. 173–4. Cf. also C. DAY LEWIS (1944) *Poetry for You. A Book for Boys and Girls on the Enjoyment of Poetry*, Basil Blackwell.
54 *PSR*, 7, 58, July 1914, p. 51.
55 *PSR*, 8, 77, December 1920, p. 168.
56 *PSR*, 17, 10 (New Series), May 1952, p. 11.
57 *PSR*, 16, 2 (New Series), October 1953, pp. 64–5.
58 *PSR*, 16, 5 (New Series), October 1954, p. 64.
59 *PSR*, 20, 1, February 1971, p. 44.
60 *PSR*, 20, 2, June 1971, p. 52.
61 *Ibid.*
62 Cf. DAVID PILGRIM (1978) 'Salute to SATIPS', *Conference*, 15, 2, June, pp. 6–7.
63 *PSR*, 19, 2, June 1966, p. 45.

Part 4

Coming to Terms with Contemporaneity

15   Much Ado about Greek

> The belief in a system of education exclusively classical is an 'idol of
> the theatre', which will not easily be obliterated from the enchanted
> glass of the public judgment.
> (Rev. F.W. Farrar (1867) *Essays on a Liberal Education*)

Greek Goes

Following up its resolutions of 1908,[1] the HMC wasted no time in reorientat-
ing the preparatory school curriculum. The moment was propitious. The
archon of antiquity, Dr James, chief opponent of change, left Rugby for St
John's College, Oxford, whilst the Board of Education had stressed the need
for better standards of English in secondary schools.[2] With the Board's
view, the Rev. the Hon. E. Lyttelton publicly agreed: his *Schoolboys and
Schoolwork*[3] (1909) though genuflecting cursorily to Greek[4] seemed to devote
his theme to the teaching of English. He wrote: 'Among languages in education
the primary place belongs to the mother-tongue.'[5] English takes pride of place
in his ideal curriculum for preparatory schools for 'to teach a young boy his
own language is to teach the power of expressing accurately the ideas that are in
the mind.[6] Since he was now headmaster of Eton, and was a member of the
common entrance board of management, his views carried weight. Moreover
his book was prefaced by Dr H.M. Burge of Winchester, the chairman of the
sub-committee of the HMC on curriculum reform for boys aged between nine
and sixteen, set up after the resolution of 1908. And when that appeared in
1909/10, Mr Gidley Robinson wrote: 'If loyally acted upon by general
agreement among the public schools ... [it] marks a definite stage in the
evolution of the preparatory curriculum and its adjustment to modern needs.'[7]

For this report, in addition to emphasizing the need for a thorough
grounding in English throughout the preparatory school course, recognized
the claims of subjects like geography and handicraft to be included too. It also
recommended that French be taught on modern lines as a compulsory and as a

scholarship subject. German, on the other hand (possibly in the light of contemporary anti-German feeling) was to be excluded. Greek was to be started only after a good grounding had been attained in English, French and Latin. Burge and his colleagues, however, with a lingering look behind, expressed the opinion that a potential scholarship winner could perhaps begin Greek two years before he left his preparatory school. So at the association's next annual conference Burge's equivocal attitude to Greek was modified. Forceful views were expressed: first, that a boy should not be allowed to begin Greek until the foundations of Latin and French had been securely laid and he had received a systematic training in English; secondly, that French and English were to be given substantial weighting in entry scholarship examinations in 'order that these subjects may not be sacrificed to a premature study of Greek'.[8]

Between the publication of the report by the HMC on the preparatory school curriculum in 1909 and the revision of the common entrance examination requirements in 1917 there was very little development in the debate on the curriculum, except perhaps for a noticeable diversity in views expounded on its future development. During this period the preparatory and public schools were largely concerned with other, if germane, questions of the inspection of preparatory schools by Board of Education inspectors,[9] and with the Board's recognition of preparatory schools as being 'secondary' in character in their logical articulation with public schools.

Typical of this diversity was the view put forward by Mr Gidley Robinson in a report of an international inquiry edited by Michael Sadler:[10] that ethical values grew from the study of history and literature. He also suggested that many preparatory schools would like to give more time to art, music and handicraft in order to cultivate a love of beauty, to aid accuracy and to provide a healthy occupation during leisure hours.[11] Contrasted with this was the opinion of a contributor to *The Times Educational Supplement*, who argued that the curriculum of the preparatory schools was a burdensome one. For to study 'Latin and even Greek (including in both cases grammar, translation and composition, and sometimes verse), arithmetic, geometry, algebra, English, French, German, Scripture, Geography, History and nature study'[12] would involve a gigantic timetable. So he recommended a weekly timetable of thirty-two hours to give a thorough grounding in mathematics, French and English. This proposed timetable for the average boy gave fewer hours to Latin than to French and none to Greek. Did this presage the nature of future development?

Other would-be reformers of the preparatory school curriculum raised their voices. The newly appointed Professor of English at Cambridge, Arthur Quiller-Couch, ritually asked for more English, especially English literature; F.W. Sanderson of Oundle made a similar case for science since his was a science school, whilst Eustace North wanted to make Latin optional for the common entrance examination.[13] Preparatory schools weathered the attacks by the 'Neglect of Science' committee on public schools during the war but by

1917 were considering a report advocating a proposed revision of the common entrance examination requirements. This revision was more concerned with arrangements for the examinations *per se* than with any curriculum change. Perhaps the most important aspect of this 1917 curriculum revision was the continuing rapport of public and preparatory schools through the Joint Standing Committee (JSC), which had first been instituted in 1907.[14]

Core Curriculum Discussed

The value of the common entrance examination and the relative merits of English language or Latin as the core subject of the curriculum were the main preoccupations of the inter-war years. Voices were raised sometimes in criticism of the common entrance examination and sometimes even for its abolition. As for Latin it was losing ground gradually to English as the needs of the average boy came to be regarded as paramount. Outside these two main areas of discussion, science was increasingly seen as being of increasing importance.

The Common Entrance Examination: Development

As the Common Entrance Examination (CEE) became more established it elicited more support. From the start some regarded it as a bureaucratic device for extending the influence of the APS Executive. Others found the examination irksome: an inconvenience in the life of the school and cause of mental indigestion among the pupils. In *Custodibus Custos*,[15] A.G. Grenfell of Mostyn House School described it as 'unspeakable' since it had 'to be conducted on sacramental lines for outsiders'.[16] He hoped for 'the coming of a new Public School or two, where the test for entrance at fourteen will be a rigid and searching examination into character with nothing tricky or recondite in scholarship requirements.'[17]

Such observations by one of the Association's more idiosyncratic headmasters were not unique. C.C. Lynam (Dragon), Chairman of the Association for 1921, described himself as 'not at all satisfied' with the Common Entrance Examination, describing its influence as 'disastrous'. He went on:

> The papers are stereotyped in form. Thousands of back copies are purchased and used as a standard and as a means of 'cramming' boys for the examination. Instead of a boy being judged by his real merit, character and attainments, he is judged by his mark-getting powers in a very specialised examination, and this seems to me to be destructive of anything like originality or individuality in teaching or training.[18]

Possibly as a measure to limit the psychological dysfunction in the early adolescent mind and probably to curtail the inconvenience to schools occasioned by the examination, the HMC and IAPS[19] agreed in 1923 to shorten the examining time to allow for two Latin, two French, two English and three mathematics papers in two days, with two optional Greek papers at the end of the second day.[20]

But such revisions did not get to the nub of the problems, prompting A.E. Lynam (Dragon), elected Chairman of IAPS (1926), to endorse his father's earlier comments by observing that the scholarship examinations were superior to the CEE because they 'test ability and good teaching ... and preclude cramming'.[21] So he suggested the introduction of a confidential report by the preparatory school headmaster and a *viva voce* examination to test the candidates' abilities in the arts, handicraft, music, drama and leadership. This proposed confidential report from the headmaster, however, aimed at *complementing* rather than abolishing the CEE.

Other critics of the examination were more ruthless. Quoting Bertrand Russell, H.C. Irving (Hazelwood, Limpsfield) proposed that CEE should be replaced by a *viva voce* examination.[22] An old critic of the Association, Tom Pellatt (Durnford), reminded readers of the *PSR* that Dr Cyril Norwood, headmaster of Harrow, had denounced the CEE as 'an examination of the worst type, making real education impossible'.[23] Pellatt quoted also from an editorial of *The Morning Post*, describing the examination as causing cramming to 'raise its head in private schools owing to the pressure of public school entrance examinations and unless it is promptly suppressed the whole purpose of liberal education will be defeated.'[24]

Critics from outside the Association weighed in. Writing in *The London Star*, Ernest Barker asked 'Should Preparatory Schools be abolished?', suggesting entry into public school at eleven to enable elementary schools to come into the picture. Such a suggestion was tantamount to a proposal for the abolition of Common Entrance,[25] a suggestion which was noted by the former headmaster of Eton, the Rev. the Hon. Edward Lyttelton:

> If rumour is to be believed, a movement is on foot for substituting a
> simple recommendation from the Preparatory Schools headmasters
> ... the gain would be immense. The Preparatory teachers could teach
> by natural methods.[26]

He added: 'Examinations begin to be pestiferous when they are used as goals for the lethargic.'[27] Lyttelton's advocacy of natural methods may seem a little strange coming from a former headmaster of Eton, but he would possibly be reflecting the impact made by H. Caldwell Cook, who as a master at the Perse School in Cambridge wrote the book, *The Play Way — An Essay in Educational Method*.[28] Although the Association has a conservative reputation it has invariably been level with, if not in advance of, contemporary educational thinking. It could warm to such naturalist blandishments.[29]

Evidence of this is to be seen in a debate in the *PSR* on the CEE and its effects on the curriculum. Dr C.A. Alington began the debate with his article on 'The education of the average man', suggesting that the average boy was judged too harshly by criteria which were more appropriate for the intellectual minority.[30]

The Nelson Touch

Responding to Alington's article, J.P. Nelson (Arden House) agreed with him that the CEE encouraged cramming. He endorsed Alington's suggestion that the curriculum should be divided into a literary and scientific stream. If a boy were allowed to choose one stream he would then have more time for the affective aspects of the curriculum like history, literature and handicrafts. Himself a very gifted artist,[31] Nelson thought that far more use should be made educationally of boys 'learning to make something and using their hands'. A more conservative member of the Association, E.L. Browne (St Andrew's), replied that the real object of the CEE was 'to enable the Public Schools to decide on the acceptance or rejection of their alumni'.[32] So the CEE continued to serve a useful purpose for him.

The Master of Wellington College, F.B. Malim, saw the CEE as a not unmixed evil. Though the physical and moral aspects of education might be neglected (even though they were inseparable from the cognitive), he did see a possibly new perspective by borrowing from the educational ideas of Professors John Adams and A.N. Whitehead. Citing Adams,[33] Malim suggested that preparatory schoolmasters teach *boys* as well as teaching *Latin* and *geometry*, by enabling them to acquire the basic skills before the age of eleven by allowing them to exercise their natural curiosity. Thus 'inert ideas'[34] (sterilized through the process of instruction) would be reactivated through activity. Seemingly, Malim had done his own homework on the two Hadow Reports which endorsed such 'naturalist' ideas.

The debate on the CEE continued well into the late 'thirties. In June 1933 an anonymous contributor to the *PSR* floated the idea of a scheme which divided the subjects into six groups:

Group I Latin, Greek
II English, History
III French, German, Spanish
IV Geography, Biology, Nature Study, General Science
V Arithmetic, Algebra, Geometry
VI Drawing, Music

This variant on Dr Alington's dichotomy of a literary and scientific curriculum was intended to enable boys to exhibit efficiency in only a minimum number of subjects and not take subjects from all groupings. Emphasis was placed on the confidential report of the preparatory school headmaster on the home background and parental influence. The anonymous author felt that if the Joint Standing Committee of the HMC and IAPS wanted reform, the IAPS was in a better position than ever before to give a lead.

J.P. Nelson (Arden House) who became a member of the executive committee in the 1940s and 1950s and Vice-Chairman in 1952, was prepared to give that lead. In an article on curriculum reform[35] his emphasis was on the competing claims of art and commerce 'to rank equal in dignity with any other calling'. He proposed first more scope for art, music, handicraft and nature study in the curriculum; secondly, the postponement of Latin till eleven; thirdly, of French till twelve; fourthly, lower standards in mathematics; fifthly, coordinated history, geography and English; and lastly, the introduction of elementary science. Time was to show how visionary Nelson was in 1936 concerning the future character of the curriculum. But if Nelson was constructive in his comments on curriculum reform, the curriculum which he wished to reform culminated for a preparatory school boy in the CEE. It was Tom Pellatt who voiced the exasperation of some when he wrote:

> Can anyone for a moment deny my statement, that this entrance examination, with its from twelve to fifteen papers, is the most diabolical instrument which could possibly be invented for enforcing cram of the worst type upon children just at the age when it does them most harm?[36]

Which Was the Core: English or Latin?

Closely linked with the criticisms of the CEE was the debate between the respective proponents of English and Latin as the core subject of the curriculum. Whilst Greek had been under attack, Latin had received little limelight. After 1909 the situation changed. The domino effect prevailed. If Greek fell the knock-on effect on Latin was inevitable, especially since 'the transfer of training theory' was giving way to other less biased vested interests. Preparatory schoolmasters were aware of this.[37]

The enormous impetus to science during the First World War reacted on the Joint Standing Committee of the HMC and APS.[38] First, they recognized that English grammar was a prerequisite for the study of any foreign language and recommended the study of a second language other than English at the age of ten. Latin was to be taken up only after a satisfactory level of proficiency had been reached in that second language, usually French. These recommendations were clearly aimed at delaying, if not relegating, the study of Latin. Eight years later, at the time of the revision of the preparatory schools curriculum in 1926 — a development contemporary with the publication of the first Hadow Report — the Joint Standing Committee emphasized the necessity for a 'thorough training in English throughout the whole period of preparatory school', adding that 'English papers should be made a substantial part of the entrance examinations of public schools, especially entrance scholarship examinations.'[39]

This elevation of English as the core subject in the curriculum, characteristic of the 1920s and 1930s, was reinforced by a simultaneous relegation of Latin as the prime study for the majority of boys. In 1933 H.N.P. Sloman (Tonbridge) inveighed against the 'tyranny of Latin'[40] and suggested that it ought not to be studied until a boy had reached the age of ten or eleven. He felt that French could be studied two years earlier, but he warned against the two languages being started simultaneously. At the annual conference of the IAPS in the same year Dr Cyril Norwood (Harrow) gave strong support to the idea that English was more important than Latin for the majority of boys. In 'defining the place of Latin in the curriculum'[41] Norwood declared that his own opinion was close to that of the Consultative Committee of the Board of Education. The right education for the great majority of secondary school pupils was 'a sound education based on our English culture intended to produce sane English citizens'.[42] For Norwood (future chairman of the Consultative Committee which produced the Report on the Curriculum in 1943) history, geography, language and literature ought to be elevated from the status of minor subjects to that of major ones. It was English then, not science, which was responsible for the successful assault on the classical hegemony of the preparatory school curriculum. Whereas science is often seen as the subject which superseded the classics in secondary schools (as suggested by the promotional efforts of the Science and Art Department from 1853 to 1899) it was in fact English and cognate subjects which, in the preparatory schools at least, forced Latin and Greek into a more lowly place. Such then was the position at the time of what the late Arthur Harrison called the 'Great Debate at the 1937 Conference'.[43]

The Great Debate of 1937

Although a major paper on science and nature study in preparatory schools was presented at the 1937 Annual Conference at the Great Central Hotel, Marylebone, it failed to make its case because of the presentation at that conference of the report of the Curriculum Committee to the Council.

This report encapsulated the curriculum reforms proposed over the past twenty years: the replacement of Latin by English as the core subject in the curriculum, and secondly the granting of more time to physical training, art, handicraft and hobbies. W.D. Johnston (Cheltenham Junior School) and Geoffrey Hoyland (The Downs, Colwall) were well to the fore in their proposal that aesthetics should have a greater share of the curriculum. Johnston proposed that the conference 'approves the principles of the Report of the Curriculum Committee and requests Council to open negotiations with the Headmasters' Conference to secure their co-operation in the reform of the curriculum'.[44] He was ably seconded by Geoffrey Hoyland, an admirer and disciple of Edward Thring who had introduced much cultural activity into Uppingham in the nineteenth century.[45] Arthur Harrison gave his impression of the great debate that ensued and accounted for the amendment to the original motion which was finally carried by almost 400 to 20 against.

In this debate the Rev. F.G. Ridgeway (St Peter's Court) swung the packed hall away from immediate reform to one of cautious exploration.[46] The proposal finally passed by Council was:

> That a Joint Commission of representatives of the Universities, Public Schools and Preparatory Schools should be appointed to consider the development of education from every angle, and to recommend what changes, if any, are desirable.[47]

This final resolution was too vague and vast in design to achieve anything. Harrison's verdict that it had killed the topic of the curriculum as 'dead as mutton for the next twenty years or more'[48] is borne out by the fact that between 1938 and 1957 the *PSR* contained very few articles or letters about the curriculum *per se*. Instead the focus of interest switched once more to the CEE and intelligence testing. Mr Pat Knox-Shaw (St Peter's, Seaford),[49] who was one of the twenty to vote against the final motion, seemingly consoled himself by writing an article for the *PSR* in which he upheld the pre-eminence of English in the preparatory school curriculum.[50] It mattered not that to a certain extent he was contradicted by P.G. Hunter, Senior Master at Stowe School, who in 1942 referred to the four pillars of the preparatory school curriculum: Latin, French, mathematics and science, with English being of only *secondary* importance to Latin.[51] In the late 'thirties and early 'forties, such discussions took second place to preparations for war and then to war itself. By the 'fifties the CEE was the main concern once more. Mr C.F.C. Letts (Oakley Hall) and Mr P.H. Vezey (Beaumont House), through their assiduous correspondence with the *PSR*, served as watch-dogs over the CEE, to be considered in further detail.

Notes

1 *PSR*, 5, 42, March 1909, p. 315, cf. p. 186–7.
2 This was reflected in the article, 'The place of English in a good general education', *PSR*, 5, 40, July 1908, pp. 223–6. See also OLIVE BANKS (1967) *Parity and Prestige in English Secondary Education*, Routledge and Kegan Paul, 3rd impression, pp. 37–9.
3 In his note to the preface LYTTELTON acknowledges his debt to Mr E.D. MANSFIELD for his advice on the preparatory schools.
4 The book is dedicated to HENRY JACKSON, Professor of Greek at Cambridge.
5 LYTTELTON, *op. cit.*, p. 17.
6 *Ibid.*, p. 21.
7 *PSR*, 6, 45, March 1910, p. 1.
8 *Ibid.*
9 Dr LYTTELTON felt that inspection would have the effect of raising standards of Latin. *PSR*, 6, 54, March 1913, pp. 348–53.
10 M.E. SADLER (Ed.) (1908) *Moral Instruction and Training in Schools*, 2 vols, Longmans and Co.
11 SADLER, *op. cit.*, p. 160.
12 *The Times Educational Supplement*, 1 October 1912.
13 R.A. HARRISON, *op. cit.*, pp. 55–7.

14 H.C. KING (1926) 'Private and preparatory schools', *The Journal of Education and School World*, April, p. 253.

15 Printed privately (1921). GRENFELL adjured his readers to 'keep this book locked up whenever boys are about'.

16 A.G. GRENFELL, *op. cit.*, p. 55.

17 *Ibid.*, p. 99.

18 C.H. JAQUES (1977) *A Dragon Century 1877–1977*, Blackwell, p. 51.

19 The Association was incorporated in 1923.

20 *PSR*, 8, 85, July 1923, p. 429.

21 *PSR*, 9, 95, December 1926, pp. 280–2.

22 *PSR*, 9, 99, March 1928, p. 432.

23 *PSR*, 9, 100, July 1928, pp. 462–3.

24 *Ibid.*, p. 462.

25 *Ibid.*, p. 451. ERNEST BARKER, a man of humble origin who had not gone through the system, was rationalizing from his own experience in advocating entry at 11.

26 EDWARD LYTTELTON (1928) *The Quarterly Review*, 251, 497, July, pp. 169–70.

27 *Ibid.*, p. 172.

28 H. CALDWELL COOK (1917) *The Play Way*, Heinemann.

29 An article on the Dalton Plan appeared in the *PSR*, 8, 86, November 1923, pp. 464–5. Cf. HELEN PARKHURST (1922) *Education on the Dalton Plan*, G. Bell and Sons.

30 *PSR*, 10, 111, March 1932, pp. 282–8. Cf. also C. ALINGTON (1938) *A Plea for a Plan — The Two Types of Education*, Longmans. This work differentiates between a later literary or scientific curriculum but postulates a common core of English, history, geography and divinity.

31 Cf. J.P. NELSON (1971) *Broad Campden*, privately printed, in which the author drew his own fine illustrations.

32 *PSR*, 10, 113, Nov. 1932, p. 351.

33 JOHN ADAMS, a neo-Herbartian in educational theory, propounded his bipolar theory in the early twentieth century. It was encapsulated in the dictum: *Magister Johannem Latinam docet.*

34 Cf. A.N. WHITEHEAD (1962) *Aims in Education and Other Essays*, London, Ernest Benn. p. 7.

35 *PSR*, 11, 125, November 1936, pp. 267–268. The article is signed 'J.P.H.' but this is almost certainly a misprint. The only headmaster with those initials in 1936 was Mr J.P. HOWARD of Copthorne School. The description of Copthorne gives no inkling of an 'aesthetic' appreciation, whereas J.P. NELSON refers to music, dancing and well equipped studio for art work in the description of his school.

36 T. PELLATT (1936) *Boys in the Making*, Methuen p. 181.

37 Cf. *PSR*, 9, 89, November 1934, pp. 85–6, article on intelligence tests. Also *PSR*, 10, 104, November 1929, p. 66, article on 'Intelligence tests — some figures and reflections'.

38 *PSR*, 8, 72, March 1919, p. 1.

39 *PSR*, 9, 96, March 1927, p. 315.

40 *PSR*, 10, 116, November 1933, pp. 423–4.

41 *PSR*, 10, 117, March 1934, pp. 468–70, 'The place of Latin in the curriculum', address to the conference.

42 *Ibid.*

43 HARRISON, *op. cit.*, p. 61.

44 *Ibid.*

45 Cf. GEOFFREY HOYLAND (1946) *The Man Who Made a School: Thring of Uppingham*, London, SCM Press.

46 R.A. HARRISON, *op. cit.*, p. 62.

47 *PSR*, 11, 129, March 1938, p. 405.

48 R.A. HARRISON, *op. cit.*, p. 62.

49 Mr PAT KNOX-SHAW was Chairman of Council in 1940 and 1943 and Vice-President 1969–70.

50 *PSR*, 11, 130, June 1938, pp. 457–8, 'A time-table and some ideas behind it'.

51 P.G. HUNTER (1942) 'The preparatory and public school curriculum', *The Journal of Education*, February pp. 62, 64.

16   Enter the Insurance Companies

Oh, dry the starting tear, for they were heavily insured.
(W.S. Gilbert.)

The Great War and the Preparatory School

The effects of the war on the APS were minimal. A sub-committee had been
formed in December 1914 to consider difficulties arising from the war. The
four main, yet seemingly trivial, concerns at that time were first, the failure of
boys to return to school after the summer holidays; secondly, non-payment of
school fees; thirdly, the non-appearance of boys for whom places had been
booked; and fourthly, the withdrawal of boys followed by the refusal of
parents to pay the usual term's fees in lieu of notice. Trivial or not, the financial
consequences of these difficulties were very serious. APS standing orders were
suspended, thus preventing major loans from Association funds, but the
Treasurer was authorized to expend £500 in helping schoolmasters in distress
during the war.[1]

Perhaps the greatest impact on the schools was the shortage of staff
resulting from the response by assistant masters to the call to fight for King and
country. This had led to the employment of more women in boys' preparatory
schools. Many schools, like St George's, Eastbourne, were forced to close.[2] But
by and large the schools were little affected by the ravages on the continent,
except for the legion of old boys killed in this 'subalterns' war'. It is possible
that the worldwide Spanish influenza epidemic of 1918/19 was more disruptive
of the even tenor of preparatory school life than the war itself. At Yardley
Court the headmaster and many others were struck down with 'flu and all
matches were cancelled for the term, which finished several weeks early.[3] At
Fonthill several boys were seriously ill and the school was forced to close down
two weeks early before Christmas to relieve the pressure on a full sanatorium.[4]
Influenza had struck the Dragon School in November, and it was closed down
for three weeks. It is doubtful whether any schools escaped this epidemic,[5]
which gave added point to the advice given in the *PSR*, after the fatalities of the

measles epidemic in 1917,[6] on 'The prevention of the spread of epidemic diseases at schools' by H. Marley Fletcher, physician to St Bartholomew's Hospital. No doubt Marley Fletcher's advice helped in some degree to contain the Spanish influenza in 1918/19, but the disrupting effects of this epidemic were great.

Despite the widespread illness there was a great feeling of optimism which was reflected nationwide in a boom period of both investment and spending. No doubt many thought that it would be possible to return to the prosperity and living standards of pre-war days. There were some who were now more prosperous than ever. In this climate of optimism and prosperity, established preparatory schools began to increase in numbers. At Yardley Court the cubicles were removed from the dormitories to make room for an increase of boys to 100.[7] This modification was insufficient to meet the demand, and in 1923 the school had to embark on a £10,000 building project to provide extra accommodation. This was the time when several new preparatory schools were started. Amongst them were Downsend, Leatherhead (1918); Brighton College Junior School (1919); Downside, Purley (1920), founded by Edgar Dodd; Chelmsford Hall, Eastbourne (1920), founded by L.C. Stevens, a young demobilized staff officer; Coventry Preparatory School (1920), founded by the Rev. Swallow; St Michael's, Barnstaple (1920), founded by H.H.H. Hockey; West Hill Park, Fareham (1920); Malsis Hall (1920), founded by A.H. Montague as a 'feeder' school for Giggleswick; Swanbourne House (1920), founded by the Wykehamist Lionel Evans; Brightlands, Newnham-on-Severn, which was to be attended by T.C. Worsley,[8] the future public school critic and writer.

New Schools

Between 1920 and 1930 at least fifty-six schools were thus founded,[9] some, strangely enough, being opened during the early years of the depression. Amongst other preparatory schools to be opened in the early 'twenties were Beech Hall, Macclesfield (1925/26); Great Walstead, Haywards Heath (1925), run on Evangelical lines by R.J. Mowll from 1925 to 1960; Haileybury Junior School (1922); Holmwood House, Colchester (1922); Ravenswood, Tiverton (1922); Sevenoaks Preparatory School (1921); Victoria College Preparatory School (1922); Stroud School, Romsey (1926) and St Hugh's, Woodhall Spa (1925), founded by Mr and Mrs George Forbes who had been assistant teachers at St Peter's School, Seaford, under the future Association Chairman, Mr Pat Knox-Shaw.[10]

Fewer preparatory schools were opened during the depression years of the late 'twenties. Amongst them were Ashfold (1927), a school attended by the late [Sir] Edward Boyle, a future Tory Minister of Education; St Aubyn's School, Tiverton (1928); and Wycliffe College Junior School (1928).

The widespread optimism of the post-war years proved to be falsely based.

The commercial and industrial boom came to an abrupt end in the winter of 1920/21. This was largely brought about by the economic situation of a country geared to the high production of goods which a war-torn Europe was unable to absorb. Overproduction led to unemployment: the old British staple industries of shipping, coal and cotton became very depressed. Britain soon abandoned post-war reconstruction. The end of the boom period signalled a period of economic difficulty for the preparatory schools. Some amalgamated, others closed, but some schools were faced with economic pressure before the 'twenties and 'thirties — even before the war ended — as a result of the government's attempt to make them subject to its excess profits duty.

The Excess Profits Duty

The crisis was occasioned by the Finance (No. 2) Act of 1915 which had sought to prevent traders and manufacturers from making abnormal profits during the war. Unfortunately the administration of this act covered all profits made *during* the war, not merely those made *because* of the war. As proprietors of private schools the preparatory school headmasters were liable to duty. The schools were advised by the Association that exemption from payment was unlikely to be granted as a general principle but that each case would have to be decided on its merits.[11] The hardest hit schools were those which were opened in the years immediately before the war and were not adequately profitable until 1914. Schools in this category would possibly include Beachborough (1912), founded by F.E. Chappell; Shardlow Hall, Derby (1911); Moor Allerton School (1914); Northwood Preparatory School (1910), more popular-ly known as 'Terry's' after its first headmaster; Tonstall School, Sunderland (1911); and Oakwood School (1912), founded by Captain R.P. Fenn, its headmaster for the next fifty years. Schools such as those found it difficult to convince the Taxation Office that their profits had risen above their pre-war level not because the war had enabled them to prosper but as the normal result of well-organized developments.

The excess Profits Duty threatened to cut some schools' profit by 50 per cent. It was the subject of heated debate at the twenty-eighth annual conference in December 1916.[12] A sub-committee was set up and a firm of accountants was hired to assist in some eighty cases. Schools were advised by the APS to appeal to the Special Commissioners in London against the assessments made on them. The response to this advice was enormous. Schools from all parts of England, from Devon, Essex, Shropshire, the Midlands, from Sussex (especial-ly), as well as from Scotland, Ireland and Wales, sought advice from the APS. The Special Commissioners in London pronounced unhesitatingly in favour of preparatory schools: though in one case an adverse decision of the local commissioners meant that the case had to be taken to the High Court. The joint heads of the school in question, Farnborough Preparatory School, Messrs E.G.H. North[13] and R.A. Ingram, won their case before Mr Justice Sankey of the King's Bench Court in June 1918 on the ground that they were concerned with the intellectual, social, moral and physical well-being of the boys under their care. This judgment[14] is of great significance for the preparatory schools in the twentieth century since it established that private preparatory schools are primarily concerned not with profits but with the welfare of boys.

This view of the preparatory schoolmasters' concern for the schoolboy was and continues to be valid despite the fact that in the early twentieth century the schoolmaster was concerned not only with the practice of his profession but also with his income and livelihood. Two facets of this pragmatic attitude were in evidence in the early 1920s. The first arose from the limitation placed upon the post-war expansion of preparatory schools by the insufficiency of public school places; the second resulted in the establishment of rules of etiquette amongst headmasters to regulate the transfer of boys from one school to another. We will look at these two facets of preparatory school development, induced by the onset of hard times.

Montauban's Initiative: Stowe

The English public schools emerged from the Great War with both strong critics and ardent supporters. Some of those who regarded the political and military leadership during the war as inadequate traced this inadequacy to the English public school system which had been developed in the late Victorian and Edwardian eras. Chief among the critics of this system was Alec Waugh, author of *The Loom of Youth* (1917).[15] C.E. Montague's *Disenchantment* (1924)[16] epitomized the disillusionment of many with the public school system.[17] On the other side stood Martin Browne, an Etonian, who opposed Waugh's view with a book based on the strength of morality, religion and chapel services.[18] Such supporters viewed the public schools as the guardians of standards in a rapidly disintegrating society. In their view the leaders of the nation — and especially the junior officers, products of the public schools — had emerged from the war with honour and distinction. It mattered not whether an alternative tradition was being created in less orthodox public schools like Clayesmore (1896), Abbotsholme (1889) and Bedales (1893): socially-aspiring parents in the early 'twenties sought places for their sons at the traditional public and preparatory schools. In numerical terms, too many parents were seeking too few public school places. Whilst the public schools were inundated with requests for entry, the preparatory schools were being frustrated in their failure to satisfy all interested parents. Symptomatic of this exigency was the precaution of J. & J. Paton, Educational Agents, of placing full-page advertisements in the *PSR* in which they stressed that:

> so many schools at present being full, some with long waiting lists, it will be an assistance to us, in dealing with the large number of inquiries daily received, if Principals likely to have vacancies for the next two terms will notify us as early as possible.[19]

The Joint Standing Committee of the HMC and APS met in January 1921 to confer on the difficulty, or perhaps crisis,[20] of 'public school congestion'. It was suggested at this meeting that boys could be registered at any age whether the registration fee was paid or not; but that at a later date, say four years before the boy was due to go to his public school, his entry should be confirmed and a substantial sum should be paid by his parents — either as entrance fee or first term's fees — returnable if he failed the CEE.[21] To facilitate this policy the APS Council set up in 1921 a sub-committee responsible for a Public Schools Vacancies Bureau which, with the cooperation of public schools, was to put members in touch with schools which had vacancies. To this sub-committee were appointed Mr A.S. Grant (Hillside, Reigate), the originator of the idea; the Rev. E.L. Browne (St Andrew's, Eastbourne); the APS Secretary, Mr H.C. King; and Mr E.H. Montauban (The Hall School, Hampstead).[22] Montauban felt that the Vacancies Bureau did not go far enough and proposed, in addition, the creation of a new public school which would go a long way towards soaking up the surplus of preparatory school boys seeking admission to public schools. This courageous and imaginative proposal was adopted by the APS and a further sub-committee, which included Montauban, was formed to investigate the possibility.

At this moment of decision there came on to the market a fine stately home, Stowe House, the family seat of the Dukes of Buckingham.[23] The house and grounds of 280 acres were sold by auction for £35,000 to a Mr Shaw. He was persuaded by Mr Montauban to make a gift of the unfurnished house and grounds to the APS for the proposed new public school. In making the gift Mr Shaw made it provisional on Montauban's securing adequate financial backing within a limited period — a challenge which Montauban was eager to accept. It was felt that £200,000 would be required to convert and endow the house for school purposes, with another £35,000 for the purchase of equipment and minor adaptations. Montauban resorted to the well-tried method, much used in the nineteenth century for the financing of proprietary schools, of selling a number of shares or 'rights' to members of the APS to meet the initial costs of equipping the house. Under Montauban's scheme £50 would purchase an 'option' to nominate a boy for Stowe at the ordinary rate; £150 secured an Exhibition which entailed also a £20 per annum reduction in the fees. Montauban planned for 400 'options' and 100 Exhibitions. Several 'options' and Exhibitions could be held by any one preparatory school.[24]

Montauban won considerable support in the APS[25] for his scheme and from Dr Cyril Norwood, then Master of Marlborough (1916/25). But he found less support, even opposition, amongst other members of the HMC. In particular the Rev. the Hon. Dr Edward Lyttelton, retired headmaster of Eton, was less sanguine than Montauban about the scheme's chances in view of the country's worsening economic situation. If the public school congestion were to ease, he argued, then Stowe would be an embarrassing rival to other public schools.[26] At first Cyril Norwood's only ally in a generally antipathetic HMC was Dr A.A. David of Rugby. However, they were soon joined by F. Fletcher

237

of Charterhouse in their support of Montauban's plan for the foundation of a new public school, and together they formed an influential caucus. A new committee, which included five representatives from the APS and five from the HMC, examined closely the logistics of the opening of the proposed new school. But time was running out, and the project seemed likely to founder on the rocks of insolvency. At this critical stage the joint HMC/APS body was rescued by another educational committee whose chairman was Lord Gisborought and one of whose members was Dr David, newly translated from Rugby to the episcopal throne of St Edmundsbury and Ipswich.[27] Lord Gisborough was but the figurehead of this committee. The driving force was its Secretary, the Evangelical the Rev. Percy Warrington, Vicar of Monkton Combe. It was Warrington who was later to gain the soubriquet of 'the financier in the surplice' because of his part in the re-establishment of Wellington (Salop) College as Wrekin College (1920) and the foundation of Canford School (1923).[28] This committee had the funding necessary to take over the work of the joint HMC/APS committee. It bought Stowe and invited Montauban to become a governor of the new school.

Stowe School opened with ninety-nine boys and twelve masters at the end of the Easter holidays with J.F. Roxburgh, from Lancing, as headmaster. Preparatory schoolmasters were interested to learn from the foundational head that as an experiment he intended to admit a number of boys through selection rather than by examination.[29] Although Roxburgh, Warrington and Gisborough were responsible for Stowe's ultimate success, the originator and architect of the scheme for a new public school at Stowe was Montauban, loyally backed by the APS. As Lord Gisborough declared at a celebratory dinner, 'the little candle Montauban then lighted has started a great conflagration in the world of modern England'.[30]

Establishing Rules of Etiquette

The exigencies of war made members of the APS very sensitive to the need for a universal recognition by members of the professional etiquette governing recruitment of pupils. The Executive reminded its members at the annual conference in December 1914 that it had been the recognized convention amongst APS members that a headmaster receiving a boy into his school should communicate with the boy's previous school. Although it was recognized that no sanctions could be applied,[31] convention had officially been established in 1908 in order to curb what was colloquially known as 'poaching' — the practice of inducing parents to change their sons' schools not by any sound educational argument but by offering a lower rate of fees. Wilkinson of Seafield House, Broughty Ferry, complained bitterly to the APS in 1918 that this practice was rife.[32]

The Association drew up a new code of professional conduct which covered (1) underbidding with fees to attract pupils from other schools; (2) the remission of fees in cases of absence through illness; (3) the legal entitlement to fees for the following term when a boy took a 'chance vacancy' at a public school; and (4) regulations concerning quarantine and the isolation of infectious diseases. Although no sanctions could be applied against offending headmasters, it was made plain that those accused of contravening the code would be expected to send the Association a brief statement of explanation.[33] At the 1923 annual conference the resolution concerning professional etiquette was incorporated into the Association's Handbook to ensure general knowledge of the ground rules amongst its members. In the following year the IAPS annual conference placed an embargo on the advertizing in the press of reduced fees when it passed a resolution that

> the IAPS, while feeling that any interference with legitimate advertising is beyond its province, are of the opinion that it is contrary to the spirit of the association and against the best interest of education that advertising offering reduced fees should be inserted in the Public Press.[34]

This resolution was again drawn to the attention of IAPS members in 1930 by the editor of the *PSR*. It was re-emphasized that fee-cutting was ungentlemanly and unprofessional. But the Association still had cause to admonish offenders as late as 1940. The Association was powerless when aided or maintained secondary schools accepted boys in mid-term. Their low fee structure made them a constant threat to preparatory schools, as Mr Paul Griffiths (The Hall, Cheshunt) observed in 1932.[35]

The Impact of Hard Times

The continuing anxiety of preparatory schools lest their fees be undercut by their rivals reflected the deteriorating economic situation as years of deflation in the 'twenties gave way to years of acute depression in the 'thirties. This was the time when there were three million unemployed in Britain, when some impoverished parents had to withdraw their sons from their preparatory schools whilst others sought fee reductions; and when some preparatory schools had to close down or amalgamate. The *PSR* gave guidance on ways in which schools might economize.

It was suggested in November 1931 that it was false economy to cut down on either food or salaries but that economies could be made in the areas of entertainment and in the conduct of the schools' sports programme. The number of matches could be halved; the extravagance of blazers and 'colour' caps could be eliminated.[36] The traditional Sunday wear of Eton collar, Eton jacket and straw boater was thought to be outmoded in times of economic stress. Shorts and stockings were not only cheaper but also more suitable for small boys than were trousers, even for cricket.[37] Studs, collars and ties were less in evidence. Flannel was increasingly replaced by drill in summer and by corduroy in winter. The ideas of H.H. Almond of Loretto concerning 'sensible' clothing, long advocated as suitable for preparatory schools by E.P.

Frederick of Wells House, and later adopted by C.C. Lynam (Dragon School), were thus extended to other schools in these times of economic hardship. Amongst proposed economies were cheaper rail tickets negotiated with the railway companies[38] for boys travelling to and from school.

Commercial firms, aware that schools were now closely scrutinizing their domestic economy, announced that their wares could be despatched direct from the factory at reduced prices.[39] Rowe's, tailors of Gosport and London, advertized a plan for reducing the cost of education by offering their products direct to the schools themselves at a corresponding reduction where they were appointed outfitters to the school.

Attempts were made to effect economies at the IAPS centre. Early suggestions for economy were the abandonment of a second Council meeting in the summer term unless there were urgent matters on the agenda, and the curtailment of the printing bill by printing the names of candidates for election to Council once only.[40] It was calculated that each Council meeting cost £50. It was suggested, therefore, that in order to reduce costs the Council should form a 'cabinet' of eight or ten members residing not more than 100 miles from London to transact business when required, the whole Council being assembled only when the Chairman thought it necessary. When this proposal was put to the annual conference in December 1932 the motion was lost. Preservation of the democratic constitution was rated higher than any relatively small economy.

The Association could have saved £2500 (the 1932 figure)[41] by abandoning the requirement that the CEE must be invigilated by 'outside' invigilators. Another suggestion was that because of the smaller entry of candidates to the CEE and the diminished membership of the IAPS the entrance fee for the CEE should be raised. All these proposals were rejected at the same time as the radically oligarchic one of instituting a cabinet based on London. In such circumstances, what hope of succeeding had the imaginative and revolutionary proposal of Mr Fred Chappell that the Association should purchase an HQ in London? Indeed 1933 was regarded as the wrong economic moment for such a proposal.[42] Chappell's proposal would in the long run have had economic advantages for communication and travel; and with the hindsight of history it can be seen that the purchase of a London property in 1933 would have been an excellent investment. Be that as it may, the officers of the Association had to continue to conduct business from their respective homes or schools. It was not until Mr Tim Dealtry persuaded the Association in 1962 to purchase 138 Church Street, a Georgian house in Kensington, that the Executive was able to work in proper conditions.[43]

Making It Easier for Fee-Paying Parents

Three significant ameliorative measures were adopted during these years of national economic depression. First, the School Fees Insurance Scheme, started in 1925, enabled parents to obtain cover against loss of schooling when their sons were absent through illness. Secondly, the Benevolent Fund was established in 1929. Supported by voluntary donations, its purpose was to help retired members and their relatives in acute distress. The institution of a Benevolent Fund underlined the need for the Association to institute a satisfactory pension scheme for assistant masters. It is a matter of surprise that such a scheme had not been established earlier. It would have been a satisfactory prophylactic measure against the unstable times. An assistant who was not likely to become a headmaster but who could look forward to an adequate pension after long service would have been a more contented and stabilizing influence in a school beset by other financial worries. The availability of the state pension scheme in the maintained system might attract assistant masters out of the preparatory school system. Excluded from participation in the Teachers' Superannuation Act of 1918 because they were working in private profit-making institutions, the assistant masters (and mistresses) were at a decided disadvantage compared with their peers in the maintained school system. It took fourteen more years of convoluted argument and complex negotiation before the IAPS introduced its own pension scheme.[44] By the end of 1933, 102 preparatory schools had joined the scheme, ninety-three were expected to join shortly and another 100 were in correspondence with a view to joining. The IAPS pension scheme was no doubt seen by many heads as a sound investment during trying times. Assistant masters presumably gained even more satisfaction from the scheme. Whatever its limitations might be, the assistant masters were now better able to face old age.

By 1933, when the IAPS pensions scheme was firmly established, the national economic depression began to recede. According to A.J.P. Taylor, home industries were boosted by increased spending.[45] This was not true of the preparatory school world. Writing in *The Preparatory Schools' Year Book* (1934), 'K.D.' observed: 'the worst of the financial crisis is now over, and we appear at last to be on the road to industrial recovery. But even so ... less money is being spent, and everyone is worse off in consequence.'[46] He further observed: 'This state of affairs is reflected in the Preparatory School world. There is an ever-increasing demand by the parents for economy in educating their children, and Headmasters are being urged more than ever before to reduce their fees.'[47] Urging moderation on both the parent and the headmaster, 'K.D.' stated bluntly that fees could not be reduced for all parents — only for exceptions. Universally lower fees would cause schools to collapse financially, as some already had. When parents sought lower fees he advised them to find cheaper schools. No doubt with the recently instituted pension scheme for assistant masters in mind, he added that massive profits for preparatory school owners were a thing of the past; and even in the past, *profit* was necessary to ensure a relatively carefree old age. At the same time he advised principals to make less onerous demands on parents for clothing and equipment. He summarized the position: 'The whole situation needs fair and open treatment on either side, as much in matters of economy as in every other question that affects the welfare of a boy for whom his parents and the Headmaster are jointly responsible.'[48] Another contributor to *The Preparatory Schools' Year Book* (1934), F.S. Jamieson, recommended that in order to ease the load in the payment of school fees, parents should take out an insurance policy to cover their children's education — a practice which still persists today.[49]

Such was the continuing hardship experienced by the Association, despite the less oppressive general economic situation, that the IAPS formed a sub-committee in 1937 to enquire into the causes of depression in the preparatory schools.[50] Two major and connected causes were discerned: the falling birthrate and competition from the local maintained system of schools.

The Declining Birth Rate

Since 1905 there had been a steady overall decline in the nation's birth rate. As Table 10 indicates, this decline was evident not only in the total number of births but also in the number of births per thousand of population. The decline in the size of the family would theoretically make it easier for parents to send an only child to a preparatory school.

A.J.P. Taylor has suggested that the baby Austin had ousted the baby; and had not the nursery given ground to the garage?[51] Perhaps middle class and upper middle class families were now preferring to invest in material goods rather than in extensive families.[52] This could have beneficent effects on the preparatory schools who relied on them for their clientèle. Many letters and leading articles in *The Times* between 1932 and 1939 drew attention to the declining birth rate and its effects.[53] In 1933 the Government Actuary estimated that there would be a decline of about one million in the number of elementary school children during the next fifteen years. Yet by the same token there should not necessarily have been fewer boys at preparatory schools during the same period.[54] Yet 'K.D.' was asserting in *The Preparatory Schools' Year Book* of 1934 that 'many schools are lower in numbers than they have been for many years, and some, whose position a few years ago seemed impregnable, have closed down altogether.'[55] In that same year Cheam moved to its present Berkshire location at Headley. During the depression years of the later 'twenties the numbers had been at a low ebb (seventy-two in 1929) and had sunk to forty-eight by September 1923. The school's move in 1934 caused the numbers to drop more dangerously. In 1935 the school had thirty-six boys — the lowest number in eighty years.[56] Elstree, another well-established school, weathered the storm, but there was no longer a waiting list for entry.[57]

There were grounds, however, for hope and optimism for some preparatory school headmasters. The declining birth rate might be seen as a blessing by boarding schools, for example. In the days of larger families it had not been possible to send the boys to boarding school because of the accumulated cost of educating so many. Now there was perhaps only one son in the family, and a boarding school education was seen as not only desirable but also financially

Table 10. Population Figures: England and Wales, 1905–35

Year	Total births in 1000s	Births per 1000 population	Year	Total births in 1000s	Births per 1000 population
1905	929	27.3	1930	649	16.3
1915	815	21.9	1931	632	15.8
1925	715	18.3	1932	614	15.3
1926	685	17.8	1933	580	14.4
1927	654	16.6	1934	598	14.8
1928	660	16.7	1935	599	14.7
1929	644	16.3			

Source: Figures extracted from B.R. Mitchell and Phyllis Deane (1971) *Abstract of British Historical Statistics*, Monograph 17, Cambridge University Press, p. 30.

possible.[58] The optimism of at least one preparatory boarding school headmaster was matched by the 'Association establishment' when Mr H.F. Pooley and the Rev. P.C. Underhill, respectively Chairman and Secretary of the IAPS, wrote to *The Times*[59] in reaction to a leading article by the headmaster of Dover College about the 'fierce competition' between preparatory schools. Pooley and Underhill, whilst acknowledging that the economic crisis of the early 'thirties and the declining birthrate had led to the closure of some schools and the amalgamation of others, nevertheless displayed great optimism for the future of preparatory schools. They were of the opinion that increased efficiency would be the mark of those schools which survived. With some pride they pointed to the raised standards arising from inspection of schools by the Board of Education (which was now a condition of IAPS membership); to the pension scheme for assistant masters; to the regular refresher courses for both headmasters and assistant masters; and to closer cooperation with the public schools on curriculum and examinations.[60] Despite the outbreak of war this mood of optimism for greater efficiency was evident also at the annual conference, held at its usual venue at the Great Central Hotel, London. There was much talk at this conference about raising the status of the Association to a level comparable with that of the BMA, the Law Society or the Bar Association.

Competition from LEA Schools

Another discernible factor contributing to the continued depression of the preparatory schools in the late 'thirties was the increasing competition from locally maintained schools, whose facilities were improving as greater investment was made in them by the LEAs (see Table 11). Yet though it was for many parents no longer a foregone conclusion that their boys would attend a preparatory school, this did not deter Marcus Maloney, an assistant master at Cumnor House School, Purley, from dropping a prospectus into every pram he met in Purley.[61] Other preparatory schools were experiencing diminished enrolments and thus smaller incomes. Not only were the LEA schools with their increased financial support better off financially than the preparatory schools but the law made LEAs a potential threat to the preparatory schools. The day preparatory schools in the towns were especially liable to interference by the LEAs which were responsible for ensuring minimum standards in all schools in their administrative areas. LEAs had power to inspect preparatory schools in their areas if so requested, but suspicion of LEA pretensions caused preparatory schools to prefer inspection by the Board of Education's inspectors.[62] A major inhibiting factor in the preparatory schools' involuntary competition with LEA schools was that the Board of Education continued to view them as schools conducted for private profit. Whilst classifying these schools as 'businesses', the state was undecided whether to encourage, tolerate or suppress them.[63]

Table 11. LEAs' Expenditure, 1900–39

Year	Expenditure of LEAs in £ 000,000s
1900	8.8
1910	27.5
1920	56.4
1925	73.9
1930	83.7
1935	86.9
1936	92.2
1937	95.0
1938	98.0
1939	100.4

Source: Extracted from B.R. Mitchell and P. Deane (1971) *Abstract of British Historical Statistics*, pp. 417–18.

Preparatory School Closures and Amalgamations

The declining birth rate and the competition of locally maintained schools led many schools to close down and others to amalgamate. Amongst those which closed was Beech Lawn School (known locally as Greyfriars), Leamington Spa, the good will of which was transferred in 1935 to Arnold Lodge School.[64] When Banstead Hall School, Surrey, closed in 1936, eleven Banstead Hall boys arrived at Elstree to boost its numbers.[65] Fonthill School was enlarged on three occasions during the inter-war period when it subsumed Hazelwood School, Oxted (1927), the nineteenth century foundation Bengeo School, Hertfordshire (1936) and Seabrook Lodge School, Hythe (1939).[66] After the Great War Eastbourne had over thirty preparatory schools, but by 1946 it had only five.[67]

Yet according to P.L. Masters some fifty-three schools were founded between 1930 and 1939,[68] some schools being opened during the depression years. Amongst these were Betteshanger School, Kent (1933);[69] Broadwater Manor House, Worthing (1930); Cumnor House School, Surrey (1931); Junior School, Felsted (1933); Grace Dieu Manor House (1933);[70] Mowden Hall School, Northumberland (1933); The Pilgrims' School (1931); Tower House (1931) and Town Close House, Norwich (1932). Others were opened when circumstances were improving. This group included Beacon School, Buckinghamshire (1934); Birchfield, Shropshire (1935); Caterham Preparatory School; St Andrew's Church Hill House, near Woking (1937); St Joseph's, Ipswich (1937), a Roman Catholic School; Treliske, Truro (1934); Vinehall, East Sussex (1938); Winchester House, Sevenoaks (1938); and Widford Lodge, Chelmsford (1935). Almost invariably these schools started in a very modest way. Widford Lodge School, for example, began with one class of nine boys in the Lodge's billiard room; Cumnor House began with only six boys. The number of new schools opened in the 'thirties fell short of the number which closed or amalgamated. Table 12 shows that there was a nett loss of approximately 264 *established* schools between 1930 and 1940.[71]

During this period approximately 431 new members joined the Association including 157 partners. At least fifty-three of these new members were responsible for new foundations. On the other hand 485 members either died in harness or retired from the Association. There was thus a loss of approximately 211 IAPS[72] member schools but only a nett loss of fifty-four individual members. The significantly new factor in these ownership figures was the increased number of those who entered partnerships. Hitherto partnerships had been a mode of promotion for assistant masters who were offered joint headships by grateful or near retiring incumbents.[73] During the 'thirties many partnerships arose from the many amalgamations.

The 'twenties and 'thirties had been hard years for the preparatory schools. Many of them had succumbed to economic and other pressures. Bengeo, Wixenford, Eastman's and many other schools had gone, taking their nineteenth century traditions with them. Those schools that survived the 'thirties were to face even more traumatic circumstances: the Second World War made even greater demands on the schools in the Darwinian process of the survival of the fittest.

Table 12. *IAPS Association Membership, 1930–40*

Year	New members	New partners	Resignations, deaths, closures
1930	33	—	23
1931	31	7	25
1932	21	17	54
1933	21	14	45
1934	23	28	53
1935	32	14	46
1936	28	10	72
1937	22	15	49
1938	22	25	34
1939	28	19	37
1940	13	8	47
TOTALS	274 – 53* = 221	157	485

Nett figure for lost established schools –264

Total of new members and partners 431

Note: *Philip Masters' figure for new foundations 1930–40, extant in 1966.

Notes

1 *PSR*, 7, 60, March 1915, p. 112.
2 LEONARD COVERLEY, (1971), *History of Chelmsford Hall*, Eastbourne, Sumfield & Day p. 1.
3 Cf. *Yardley Court 1898–1973*, p. 28
4 M.A.F. COOPER (Ed.) *Fonthill, 1970*, p. 33.
5 Cf. C.H. JAQUES, *op. cit.*, p. 83.
6 *PSR*, 7, 70, July 1918, pp. 387–8.
7 *Yardley Court, 1898–1973*, p. 30.
8 Cf. T.C. WORSLEY (1967) *Flannelled Fool — A Slice of Life: The 'Thirties*. Alan Ross, p. 36.
9 P.L. MASTERS, *op. cit.*, p. 108.
10 H.D. MARTINEAU, (1975) *Half a Century of St Hugh's School*, Horncastle, Cupit and Hindley, p. 2.
11 *PSR*, 7, 64, July 1916, pp. 224–6.
12 *PSR*, 7, 66, March 1917, pp. 279–80.
13 Future Chairman of the Association in 1920 and 1928.
14 Sir J. SANKEY, a high court judge and later Lord Chancellor in the Labour Government of 1929, headed several commissions which pronounced on issues under dispute.
15 ALEC WAUGH (1917) *Loom of Youth*, Grant Richards.
16 C.E. MONTAGUE (1924) *Disenchantment*, Chatto and Windus.
17 *Ibid.*, pp. 215–6.
18 MARTIN BROWNE (1919) *A Dream of Youth*, Longmans, Green and Co.
19 For example, *PSR*, 8, 73, July 1919, advertisement page.
20 According to the late R.A. HARRISON it was impossible to find a vacancy at any of the leading public schools for a boy who was nine years or older. Cf. R.A. HARRISON, *op. cit.*, p. 116.
21 *PSR*, 8, 78, March 1921, p. 211.
22 E.H. MONTAUBAN was first elected to the Association in 1898 when he was headmaster of St Bede's, Eastbourne. He was headmaster of Dover College Junior School before taking over Belsize Junior School (The Hall), Hampstead. He was elected to the Council in 1921 at the twenty-fifth annual conference. He founded Selwyn House Girls' School in London, NW. He died in 1954. Cf. P.G. DRURY-LOWE (Ed.) (1964) *The Hall School, Hampstead*, Monmouthshire, Starling Press pp. 46–9.
23 The third Duke of Buckingham died without a male heir and the house passed through the female line to Lady KINLOSS whose son was killed in the Great War. Cf. NOEL ANNAN (1966) *Roxburgh of Stowe*, Longmans, 2nd impression, p. 51.
24 *PSR*, 8, 81, March 1922, p. 287.
25 *Ibid.*, p. 293. At the 1921 conference voting was 85 to 30 in favour of backing Stowe.
26 Cf. *The Times*, 29 and 30 April 1922.
27 ALBERT AUGUSTUS DAVID (1867–1950), headmaster of Clifton College 1905–09, of Rugby 1909–1921, Bishop of St Edmundsbury and Ipswich, 1921–23 and Bishop of Liverpool, 1923–44.
28 NOEL ANNAN, *op. cit.*, pp. 79–80. Cf. also B.C.W. JOHNSON, *Wrekin College 1880–1964*, Shrewsbury, p. 49.
29 *PSR*, 8, 85, July 1923, p. 429.
30 Quoted from R.A. HARRISON, *op. cit.*, p. 119.
31 *PSR*, 7, 60, March 1915, pp. 111–12.
32 *PSR*, 7, 70, July 1918, p. 408.
33 *Ibid.*, p. 395. Cf. IAPS Green Book. *Notes for the Guidance of Members*, March

1978 for full statement of the acknowledged ground rules.
34 *PSR*, 10, 107, November 1930, p. 171.
35 *PSR*, 10, 113, November 1932, p. 353.
36 *PSR*, 10, 110, November 1931, p. 249.
37 *Ibid.*, pp. 259–60.
38 *PSR*, 10, 112, June 1932, p. 305.
39 *Ibid.*, advertisement page.
40 *Ibid.*, p. 305.
41 *PSR*, 10, 114, March 1933, p. 383.
42 *PSR*, 10, 117, March 1934, p. 467.
43 *PSR*, 19, 3, October 1970, pp. 15–16.
44 *PSR*, 10, 113, November 1932, pp. 335–6. Each master was to contribute 5 per cent per term irrespective of salary. The basis of payment was to be 50:50 between the school and the master. The pensionable age was to be sixty.
45 A.J.P. TAYLOR, (1965) *English History 1914–1945* Oxford University Press, p. 342.
46 H. OLDFIELD BOX (Ed.) (1934) *The Preparatory Schools Year Book*, Churchman Publishing Co., p. 72. Only the writer's initials are given. Attempts to break the anonymity have not been successful.
47 *Ibid.*, p. 73.
48 *Ibid.*, p. 76.
49 *Ibid.*, pp. 79–80.
50 *PSR*, 11, 129, March 1938, p. 407.
51 A.J.P. TAYLOR, *op. cit.*, p. 302.
52 Cf. GRACE G. LEYBOURNE 'The Influence of the cost of education on the size of the family', Eugenics Society 1938, pp. 16–17. Cf. also MONTAGUE COOKSON (1872) 'The morality of married life', *Fortnightly Review*, October 18, pp. 402–4, p. 412. Cf. also HAROLD COX (1922) *The Problem of Population*, Jonathan Cape, pp. 98–9.
53 Cf. *The Times*, 4 June 1932; 23 January, 21 June, 29 August 1933; 27 June, 2 August 1934; 28, 29 September and 1, 2, 3, 7, 8, 9, 10 October 1936; 11, 16, 17 February; 17 April; 19 June and 24 September 1937; 5 January, 28 May; 3 June, 2 July, 16 July, 3 August 1938; 18 January, 20 February, 10 March, 24 May and 29 June 1939.
54 *PSR*, 10, 115, June 1933, p. 396.
55 H. OLDFIELD BOX (Ed.), *op. cit.*, p. 73.
56 EDWARD PEEL, *op. cit.*, p. 237.
57 I.C.M. SANDERSON, *op. cit.*, p. 60.
58 *PSR*, 11, 129, March 1938, p. 407.
59 *The Times*, 14 April 1939. This letter was reproduced in the *PSR*, 12, 133, June 1939, p. 46.
60 *Ibid.*
61 H. MILNER GULLAND (1976) *School Story*, Guildford, p. 11.
62 *PSR*, 10, 112, June 1932, p. 310.
63 *PSR*, 10, 114, March 1933, p. 374.
64 *Leamington Spa Courier*, 26 July 1935.
65 I.C.M. SANDERSON, *op. cit.*, p. 65.
66 M.A.F. COOPER (Ed.) (1970) *Fonthill*, Fonthill, p. 13.
67 LEONARD COVERLEY, (1971) *Chelmsford Hall 1920–1970*, Eastbourne, Sumfield and Day, p. 41.
68 P.L. MASTERS, *op. cit.*, p. 108.
69 EDWARD and ROBERT KENNEDY attended the school for a short while.
70 A Roman Catholic School attended at NORMAN ST JOHN STEVAS.
71 The statistics have been extracted from figures given in the issues of the *PSR* between March 1930 and June 1940.

72 The figure can only be approximate to allow for wastage also amongst partners.
73 Others acquired their schools in other ways: many partners bought for themselves a financial share in the business, then perhaps over a period bought the whole school from the headmaster, who had by then retired.

17   The Men in the Engine Room

Put on the whole armour of God.
(IAPS motto)

The Incorporation of the Association

As the APS had no charter and was not incorporated, the Association's legal adviser, when the war broke out, advised that a trustee should be appointed to act as custodian of investments and surplus funds in a time of emergency. In December 1914 Lloyds Bank was appointed,[1] but this was an interim measure. In 1919 the Association began to consider the legal step of becoming incorporated. Significantly, Mr J.S. Norman (The New Beacon, Sevenoaks) was Chairman of Council both in 1914 and 1919.

The Association needed to be recognized as a legal body for insurance purposes — and particularly to make it possible to set up the Association's own pension scheme.[2] Despite initial and ritual objections from the Board of Trade, incorporated status was granted in 1923 when the APS became the IAPS and received its charter.[3]

The Case for Admitting Women

Loath as the AHPS had been to admit lady principals to its ranks, a lady principal had complained in the first issue of the *PSR* that their exclusion from membership unfairly handicapped boys' preparatory schools conducted by her sex.[4] They had to be represented by men. For example, between 1896 and 1927, when Windlesham House was being run by Mrs Charles Malden, she was represented by her brother-in-law, Mr H.M.S. Malden. Exceptional though she was as a preparatory school principal, as a woman she was excluded from the Association. Such masculine dominance was expressed by J.E.C. Welldon of Harrow saying at a meeting of his fellow headmasters that preparatory schools run by women were inferior.[5] Nevertheless pressure for the admission of women heads to the Association was very evident from time to time in the early years. One letter addressed to the editor of the *PSR* in December 1897 was so sarcastic that there are grounds for believing it to have been written by an *'agent provocateur'*. It read: 'If you were gracious enough to offer us these opportunities of acquaintance with the Lords of the Profession, we should gratefully accept no doubt. But all this we leave to your High and Mightinesses.'[6] The next edition of the *PSR* carried an article on the same theme signed 'Justitia'.[7] The lady principals aspiring to membership found both champions and antagonists among Association members. Mr C.C. Lynam, editor of the *PSR*, strongly pressed the case of his neighbour school, Summer Fields, which had been founded by a lady principal, Mrs Maclaren. This partisanship might account for the inclusion in the *PSR* of several letters in favour of the ladies' cause. Mr H.R. Heatley, Beaudesert Park, Henley-in-Arden, on the other hand, was one of their most determined opponents.[8]

Attempts like that of C.D. Olive (Rokeby)[9] to secure admittance of lady principals to the Association were overwhelmingly rejected. Just before Lynam resigned from the editorship in December 1900, he published a letter signed 'Madam' — perhaps representing the editor's last attempt to influence his colleagues in which the correspondent asked for the matter of lady principals to be raised once more at conference. She claimed to be the owner of 'a fairly large preparatory school' in the south of England where all the boys went on to public schools and left before fourteen — surely Mrs Malden! With the exception of her sister who taught the juniors, all her staff were male graduates.[10] What logic, therefore, excluded her school from the benefit of full membership with the Association?

The new editor of the *PSR*, F. Ritchie, published a letter by a headmaster rejecting once again the case for lady principals on the grounds that women were unsuitable for dealing with boys over the age of ten. In recognizing their value in the education of very young boys the correspondent suggested that lady principals ought to confine their activities to girls' schools, or if they took on young boys in their school to join the Parents' National Education Union (PNEU) which catered more for the pre-preparatory stage.[11] C.C. Lynam made a further attempt in the cause of lady principals when he proposed an amendment to the Rules of the Association at the tenth annual conference in December 1901. On this occasion he was strongly opposed by the Rev. W. Earle (Bilton Grange) and the Rev. E.L. Browne (St Andrew's, Eastbourne) on the grounds that women were unsuitable for dealing with the moral problems of growing boys. The amendment was lost.[12] The battle was over for a while and the Association got down to other problems such as the curriculum, a common entrance examination and preparatory school relations with the Royal Navy.

Enter the AHMPS

The admission of lady principals, however, continued to be the concern of Lynam, who almost two decades later tried to amend the Rules to include women at the conference in December 1920. On this occasion he was seconded by E.H. Montauban — Stowe's co-founder — but once again the motion was heavily defeated (65–10).[13] This was Lynam's last attempt. Mr H.F. Pooley (Dane Court, Pyrford)[14] took on Lynam's mantle of 'Sir Galahad' but at both Council meetings in March and December 1932 he was unable to secure a seconder to his motions urging their admission. His pleas for commonsense had fallen on deaf ears.[15] Meanwhile the headmistresses had in 1929 formed the Association of Headmistresses of Preparatory Schools (AHMPS). In the late 'sixties members of the AHMPS enjoyed affiliation with the IAPS. But it was not until 1971 that lady principals *per se* gained access to the IAPS, thus forming part of the social revolution of the late 'sixties and early 'seventies when bastions of male exclusivity were successfully assaulted by women.

The 1971 decision opened membership to headmistresses whose schools were recognized as efficient by the Department of Education and Science and had at least thirty-five boys under fourteen years of age. The first lady principal to become a full member of IAPS was Mrs K.T. Wilson, Principal of St David's Preparatory School, Huddersfield. As she had been running this school of 140 boys since 1937, her election illustrated the commonsense nature of the reform.[16] William Hickey in the *Daily Mail* reported on the changes that were necessary to the IAPS constitution because of the election of its first woman member. He indicated that the retiring chairman, Mr James Hornby (Clifton), had observed: 'We went through adding "and headmistresses" whenever the word "headmaster" appeared. But we were stumped when we came to the final paragraph which read: "Members should try to promote intercourse among headmasters".'[17]

During the 1970s the two associations moved closer to each other. At the general meeting of the AHMPS in October 1976 the president, Miss Barkley, declared that the two associations ought to merge.[18] Between 1976 and 1980 discussions took place in which it was recognized that it was illogical that preparatory schools should have two associations whose aims were so similar. The growth of co-education in IAPS schools — 7425 girls were attending IAPS schools in 1980 — added force to the arguments for amalgamation which had already been recognized by plans to amalgamate the Common Entrance Examinations for boys and girls. Amalgamation between the two Associations took place formally on 1 January 1981. The efforts of 'Skipper' Lynam, C.D. Olive and H.F. Pooley were at last vindicated.

The Reconstitution of the Council

The changes to the IAPS Council brought by the amalgamation of the two Associations in 1980/81 were not the first changes to be effected since Lionel Helbert's innovations in 1908–9 gave the Council an established local representational character. Just after the passing of the 1918 Education Act, it seemed that local education authorities in the maintained system were likely to gain more powers over schools conducted in their several areas and were seen as a possible threat to the independence of preparatory schools. The APS reacted in a defensive way. In 1919 they further increased the *local* character of the Council by scheduling twelve local associations centred on London, Broadstairs, Eastbourne, Bristol, Bournemouth, Birmingham, Liverpool, Durham, Cambridge (or Bedford), Oxford (or Reading), Scotland and Ireland. Day schools and small schools with fewer than forty boys, considered to be particularly vulnerable to both threats, were to be represented by specially nominated members among the twelve 'general' representatives — as opposed to 'local' representatives — on Council.[19] These changes in 1919 seemed to have required no major modification until 1933/34 when factors other than threatening LEAs brought about further changes to the IAPS constitution.

In the 1930s there was a general feeling that the then current 12:12 division of seats in Council between general and local representatives gave insufficient emphasis to the interests of the local districts. Moreover, local representatives were elected annually whereas general representatives were elected for three years. Another anomaly was that members were free to attach themselves to any district they preferred irrespective of the location of their schools. This arrangement reflected the fact that it was the headmaster, not the school, who was elected to the Association. After much discussion the general representatives were reduced in number to nine whilst the local representatives were increased to fifteen. London, Sussex and the North of England each gained an extra local representative and each district was given a definite geographical boundary. A headmaster was to be a member of the district in which his school was located. The object of these changes was to foster more local participation in the governance of the Association.[20]

There have been other minor amendments to the constitution but today (1982) the Association consists of twelve IAPS districts, with members again free to make their own choice of district, though it is likely that heads will choose to belong to the district in whose area their school lies. Of the twenty-two representatives, each serving for three years, thirteen are district representatives and nine are general representatives. The Chairman is elected by Council from its number and he, in turn, nominates the Vice-Chairman. Both Chairman and Vice-Chairman serve in that capacity for one year only.[21] The Council is served by several committees. The General Purposes Committee deals with matters concerning membership and etiquette (see 238–9); gives advice on salaries, or bursarial and insurance matters; and on general policy. There is also a Finance Committee to look after the Association's funds. A Training Committee is concerned with courses and seminars, especially the annual four-day refresher courses at Oxford, and keeps contact with colleges of education. A Consultative Committee advises the Chairman on larger issues of policy, whilst the Public Relations Committee is in constant contact with the Independent Schools Information Service (ISIS) over all public relations matters. Finally, the Advisory Committee representatives sit with representatives from industry, commerce and public affairs to their mutual benefit.[22]

This highly organized Association, which operates from its HQ at 138

Kensington Church Street, London, maintains close contact with other independent school organizations through the Independent Schools Joint Council (ISJC) and with the public schools through the Joint Standing Committee of the HMC and IAPS. The Association has representatives on twenty-five other bodies of various kinds. This superstructure of Association committees is responsible for the continuing welfare of 441 schools in the United Kingdom and Eire and fifty-one overseas (1980 figures) whose heads are IAPS members. The Association's united front and efficient organization ensure the continuing participation of these schools in the education of some of the nation's children between the age of eight and thirteen.

The Preparatory Schools Review

The journal of the Association, the *Preparatory Schools Review*, is one of the chief instruments in giving a sense of unity to the preparatory schools. There can be few, if any, English educational journals which can boast of Victorian origins. By comparison, *Conference*, the journal of the HMC, has a history going back only to 1963. Since the first issue of the *PSR* in July 1895 the journal has reflected both the official aims of the Association and the individual differences of members. It has been published almost continuously for eighty-eight years, the only break being when it ceased to appear in 1940 after the death of its editor, Lord Wrenbury, and was prevented by the exigencies of war from reappearing until 1945. The first editor, C.C. (Skipper) Lynam (Dragon School), was probably the most idiosyncratic, as his championship of lady principals has shown. At a very early stage he was in favour of constitutional changes in the Association and tended to push his views in the columns of the *PSR*. This led to a crisis in 1899 when the Rev. Herbert Bull, Chairman at the eighth annual conference, referred to 'the enthusiasm' of Lynam that 'outran his discretion ... for our particular branch of the profession'.

Lynam tendered his resignation but the Council refused to accept it.[23] Lynam's successor a year later, Mr F. Ritchie, was less mercurial and it was during his editorship (1901–6) that the very weighty matter of introducing the Common Entrance Examination was widely discussed in the columns of the *PSR*. The tradition was that the *PSR* should report the annual conference and Council meetings, and include articles on many aspects of preparatory schools. In 1903 Ritchie attempted to broaden the scope of the journal by recommending its purchase by parents as well as by schoolmasters. He introduced the practice of advertizing vacant posts, requests for posts, partnerships and school transfers, as well as vacancies for matrons and domestic servants. In 1914, during the editorship of Mr Gidley Robinson, there was an experiment in the reprinting of articles from the *PSR* in a 'Reprint Volume'. This sold sufficiently well for the reprints to be reprinted in 1917. In the 1930s the Association engaged in the production of two further publications: the *Public and*

Preparatory Schools Year Book (PPSYB) and *The Bulletin*. The *Public Schools Year Book*, published annually since 1889, was the *vademecum* of public schools. In 1933 the IAPS Council decided to join forces with the public schools in the production of a joint year book. This was first published in 1934. At first some IAPS members opposed this move in view of the inequitable terms offered to the junior partners.[24] But since 1934 the *PPSYB* has been a most useful compendium of knowledge about both public and preparatory schools. The *Bulletin* was circulated to every member of the Association from 1938 to pass on information about general administrative matters, thus lubricating the workings of the Association. It gave notice of district meetings, offered details of insurance and notified vacancies in headships. This *Bulletin* was to continue during the early 'forties when the *PSR* itself had ceased to function.

The *PSR* was launched once more in June 1945 with a new cover design. This issue earned the appreciation of J.F. Wolfenden, then headmaster of Shrewsbury, since it restored the links, attenuated by the war, between the public and preparatory schools. Wolfenden looked to the *PSR* as representative of a body which knew where it was going for 'statements of policy; reports of conferences; discussion of principles and letters about matters of controversy'.[25] In the post-war *PSR* there were a number of changes. Book reviews were published. Personal advertisements appeared. The journal resumed the functions given in 1938 to the *Bulletin*, which after thirty-four issues ceased in 1948 to be published.

As the chief organ of public relations for the IAPS, the *PSR* was more than an adequate instrument. But in the late 'forties the efforts of R.J.S. Curtis (Hurst Court, Ore), Secretary of the Public Relations Committee (1942), led to a decision to publish a book on the preparatory schools which would make their virtues known to the public at large. This plan bore fruit in the publication by IAPS in 1951 of *The Preparatory Schoolboy and His Education*.[26] This was the work of several IAPS members including Gilbert Ashton (Abberley Hall), R.J.S. Curtis, Pat Knox-Shaw (St Peter's, Seaford), 'Joc' Lynam (Dragon), O.E.P. Wyatt (Maidwell Hall) and the Rev. P.C. Underhill (Secretary of IAPS).

Engine Room Personnel

The successors of Herbert Bull, E.D. Mansfield, C.C. Lynam, F. Ritchie and C.C. Cotterill were Hugh C. King (The Downs School, Bristol), The Rev. P.C. Underhill (Wellington House) and L.P. Dealtry (The Leas, Hoylake). When Hugh King, having been Chairman in 1915, died in office in 1937 he had been Secretary of the Association for nineteen years. His years of office covered the long and demanding period of recession and depression of the 'twenties and 'thirties and the historic incorporation of the Association. He represented the IAPS on the Teachers' Registration Council and on the executive of the Royal Society of Teachers. Despite the demands of the secretaryship and his poor health, King also found time to be Chairman of the Council of St John's School, Leatherhead; Vice-Chairman of the Professional Classes Aid Society; a member of the Beaconsfield Urban District Council; and editor of the Beaconsfield Parish Magazine.[27]

Though King was a somewhat remote figure to his junior colleagues,[28] King's successor the Rev. P.C. Underhill, a genial giant of a man was friendly and efficient in his tenure of the Association's key post. A former headmaster of Herbert Bull's old school — Wellington House, Westgate-on-Sea — Underhill made his office, in the small town of Henley-on-Thames, the hub of the Association for some twenty years, being Secretary not only to the IAPS, but also the Common Entrance Board. He was also vicar of two parishes.[29] Yet he coped with the pre-war period of anxiety, the war time involving the evacuation of so many schools, and the shift of annual venue from the Grand Central Hotel, London, to Oxford. This move greatly assisted the development of the Association's activities. After the war he had to meet the demands of a burgeoning association which was reacting to the challenges implicit in the Fleming Report. R.A. Harrison, in his assessment of Underhill, gave him credit for recreating the IAPS after the doleful years of the 'twenties and 'thirties.[30]

In 1957 he was succeeded by Mr L.P. (Tim) Dealtry, who had been his assistant since 1946 and also Treasurer since 1952. A sensitive and shy man by contrast with his clerical predecessor, Dealtry consolidated the considerable achievements of Underhill. In the list of secretaries of the Association his is the only name which does not also appear in the list of Chairmen of the Association, although he had been a member of Council intermittently for a total of six years. His was a quiet leadership style, but he purchased and established the permanent central office at 138 Church Street, Kensington.

> Almost all the more important educational strategic developments with which the IAPS was concerned in the post-war years were the product of his logical, pliant, constructive, imaginative and unfailingly prescient mind,[31]

said R.A. Harrison of Dealtry, who communicated to the Association his own sense of concern about its future at a time when it was enjoying unprecedented prosperity. He had urged the formation of a policy committee in which leading IAPS members discussed the schools' problems with industry. He had revived the refresher courses and put a new emphasis on the training of assistant masters with the introduction of eighteen month in-service courses. He also edited the *PSR* from 1947 to 1956. Two weeks before he died in 1963 he was made a Vice-President of the Association.[32]

Successively guiding the Association from 1919 to 1963 through the difficult times of pre-war depression, war-time evacuation and post-war expansion, King, Underhill and Dealtry were helped by others such as Mr Pat Knox-Shaw who became headmaster of St Peter's School, Seaford, in 1934. He joined the Council in 1938 and with 'Joc' Lynam (Dragon) and Oliver Wyatt (Maidwell Hall) kept the Association going during the war years.[33] Vice-

Chairman in 1939, he was Chairman in 1940 and again in 1943 when administration of the Association was at its most difficult. War-time evacuation of his school to Barnstaple made communication with his colleagues difficult. Knox-Shaw was a skilful cricketer[34] and a practising Christian whose school chapel was 'his pride and joy'. He led the IAPS delegation which the Fleming Commission consulted in 1943/44. After his retirement in 1955 he began a fifteen years' career firstly as an assistant to the Rev. P.C. Underhill at Henley and then as the Secretary of the IAPS Training and Refresher courses. In 1956 he relieved 'Tim' Dealtry as editor of the *PSR*, which he was still editing when he died in 1970.

J.H.R. Lynam was a second IAPS figure who kept the Association alive during the war years. The last of the Lynam dynasty, he was Chairman in two consecutive years, 1941/42, and served on the Council intermittently for a total of eighteen years between 1936 and 1960, retiring from the headmastership of the Dragon School five years later. The other member of the wartime 'triumvirate' was Oliver E.P. Wyatt, MC, who died preaching in his local church in Suffolk in 1973.[35] A man of many interests, he played a full role in the IAPS, being Chairman in 1944 and in 1948. While he was at Maidwell Hall in Northamptonshire he was a magistrate and Chairman of the Rural District Council, church warden, lay reader and squire of his parish. It was he who led the rearguard action against the Fleming Committee's proposal that all preparatory schools should become 'Charitable Trusts'. Another leading member of 'the second generation' of the Association was Mr Fred Chappell (1881–1980) who died fifteen months short of his 100th birthday. Elected to membership in 1913, he served on the Council for twenty-one years and was its Chairman in 1936. Like Pat Knox-Shaw and Oliver Wyatt, Fred Chappell was a devout Christian.

A 'third generation' of IAPS leaders can be discerned amongst three of the present Vice-Presidents: R.J.S. Curtis, the Rev. Robert Wickham and L.H.A. Hankey, all of whom have served the Association with great distinction. A fourth Vice-President who died in 1980 was R.A. (Arthur) Harrison. Whilst headmaster of Marlborough House School he served as Chairman of Council in 1952. He shared the distinction with Mr Henry Brooke, the then President of the Association, of launching the Bursary Scheme for the sons of IAPS assistant masters at public schools. After retiring from his school in 1957 he became IAPS Treasurer and for six years in 1962 was also Secretary, after the sudden death of 'Tim' Dealtry. In his later years Harrison devoted much of his energy to the promotion of the IAPS orchestra at Snape in Suffolk.[36] The late Gilbert Ashton (Abberley Hall), who was Chairman of Council in 1937 and 1946, Chairman of the IAPS Pensions Scheme for twenty-five years from its inception in 1936, and Council member intermittently for fifteen years, ought to be added to that group of, to adopt Alicia Percival's phrase, 'very superior men'.[37] Today a 'fourth generation' can be perceived who at the moment fulfil leadership roles within the Association: men like Mr J. Hornby (ex-Secretary), Mr T.H.B. Bowles (Bramcote, Gamston), Mr J.R.G. Higgs (Beechwood Park,

St Alban's), Mr A.H. Mould (St John's College School), Mr H.E.P. Woodcock (DCPS), Mr Jack Dodd (former Secretary and now Vice-President) and Mr W.L.V. Caldwell (Editor, *PSR*) — all of whom have been Chairmen of the Association and continue to serve the Association with great élan.

Notes

1 *PSR*, 7, 60, March 1915, p. 108.
2 *PSR*, 8, 75, March 1920, pp. 117, 123–4.
3 *PSR*, 8, 83, December 1922, p. 371, also *PSR*, 8, 84, March 1923, p. 414.
4 *PSR*, 1, 1, July 1895, p. 18.
5 Cited by G.H. WILSON (1937) in *Windlesham House School 1837–1937*, McCor-quodale, pp. 56–7. There is no sign of this in the AGM report of the HMC for 1890. The HMC confirms (letter dated 19 October 1971) that no record of this comment is to be found in the Report of either the 1890 or 1896 AGM. It seems likely that it was made *en passant* in 1896, possibly outside committee.
6 *PSR*, 1, 8, December 1897, p. 94.
7 *PSR*, 1, 9, March 1898, pp. 24–5.
8 *PSR*, 1, 10, July 1898, p. 46.
9 It is not without significance that Mr C.D. OLIVE wrote on Dame Preparatory Schools in the Board of Education Report on *Preparatory Schools*, in 1900.
10 *PSR*, 2, 17, December 1900, p. 193. Miss ROSE MALDEN, Mrs CHARLES MALDEN's sister-in-law, taught at Windlesham.
11 *PSR*, 3, 18, March 1901, p. 34.
12 *PSR*, 3, 21, March 1902, p. 99.
13 *PSR*, 8, 78, March 1921, p. 204.
14 POOLEY was chairman of the IAPS in 1939.
15 *PSR*, 10, 112, June 1932, p. 305; *PSR*, 10, 114, March 1933, p. 369.
16 *PSR*, 21, 2, June 1972, p. 3. See also *PSR*, 30, 1, February 1981, pp. 3–5.
17 *Daily Mail*, November 1971.
18 From the official proposals for amalgamation, May 1980, p. 3.
19 *PSR*, 8, 73, July 1919, pp. 45–51.
20 *PSR*, 11, 119, November 1934, pp. 38–42.
21 Amalgamation Document, 1.
22 *Ibid.*
23 *PSR*, 2, 14, December 1899, pp. 36–7. See also *PSR*, 2, 15, March 1900, p. 83.
24 *PSR*, 10, 120, March 1934, p. 464.
25 *PSR*, 14, 2, November 1945, p. 3.
26 *PSR*, E.H. ALLEN and L.P. DEALTRY (Eds) (n.d.) *The Preparatory Schoolboy and His Education*, Evans Bros.
27 *PSR*, 11, 127, June 1937, pp. 333–4.
28 R.A. HARRISON, *op. cit.*, p. 136.
29 *Ibid.*, p. 137.
30 *Ibid.*, p. 138.
31 *Ibid.*, p. 140.
32 *PSR*, 18, 9, February 1964, p. 3.
33 *PSR*, 20, 1, February 1971, p. 11.
34 KNOX-SHAW played cricket with ALEC WAUGH and was in one of the teams in the match with A.G. MACDONNELL depicted in *England, Their England*.
35 *PSR*, 22, 2, June 1973, p. 44.
36 *PSR*, 29, 3, 1980, p. 15.
37 Cf. ALICIA C. PERCIVAL (1973) *Very Superior Men*, Charles Knight and Co.

18   War and Schemes of Symbiosis

Could our present rulers help the independent schools they would ease the position of the middle class parents and ensure that independent thought and action in education would be able to be continued in this country.
(J.H. Leakey (1951) *School Errant*)

Preparation: Ninety Schools Evacuated

In the Second World War 60,000 civilians were killed from air attack compared with some 1117 civilian deaths in the first.[1] The Zeppelin raids of the First World War were trifling compared with the systematic bombing of cities such as London or the 'blanket' bombing of other cities such as Coventry in the second. Whereas the civilian population of Britain in the First World War was physically detached from the muddy trench warfare on the continent, in the Second World War it was heavily involved in a total war which demanded early national conscription; a constant vigilance at home leading to the formation of the Local Defence Volunteers (later Home Guard); constant personal discomfort and permanent anxiety in the face of an enemy whose victories, at least in the early years, were staggering; and the preparatory schools suffered with the rest.

Anticipating this, some individual schools took early measures to minimize the threat. One master at the Dragon School in Oxford was given responsibility in 1938 for studying the city's plans for Air Raid Precautions (ARP) so that the school could coordinate its efforts. Soon after, a long zig-zag trench was dug in an adjacent field and fitted with wooden props and duckboarding, where boys were to repair in case of enemy air-raid. Meanwhile, arrangements were made (but were never implemented) for the boarders to evacuate to a large hotel in Cornwall.[2] Yardley Court, Tonbridge, also took heed of the warning signs from the Munich crisis and immediately began the building of a large air-raid shelter in the school grounds which could accommodate twenty beds and seating for 150.[3]

At Bramcote School, Scarborough, an air-raid shelter was constructed under a school lawn at a cost of more than £1000. This relatively heavy expense was singularly misplaced: the shelter was used only three times before it was decided to evacuate the school to Eshton Hall, near Gargrave, because of parental fears of invasion.[4] At Northwood Preparatory School, in Middlesex, three air-raid shelters were similarly constructed under the school lawn. Northwood School, however, remained *in situ* throughout the war. The air-raid shelters became almost a part of the boys' daily life since interrupted lessons were continued in the shelter. Other early precautions were the gas-proofing of gymnasia, changing rooms, kitchens and cellars; the total 'blacking-out' at night of windows which in many areas were also protected with sticky tape against shelling and bomb-blasting; the carrying of gas-masks by boys and staff alike[5] and the learning of first aid by staff members.[6] Some of these measures turned out to be unnecessary: at Lambrook in Berkshire the zig-zag trench and underground shelter were never used.[7] The Editor of the *Bilton Record* encapsulated this process of adaptation in December 1939 when he wrote

> War has brought to us, as to everyone, its problems and its complications; we have had to face strange, unwanted situations, but life has speedily resumed the even tenor of its way. Blackout — a formidable proposition at the outset — has now become an accepted and most natural part of the day's routine. ARP practices are a regular feature

But the greatest single precaution by any school was its removal to a place of greater safety, a process known as 'evacuation'. The evacuation of certain preparatory schools was carried out in conjunction with the national scheme organised by the Ministry of Health.[8] The evacuation scheme divided the country into three categories, the 'evacuable' (regarded as vulnerable either because of population density or because of the likelihood of their being bombing targets), 'neutral' (where there was to be no evacuation of population but where no evacuees were to be received) and 'reception' (which were to receive evacuees).[9] Though 'largely unprepared' at the time of the Munich crisis in September 1938,[10] IAPS sent at twenty-four hours' notice a circular to schools, the replies to which formed the basis of its scheme.

Launched in January 1939 at the same time as the launching of the National Scheme, in liaison with Mr Norman Lowndes at the Ministry of Health, schools were able to make their own arrangements for evacuation. This usually entailed the headmaster's going off in his car to reconnoitre likely areas of refuge and returning to make contact with the Ministry and IAPS. To ensure that such a move would not snarl up other evacuation arrangements,[11] the IAPS set up a committee in response to the Ministry of Health's invitation to consider the question of evacuation. During the ensuing months schemes of affiliation or adoption were worked out whereby preparatory schools in 'evacuable' areas were to join schools in 'reception' areas. Other alternative accommodation was sought in large country houses, hotels and public schools.

In all some ninety preparatory schools were evacuated by the end of the year.[12] The Association facilitated matters by giving advice on what might be a fair *per capita* charge between schools for board and lodging and published an up-to-date list of schools 'in evacuation quarters' as agreed at the Council meeting on 2 February 1940.[13] Perhaps the Association's most useful contribution at this time was on the delicate subject of fees in lieu of notice and refunds. With the wisdom of Solomon the Council adjudged, in October 1939, that where a school remained in an area scheduled as 'evacuable', the school could not hope to recover fees in lieu of notice from parents. The Council agreed to discourage all legal action against such parents. They decided, too, that in cases where boys were received into other preparatory schools and no arrangement had been made either between the losing school and the parent or between the receiving and the losing school, then 10 per cent of the losing school's fees for three terms should be refunded by the receiving school. Further, in cases where a boy was withheld from school and kept at home the parent was to be pressed to pay half fees for the term or, alternatively, full fees on the understanding that such fees should cover the term when the boy returned to the school.[14] When considered against the background of national emergency these decisions of the IAPS may seem hairsplitting and even trifling, but schools which had survived the precariously hard times of the 'twenties and 'thirties saw a necessity to clarify such issues.

'Phoney War' and the Moving of Schools

The 'phoney' war saw some three million child evacuees, many of them from independent schools, adapting themselves to a new environment. This period of stress and turmoil was the basis of one playwright's creation, *The Happiest Days of Your Life*,[15] in which two schools were merged for the duration. During this period of the 'phoney' war many preparatory schools underwent similar processes of affiliation or moved into a different domicile.

Often school buildings were requisitioned at very short notice by military or other authorities. I.C.M. Sanderson, headmaster of Elstree, was informed on the 5 September that 150 men and eleven officers from the 11th HAC Regiment, Royal Horse Artillery, were to be billeted on the school for an indefinite period, and within seventeen days the school had moved to its present location at Woolhampton in Berkshire.[16] In October 1939 Colet Court's (London) buildings were to be requisitioned as sleeping quarters for recruits. But already the bulk of the school had moved to Bigwood Camp, temporary accommodation near Radley School, and to Danesfield, a large house near Marlow which accommodated forty boarders.[17] At a later stage Colet Court was taken over by the Royal Army Medical Corps (RAMC). In May 1940 R.J.S. (Dick) Curtis, headmaster of Hurst Court, Ore, received twenty-four hours' notice from the military to move out of his school.

Fortunately Curtis had made arrangements that in such an emergency the school should be removed to Wrekin School, Shropshire. Thither Hurst Court moved the next day in two large buses surrounded by books, bats and bedding.[18] West Downs had to move from Winchester to Blair Castle, Scotland, to make way for a succession of military units,[19] including US General Bradley's HQ Staff. But Chafyn Grove, Salisbury, twice successfully resisted attempts to requisition its buildings — in 1939 and 1944 — no mean feat in view of its location.[20]

Some schools moved not because their buildings were requisitioned by the military but simply because they were in what they felt were danger zones. On the outbreak of war Hawtrey's, at Westgate-on-Sea, moved immediately to Llangedwyn Hall in North Wales;[21] Heatherdown, Ascot, moved to Herefordshire;[22] and St Wilfrid's School, Seaford, moved to Llanidloes, in Montgomeryshire.[23] After the fall of Amiens in May 1940 Mr R.A. Harrison at Marlborough House, Hawkhurst, was inundated with telephone calls from anxious parents. Until then Kent had been regarded as a 'safe' area because it seemed an unlikely target for bombs. But with the invasion and collapse of France, Kent and Sussex seemed likely to be on the invasion route. Once the decision was made to move Marlborough House on Devon, it was executed virtually overnight.[24] Cumnor House, a Sussex school, was similarly moved to Littleworth Cross, Seale, in Surrey to escape from the invasion threat. For similar reasons Chelmsford Hall and St Andrew's both moved from Eastbourne to safer locations in the summer of 1940 after their cricket matches had been played to the accompaniment of artillery fire as the Germans reached the French channel ports.[25] Chelmsford Hall was later (1942) requisitioned by the Royal Navy and became part of *HMS Marlborough*, No. 2 Torpedo School, whilst St Andrew's became Ack-Ack Regimental HQ.

Perhaps the exemplar of schools which experienced evacuation and its attendant disruption was Dulwich College Preparatory School (DCPS) — then among the three largest preparatory schools. A whole book has been written on the topic of this school's experiences during the Second World War.[26] Dulwich College Preparatory School — closely linked with Dulwich College (1619), but independent of it — experienced three periods of evacuation. The first occurred as early as 1938 at the time of the Munich crisis, when an experimental evacuation camp was set up at Coursehorn near Cranbrook School, in Kent. When war did break out a contingent of boys and staff from DCPS went to Coursehorn and stayed for about a year. With the fall of France in 1940, Coursehorn ceased to be a suitable place of refuge and Mr Leakey, the headmaster, had to find an alternative. He hit on the 'Royal Oak Hotel' at Betws-y-Coed, North Wales, where the school stayed from 1940 to 1945.

The policy pursued by Mr D.J.V. Hamilton-Miller, headmaster of Shrewsbury House, Surbiton, was unorthodox even if, like that of Leakey, it was the product of careful planning. After Munich, Hamilton-Miller set about discovering from his 120 sets of parents what their wishes were. Opinion was fairly evenly divided (55:65) on whether to send the boys as boarders to a 'safe' area or to remain in Surbiton. The head decided that this division should be faithfully reflected by splitting the school in two. He then faced the three possibilities for the boarders: to take a large house in a rural area where boys could live as boarders; to join up with another preparatory school; or to find accommodation in a public school which had not yet recovered from the hard times of the 'thirties.[27] Rejecting the first solution, Hamilton-Miller considered the second. But he concluded that if two schools occupied the same premises, each would suffer restrictions. He plumped for the third. He sent his fifty-five boarders to Kelly College, Tavistock, where they stayed during the 'phoney war'. By the summer term of 1940 the parents of the boarders felt that, with the danger apparently receding, the school should return to Surbiton. Hamilton-Miller, who had meanwhile offered the main building at Surbiton to the War Office, succeeded in redeeming it for resumed use by the preparatory school.[28]

Evacuating Boys Abroad

When France fell in June 1940, some schools regarded Churchill's 'finest hour' as also 'the darkest hour'. Arrangements were made for boys to be evacuated to the USA and to Canada. Some boys left Aysgarth School, Yorkshire, to cross the Atlantic but most of them remained.[29] David Frost, the future television personality, was one of those who left St Hugh's School, Woodhall Spa, for refuge in Canada.[30] Boys went from Yardley Court to go not only to North America but also individually to join their parents in China, Brazil, Syria, Egypt, Australia, South Africa and India.[31] The Dragon School contemplated starting a branch in Canada but abandoned the scheme because of financial and transportational difficulties.[32] The late Lord Boyle's old school, Ashfold, left Buckinghamshire for Canada in 1941 and stayed there till 1945.

Many preparatory schools stayed put. The Dragon School, after much contemplation of moving, decided to stay, enjoying a certain immunity from the war in the 'open city' of dreaming spires. Wolborough Hill School, which did not move from its home at Newton Abbot, was less fortunate. During the six years of the war there were 615 alerts in the area of the school, and at one stage the headmaster, Lt. H. Jeffreys-Jones, spent eleven days and nights without going to bed.[33] Yardley Court, despite its vulnerable position stayed in Kent throughout the war experiencing 'the full weight of the flying bomb attack' in 1944.[34] Lambrook, which must be one of the few nineteenth century schools to have a continuous record of occupancy of its original buildings, remained in Berkshire. So did several of its nearby neighbours: Woodcote House, Windlesham; Sunningdale; Bigshotte and St George's Windsor.[35] Temple Grove remained at Uckfield in Sussex.

All preparatory schools, whether they remained in their own school buildings or sought refuge elsewhere, suffered because of the war. Some suffered a fall in numbers. Homefield, a school of 200 at the beginning of the war, was down to 125 by the end of hostilities.[36] Yardley Court lost sixty-five boys out of 137 during the summer holiday of 1940,[37] whilst at Cumnor House the number dropped from 100 to twenty-nine.[38] Widford Lodge School, in Essex, came near to extinction when it was reduced to five pupils, three of whom were sons of the headmaster. The latter, less occupied than heretofore, devoted much of his time to Air Raid Precautions. The school had become the main ARP depot in Chelmsford, and he himself was ARP director.[39]

The Benefit to Rural Schools

Numbers, however, were not dwindling everywhere. Rural schools located away from the east and south-east coasts tended to increase their numbers as others lost theirs. Abberley Hall in Worcestershire was so inundated with requests for places that it increased its accommodation.[40] Maidwell Hall in Northamptonshire also benefited from its rural site far from industrial targets. It increased its numbers and strengthened its links with Eton College.[41] 'These were years of growth', too, for Swanbourne House.[42]

If many schools experienced a decline in numbers during the early years of the war, there was also a general loss of assistant masters. Although schoolmasters over twenty-five years old were to be in a reserved occupation *pro. tem.*,[43] many rushed to join the Colours, leaving some schools denuded of young assistant masters. At Marlborough House, Hawkhurst, the headmaster, R.A. (Arthur) Harrison, lost some of his young masters immediately and by 1940 was left with only his second master from his original staff.[44] The choir school, St Michael's College, Tenbury, was substantially weakened in 1940 by the departure first of its choirmaster and then of its warden.[45] Once again Abberley Hall, St Michael's neighbour, fared well, losing only two staff to His Majesty's Forces and gaining two very satisfactory replacements.[46] Gaps in teaching staff were filled by the employment of retired male teachers; by increasing the number of qualified lady teachers; and by encouraging public school boys, not yet of an age for military service, to give a hand.[47] War had encouraged the return of 'birds of passage'. Retired army officers were often found in this emergency teaching force: at Elstree a retired Major-General taught mathematics and physical training for two years.[48]

When domestic staff entered the armed forces or the factories there were no such remedies. The headmaster's wife became more invaluable than ever in the successful running of the school. At Chelmsford Hall,[49] as in many other schools, the boys had to make their own beds, clean their own shoes, keep their rooms clean and tidy and wait on each other in the dining hall. (As late as January 1942, however, St Michael's boys had not been asked to perform these extra duties.)[50] Schools shared many hardships with the nation at large. Food and clothes were rationed. Many school grounds were given up to the growing of fruit and vegetables and some boys learnt much about animal husbandry because of the war years. Corduroy shorts and jumpers took the place of flannel trousers and jackets. Thus the war accelerated the changes in clothing and styles of clothing which had started during the harsh period of the 'thirties. At Elstree the school ran a used-clothing store which was well patronized.[51] The war made the Eton Collar and top hat almost, if not totally, obsolete.

The war brought hardship and disruption to the sporting field too. Because of the evacuation of some schools and the closure of others, traditional inter-school sporting programmes were reduced in the 'evacuable' areas. At Yardley Court there were no rugby matches for three seasons, and one period of four consecutive terms saw a total of one match of any kind. Shortage of opponents had conspired with the usual epidemic diseases and with transport difficulties to render the school's programme nugatory.[52] The transport difficulties were largely caused by the increasing shortage of petrol, which was the subject of discussion at the General Purposes Committee of the IAPS Council on 14 October 1942. The Committee agreed to suggest to the schools that they ought not to go out of their way to play additional matches.[53] The ploughing up of playing fields (as for example at Dunchurch-Winton School) for vegetable allotments and other war efforts further limited sporting programmes.[54]

Affiliations, Amalgamations and Closures

As we have seen, the economic pressures of the 'thirties compelled many schools to amalgamate or close. The Second World War accelerated the process. Some headmasters refused to surrender to adversity. When war came and they found themselves in an 'evacuable' area, they affiliated or amalgamated temporarily with another school. Winton House (1863), at the beginning of the war, affiliated with Bilton Grange (Rugby) for about a year[55] before amalgamating permanently with Dunchurch Hall (Rugby) in 1940. When Mr Lesley Fawcus, the headmaster of Winton House, brought his boys to Dunchurch Hall to form the new school, Dunchurch-Winton Hall, he enlarged the school from thirty-five to sixty boys, thus making it a viable economic proposition.[56] In the case of Winton House, the school was able to retain continuity by joining its name to that of the host school (as did Brunswick House when it amalgamated with Stoke House in the 1960s to form Stoke Brunswick School). Other schools, less fortunate, did not survive amalgamation. Farnborough School and George Orwell's old school, St Cyprian's, Eastbourne amalgamated in 1939 and 1942 respectively with Summer Fields, Oxford and both lost their identity.[57] Similarly The Limes School, Croydon was submerged in Heath Mount School,[58] Hertfordshire, as was Aldwick Grange, in January 1941 with Hawtreys.[59] Other schools such as St David's, Surrey (1939)[60] and Seacroft School, Skegness (1940)[61] just closed their doors. A detailed sample of schools which either closed or amalgamated during the 'thirties and 'forties is given in Appendix 3.

The War Effort and Preparatory Schools

Both boys and remaining assistant masters at preparatory schools contributed to the war effort in their several ways. 'Digging for victory' in the school gardens, filling sand-bags and putting on displays of art, music and gymnastics to boost savings weeks' campaigns were common activities, whilst many masters joined the local ARP or Home Guard — the successor of the Local Defence Volunteers (LDV). In keeping with this defence-keeping rôle it was suggested at a district meeting of IAPS that schools arrange to have the staff, not the boys, handle the stirrup pumps and other fire-fighting equipment.[62]

Throughout the war many schools ran National Savings Groups and made especially great efforts at saving during 'Warship Week' in 1942, 'Wings for Victory Week' in 1943 and 'Salute the Soldier Week' in 1944.[63] The Mall School, Twickenham, like other preparatory schools, joined the Ship Adoption Society and was thus linked with a certain Captain Bedford, of the Merchant Navy, and his ship.[64] Similarly Bilton Grange (Rugby) had a close association with the destroyer *HMS Vanquisher*. A photograph of Bilton Grange hung in the wardroom of *HMS Vanquisher*, as did a picture of *HMS Vanquisher* in Bilton Grange.[65] The school sent parcels of comforts like hand-made woollen mittens, books and games to the sailors of *HMS Vanquisher*. These 'adoptions' were not mere formalities. A letter from Lt. Commander Osborne of *HMS Vanquisher* to Mr Machin, the headmaster, records a request for 'seven electric irons (110v D.C.), some shoe leather for mending shoes' and some cricket equipment — items which the ship could not obtain.[66]

The IAPS as a body showed the same thoughtfulness and concern but on a larger scale. In 1940 the Lord Mayor of London appealed for money on behalf of the Red Cross and St John's Fund. Over 200 preparatory schools raised £620 — more than enough to purchase a preparatory schools' ambulance for use by the Red Cross.[67] At about the same time the IAPS appealed to its members for sports equipment of all kinds to give to 'convalescent homes for temporarily shocked airmen'.[68] Like the population at large, the preparatory schools were affected by the wartime spirit of cooperation. It was a similar camaraderie that sustained Londoners during the 'Blitz' and boosted their morale. The sharing of a common experience is perhaps epitomized in a letter, (with the original spelling retained) a preparatory schoolboy addressed to Mr Chamberlain at the time of the Munich crisis,

> Dear Sir,
>
> I ask you what we can do? I am 12, nearly 13, if there is a war what can I do? If I cood serve my country I would be ready to give up a good eduecation for it. It would give me satisefaction. Fighting is not nesesarily my ambishion. But there are many other things, as farming, stabel boy in the Army, assistent cook field ambulance boy or eaven despatch rider....[69]

The Fleming Report, 1944

In the dark days of the early 1940s it was part of the strategy of the British Government to keep up morale by planning for the post-war era. A committee of Senior Officials on Post-War Educational Reconstruction was formed in November 1940 by the Board of Education. This committee became the catalyst for educational planning. The White Paper on *Educational Reconstruction* (1943) in turn foreshadowed the 1944 Education Act — a major ingredient of the post-war welfare state. During these war years the coalition government created committees to examine several areas of education. The curriculum and examinations in secondary schools were examined by a committee under the President of St John's College, Oxford, Cyril Norwood. The future training and supply of teachers became the province of the Vice-Chancellor of Liverpool University, Arnold McNair. The public schools and the general educational system were to be examined by a committee chaired by the Scottish judge, Lord Fleming. The preparatory schools *per se* were not within Fleming's brief. But since recommendations for the future of the public schools would have repercussions on the preparatory schools, the IAPS took a keen interest in the Fleming Committee and its deliberations. It submitted evidence to the Committee, and four members of the Association, Mr Pat Knox-Shaw (St Peter's, Seaford and Chairman), the Rev. P.C. Underhill (Secretary), Mr J.H.R. Lynam (Dragon School) and Mr Oliver E.P. Wyatt (Maidwell Hall), gave evidence individually.

In his examination of the Fleming Committee Professor Gosden adopted a mild 'conspiracy' view of their deliberations when he wrote:

> The establishment of the Fleming Committee came about not so much in an endeavour to 'democratize' the public schools — even though that appeared to many to be its purpose — but rather out of an attempt to find a politically acceptable way of bringing state-supported pupils, and therefore public money, to the salvation of the financially unstable and threatened boarding schools.[70]

Before reaching this conclusion Professor Gosden had examined in great detail the behind-the-scenes activity between senior officials in the Board of Education and members of the HMC.[71] He attributed motives to the public schools' lobby, led by Dr Spencer Leeson, headmaster of Winchester and Chairman of the HMC, in the passing of the Public Schools and other Schools (War Conditions) Act of 1941 which allowed schools to divert parts of their endowments to purposes other than those originally intended. This Act served to underline the financial plight of some public schools which led to, and formed their attitude to compromise with, the Fleming inquiry. As Professor Gosden himself records this alleged attitude was explicitly denied by Sir Maurice Holmes, Permanent Secretary of the Board of Education when he suggested that a greater association between the public school and maintained schools had some considerable merit.[72] But there is, nevertheless, still a need to examine the allegation of compromise, at least as far as the preparatory schools themselves were concerned.

One of the main proposals of the Fleming Report was that boys and girls from elementary schools who were capable of benefiting thereby should be enabled to enter public schools irrespective of the income of parents. Since elementary schools kept their pupils only till the age of eleven, the question arose what was to happen to the selected children until they were ready to move to public schools at thirteen. The junior forms of day secondary schools would not provide suitable preparation. The only acceptable alternatives were to send them either to a junior school of a public school or to a private preparatory school.[73] From the beginning the Association was not united in its official attitude towards the Fleming Committee so that the division of opinion in the IAPS vitiates any 'conspiracy' theory at least by that association.

Eliminating Private Profit?

The idea of public money being spent in the provision of preparatory boarding education went back much further than the anxiety in the 'thirties of public and preparatory school headmasters about the declining numbers in their schools. The Bryce Report of 1895 had proposed that local authorities should provide preparatory boarding schools,[74] a suggestion which received the approval of the then Bishop of London[75] and was supported by other witnesses who gave evidence. Mr E. Storr, the chief master of modern subjects at Merchant Taylors' school, claimed that the then High Master of St Paul's, Mr F.W. Walker, proposed that a preparatory school for former elementary school boys should be set up at public expense. Instead of the scholarships' being given at St Paul's School to elementary scholars, he wanted to see a preparatory school established, that is a school on the lines of Elstree and such well-known schools, for scholars drafted from elementary schools.[76] On the other hand, HM Inspector James W. Headlam, who reported in 1894/95 on the system of secondary education in Surrey, recommended that public schools ought to have preparatory schools attached as junior schools. The suggestions of both High Master Walker and HM Inspector Headlam had some bearing on the discussions in the twentieth century about the proposed articulation between the elementary school and public school systems.

It is significant that more than a year before the formation of the Fleming Committee two members of the IAPS — Mr L.P. Dealtry (The Leas, Hoylake) and Mr W.P. Johnston (Cheltenham Junior School) — should have formulated a proposal to eliminate private profit from the preparatory schools.[77] Two months later the General Purposes Committee of the Association was discussing the possibility of preparatory schools forming into limited companies and even of regional groups of preparatory schools controlled by a board of governors.[78] Such measures would remove the seeming handicap of private ownership and give the schools a 'charitable' rather than a 'proprietorial' basis.

In May 1941 the Council resolved: 'In order that we may take the greatest possible share in the future education of the nation the Council is of the opinion that it is a necessary first step to eliminate the element of private profit from our schools.'[79] This resolution of the IAPS even before the formation of the Fleming Committee had enormous repercussions on the development of preparatory schools after the war. Meanwhile it was an earnest of their good intentions. Since the time of the Bryce Commission their relatively high fees had been seen as standing in the way of the attendance of potentially able elementary school children. Later, when the free inspection of schools was a subject of controversy, their private, fee-paying and profit-making character had been held against them. It is thus of some significance that the Fleming Report of 1944 was likewise to discriminate against those preparatory schools — the majority — which were private profit-making. In this sense the memorandum of Dealtry and Johnston in 1941 and the resolution which followed were extremely timely.

In 1941 the Rev. F.G. Ridgeway further developed the ideas of Dealtry and Johnston when he wrote a memorandum suggesting that the conversion of preparatory schools into charitable institutions would enable them to maintain their contribution to the educational life of the nation. The schools were to be seen as 'preparatory' rather than 'private' schools.[80]

Anticipating the recommendations of the Fleming Report, Radley College made tentative overtures to the IAPS in 1942 to cooperate with them in a scheme of bursary scholarships for elementary school boys. Radley's initiative met strong opposition from Mr Oliver Wyatt (Maidwell Hall), who deprecated the idea that preparatory schools should become 'charitable' institutions in order to help boys from the maintained system. Mr W.D. Johnston (Cheltenham Junior School) was in support of the Radley scheme, which articulated well with his own proposals for converting preparatory schools into charitable trusts. Wyatt then reminded Johnston that 90 per cent of the preparatory schools were 'private profit' concerns.[81]

Two months later, at a Council meeting in July 1942, Johnston and Wyatt were again in conflict when Mr R.W. Thompson (Aysgarth) supported the principle of eliminating the private profit motive from preparatory schools. On this occasion Mr W.D. Johnston suggested that the IAPS should set up an experimental unit as a charitable trust, since it would put the preparatory schools on a better footing for any proposals to integrate with the maintained system which might arise from the Fleming Committee's deliberations.[82]

It is clear, therefore, that although the IAPS was divided in its views on charitable trusts, the Association was already thinking along the lines of the Fleming Committee's terms of reference: 'To consider means whereby the association between the Public Schools . . . and the general educational system of the country could be developed and extended. . . .'[83] It was known that the Fleming Committee was considering the idea that HMC schools should be encouraged to open junior branches. This caused some disquiet.[84] Such junior branches would have a decided advantage over private preparatory schools run on private-profit lines.

The Randolph Hotel Meeting

The Fleming Report was published in July 1944. It is significant that Mr Oliver Wyatt, the arch-opponent of the charitable trust movement, was Chairman of the IAPS in that critical year. On 10 September 1944 a special Council meeting was held at the Randolph Hotel, Oxford, to consider the preparation of a memorandum in response to the Report. The task was deputed to Mr Oliver Wyatt, Mr 'Joc' Lynam and Mr Pat Knox-Shaw — all of whom had given evidence to the Fleming Committee — who were to be joined by Mr T.C. Elliott (Fan Court, Long Cross, and IAPS Chairman in 1945). The Randolph Hotel meeting shows clearly the influence of Wyatt, even though he was in a minority. The Minutes included the following statement:

> That together with the Council's opinion of the Fleming Report it should be placed on record that there yet remained members of the IAPS who feel strongly that some preparatory schools should continue to exist which are completely free from any form of state restriction or interference whatsoever *even to the point of their refusing to accept state bursars* [my italics].
>
> In placing this on record these members wish to emphasise that they are in no sense unmindful of the dangers of their attitude in view of their being possibly in a minority and the overwhelming flood of political and public opinion against private enterprise in education at the moment.
>
> They nevertheless feel that some schools must persist in England either in the IAPS or out of it, which are completely free from any danger of political influence being injected by degrees of state control, both for the benefit of world education as a whole and for the maintenance of English liberty of thought.[85]

This was no equivocal comment with an eye to the main chance. This was a statement of principle against the main trend. Oliver Wyatt in 1944 was showing as much independence of thought as had Tom Pellatt in the early years of the century.

It is a commonplace of educational history that the Fleming Report was shelved largely because the LEAs did not wish to join in a scheme which helped to cream off their most promising pupils for public schools and at the same time place public funds in public schools' hands. On the other hand it could be argued that the preparatory schools, which by 1944 formed an essential infrastructure to the public school system, had been badly treated by the Fleming Committee. They were part of the public school system yet were not given adequate consideration as such. The only major reference in the Report to the preparatory schools was in Section 181 which dealt with the 'problem of the period from 11 to 13'[86] in which the preparatory schools were criticized for being conducted for private profit. The Fleming Committee did not consider possible ways in which this situation could be changed, yet implicitly assumed that preparatory schools should continue to service the public schools. The Fleming Committee's condemnation of private profit as the financial basis of the schools made them deeply anxious about their future. The whole Fleming episode has one lasting effect on the preparatory schools: they have gradually become charitable institutions. By 1965 110 schools out of a total of 494 were charitable institutions: some 22 per cent of the preparatory schools.[87] These charitable institutions were to greatly outnumber the proprietorial ones by the 'seventies. In 1974 309 out of 464 were charitable institutions: in 1981 exactly 75 per cent — 330 out of 440 boys' IAPS schools — had ceased to be proprietorial.

Notes

1 Quoted from A.J.P. TAYLOR, *op. cit.*, p. 44 and p. 411. His figures for the Second World War were quoted from TITMUSS, *Problems of Social Policy*, 13, pp. 324–6 and Note A437.
2 C.H. JAQUES, *op. cit.*, pp. 147–149.
3 ANON., *Yardley Court 1898–1973*, p. 46.
4 ANON., *A short history of Bramcote School*, p. 2.
5 Cf. IAPS *Minute Book*, Vol. III. December 1938–December 1948, Council Minutes of meeting of 1.12.1938 concerning ARP and the use of gas-masks.
6 At Widford Lodge, Chelmsford, for example, all the staff including the headmaster and his wife learnt first-aid.
7 For this information I am grateful to Mrs FLORA FORBES, the widow of A.H. FORBES, a former headmaster of Lambrook.
8 G.A.N. LOWNDES, (1969) *The Silent Social Revolution*, 2nd edition, Oxford University Press, pp. 188–211. NORMAN LOWNDES played an important part in the original planning of the evacuation scheme, and in some sense Chapter 12 of *The Silent Social Revolution* can be seen as an apologia for that scheme. See also P.H.J.H. GOSDEN, (1976) *Education in the Second World War*, Methuen, pp. 7–31.
9 G.A.N. LOWNDES, *op. cit.*, pp. 199–200.
10 *PSR*, 12, 234, November 1939, p. 82.
11 P.H.J.H. GOSDEN, *op. cit.*, pp. 11–12.
12 *PSR*, 12, 135, March 1940, p. 114.
13 *Ibid.*, p. 108.
14 IAPS *Minute Book*, Vol. III, 6th October 1939.
15 JOHN DIGHTON: *The Happiest Days of Your Life* (1951).
16 I.C.M. SANDERSON, *op. cit.*, pp. 67–69. In due course Elstree was occupied by the Welsh Guards; the Coldstream Guards; the London Irish Regiment and the W.R.A.F.
17 JAMES BEWSHER et al., (1963) *The Story of Colet Court*, Eastbourne p. 22.
18 I am grateful to Mr R.J.S. CURTIS, OBE, for this information.
19 I am grateful to Mr J.F. CORNES, headmaster of West Downs for this information.
20 ANON., *Portrait of a School*, 1976, p. 4.
21 From an undated typescript in my possession on the history of Hawtreys. I wish to thank Mr G.E. WATTS, headmaster of Hawtreys, for this information.
22 From information given in a letter of 6 February 1978 from Mrs A.H. FORBES, widow of the former head of Lambrook School.

23 From information given in letter of 3 November 1977, ERIC LOUSADA, of St Wilfrid's School, Seaford, Sussex.
24 R.A. HARRISON, *op. cit.*, pp. 41–2.
25 Cf. PAUL SPILLANE, *op. cit.*, p. 63 and L. COVERLEY, pp. 29–30. St Andrew's went to Thurlestone in South Devon before going to Oakash, Chaddleworth, Berkshire. Chelmsford Hall moved to Wellington School, Somerset.
26 J.H. LEAKEY (1951) *School Errant*, Queensgate Press, p. 99.
27 D.J.V. HAMILTON-MILLER and R.P. IRVING (Eds) (1965) *Shrewsbury House Magazine*. Century Supplement, pp. 19–20.
28 *Ibid.*, p. 23.
29 E. THOMPSON (1977) *Out of the Oak; the Story of Aysgarth School*, Stockton, p. 38.
30 H.D. MARTINEAU, *op. cit.*, p. 12.
31 ANON., *Yardley Court, op. cit.*, p. 46.
32 C.H. JAQUES, *op. cit.*, pp. 153–4. Chelmsford Hall had a similar decision to make about an offer from the USA in 1940. Cf. L. COVERLEY, *op. cit.*, p. 32.
33 RICHARD WATTS, *op. cit.*, p. 31.
34 ANON., *Yardley Court, op. cit.*, p. 48.
35 Information from Mrs FLORA FORBES.
36 DAVID WARREN (1970) *A History of Homefield*, Charlmont Press, p. 13.
37 ANON., *Yardley Court, op. cit.*, p. 46.
38 H. MILNER-GULLAND, *School Story*, Guildford, p. 11.
39 History of Widford Lodge School (1967) *East Anglia Life*, 9, 69, July, p. 2.
40 I am grateful to the late Mr GILBERT ASHTON, ex-headmaster of Abberley Hall, for this information.
41 I am grateful to Mr J.A.H. PORCH, ex-headmaster of Maidwell Hall, for this information.
42 *Swanbourne House School Magazine*, June 1970, p. 44.
43 Cf. IAPS Council Minute dated 6 October 1935.
44 R.A. HARRISON, *op. cit.*, p. 41.
45 M.F. ALDERSON and H.C. COLLES (Eds), *op. cit.*, pp. 66–7.
46 From information given by the late Mr G. ASHTON.
47 *PSR*, 12, 135, March 1940, p. 114.
48 I.C.M. SANDERSON, *op. cit.*, p. 78.
49 L. COVERLEY, *op. cit.*, p. 75.
50 M.F. ALDERSON and H.C. COLLES (Eds), *op. cit.*, p. 68.
51 I.C.M. SANDERSON, *op. cit.*, p. 79.
52 ANON., *Yardley Court, op. cit.*, p. 48.
53 *Council Minute Book*, Vol. 3.
54 *Ibid.*, Minutes of Meeting, dated 15 October 1942. Cf. also typescript history of Dunchurch-Winton at the school.
55 *Bilton Record*, 13, 5, July 1940.
56 Unsigned typescript history of Dunchurch-Winton Hall.
57 RICHARD USBORNE (Ed.), *op. cit.*, p. 280.
58 I am grateful to Mr R.C.J. ROBERTSON, headmaster of Heath Mount School, for this information.
59 I am grateful to Mr G.E. WATTS, headmaster of Hawtreys, for this information.
60 EDWARD PEEL, *op. cit.*, p. 239.
61 H.D. MARTINEAU, *op. cit.*, p. 9.
62 *PSR*, 12, 136, June 1940, p. 139.
63 Cf. ANON., *A History of the Mall School 1872–1972*, p. 13, also J.H. TERRY, *Northwood Preparatory School 1910–1960*, p. 18, also PAUL SPILLANE, *op. cit.*, p. 68.
64 *Mall School, op. cit.*, p. 12.
65 *Bilton Record*, 13, 4, April 1940.

66 *Ibid.*, 17, July 1944.
67 *PSR*, 12, 136, June 1940, pp. 139–40.
68 *Ibid.*, p. 141.
69 *Ibid.*, pp. 152 and 154.
70 P.H.J.H. GOSDEN, *op. cit.*, pp. 332–3.
71 *Ibid.*, pp. 333–8.
72 *Ibid.*, p. 350.
73 Board of Education *Report of the Committee on Public Schools appointed by the President of the Board of Education in July 1942* (FLEMING) 1944, HMSO, p. 68.
74 Royal Commission *Report on Secondary Education* (BRYCE) Report 1895, Vol. I, p. 285.
75 *Ibid.*, Vol. 2, p. 452. Minutes 4777–4780.
76 *Ibid.*, Vol. 3, p. 127. Minute 7461.
77 *IAPS* Council Minutes Vol. III. Minutes of Meeting of 6th February 1941.
78 *Ibid.*, Minutes of Meeting of 7th April 1941.
79 *Ibid.*, Minutes of Meeting of 15th May 1941.
80 *Ibid.*, Minutes of Meeting of 15th July 1941.
81 *Ibid.*, Minutes of Meeting of 21st May 1942.
82 *Ibid.*, Minutes of Meeting of 9th July 1942.
83 Fleming Report, p. 1.
84 Minutes of the IAPS, Vol. III. Minutes of Meeting of 4th March 1943.
85 *Ibid.*, Minutes of Meeting of 10 September 1944.
86 FLEMING Report, p. 68.
87 P.L. MASTERS, *op. cit.*, p. 107.

19   Change in a Post-War World

Today there is a stirring in the educational world at large which seeks to relegate examinations to a suitably subordinate position, and to allow teaching to be directed towards its proper ends.
(J.H. Dodd, Chairman of IAPS, 1965)

The Return to Normal

By the time the Fleming Report was published the war had less than a year to run its course. The German occupation of Europe was progressively contracting after the successful Normandy landings in June 1944. At home, only the launching of the V1 and V2 rockets was to cause any further serious discomfort. Sensing that the end to hostilities was not far off the Association set up a Committee in September 1944 to deal with the process of de-requisitioning schools.[1] In an atmosphere of great optimism headmasters were advised, before the end of 1944, to write to the local MP if there were any difficulties about the return of school buildings by their occupying authority. St Hugh's School returned to Woodhall Spa, Lincolnshire in the autumn of 1944 from Storrs Hall at Ingleton, in North-West England.[2] The local MP helped Bramcote School to return to its Scarborough home in March 1945.[3] A number of evacuated schools had thus been restored to their original locations in time to celebrate the victory in Europe in May 1945 when bonfires were lit and effigies of Adolf Hitler were burnt. Soon after this the headmaster's wife at St Andrew's, Eastbourne, Mrs J.A. Fewings, went to the War Office to demand the de-requisitioning of that school to allow its return;[4] meanwhile, Ashfold School returned from Canada to Aylesbury.

The process of resettlement continued immediately after the war in a spirit of optimism and hope, even though the rationing of clothes, petrol and food continued for a while in 'austerity Britain'. The Rev. F.G. Ridgeway (St Peter's Court, Broadstairs) had forecast before the end of the war that preparatory schools, which had experienced great hardship in the 'thirties and 'forties, would enjoy a period of unwonted prosperity after the war.[5] He was right. The war was succeeded by decades of unparalleled prosperity when many preparatory schools had to extend their buildings to meet the demand for the education they offered. Commander I.C.M. Sanderson at Elstree School was dealing with up to five applications a day. After a while the school could only accept bookings from parents whose boys were still in the nursery.[6] The small school of Chafyn Grove (Salisbury) jumped in number from sixty-eight to eighty-seven in 1946.[7] Similarly, after St Wilfrid's, Seaford, returned from Llanidloes, Montgomeryshire, its numbers grew at a rapid rate.[8] During the first term back at Scarborough, Bramcote School increased its numbers by twenty to bring the total in 1945 to seventy-seven boys[9] — an increase of about 26 per cent in one term. The numbers at St Hugh's, Woodhall Spa, increased at such a rate that it became necessary to extend the dining hall to accommodate forty more boys.[10] The numbers soon reached 193 in what before the war had been a moderately sized school of seventy boys.[11] A larger school like Colet Court (London) increased from 200 to 250 over the first four years.[12] This expansion amid the post-war euphoria was a universal phenomenon amongst preparatory schools.

Education as Investment

There were reasons for this rush to enter boys in fee-paying schools. Many who had not themselves enjoyed a preparatory/public school education were better off than their parents had been and decided that a good education was a good investment for their children. At the other extreme were those who had attended independent schools themselves, but were now living in reduced circumstances because of the war. Many such men were using their gratuities while their wives went out to work in order to find the money to send their children to preparatory or public schools. Whatever the reasons for this great influx of boys, the pre-Stowe situation had returned: there was a shortage of places in the public schools and a surplus of preparatory schoolboys to fill them. The early 1950s saw several hundred more boys trying to enter public schools than there were places.[13] The standards of the CEE inevitably rose, and competition was keen. In the late 1950s the situation was aggravated as boys born during the post-war birthrate bulge began to move from the preparatory to the public school.

The continuing shortage of assistant masters at the end of the war led the IAPS to ask the HMC to alert boys awaiting call-up that teaching vacancies existed in preparatory schools. Men invalided out of the forces were also encouraged to join preparatory schools staffs.[14] In May 1945 the Council voted unanimously for the immediate return of assistant masters from the forces and sent a memorandum to this effect to the Ministry of Education.[15] As was to be expected, there was a period after the war when adjustment between assistant masters returning from the forces and incumbent assistants formed part of the overall settling down process.

Whereas shortages of teaching staff were made good by the return of masters from HM Forces, the gap created by the war-time migration of domestic staff to the factories and other well-paid employment was less easy to fill. The void was partly filled by the hundreds of *'au pair'* girls who came from Europe to study English, many of whom found their way into preparatory schools.[16]

One of the major post-war changes to be wrought amongst preparatory schools was the large scale alteration in the status of schools from 'proprietary' to 'charitable trust'. As already observed, this was a direct result of the criticism by the Fleming Committee of preparatory schools for being private profit-making institutions. One early metamorphosis was that of the Dragon School, which from 1953 has been governed by the Dragon School Trust.[17] In the same year 'Terry's' became an educational trust known as Northwood Preparatory School Trust (Terry's) Limited.[18] Amongst other schools which became educational trusts in the 1950s were Bramcote School and St Andrew's, Eastbourne, both in 1957. It is likely, however, that Chafyn Grove School (1876) which became a preparatory school in 1916 has the longest history of 'trust' status amongst preparatory schools since it became an educational trust in the 1890s and was thus already a charity at the time of its metamorphosis.[19]

Avoiding the New 11+

Barred from paying for their children to go to a grammar school when secondary school fees were abolished by the 1944 Education Act, some parents sought places for their children in preparatory schools. As the 11+ examination became more and more competitive, and as poor or laggard LEAs failed to provide enough grammar school places, the diversion of middle class children increased until with the second bulge pressure began to build up for the abolition of the grammar school and the selection procedures. Criticisms began to be levelled against the 11+ examination; its validity was doubted, its justice called into question. Such problems of selection (or 'allocation' as the LEAs called it) were greatly aggravated by the birth 'bulge' of the 'fifties and early 'sixties.

Similar problems were experienced in the preparatory schools. The birth bulge created a shortage of places in public schools which affected the 'feeder' preparatory schools. As with the 11+ this situation led almost inevitably to intensive coaching or 'cramming' and finally to intensive criticism.

Higher standards for entry into the public schools[20] in the 'fifties caused P.H. Vezey (Beaumont House) and C.F.C. Letts (Oakley Hall) to demand that guidance be given as to the mark-values for questions in the CEE,[21] to ensure masters marked consistently. Mr Letts reproached the public schools for allowing the law of supply and demand to operate to the detriment of education.[22] The worst fears of Letts and Vezey were realized when the IAPS council warned that because of the 'bulge' there would be fewer places available for the common entrance candidates' pool and offered, as a sop to preparatory schools, help in finding places for less able boys in non-HMC schools.[23]

Donald Lindsay (Malvern College) attempted to placate the preparatory schools by suggesting that pass-marks in the CEE were bound to fluctuate according to supply and demand. He suggested, however, that pass or failure in the examination should be determined by a candidate's showing only in the four main subjects. Elsewhere in the curriculum he felt 'adventurous methods' should be used in teaching. He favoured due emphasis on the arts, which ought to be the subject of inquiry by the Joint Standing Committee. He concluded that a confidential report could include questions to gain knowledge of a boy's initiative or sense of responsibility.[24] C.F.C. Letts, the self-appointed watch-dog of the CEE for the IAPS agreed with Lindsay that a better 'personal profile' questionnaire to assess the true potential of a boy was necessary in the CEE but suggested also the creation of more public schools (as in the 'twenties when Stowe and Canford were founded) and the lowering of the pass mark in some subjects.[25]

Further feeling about Common Entrance: Admit to Public Schools at Eleven?

Towards the end of the 1950s, feeling concerning the CEE had reached crisis point. This feeling was probably best exemplified by W.L.V. Caldwell (Belhaven Hill), who averred that the misuse of the CEE 'threatens to undermine our ... character and destroy the purpose of our existence'. He advised his colleagues: 'We must disseminate information about preparatory schools, when we have decided what we are'. To become cramming institutions of 'feverish extra work'[26] would be a denial of what preparatory schools had previously aimed at namely — the production of 'a well-mannered person with cultivated interests and a sense of responsibility'.[27] D.R. Wigram (Monkton Combe) offered a solution to the problem by suggesting that boys should be allowed to qualify for public school when they were ready. For some, this could be at eleven.[28]

The Bulge and Its Consequences

Between 1947 and 1952 preparatory school numbers had risen by 5,000. This was partly due to the nationwide birthrate 'bulge' and partly to the embourgeoisement of the upper working class. Hence J.S. Peel (Taverham Hall) felt the need to defend the CEE, which he did by applauding the raising of standards in the examination. Statistics for his own school made the point sufficiently.

Table 13.   Taverham Hall Examination Statistics

Date	Number of boys	Number doing CEE	Number getting over 60%	% getting over 60%	Average age
Nov. 1951	55	19	4	7	12.5 months
Nov. 1957	74	33	14	19	11.10 months

Neither the widening of the bottleneck (Wigram) nor complacency (Peel) satisfied Mr Letts. Recalling a similar position after the First World War when places in public schools were hard to obtain, he noted that the situation rapidly improved and the pass mark fell quickly. No doubt the creation of Stowe, Canford and Rendcomb was partly responsible for this. Letts suggested that a solution might be the abolition of the CEE and the institution of a 'Junior Certificate of Education' administered by the preparatory schools themselves.[29] Letts was not to be dissuaded by the argument of the Rev. R.G. Wickham (Twyford) that the preparatory schools were experiencing 'a rising tide of prosperity and popularity' which inevitably led to competitive cramming for examination[30] and had to be tolerated. He called for the creation of another public school to absorb the overflow of applicants from preparatory schools.[31] Such was the critical state reached with the curriculum and common entrance when the IAPS published its blue-print, *Foundations*, in 1959.

Foundations appeared just as a second bulge was discerned coming up the tideways. Its terms of reference had instructed its authors to consider 'the possibility of boys entering (preparatory) schools or leaving them as a result of the 11+ examination'.[32] These terms of reference can be traced back to the advice given by Lord Hailsham in April 1957, when he was Minister of Education, that the IAPS should take a long careful look at its curriculum in the light of educational developments outside the world of public and preparatory schools.

The preparatory schools clearly found themselves torn between two diverse philosophies: the one which urged that the preparatory school curriculum should be designed to fulfil the schools' prime function of enabling boys to enter public schools; the other which eschewed examinations and sought to implement 'modern education' by concentrating on the development of character. The authors of the report[33] produced what they called the Creed of Preparatory School education based on three basic beliefs. These were: (1) the need for boys to learn that individuals were less important than the group; (2) the need for boys to work hard at tasks which must often prove uncongenial; and (3) the need for boys to develop their own abilities in order to use them for the good of others.[34]

As there were more preparatory schoolboys than the public schools could take, and since the maintained primary schools were becoming increasingly efficient, there was an increasing two-way traffic between the maintained and the public/preparatory school system at the age of eleven. One of the main tasks of the committee which produced *Foundations* was to identify the best ways of facilitating such transitions. This could best be done, it felt, through a closer liaison between IAPS and primary school heads at a local level. Committee members collected their data from a variety of sources. They met experts who were invited to give their views; they sent questionnaires to 150 preparatory schools; they monitored a conference on 'Science and Young People' organized by the Shell Petroleum Company Ltd and the IAPS (an important development for the later emphasis on science in the curriculum); they received written reports from acknowledged subject experts and they also took much benefit from the Association's annual conference which was geared very largely to curriculum considerations.

The main conclusions arising from the Committee's survey of evidence and witnesses were first, that there was extensive anxiety concerning the effectiveness of the CEE and secondly, that some feared the undue emphasis on science in future curriculum planning. Whilst recognizing that schools were individually responsible for the shaping of their individual curricula, the Committee made seven major recommendations for consideration by the IAPS. These were:

1   A later start in Latin, at about the age of 10 to 11.
2   Latin to be taught to only those academically able to benefit from it.
3   Introduction of some science, either formal or informal.
4   A greater emphasis on English to achieve greater literacy.
5   More attention to cultural aspects, especially music.
6   More attention to both geography and physical education.
7   Greater emphasis on flexibility of arrangement to take account of boys' differing educational needs.[35]

Foundations contained in its forty-seven pages a mixture of 'progressive' and traditional ideas. It advocated, for example, the inclusion in the timetable of periods run on a very modified Dalton plan whilst at the same time advocating training in formal English grammar.[36] The report was not averse to admitting 'the duty of insisting on hard work and a modicum of drudgery' in history,[37] whilst recognizing the need in the curriculum for science *per se* being an extension of the already established nature study. According to the report, 'Science should be regarded as a means of stimulating interest in natural things and of supplementing a boy's inherent interest in how things work'.[38]

It was launched in a blaze of publicity with a press conference and the sending of copies to MPs, to members of the HMC and to local education authorities. The first copy went to the Duke of Edinburgh, whose eldest son was at Cheam School.[39] By the criterion of copies published and sold — constant reprints were necessary — the impact of *Foundations* was both instant and extensive. Many regarded the report as 'progressive' and a means for the great improvement of the curriculum. Harrison, at the heart of the discussions and debates, was less sanguine. As he indicated later, the IAPS was still subject to the dictates of the CEE and of the scholarship examinations. Similar disquiet was expressed by the Rev. R.G. Wickham (Twyford), a fellow *Foundations* committee member. In an article, 'If the Foundations be destroyed' (1960),[40] he argued for a new conception of the CEE. He suggested a more flexible approach in which there should be only three 'basic' or 'compulsory' subjects — Latin, mathematics and English — with a complement of voluntary subjects. Such a change, argued Wickham, would give breadth of knowledge, as well as assessing candidates' intelligence.

The 'Piper Report': *Prospect* 1965

Ironically, as the bulge began to reach a peak, a second committee on curriculum reform under the chairmanship of Mr D.S. Piper (St Anselm's, Bakewell) was formed. This committee of seven members contained five from the previous one[41] so that the Report of 1965, *Prospect*, is to be seen as a close sequel to *Foundations*. During the intervening six years the birth rate had been steadily rising again which rendered the *Foundation's* recommendations some-what irrelevant, especially (as Mr Jack Dodd, the Chairman of Council, in his foreword to the report mentioned) fresh ideas were abroad: 'a new conception of mathematics, the exploration of science for the young, a less formal approach to the teaching of French and, above all, a more liberal approach to the study of our own language.'[42] The state system of secondary schools was also changing as the comprehensivization, long advocated by the Labour Party, was implemented (by *Circular 10/65*). LEAs were obliged to comply.

In such a climate the orientation of *Foundations* towards the eleven plus examinations seemed irrelevant. If the grammar schools *per se* were to disappear (despite Mr Harold Wilson's assertions to the contrary) through a process of comprehensivization, then the pivotal point of *Foundations* would be of less significance.[43] There is no mention of this socio-political point in the pages of the *Prospect* report but it is against such a background that the sequel to *Foundations* perhaps ought to be seen. The preamble to the *Prospect* report itself admits that in 1959 'circumstances in both public and preparatory schools [had been] unfavourable to any immediate or radical change'.[44]

It recommended yet another HMC/IAPS committee to consider the whole examination structure which bound the schools together. It was the lack of reference to the CEE and scholarship examinations which had partly rendered *Foundations* ineffectual. The proposed abandonment of Latin for all but the ablest boys during the first two years of preparatory schooling would go some considerable way towards the broadening of the curriculum and provide a bridge between the curricula of the primary and the preparatory schools. It was also recommended that in dealing with the curriculum for the younger boys, their basic educational needs should take priority over the requirements of an examination they would take five years later. During a boy's last three years at preparatory school two or three periods of his weekly timetable would be devoted to science — a subject at that time being promoted heavily by industry. The replacement of Latin by English as the core subject for the less able boy was another major recommendation and endorsed previous trends in the relative values of those two subjects for the preparatory school curriculum.

A closer rapport with primary schools was advocated in view of the application of new techniques in mathematics and French and of the new importance of science to both primary and preparatory schools. Finally, the recommendations laid new emphasis on the importance of 'out of school activities' in increasing leisure opportunities.[45]

Prospect sought to bring preparatory schools into the mainstream of educational development. But it also insisted on the preparatory schools' 'right to retain religious principles on which so much of their work [was] based' and to retain 'the freedom to make their own educational experiments'.[46] These rights of freedom were embodied as leading objectives of preparatory school education. These were:

1 to provide the spiritual, moral and physical foundations on which it is possible to build a life which is useful to society and satisfying to the personality of the individual boy himself;
2 so to stimulate the interest and imagination of boys that the pursuit of useful knowledge becomes a habit of mind instead of a duty;
3 to combine the attainment of knowledge and the power to think and reason with the disciplines of hard work;
4 to prepare a boy for the next stage in his educational career; and
5 to make the fullest contribution to the education of the country as a whole.[47]

Of interest is the order: preparation of a boy for public school is listed no higher than fourth thus seemingly giving low priority to the importance of examinations in the total process. *Prospect* was meant to take *Foundations* a stage further by giving practical suggestions for the implementation of ideas enunciated in the earlier document. There are grounds for believing, however, that *Prospect* made even less impact than did *Foundations*.[48]

Science and the Preparatory School Curriculum[49]

Real progress in the development of the curriculum was the extensive adoption of science in the 1960s. Though as early as 1897 an article on science teaching in preparatory schools appeared in the *PSR*,[50] to be followed in a succeeding issue with an article on the ideal curriculum by C.C. Lynam (Dragon) which included natural history and the cultivation of the habits of observation,[51] they were merely straws in the wind. By and large, schools of the APS were not interested in science in the nineteenth century and regarded it as no part of their function to be so.

One major exception to this generalization was the Rev. Walter Earle, headmaster of Yarlet Hall School, Staffordshire (1873–1887) and later of Bilton Grange, Rugby (1887–1922), who ensured that all boys at his schools were taught science. Similarly, C.C. Lemprière of Carteret House, Harrogate (c.1890–1902) and later of Red House School, Moor Monkton, (1902–c.1920) had science taught on a regular basis at his schools in conformity with his belief that science was the soundest method of teaching boys to think.[52]

A major advance in the teaching of science in preparatory schools was made in 1907 when, at a joint conference between the HMC and the APS, the Joint Standing Committee was created. This Joint Standing Committee (JSC) drew up a suggested curriculum for preparatory schools and in so doing they consulted the Association of Public School Science Masters (APSSM) over a science section. Influenced also by the ideas and practice of Miss Charlotte Mason, the foundress of the Parents' National Education Union (PNEU) and those of the Froebel Institute, the JSC adopted a practical approach to science in the preparatory schools' new curriculum by emphasizing nature study. This emphasis amongst those minority schools which taught science continued into the early 1920s, by which time the concept of general science, at least for the senior preparatory school boys, was beginning to be added to that of nature study. In many ways however general science, with a biological emphasis on the environment, differed little from nature study with its emphasis on observation. So there was a natural progression from the nature study of the younger boys to the general science of the older ones. Revisions of the suggested preparatory school curricula in 1922, 1926 and 1935 contained sections on nature study and general science.

During this very early period in the teaching of preparatory school science there were factors which both encouraged and discouraged its permanent establishment. Amongst the former were the scientific inventions of the early twentieth century which led, in the case of Twyford School, to a scientifically-minded master transmitting wireless from about 1913 onwards. From c.1912 to c.1930 regular lectures were given at Twyford on subjects like sound, light, electricity, mechanics and chemistry.[53] It would seem, too, that the scientific and technical activities of F.W. Sanderson were bearing fruit in at least one preparatory school. St Piran's at Maidenhead could boast of a small laboratory as early as 1919/20[54] and by 1923/24 possessed an engineering workshop, wireless room, technical library and photographic developing room.[55] The comprehensive report of the Prime Minister's Committee on Natural Science, published in 1918, which formed part of H.A.L. Fisher's programme of educational reform, made definite proposals concerning science in preparatory schools and can be thus seen as another encouraging factor.

First amongst the factors discouraging the advance of science as a preparatory school curriculum subject was the perennial question as to what could possibly be omitted to make room for science's inclusion; established subjects had a tendency to cling to their time allocation.[56] Secondly, the high cost of providing science laboratories ensured that science was taught either not at all or only along the lines of nature study where capital investment was negligible. Schools which were maintained solely from school fees were not readily able to invest in this insufficiently established part of the curriculum. Such schools were reinforced in their reticence by some public schools which urged that the teaching of science should be left to a later stage. Moreover, where were the preparatory schools to obtain trained personnel in scientific subjects? Against such a background of adverse factors there is little surprise in finding that *Foundations* (1959) recommended that science should not be a compulsory paper in CEE. Within a decade, however, the situation was to be transformed.

A major breakthrough in the establishment of science in preparatory schools occurred in 1960(?) with the publication of a pamphlet, *Natural Science*, by Crispin Hill (Aldro School). This pamphlet emphasized the need for some science to be taught to boys before arriving at their public schools. Its concern was to establish the habit of keen observation in order to foster a scientific attitude. Hill was careful to state early in the pamphlet that he was not advocating that science become a subject in the CEE but merely that some early but well-considered steps be made towards the creation of a scientific outlook. The objective of his suggested course was 'to open the boys' eyes to the richness of the world around them.'[57] He would include in such a course the topics of heat, pressure, measurement, machines, chemistry, light, nature study, magnetism and electrostatics, current electricity, astronomy and the weather chart.

Before even Nuffield Science got under way in either public schools or the maintained secondary system, the Shell International Petroleum Company arranged for a most important conference at Shell Lodge, Teddington in January 1962. This was, in fact, the third Shell/IAPS Conference.[58] Science had been discussed at two previous conferences in 1956 and 1958, but these were before the publication of *Foundations* which had advocated the study of science in preparatory schools. If, therefore, *Foundations* had been a largely ineffectual document for the general reform of the preparatory school curriculum, in one respect it led indirectly to a transformation of it in the 1960s and 1970s.

The third Shell/IAPS Conference, with the theme of 'Science in Preparatory Schools', was attended by twelve preparatory school headmasters, chosen on a regional basis, together with Donald Lindsay representing HMC and representatives from Her Majesty's Inspectorate of Schools, the British Association for the Advancement of Science (BAAS), the London Institute of Education (the late Professor Joseph Lauwerys), the University Appointments Board and from provincial museums. The conference had a profound influence on the future of science in preparatory schools. It was agreed that there were compelling reasons for boys between eight and thirteen to be taught science and that such teaching should be first informal and heuristic, then formal in preparation for O-level examinations. It was prudently felt at this stage that science should not be a subject for CEE; it was sufficient for boys to have been given an insight into the scientific outlook in preparation for their continuing scientific studies in their public schools. To facilitate the general adoption of this policy a syllabus was to be drawn up, prepared by the IAPS Science Committee, in consultation with the Science Masters' Association (SMA);

science was to be included in IAPS training courses. Ways and means of providing staff and facilities were to be explored, including turning to the BAAS and museum services.

It would, however, be misleading if the reader were to gain the impression that before the third Science Conference all was darkness in the preparatory school scientific world and all was light afterwards. As Mr D.S. Piper (St Anselm's, Bakewell) suggested at the conference, some 250 preparatory schools were interested in science as a result of the two previous conferences and the John Lewis teaching kits[59] used by many schools. Undoubtedly a revolution in thinking had been achieved. But had it gone far enough? For Mr C.F.C. Letts (Oakley Hall) — who was not present at the conference — it had not. He felt that public schools were hindering initiative which the preparatory schools were willing to take because they still maintained that Latin, not science, should be the main subject in the CEE.[60] No doubt Letts was reacting against the opposition expressed by [Sir] Desmond Lee (Winchester) at the 1962 IAPS annual conference to the examination of science.[61]

Letts's doubts concerning the attitude of the public schools to science in preparatory schools were perhaps assuaged by a one-day conference that took place at the Shell Centre in November 1962, at which the IAPS made plain their future plans for science in preparatory schools. The Rev. R.G. Wickham (Twyford) and Mr D.S. Piper (St Anselm's, Bakewell) had been responsible for much of the preparatory work since January, and came prepared to discuss a proposed syllabus and ways in which time would be made for science in an already crowded curriculum. The customary closeness between the two head-masters' associations ensured a successful outcome of the deliberations. Sir George Allen, Secretary of the BAAS, was present at this meeting, as was Farrer-Brown, Director of the Nuffield Foundation. The representatives from the HMC, R.J. Knight (Oundle), B.W.M. Young (Charterhouse) and F.L. Allan, the HMC Secretary, accompanied by R.R. Pedley, president-elect of the Incorporated Association of Headmasters, complemented a meeting involving all interested parties who discussed contemporary development in Nuffield Science both in preparatory and in maintained primary schools. Soon after this important meeting Esso Petroleum was supplying science kits, each built around one textbook from 'The March of Science' scheme, which were to circulate around preparatory schools. Eventually some 400 schools took the Esso Kits.[62]

The 'new view' of science was reflected in the IAPS *Prospect* (1965) which stated:

> The time has come when it is plain that two, or preferably three, periods a week must be found for science teaching in the last three years ... and it might therefore be well to plan for the teaching of science throughout the whole of a boy's preparatory school career.[63]

Since the Committee which produced *Prospect* had D.S. Piper as its Chairman and the Rev. R.G. Wickham as its principal member, and since both were pioneers of preparatory school science, *Prospect's* attitude to the subject is not surprising. The success of their efforts became quickly evident. In the 1963/64 survey of IAPS schools, 19 per cent of the schools were teaching science throughout the school, 55 per cent had started science by the middle division stage and 78 per cent had specially appointed science rooms.[64] Thereafter progress was very swift. In a survey conducted in 1966 only 7 per cent of schools were doing no science at all, whilst 50 per cent were working on the Nuffield Science project.[65]

The final stage in the recognition of science as a major part of the curriculum was reached in 1970 when it became a compulsory subject in the CEE.[66] In order to enable the schools to cope with this development, courses in the teaching of science were instituted at public schools like Malvern, Uppingham and Denstone.

Coda

Over a period of almost a century the preparatory school curriculum has been metamorphosed from one which concentrated largely on the classics in order to fulfil the preparatory schools' function of 'feeding' public schools, to one which recognizes more clearly the views of society at large. By slow degrees, often with the public schools following rather than leading, the curriculum has severely limited the teaching of Greek; to a lesser extent, it has limited the teaching of Latin; it has recognized the value of English as the core subject; it has recognized the need for boys' aesthetic appreciation, and has so recognized the worth of science that even Herbert Spencer would be satisfied with the position it now holds in the preparatory school curriculum. In the 1970s these developments were complemented by the deliberations of the HMC/IAPS Working Party under the chairmanship of Roger Ellis, Master of Marlborough, on the curriculum of preparatory and public school boys from the age of eleven to O-level, to which reference is made in the penultimate chapter, 'The ISIS Citadel'.

Notes

1 Minutes of the IAPS Council, Vol. 3. Minutes of Meeting on 8 September 1944.
2 H.D. MARTINEAU, *op. cit.*, p. 13.
3 *Bramcote School History*, pp. 2–3.
4 PAUL SPILLANE, *op. cit.*, p. 70.
5 R.A. HARRISON, *op. cit.*, p. 42. See also H.O. EVENNETT (1944) *The Catholic Schools of England and Wales*, Cambridge University Press, p. 78.
6 I.C.M. SANDERSON, *op. cit.*, p. 82.
7 *Chafyn Grove History*, p. 4.
8 I am grateful to ERIC LOUSADA of St Wilfrid's for this information.
9 *Bramcote School History*, p. 3.
10 H.D. MARTINEAU, *op. cit.*, pp. 14–15.
11 *Ibid.*, pp. 8, 15.

12 JAMES BEWSHER *et al.*, *op. cit.*, p. 32.
13 L. COVERLEY, *op. cit.*, p. 42.
14 Minutes of the IAPS Council, Vol. 3. Minutes of Meeting of 29 December 1944.
15 *Ibid.*, Minutes of Meeting of 17 May 1945.
16 L. COVERLEY, *op. cit.*, p. 40.
17 C.H. JACQUES, *op. cit.*, p. 196.
18 J.H. TERRY, *op. cit.*, pp. 21–2.
19 I am grateful to Mr J.S. SINGLETON, headmaster of Chafyn Grove School, for this information.
20 Cf. *PSR*, 17, 5 (New Series), October 1950, p. 34.
21 Cf. *PSR*, 17, 6 (New Series), February 1951, p. 20; *PSR*, 17, 8 (New Series), October 1951, p. 34; *PSR*, 17, 9 (New Series), February 1952, p. 20; *PSR*, 17, 12, February 1953, pp. 5–6.
22 *PSR*, 16, 9 (New Series), February 1956, pp. 32 and 34.
23 *PSR*, 16, 10 (New Series), May 1956, p. 5.
24 *PSR*, 16, 11 (New Series), October 1956, p. 11.
25 *PSR*, 16, 12, February 1957, pp. 5–6.
26 *PSR*, 17, 3, February 1958, 9.
27 *Ibid.*
28 *PSR*, 17, 4, May 1958, pp. 3–5.
29 *PSR*, 17, 8, October 1959, pp. 12–13.
30 *PSR*, 17, 9, February 1960, pp. 6–7.
31 *PSR*, 17, 10, June 1960, p. 8.
32 *Foundations, a reconsideration of the aims of teaching in preparatory schools*, IAPS 1959, p. 7.
33 H.J.G. COLLIS, (Chairman, St Paul's Junior School); C.B. COOK (St Michael's, Tawstock Court); L.H.A. HANKEY (Clifton College Preparatory School); J.W. HORNBY (Bramcote, Scarborough); R.C. MARTIN (St Dunstan's Burnham-on-Sea); G.W. PAGET (Director of Training, IAPS — former HMI); D.S. PIPER (St Anselm's, Bakewell); Rev. R.G. WICKHAM (Twyford); R.A. HARRISON (Secretary, formerly of Marlborough House, Hawkhurst)
34 *Foundations*, p. 5.
35 *Ibid*, 9, Cf. *PSR*, 17, 10, June 1964, pp. 3–8, for report of opening address by A.R.D. WRIGHT of Shrewsbury at the 1964 Oxford Refresher course where he quoted the main recommendations of *Foundations*.
36 *Ibid.*, pp. 13, 15.
37 *Ibid.*, p. 21.
38 *Ibid.*, p. 29.
39 Cf. R.A. HARRISON, (1975) *How Was That, Sir?*, Woodbridge, Baron Publishing, p. 63.
40 *PSR* 17, 11, October 1960, p. 79.
41 The committee consisted of *D.S. PIPER, J.H. DODD (Downside School, Purley), H.A.C. EVANS (Swanbourne House); *J.W. HORNBY; *G.W. PAGET; *Rev. R.G. WICKHAM; *R.A. HARRISON. *members of the *Foundations* Committee.
42 *Prospect, The Purposes and Practice of Teaching in Preparatory Schools*, IAPS 1965, V.
43 *Prospect*, lacking the hindsight of later years, reiterated the point about the interchangeability of boys between the independent and maintained system but it would be fair to say that it held a less prominent position in this later report.
44 *Ibid.*, p. 1.
45 *Ibid.*, pp. 3–4.
46 *Ibid.*, p. 2.
47 *Ibid.*

48 According to ARTHUR HARRISON the demand for *Prospect* was smaller and fewer copies were circulated. HARRISON. *op. cit.*, p. 64.
49 I am very grateful indeed to the Rev. R.G. WICKHAM for much of the background information on the full-scale introduction of science into the curriculum.
50 *PSR*, 2, 7, July 1897, pp. 75–76.
51 *PSR*, 2, 8, December 1897, pp. 107–108.
52 Cf. D.P. LEINSTER-MACKAY, Durham University Ph.D. thesis, Vol. 1, 125. See also *The Durham and Newcastle Research Review*, 9, 48, Spring 1982, pp. 340–343.
53 From information given to me by the Rev. R.G. WICKHAM, ex-head of Twyford School.
54 *St Piran's Magazine*, (1974/5), p. 31.
55 *St Piran's Year Book*, 1923/4, pp. 2–5.
56 Cf. letter to Editor of *The Times* April 4, 1916 by OSWALD H. LATTER, an assistant master at Charterhouse on the occasion of the withdrawal from the common entrance examination of the science paper as an alternative to Latin verse. Cf. also *Foundations*, p. 29.
57 CRISPIN HILL, *Natural Science*, IAPS pamphlet N. 20, p. 133.
58 There was also another less official Shell Conference for Preparatory School headmasters at Trinity College, Oxford in 1961 in conjunction with representatives of the British Association for the Advancement of Science.
59 J.H. LEWIS, Science Master of Malvern College was the original architect of the scheme which culminated in the Shell/IAPS pact.
60 Letter to Editor. *PSR*, 18, 4, June 1962, p. 6.
61 Cf. *The Times*, 17 September, 1962, p. 7.
62 From information supplied to me by the Rev. ROBERT WICKHAM. Cf. advertisement in *PSR*, 18, 4, June 1962, p. 45, in which kits on air and water; weather and earth; energy and engines; hearing and seeing; electrical currents; and heating and cooling were noted.
63 IAPS, *Prospect*, p. 3.
64 Cf. IAPS evidence submitted to the Public Schools Commission, January 1967, p. 19.
65 *Ibid.*
66 Cf. IAPS circular letter, 13 December 1967, entitled 'Science paper in entrance and scholarship exams' [*sic*].

A preparatory school is like a shop: its goodwill depends on the continual supply of an article which its customers want.
(L.A.G. Strong (1961) *Green Memory*)

Objections Answered

Preparatory schools have been criticized for being old fashioned institutions run for private profit; for being socially divisive; and for *separating* young boys from parents — sometimes at a very young age. It is the purpose of this chapter to meet these criticisms in a constructive manner, to identify the ideas for which the preparatory schools stand, and to outline the measures that are being taken to achieve their ends.

In his address to the IAPS Conference in 1966 Dr Royston Lambert spoke of the public's ignorance of the preparatory schools. An attempt was made to dispel this by the publication in 1966 of Philip Masters' book, *Preparatory Schools Today — Some Facts and Inferences*. Masters indicated that 161 out of 494 preparatory schools (32 per cent) were of a proprietary constitution in 1966 whilst only 110 (22 per cent) had become charitable trusts.[1] Eleven years later there were only sixty-five proprietary preparatory schools, whilst the charitable trust schools numbered 316 out of a total of 449 — some 70 per cent.[2] By 1981 this percentage of charitable trust schools had risen to 75. By far the majority of preparatory schools is not run now for private profit.

Accompanying this has been a radical change in the preparatory school curriculum. There is of course wide variation between school and school. But it is in general true that the preparatory schools have broadened and 'modernized' their curriculum considerably in the last fifteen to twenty years. They were pioneers of the new mathematics[3] and audio-visual French[4] and, thanks to Shell, Esso and other industrial firms,[5] have promoted Nuffield Science Schemes. This orientation of preparatory schools towards the needs of commerce and industry occurred as early as the 1950s. A lecture entitled

'Education and training in a modern age', given by Sir Frederick Handley-Page in 1957 to the IAPS Oxford University Training Course,[6] epitomized this new emphasis. Hitherto preparatory and public schools had orientated their curriculum to prepare boys largely for the City, the Civil Service, the church, the law and the fighting services. The 'fifties and 'sixties saw commerce and industry recruiting more and more boys from the growing science departments in the schools. Preparatory schools cooperated with public schools in the development of science. In 1967, for example, the High Master of St Paul's School invited preparatory school heads within his 'catchment area' to discuss with him the implications of CEE science examinations.[7] Three years later science had become a compulsory subject in the CEE, Latin having already ceased to be so in 1968. In addition to the academic subjects, aesthetic subjects such as art, craft, drama, musical appreciation and singing are given time on the average school timetable. Extra-curricular activities make further contributions to the enrichment of the boys' education.[8] In orchestral music the IAPS, with its own orchestra, has reached unusual heights of excellence for schoolboy musicians.

The broadening of the preparatory school curriculum has been accompanied too by the achievement of high standards of excellence. The Labour MP, John Dugdale, recognized the disparity between the standards of preparatory schools and maintained schools when he observed: Very many [preparatory schools] are of a high standard, and give an education that is far better than any that can possibly be given at present for boys under thirteen in most state schools.'[9] John Dancy, writing in 1963, confirmed this view:

> The best ten per cent or so of preparatory schools give a better academic education than any other schools coping with that age in England — and, for all I know, in the world. The worst however are distinctly inferior as places of education to a good maintained primary school.[10]

The seemingly low percentage of preparatory schools to which Dancy attributed such excellence represented more than a mere 10 per cent of the IAPS schools — some fifty or so schools — since at the time there were probably more than a thousand non-IAPS schools.[11] All IAPS schools were 'recognized as efficient' by the Ministry of Education, so that Dancy's 10 per cent would possibly include about 150 preparatory schools — about a third of the total. Such had been the high academic standard achieved by many preparatory school boys that the IAPS was able to claim in 1967 that in some subjects a good common entrance candidate might well have covered a great part of his O-level work before he reached his public school.[12] Scholarship papers for entry to public school were in many cases up to GCE O-level.[13] In catering for some of its high-fliers one school, Clifton Preparatory School, has some boys attending courses at Bristol University.

From the foregoing it can be seen that IAPS preparatory schools have been largely transformed into non-profit making institutions enjoying a broad curriculum and a rich extra-curricular programme.

Sharing Facilities

When Sir John Newsom[14] was charged with examining ways of reducing the social divisiveness of the public schools (and by implication, of the preparatory schools), the IAPS denied 'absolutely that ... [they] consciously influenced [their] pupils to regard themselves as belonging to a superior social class — or indeed to any class at all, superior or otherwise.'[15] They claimed they were concerned with the production of excellence in intellectual endeavour and social behaviour and of an ethos that helped to achieve those aims. An excellent reputation had nothing to do with social divisions since no section of society had a monopoly of that. Attacking the myth that the 'old school tie' system secured the best jobs, the IAPS denounced any alleged injustice arising from preparatory and public school boys' acquiring the best jobs over the heads of better individuals — if indeed that were the case. The open competitive examination, however, ensured to a very large extent that this was not the case. If, on the other hand, their pursuit of excellence caused their boys to obtain the best jobs then, in terms of Aristotelian distributive justice, so be it.

The more pragmatic amongst the IAPS fraternity, despite the post-war boom years, remembered the hardships of the 'thirties and the abortiveness of the Fleming Report which had tried to bring the English public school into the mainstream of English education. Since the war, the preparatory schools have made a brave attempt to create a dialogue both with the maintained system and with the world at large outside the school. Many preparatory schools, especially those with a large proportion of day-boys, are able to share their facilities with the locality, as does Bramcote School, near Retford, where the school hall is used as a village hall by the local inhabitants of Gamston. Playing fields and swimming baths are often used by local clubs and maintained schools in a spirit of cooperation. Often there is close contact between staffs of preparatory schools and primary and secondary schools. A good example of this interchange is to be found at Clifton Preparatory School, Bristol, where Mr L.H.A. Hankey, headmaster from 1946 to 1967, and his successor, Mr J.W. Hornby, both pursued a policy of integration with the locality. Being a mixed boarding-day school it can forge close links. The school hall is used for local functions and the school participates in local galas and carnivals. Clifton Preparatory School has a Primary Schools Scholarship Scheme whereby primary school pupils are able to compete for places in the school. College of education students do their teaching practice there and the headmaster lectured (1980) at the local colleges of education. Such reciprocity may not be as strong in the rest of the country as it is in Bristol, but many schools are at pains to establish close contacts with the outside world. In some cases the response to preparatory schools' overtures has not been strong. The publication, *The Preparatory Schoolboy and his Education* (1951), was a public relations exercise. Two of its chapters were headed 'The preparatory school and the nation' and 'The preparatory school as a good neighbour'. There is little doubt that, at the centre at least, a concerted effort has been made since the Second World War to bring the two systems closer together whilst insisting on the continuing existence of the independent one.

One measure of the links between the two systems is the increasing number of pupils who go from preparatory school to maintained school. Though they form a small percentage, the numbers have increased from 511 boys out of 10,652 in 1973 to 717 boys out of 10,196 in 1977.[16] But of those leaving preparatory school before the age of thirteen a much larger and increasing proportion goes to maintained schools rather than to independent schools. Some are no doubt 'drop-outs' from the preparatory system, but the numbers reflect increasing contact between the two systems. In 1973 of these 'early leavers' 1357 went to HMC schools, whilst 558 boys went to maintained secondary or middle schools; in 1977 the figures were 1527 and 1009 boys respectively.[17] It is perhaps surprising to find that the ratio of boys going to HMC schools as opposed to maintained schools is only 3:2. It provides an answer to Dr Royston Lambert's statement that preparatory schools play so little part in the educational system of the nation that they are irrelevant to it.

Other post-war developments have diminished the isolation of preparatory schools. Chief amongst these is the trend away from boarding education. In 1967, 50.5 per cent of IAPS preparatory school boys were boarders while in 1977 only 38.4 per cent were.[18] More and more preparatory schoolboys enjoy the daily contact with their families and neighbourhood. Many boarders attend schools quite near their homes. It is a recognized fact in the preparatory school world that the increased facility of the motor car has not extended the distance parents are prepared to go to place their sons. Many parents seek schools within a fifty miles radius of their homes so that they can see their sons at weekends. Decreasing supplies of fossil fuel and rising prices are likely to increase this tendency.

The gradual adoption of co-education as an economic measure on the part of some, and as an educational policy on the part of others, is making the preparatory schools less monastic. Perhaps the best exemplar of this trend is to be found at Windlesham House in Sussex, where Mr Charles and Mrs Elizabeth-Ann Malden are co-heads of a school in which at least one third of the pupils are girls.[19] The change to co-education at Windlesham derived not from motives of economic expediency but from a firm conviction of its 'rightness'. Overall the number of girls in IAPS schools increased from 1266 in 1969 to 7197 in 1981.[20] With the increased presence of girls in preparatory schools, the quality of life is changing. There is more opportunity for mixing socially and for boys to engage in activities such as cooking which were hitherto regarded as being outside the sphere of masculine interest.

A third major educational change affecting the preparatory schools since the 1960s has been the introduction in the maintained system of middle schools catering for the age-range of 8–13. The Plowden Report (1967) encouraged this departure from the traditional practice of transferring children to secondary schools at the age of eleven plus. The preparatory schools, representing a mere 2 per cent of the boy population in the relevant age-group, were then isolated from the maintained schools because of their transfer age at thirteen. The situation has now changed dramatically. In 1973 there were 70,000 pupils in IAPS schools compared with 250,000 pupils in LEA middle schools. This change in LEA practice gave a further opportunity for liaison with the maintained sector. Mr A.H. Mould (St John's College School), the Rev. R.G. Wickham (Twyford School) and Mr H.E.P. Woodcock (Dulwich College Preparatory School) visited primary, middle and preparatory schools over a period of eighteen months to determine what were the best aspects of English education in the 7–13 age-range. After examining the aims, methods and content of the respective types of schools, they published their conclusions in June 1973 under the title of *The Preparatory Years*. Yet W.A.L. Blyth, in *The Social Significance of Middle Schools* (1977), makes no reference to their precursors, the preparatory schools. They may as well not exist.

How Important Is Boarding in the Age of the Motor Car?

Dr Royston Lambert, who has carried out much research[21] on English boarding education, gave his opinion in his address to the 1966 IAPS conference that the overwhelming majority of parents in England do not wish their children to board at the primary level. There are many preparatory day schoolmasters who would agreed with him that it is better for very young boys to be brought up during their formative years in the warmth of the family circle. Some headmasters[22] support boarding from eight to eighteen, whilst others think it should be deferred till the last two of the preparatory years. Some oppose boarding altogether.

One point of boarding education which Lambert's studies highlighted is its capacity to fulfil certain defined needs. There have always been parents living abroad. Boys whose fathers have been colonial administrators or serving soldiers have been educated in boarding schools as a matter of course. In this century, broken marriages have caused many parents to give their boys the benefit of the security and regimen of a boarding preparatory school. Often the headmaster's wife has become the surrogate mother for several boys.

In an age steeped in the nostrums of Dr Bowlby and Dr Spock condemnation of boarding is part of the new orthodoxy. This orthodoxy is probably most applicable to the very young — a view partly accepted by the IAPS in its evidence submitted to the Public Schools Commission.[23] But the atmosphere in the schools is more friendly and relaxed than formerly. The presence of girls in some schools has contributed to making them less tough and less noisy. In many boys' preparatory schools the headmaster's wife, or the matron or both play a leading part in the life of the school and provide feminine sympathy. The *routine* of a boarding school, too, offers a certain security, as readers of the educationist, Sir Percy Nunn, will readily recognize.[24] The case for boarding has already been argued very cogently by John Dancy in his *The Public Schools and the Future* (1963).[25]

VAT, SET and Other Burdens

Immediately after the war the economic anxieties of the 'thirties appeared to have been dissipated by long waiting lists, expansion in classroom and living accommodation to meet the growing demand, the buoyant hope for the future. Writing in *The Quarterly Review* in 1954, James Nowell sensed that the current prosperity was merely transitory. Parents were often paying for their children's boarding education out of capital; and capital, decimated by death duties, could not last forever.[26] Only a few boys could ease the strain on their parents' pockets by winning scholarships; for the rest, insurance schemes only partly eased the pressure. Costs of running a school were now such that fees could not be reduced. If numbers in the schools were to drop, as they had done in the 1930s, many smaller schools would not be able to continue. Despite the boom the situation was precarious. For the headmaster who owned his own school, a major problem would be to find a possible successor who could raise £60,000 or more to buy him out. Having bought the school, the new headmaster must sooner or later face the problem of financing improvements and extensions, let alone staff salary increases. Fees had to be raised to meet rising costs which had been aggravated by inflation, the Value Added Tax (VAT) and the Selective Employment Tax (SET). The problem was essentially one of resolving 'the opposition between the need to spend money and improve quality, and the need to cut their costs to a minimum for the sake of the parents' pockets.'[27]

In 1954 when Nowell was analyzing the future chances of independent schools, some seventy-two IAPS schools had increased their numbers whilst twenty-four had experienced a decrease, the remaining 262 out of 358 schools maintaining their numbers at about the 1953 level.[28] His observations, therefore, were made at a time of relative stability. A decade later the picture had completely changed. In September 1957 Part III of the 1944 Education Act was implemented. This gave the Ministry of Education powers to inspect all private schools and to close them if they failed to reach appropriate standards in buildings, instruction and suitable ownership.[29]

From 1959 to 1965 private schools were closing at a net rate of 100 a year[30] and a few of those were IAPS preparatory schools, though not necessarily because of low standards in their case, but through financial exigency. The problems of maintaining standards served to compound the difficulties associated with rising costs, so that even some well-established preparatory schools, such as Rottingdean School (1890–1962), had to close their doors.[31]

The higher taxation of parents and the selective employment tax of schools, which had the nett effect of cutting down staff, combined to render the position of preparatory schools precarious indeed. Between 1970 and 1977 some forty IAPS schools were forced to close. Among them were some Victorian foundations like Stone House, Broadstairs (1970), Wellington House, Westgate-on-Sea (1970), the Knoll, Woburn Sands (1974), XIV School, Bristol (1977) and Ladycross, the Roman Catholic School at Seaford (1977). Others amalgamated to stave off closure,[32] such as Upcott House with Buckland House, Shebbear, Devon. One of the Victorian schools which closed down in 1970 was Moorland House, Cheshire (founded by L.J. Dobie in 1860). Its problems were probably typical of the schools which closed in the 'seventies: astronomical increases in the fees leading in turn to the dwindling numbers giving rise to a further need for fee increases. This vicious circle was stopped in the case of Moorland House only by the retirement of the headmaster, Mr Anthony Newsom, and the closing of the school.[33] Almost all the schools which have become defunct since 1973 were schools of fewer than seventy boys. Of those small schools which survived, most have since increased their numbers considerably. In 1939 a school with between thirty and sixty boys was financially viable and the average number was sixty. In the late twentieth century a school needs to range from about 100 to 160 pupils to be viable. This does not mean that all schools have approximately 160 pupils. In 1977 there were 258 schools having between 100 and 199 pupils; 100 schools with more than 200 pupils; sixty-four between seventy and ninety-nine, and twenty-seven schools with under seventy pupils.[34] Some small schools, such as Twyford with eighty-five pupils, have remained 100 per cent boarding. Others have adapted themselves to the changing times. Holme Grange, Wokingham, has not only abandoned boarding altogether but has also introduced a pre-preparatory department for boys and girls, thus converting a 50:50 boarding/day school into a 150-strong day school.[35]

The areas of the country where the preparatory schools were hardest hit were in the Midlands and Wales, whilst schools in the Home Counties, especially in Surrey, benefited from the increased tendency of parents to send their sons to boarding schools within a fifty miles radius of the home. Amesbury School, Hindhead, for example, increased its numbers from fifty-nine in the Lent Term of 1971 to 134 in the Summer Term of 1977.[36] Despite the prosperity of some schools such as Amesbury, the overall picture was one of contraction until 1979. In 1975 73,555 pupils attended 453 IAPS schools; in 1977 72,058 pupils attended 449 schools;[37] since 1977 there has been a concerted publicity scheme in operation in which leaflets advertizing the virtues of IAPS schools have been left in doctors' and dentists' waiting rooms, in golf clubs and estate agents' offices.[38] In 1981 79,682 pupils attended 440 IAPS schools.[39]

The closure of some preparatory schools in the 'sixties and 'seventies rendered the careers of assistant school masters aspiring to headships precarious. It was possible to leave a senior post in a thriving preparatory school to take over a headship of a small school, a natural move in normal times, only to find that school moving swiftly towards insolvency. A particularly bad 'near miss' was the case of Mr Courtney, of Cargilfield, Edinburgh. He had been there since 1947 and was tempted to apply for three headships in the south of England but was dissuaded each time by his headmaster. By 1977 all three English schools had become defunct.

The Failure of Fleming

One major way of relieving the economic pressures on preparatory schools was seen to be some kind of national implementation of the Fleming Report of 1944, a report which had largely been a dead letter. The Chairman of the Association in 1945, Mr T.C. Elliott (Fan Court, Long Cross) probably expressed the general attitude of the Association towards the Fleming Report when he declared:

> We are ... concerned to find ways in which the living values and standards we have already reached may be improved and ways in which we may place our accumulated and unique experience of work with small school units at the disposal of the Ministry of Education. We want to find a right place in the educational framework of our country and we have made our desire clear to the Minister.[40]

The Fleming Report had proposed means of bringing together the independent and maintained schools in a way which would have benefited the former financially. The neglect of these proposals maintained the distance between the independent and maintained sectors.[41] The neglect of the Fleming Report was due to the majority of the independent schools, in the post-war euphoria of full classrooms and full booking-lists, paying no more than lip-service to the idea of closer cooperation; for their part the LEAs showed no enthusiasm for a scheme which would transfer their most able pupils to the independent schools. Despite this opposition to change, there were those who saw that such a scheme would not only give the independent sector a stronger financial base but would also enable wider clientèle to enjoy the benefits of a preparatory/public school education. James Nowell, writing in 1954, felt that if more 'spade-work' could be done with the two examinations at 11+ and 13+, it might be possible for the practical aspects of the Fleming proposals to be revived in a revised scheme.[42]

Nowell's concern for the continuation of the independent schools was shared by John Dugdale in 1957 when he pointed out that the newly implemented Part III of the 1944 Education Act could threaten preparatory schools. Whilst agreeing that schools should be, as were factories and slaughter-houses, subject to minimum standards, Dugdale was concerned about the preparatory schools' continuance. He suggested a five-point plan to ensure this: first, the curriculum ought to be modified to cater for more than just the preparation of boys for public schools;[43] secondly, the schools should cease to be run for private profit; thirdly, more experimental work ought to be conducted in the schools, thus justifying their independence; fourthly, boarding education should be seen as the main contribution of preparatory schools; and fifthly, publicly financed free places should be given to those children from the primary sector who passed an entry examination.[44]

It was clear from the sixty-seventh IAPS annual conference in 1957, whose theme was 'The future of Independent Education', that Dugdale's proposals had not fallen on deaf ears. Many of the speakers spoke with optimism not of a *bleak* future but of a *different* one. Mr Angus Maude MP, President of the IAPS, spoke of his political opponent Dugdale as one who 'roared as gently as any sucking dove'. Preparatory school heads accepted the necessity of some form of state connection, with up to 50 per cent of their places allotted to pupils whose fees would be paid from public funds.[45]

Even less attractive to the preparatory schools was the Eccles Plan, named after Sir David Eccles, a Conservative Minister of Education, who advocated the use of primary schools by future public school boys as being of social advantage — a recommendation which pre-empted the charges of the Public Schools Commission about 'social divisiveness'. If this suggestion had been adopted as a post-Fleming compromise it would have been very harmful to the continuing institutional health of the preparatory schools as an integral part of the public school system. One recalls the fears expressed by Mr O.C. Waterfield (Temple Grove) in the nineteenth century lest the competition from dame preparatory schools at one end of the preparatory age spectrum and from public schools' junior schools at the other would lead to the early extinction of classical preparatory schools.

Throughout the 1950s and 1960s there were constant pleas both on behalf of the independent schools and of the nation for closer ties between the independent and maintained sectors.[46] The desire by the IAPS to fall in with such suggestions — possibly because of the threat of the Eccles plan — was evident in their submission to the Public Schools Commission in 1967. They declared:

> Nevertheless, it is a matter of regret to us that admission to preparatory and public schools is for the most part restricted to boys whose parents are wealthy enough to afford the fees.... None of the principles which we hold dear is offended by the proposal that our intake should be broadened.[47]

The Genesis of ISIS and ISJC

Although the post-war economic pressures have been sufficiently harmful to close many long-established preparatory schools, the economic threats to these schools pale into insignificance by comparison with the political threats which they now face. The Labour Party, as was made clear in the terms of reference (probably more appropriately styled 'terms of direction') of the Public Schools Commission, seeks the dismantling of independent education in Britain. The recommendations of this Commission have led only to the abolition of the Direct Grant, thus driving many academically excellent schools, which were providing a valuable bridge between the independent and maintained sectors, into the status of fully independent school, no longer accessible to the clever children from lower socio-economic groups. Since the publication of the second (Donnison) report of the Public Schools Commission (1972), the Labour Party has become more determined to abolish the independent sector as it now exists. In 1983 outright abolition forms part of the policy which the Labour Party intends to implement when it next comes to power. The political threat from the Labour Party in 1980s is more real than the threats of 1869 and 1902.[48] This time it is based not on educational grounds but purely on the political belief that education ought not to be a vendible commodity insulated against the state.

In April 1978 Mrs Shirley Williams, Secretary of State for the Department of Education and Science in Mr Callaghan's Labour Government (1976–9), discontinued the designation 'recognized as efficient', together with the system of full-dress inspections by Her Majesty's Inspectorate as an outcome of which a school had been able to acquire the accolade of 'recognized'. IAPS preparatory schools were not immediately affected, because all had earlier acquired 'recognized' status as a condition of IAPS membership. But since the DES would no longer conduct inspections for renewal of recognition, it was clear that in future years they could no longer rely on 'erstwhile recognition' as evidence of quality. As with the abolition of Direct Grant schools, the withdrawal of 'recognition status' from highly efficient schools is a serious slur. A more generous interpretation of this DES measure might be that, as Mr Michael Henley, CEO of Northamptonshire, has recently suggested to me this: was part of a wider campaign by the DES to economize.

So the Independent Schools Information Service (ISIS), with Donald Lindsay, ex-headmaster of Malvern School as its first director, came into being at national level in October 1972 to give information to parents about the opportunities in independent schools. Indirectly it serves as a defender of independent education. By disseminating information it provides a major defence against the predations of the Labour Party. ISIS is not a scholastic agency like Gabbitas-Thring but an information agency which can advise on options available. In addition to the ISIS headquarters in London there are seven ISIS regional branches in the United Kingdom.[49] These branches give information about individual independent schools in their region. The main significance of ISIS lies perhaps in its being an organization to which all 'recognized as efficient' — now 'formerly recognized' — independent schools can belong, enabling them to speak with one voice about the virtues and ideals of independent education.

Educational consultancy is only one part of the function of ISIS; it also aims at informing the public about independent education and the ideals on which independent schools are based. It has no political ties but seeks to organize 'the defence of independent education whenever it comes under political attack'.[50] In defence of its ideals ISIS and the body behind it, the Independent Schools Joint Council (ISJC),[51] are inevitably in conflict with the Labour Party whose attitude towards an independent school sector was becoming progressively more hostile and intolerant.

The Socio-Economic Case

As Alan Peacock and Jack Wiseman of the Institute of Economic Affairs argued in 1964, education has become increasingly more subject to political control — and worse, to political caprice.[52] It is not without significance that in 1962 some 91.9 per cent of children were educated in the United Kingdom by the state, and that higher education students were assisted from public funds more extensively than in many other Western countries.[53] It needs to be reaffirmed that it is the duty of the Secretary of State for Education and Science to *promote* education, not to *control* it; that it is the duty of LEAs to *contribute* towards, not to *monopolize*, the community's development; and that it is the parents' *duty* to see that children of compulsory school-age receive efficient full-time education.

There are positive advantages to the nation in the retention of an independent schools sector. The existence of an alternative to the 'state controlled' maintained system is politically and educationally healthy. On the one hand it provides a defence against the sort of monolithism which could promote a totalitarian state; on the other it serves as a yardstick of 'best' and 'worst' schools against which the Department of Education and Science and LEAs can measure their own schools.[54] An independent school does not have to convince a body of officials or an Education Committee before it can experiment, or indeed before it can make a decision to retain those traditions that it regards as valuable. The participation of the preparatory schools in the trial stages of the Nuffield Science and Mathematics schemes was significant. Since maintained primary schools by and large have less autonomy than maintained secondary schools, the independent preparatory schools are of added value to the education of the youngest of the nation.

Closely associated with the ideal of the independence of independent schools is that of freedom of parents to decide the kind of education their children shall receive. Article 13 of the United Nations' Covenant on Economic, Social and Cultural Rights states:

> The States Parties to the present Covenant undertake to have respect for the liberty of parents and, when applicable, legal guardians to choose for their children schools, other than those established by the public authorities, which conform to such minimum educational

standards as may be laid down or approved by the State and to ensure the religious and moral education of their children in conformity with their own convictions.[55]

The right of parents to choose the kind of education they desire for their children could not be more explicitly stated. Parental liberty to choose the schools for their children is endorsed by government policy in countries as diverse and as far apart as Holland and Australia. It is a strange form of twentieth century benevolent despotism which denies this right to some parents on the ground that not all parents have the same opportunities to exercise it. If the maintained system of primary education in England and Wales is of a lower standard than that of the IAPS preparatory school (a proposition denied by the Plowden Report), then it is the duty of LEAs to raise the standard of their schools. If they were to do so, it would not be necessary to proscribe the preparatory schools on grounds of inequality: they would be able still to provide a yardstick against which all primary schools could be measured.

The case for the continued existence of the preparatory schools is admirably made in the ISIS document, *The Right Start*, which admits that there are 'many fine state schools' suitable for the children of many parents. But it also acknowledges that children differ in their needs. 'Children can be robust or sensitive, athletic, musical, highly intelligent or in need of remedial teaching. Not every school is right for, indeed not every school can adequately provide for, every child.'[56] It is the *choice* offered by preparatory schools that is so important in this context. For those aesthetically inclined, schools such as The Downs, Colwall, and Old Buckenham Hall School offer great opportunities for personal development. Moreover the religious and moral aspects of education are more in evidence in preparatory schools, where many have their own chapel and where high standards of good behaviour are inculcated. Parents ought to have the right to spend their money on these values, especially if they have already fulfilled their tax-paying obligations and have thus contributed to the education of the children of others.

If ISIS is concerned with the public endorsement of ideals in education, it is also pragmatic in their promotion. Mr Tim Devlin, the new Director of ISIS, is a man of great energy and ideas who, thriving on a siege mentality engendered by the declared hostility of the Labour Party to independent schooling, is organizing the defence of the ISIS citadel. The going into the market place to extol aloud the virtues of independent preparatory schools is symptomatic of this energetic self-defence. The first ISIS shop, organized in Bristol in 1978 for this purpose, had the effect of increasing the already close rapport between independent schools in Bristol and its citizens. The IAPS, in particular, is a pragmatic body which has done much to strengthen the ISIS ramparts. It was the first body, amongst independent schools associations, to have a public relations officer. It responded positively to the withdrawal of the Department of Education and Science in 1978 of the status of 'recognized as efficient' through the discontinuance of inspections by HM Inspectorate. Within a brief period the IAPS had organized its own inspections. Such a pragmatic action will do something to mitigate the harm done by the withdrawal of Department's 'recognition'.

The Initiative of IAPS

In another area the IAPS has given evidence of its energetic leadership amongst independent schools associations. The Joint Education Trust (JET), inspired by Mr Charles Malden (Windlesham House) and Mr Raymond Cooper (formerly of the Hall School, Hampstead), is concerned with placing disadvantaged children in independent schools. The HMC has responded to this IAPS initiative and public schools offer secondary education to disadvantaged children. The number of JET-assisted children is steadily increasing and has been assisted by IAPS Council, though it is totally independent.[57]

The pragmatism of IAPS is evidenced, too, in the steady conversions of schools from private profit institutions to charitable trusts. From as early as 1945 when Bilton Grange, Warwickshire, became Bilton Grange Trust Ltd — one of the earlier preparatory school trusts — to 1958 when Hawtreys took on charitable trust status, the number of charitable trusts grew slowly. But, as indicated by the Association's latest census figures, there are now very few proprietary schools in the 'Wyatt' tradition. An even more pragmatic measure taken by Mr William Van Straubenzee and Mrs Margaret Thatcher at the Department of Education and Science before they relinquished power to the third Wilson Labour Government was to ensure the permanent legality of the charitable trust status of the preparatory schools.[58] More recently the amalgamation of the IAPS and the AHMPS in January 1981 will, in the long term, strengthen the hands of the preparatory schools against charges of possible irrelevance in the context of the almost universal adoption of co-education.

The IAPS constantly has its attention focussed on the future. Its Advisory Committee with Industry, which IAPS President, the late Mr John Davies MP, did so much to promote, keeps the schools abreast of industrial and commercial developments; its Public Relations Committee ensures they are no longer isolated from the public at large; the HMC/IAPS JSC ensures constant contact with the HMC; and the ISJC gives the IAPS a positive part to play in the work of ISIS. James Nowell observed in 1954: 'In the years ahead they should never cease to examine themselves and see if any further improvement can be made.'[59]

This interest in constant improvement by the IAPS schools was the *raison d'être* for such inquiries and reports as *Foundations* (1959); *Prospect* (1965);[60] the Ellis Report (1972), which examined the syllabi of upper preparatory school forms and lower public school forms from the age of eleven to fifteen to improve the cohesion of the two; *The Preparatory Years* (1973), which examined the best in English education from the age of seven to thirteen; and *Learning to Live* (1976), a report of the HMC/IAPS working party on 'the implicit curriculum'. All these reports have received less publicity than the Plowden and Newsom Reports, but their objective was similar: to improve preparatory school education so that it can better play its role as a contributing partner in the education of the nation.

The preparatory schools of the IAPS are schools whose aim and achievement is one of excellence. They have shown themselves capable, especially since the Second World War, of adapting to the changing world around them. They have much to offer the nation in terms of intellectual and aesthetic excellence and in high standards of behaviour and conduct. Is it too much to hope that in its relationship with the maintained sector these strengths of the preparatory school will be recognized and upheld as ultimately of benefit to the nation? Thus the IAPS motto 'Having the light we shall share it with other' — would be ripe with meaning.

Notes

1 P.L. MASTERS, *op. cit.*, p. 107. The remaining schools in MASTERS' survey are accounted for in Private Company Schools: 155, and Junior Departments of Public Schools: 64. Four schools did not answer this question.
2 *IAPS Census* (1977) p. 3.
3 Mr DENYS STRAKER of Downsend School, Leatherhead, has been one of the leaders in mathematics reform.
4 Mr NIGEL CHILVERS of Windlesham House has been an exemplar of teaching in this field.
5 Cf. Rev. R.G. WICKHAM, 'Esso and after', *PSR*, 18, 12 February 1965, pp. 14–15, also *PSR*, 16, 11 (New Series), October 1956, pp. 4–5.
6 *PSR*, Vol. 16, 12, February 1957, pp. 8–11.
7 *The Willington School Magazine*, November 1967.
8 Cf. ISIS (1975) *The Right Start — in a Preparatory School*, ISIS Document No. 10. One preparatory school is cited as offering the following extra-curricular activities: Agriculture; Art; Boxing; Bridge; Chess; Computers; Cricket; Current Affairs; Drama; Fencing; Gymnastics; Handicrafts; Heraldry; History Tours; Judo; Maps; Mechanics; Nature Study; Photography; Printing; Shooting; Silk-Screening; Speech-Training; Squash; Surveying and Tape-Recording.
9 *The Times Educational Supplement*, 12 April, 1957, p. 507.
10 JOHN DANCY (1963) *The Public Schools and the Future*, Faber and Faber, p. 141.
11 Cf. *The Times*, 4 August 1965, 5c.
12 The INCORPORATED ASSOCIATION of PREPARATORY SCHOOLS, evidence submitted to the Public Schools Commission, January 1967, p. 18.
13 *Ibid.*, p. 12.
14 Public Schools Commission (Newsom) First Report, 1967, Vol. 1, p. vii.
15 IAPS Evidence, *op. cit.*, p. 23.
16 *IAPS Census*, (1977) p. 9.
17 *Ibid.*
18 *Ibid.*, p. 4. One view might be, however, that this is not at all a fair comparison. The percentage is different but the *number* of boarders is much the same. The number of day boys rose causing a hardly diminished number of boarders to constitute a lower percentage of a larger whole.

19 According to Mr and Mrs MALDEN it has been necessary to limit the numbers of girls in the school lest they swamp the boys who achieve maturity at a later stage.
20 *IAPS Census*, (1981), p. 2. With the merging of AHMPS with IAPS 18,992 girls were in IAPS schools in 1982.
21 Cf. ROYSTON LAMBERT (1966) *The State and Boarding Education*, Methuen; ROYSTON LAMBERT and SPENCER MILLHAM (1974). *The Hothouse Society*, Penguin Books; and ROYSTON LAMBERT *et al.* (1975) *The Chance of a Life-Time?* Weidenfeld and Nicolson.
22 Mr P.G. SPENCER, headmaster of Red House School, near York, resigned in 1972 because of a policy clash with his school governors. SPENCER wanted to retain the 100 per cent boarding character of Red House School. *Daily Mail* (Irish edition), 4 July 1972.
23 Evidence, 1967, pp. 20–1.
24 Sir PERCY NUNN (1926) *Education: Its Data and First Principles*, Arnold.
25 Cf. *op. cit.*, pp. 81–102.
26 JAMES NOWELL, 'The prospects of independent schools', *The Quarterly Review*, 292, 601, July 1954, p. 340.
27 JAMES NOWELL, *op. cit.*, p. 345.
28 *PSR*, 16, 3 (New Series), February 1954, p. 54.
29 H.C. DENT (1955) *The Education Act 1944*, University of London Press, 5th ed., 1955. Part III, Sections 70–75, pp. 63–5 dealt with independent schools.
30 *PSR*, 18, 12, February 1965, p. 8.
31 From letter dated 20 October 1977 by Mr R.N.C. WEBSTER, ex-assistant headmaster of Rottingdean School.
32 Cf. IAPS Bulletin 29, October 1963. This Bulletin, started in March 1958, published thrice annually for the information of IAPS members, is not to be confused with the *Bulletin* which was published during the war years.
33 I am grateful to MICHAEL SMITH, former pupil of Moorland House, for this information.
34 *IAPS Census* (1977), p. 5.
35 *PSR*, 26, 2, June 1977, pp. 14–15.
36 From school lists of Amesbury School.
37 *IAPS Census* (1977) p. 3.
38 *The Times Educational Supplement*, 9 September 1977.
39 *IAPS Census* (1982) p. 1.
40 *PSR*, 14, 1 (New Series), June 1945, p. 3.
41 Only a few LEAs, such as Middlesex and Surrey, availed themselves of the 25 per cent places made available in the Grade B public schools for children who had attended maintained primary schools.
42 JAMES NOWELL (1954) *The Quarterly Review*, 292, 601, July p. 345.
43 This was before the major decline in Latin and the major onset of science in the preparatory school curriculum.
44 *The Times Educational Supplement*, 12 April 1957, p. 507.
45 *Ibid.*, 20 September 1957, p. 1226.
46 Cf. *The Times*, 9 March 1962, p. 6; *ibid.*, 9 April 1963, p. 14; *ibid.*, 13 September 1963, p. 14; *Ibid.* 14 September 1963, p. 4; *Ibid.*, 14 September 1964, p. 6; *ibid.*, 9 September 1967, p. 2; *ibid.*, 15 September 1967, p. 9.
47 IAPS Evidence, 1967, p. 25.
48 This is not the first time, of course, that the independent schools have found themselves the target of extraordinary political attack. It was concern about the Schools Inquiry Commission that caused EDWARD THRING and his colleagues to form the Headmasters' Conference in 1869. Furthermore, the 1902 Education Act, providing the newly formed LEAs with power to provide secondary education, had been seen as political threat to the continuation of independent schools. Many

private adventure schools had been unable to withstand the competition from LEAs even though the public and preparatory schools had continued to thrive.

49 The seven regions are Central, London and South-East England, Eastern England, South and Mid-Wales, South and South-West England, Scotland and Ireland. The beginnings of ISIS can be traced back to 1966 when Mr J.R. SINGLETON (St John's, Chepstow — now of Chafyn Grove), Mr J. SHARP (Christ's College, Brecon) and Mr J. CRAMPTON (St John's, Porthcawl) formed a group to consider recruitment in independent schools in South Wales. This first established branch of ISIS consisted of six preparatory and three public schools. By 1970 the idea had spread to the Midlands where a second branch was created. From there the organization spread first to East Anglia, then North and then to London and the South-East before a national ISIS was formed.

50 ISIS (1975) *The Independent Schools Information Service and How It Operates*. ISIS Document No. 1, 3rd ed., July.

51 The sponsoring authorities of ISIS were the Association of Governing Bodies of Public Schools (GBA); the Association of Governing Bodies of Girls' Public Schools (GBGSA); the IAPS; and the Association of Headmistresses of Preparatory Schools (AHMPS). The ISJC, constituted in 1974, has nine constituent bodies and speaks collectively for them.

52 *PSR*, 18, 11, October 1964, p. 6.

53 Lord ROBBINS (1963) *Higher Education*, London, HMSO, Vol. 1, p. 40.

54 *Ibid.*, p. 7.

55 Cf. *PSR*, 26, 1, February 1977, p. 3.

56 ISIS (1975) *The Right Start in a Preparatory School*, ISIS Document No. 10, September.

57 *PSR*, 27, 3, October 1978, p. 6.

58 *PSR*, 22, 2, June 1973, pp. 28–30; *PSR*, 30 3, October 1981, pp. 12–13.

59 *The Times*, 7 September 1974.

60 *The Quarterly Review, op. cit.*, p. 343.

21 PREP Schools or PEP Schools? Will Vouchers Help?

All the higher, more penetrating ideals are revolutionary. They present themselves far less in the guise of effects of past experience than in that of probable causes of future experience.
(William James, *The Moral Philosopher and the Moral Life*)

No Comfort in Comprehension

The only avenue to Utopia in Britain today is to win the football pools, an exercise in irrationality and improbability which provides the week-end dose of hope once provided by the numerous chapels and churches in the grim country north of Watford. The chapels have now become either, as in Bradford, Sikh gurudwaras or Hindu temples, or, as elsewhere, garages for the sale of second-hand Japanese, French or German cars. Of the churches the less said the better, as caparisoned gay priests hitch their cassocks to dance to some rock tune for the worship of Christ the homosexual. The fact is that the author of an article suggesting that Christ had an affair with a centurion barely raised a brow over the glazed eyes of those filling in the pools.

If the pools have occupied the parents, the schools have preoccupied the young: preoccupied them perhaps, but have they educated them in the European heritage (which by Article 57 of the Treaty of Rome they were obliged to do)? Certainly not. French, German, Belgian, Dutch, Spanish and Swedish boys and girls can speak English but most English boys and girls (if the DES statistics are any indication) can barely mumble 'Bonjour'.

The sustained campaign by twentieth century egalitarians to offset the findings of Margaret Mead and the cultural anthropologists by rhetoric is (if the title of a book by two of them is to be taken seriously) rather like the demolition of Liverpool. The demolition of the 11+ examination and the grammar schools, especially the direct grant grammar schools (those express-ways to excellence for working class boys and girls of flair and imagination) is tragic, for the destruction of the direct grant schools in 1976 demolished the surest route for those with high ability to overcome their environmental handicaps. Sociologically, the percentage may have been small, but it was greater in the numbers gaining access to the universities.

These too have expanded and contracted like a pair of bellows, taking in and then ejecting the well established teacher training colleges in a *volte face* designed to cause maximum confusion. It has left higher education as 'tripartite' as secondary education once was with universities, polytechnics and metropolitan institutes of higher education in competitive disarray.

Problems of standards beset both secondary schools (which have to cater for non-academic sixth formers) and colleges of higher education, polytechnics and universities (which have to provide remedial classes in essay writing and note-taking for weak students).

Though hotly contested by 'egalitarians', this decline of standards is reflected also in the primary schools as the Bullock Report on Reading (1975) and the Great Education Debate of the 'seventies, inaugurated by a Labour Prime Minister, acknowledged. There would seem to be, therefore, ample evidence of *malaise* or disease at least in English education. Of the remedies put forward to combat the decline of belief in 'education' as a panacea, 'back to the basics' has been the most insistent. The *Black Papers*[1] have given conservative critics such as Professors Geoffrey Bantock, C.B. Cox and A.E. Dyson the opportunity to expose the inadequacies of primary school practice, comprehensive schools and progressive teaching methods alike. The subsequent pressure for a return to a mastery of the three Rs as the only valid basis for educational advance led to the establishment of the National Council for Educational Standards.

Back to Section 76

Even the devotional manuals of the 'deschoolers' — if Ivan Illich's writings can be so designated — identify the bureaucratization of the existing system of maintained schools as being a cause of much of this malaise. It is argued that such a school system, supported by rates and organized by local education authorities is unlikely to respond diligently to the stated needs of its customers, the parents, because of its entrenched position. And when local education authorities (LEAs) actually allocate children to schools by areas (a measure ostensibly analogous to bussing in the USA but actually based on administrative convenience) those responsible are breaking Section 76 of the 1944 Act which gives to parents as a general principle the right of ultimate say in the education of their children.[2] It is not uncommon for state systems of education abroad, such as those in Australia, to find themselves under considerable pressures of rivalry from private systems, largely on the question of choice. Such insistence by parents on choice of school for their children is often denounced by egalitarians on the ground that choice is not available to everyone. They insist that equality through uniformity is of greater value than freedom of individual choice, if that choice is limited only to those who can afford to pay for it.

Such objections — it is argued — can be overcome by giving choice to parents who could not otherwise afford to exercise choice. With all parents having, through a national voucher system, an element of choice in their children's education, schools would feel it incumbent upon them to keep their standards high if they were not to suffer from what economists would call 'adverse market-forces'. As a professor in the economics of education put it:

> The key to the voucher scheme is the distribution to all parents of vouchers exchangeable for education at any school, state or private, that satisfies minimum educational standards, the value of the voucher being related to the average costs of education according to the age of the child. State schools would charge cost-covering fees, and after that, would compete with private schools on equal terms. Parents could supplement the voucher out of their own pockets as much as they liked at private schools that might charge fees above the standard levels. Education could still be compulsory up to a legal school leaving age but parents would now be free, as with compulsory third-party automobile insurance, to choose among alternative suppliers of the compulsory service.[3]

Another professor of Education pointed out that vouchers were first proposed by Cardinal Bourne, fourth Archbishop of Westminster, in 1926 at the National Catholic Congress, held in Manchester.[4] Cardinal Bourne's scheme was not put forward in the context of the present discussion but had a limited application for Roman Catholics in the wake of the Hadow Report on *The Education of the Adolescent* (1926) which was to increase the financial burdens of the Roman Catholic community towards their schools. As such it is not our present concern, but it does serve to emphasize that the present voucher proposal does have some historical basis and is no mere passing fad. So when Milton Friedman proposed educational vouchers in 1955[5] he was merely endorsing a familiar expedient as Professors A.T. Peacock and J. Wiseman realized in *Education for Democrats* in 1964.[6] Experiments conducted in both the USA and the UK,[7] demonstrate that educational voucher schemes do have practical application.

The competition between schools to be 'chosen' through 'vouchers' offers a possibility of raising standards of education in that striving for excellence would be at a premium. The shared tradition of excellence, entertained by Greeks, Romans and men of the Renaissance respectively in their concepts of *aretē*, *virtus*, and *virtù*, has for long been given a lower order of priority: in the pursuit of equality, quality has often been overlooked.

Look at the Russians Now

Even Marxists or quasi-Marxists need to re-examine their position once more if the revelations by John Dunstan, published by the National Foundation for Educational Research, are to be taken seriously. For in his *Paths to Excellence and the Soviet School*,[8] Dunstan has shown how the Soviet Union has entertained the concept of differentiation within equality. According to him, 'The school has a duty to foster all the positive endowments of all the children within its charge, and not only the individual but the whole society will be the beneficiary.'[9] Though adhering to the principle of comprehensive schools Soviet authorities have since the 1960s espoused diversification by opting for special schools for clever children. As a consequence there are schools for the arts, sports schools, language schools, and mathematics and physics boarding schools.[10] These are regarded as 'strategies for encouraging special talent'. Often social considerations are allowed to influence such cognitive strategies by suggestions that clever children when segregated, as in the English tripartite system or in the public/preparatory schools system, become arrogant and conscious of their status in society. This followed the claim of Blonsky the Soviet educationist, as early as 1928, that gifted children came to the top in an undifferentiated schools' system but then formed in school an arrogant aristocracy. Blonsky argues, 'but if such children were brought together with their intellectual equals, they lost their arrogance along with their superiority.'[11] As Blonsky put it, ordinary children, when left to themselves, and segregated from the clever ones, came into their own. If Blonsky was right then far from differentiation entailing a social handicap it is of positive benefit to the less gifted. As such it ought to be encouraged by egalitarians rather than discouraged.

The commitment of the Soviet Union to differentiation is no ephemeral educational experiment. The oldest special school for children gifted in the arts goes back to Tsarist times: the Vaganova (Kirov) Ballet School of Leningrad was founded originally in 1738. In 1958 there were five fine art schools but by the late 1960s there were fifty. In the late 1960s there were eighteen ballet schools in the USSR. These figures show to what extent the Soviet authorities are committed to differentiation or the promotion of talents. It is significant that Dunstan, in his examination of the Soviet scene, is able to refer to 'egalitarians' and 'differentiators' as being rival factions. Academics and politicians associate the cultivation of talents with the economic and political pre-eminence of the country.[12] Herein lies the strength of differentiation within the Soviet Union.

Invoking Tom Paine

The case for both differentiation (the fostering of talent) and the institution of a universal voucher scheme in England is one of 'the basic rights of man'. Certainly Tom Paine, author of a book of that name, thought so, since he floated the idea of a voucher scheme in the eighteenth century. E.G. West cites this in his contribution to *Education: A Framework for Choice*.[13] West has also altered masterfully the perspective of the history of education in the nineteenth century with *Education and the State* (1965) and *Education and the Industrial*

Revolution (1975). Both show how the process of the government financing education through the enlarged network of schools after 1870 was but one alternative and that an adequate network of private schools already existed in the late Victorian period which alternatively could have been financed indirectly by a voucher system offered to parents. Philosophers and statesmen, such as John Stuart Mill and Robert Lowe, also favoured private schools so that the demise of these schools was by no means a foregone conclusion.[14] West goes on to develop his theme by referring to the controversial Section 25 of the 1870 Education Act which provided for the payment of school fees of needy children attending church schools. This measure, West claims, was a form of 'voucher' scheme since it paid money to parents for school fees arising from their choice of school for their children. As such, Section 25 of Forster's 1870 Education Act becomes part of the argument in favour of a voucher scheme in England in the twentieth century. West highlights this point when he draws readers' attention to the difference in outlook in 1870 from that of a century later when the Donnison Report of 1970 set out to inhibit parental choice by its proposal to abolish direct grant schools. West makes this startling comparison in his 'Introductory essay to the second edition' of *Education and the State*.[15] In this he considers problems of social mix, family education grants (vouchers), social separatism, educational 'apartheid', the impoverishment of the state sector, and the higher income groups' advantage in a state-provided system. West completes his introductory essay by establishing a case for experiments with vouchers in England, similar to those then (1970) being considered in the USA.

Fostering Talent

The fostering of talent (or the principle of differentiation) has a long and sustained history in the form of the awarding of scholarships to deserving candidates by public schools. Has not the time come for the two educational phenomena considered in this chapter — the pursuit of excellence and vouchers — to coalesce for the cure of the malaise mentioned earlier? The last four chapters have shown how preparatory schools have been pursuers of excellence and have achieved much in their endeavours. Could not *prep* schools become *pep* schools to an ailing system? The time is surely ripe for preparatory schools to be the pivotal point of an experiment in establishing a voucher scheme, which in turn would bring them into the mainstream of English education. Time and time again, preparatory schools have shown themselves to be pragmatic educational institutions, capable of adapting successfully to the changing scene. They have already shown exceptionally high standards in mathematics, science, art and music and other subjects; they offer a Christian ethos in many schools, much prized by parents who are worried about the effects of a permissive society; they offer co-education in many cases, thus showing themselves to be in the van of educational change amongst private schools; they enjoy charity status, thus facilitating the receipt of public moneys in the form of vouchers; and they offer increased day educational facilities. Education at such preparatory schools could be said to be 'a good buy' for hard-nosed parents who seek value for money and who both have to work for a living; for the working mother, in these days of women's emancipation, would probably be a better worker could she feel free of guilt about her children. Would-be destroyers, therefore, of the preparatory school system should perhaps recall Oliver Cromwell's injunction to the General Assembly of the Church of Scotland in 1650: 'I beseech you, in the bowels of Christ, think it possible you may be mistaken.' In other words, let commonsense prevail: the English educational system needs the preparatory schools just as much as the preparatory schools need to be linked with the maintained system on a fair and just basis.

Notes

1 The *Black Papers* were a source of conservative criticism of English education from 1969 to 1977.
2 Section 76 does not say that pupils must in all cases be educated in accordance with the wishes of parents but clearly the spirit of Section 76 aims to give parents more say than they have perhaps at present.
3 MARK BLAUG, 'Economic aspects of vouchers for education' in A.C.F. BEALES *et al* (1967) *Education: A Framework for Choice, Readings in Political Economy I*, The Institute of Economic Affairs.
4 *Ibid.*, (1967) p. 34. See also A.C.F. BEALES, 'Historical aspects of the debate on education', p. 7.
5 R.A. SOLO (Ed.) (1955) *Economics and the Public Interest*, M. FRIEDMAN, 'The role of government in education', Brunswick, NJ, Rutgers University Press.
6 A.T. PEACOCK and J. WISEMAN (1964) *Education for Democrats*, Hobart Paper 25, IEA.
7 In some respects the assisted places scheme of the present Tory Government is a form of 'voucher' subsidy.
8 DUNSTAN (1978) *op. cit.*, NFER Publishing Co.
9 *Ibid.*, p. 11.
10 *Ibid.*, pp. 12–13.
11 Quoted in *Ibid.*, p. 23.
12 *Ibid.*
13 A.C.F. BEALES *et al. op. cit.*, IEA, pp. 51–85. See also *Southern Economic Journal*, January 1967, pp. 378–82.
14 E.G. WEST (1965) *Education and the State*, 1st ed., IEA pp. 136–57.
15 E.G. WEST (1970) *Education and the State*, 2nd ed., IEA.

Bibliography

Unless otherwise stated books included in this bibliography were published in London.

This bibliography is neither a full one nor a select one in the usual sense of the term 'select bibliography'. It is not a full one since many (though not all) of the biographies and autobiographies used in the text have not been included (details of these may be found in the footnotes). Nor is it a strictly select bibliography since, for example, it contains references to school magazines and articles in periodicals. This bibliography is, therefore, a compromise between the two. As such it has been arranged in strict alphabetical order within the categories of books, periodicals, official publications, theses, school magazines, prospectuses and unpublished source material.

1 *Books*

ALDERSON, M.F. and H.C. COLLES (Eds) (1943) *History of St Michael's College, Tenbury*, SPCK.

ALINGTON, CYRIL (1938) *A Plea for a Plan — The Two Types of Education*, Longmans.

ALLAN, G.A.T. (1937) *Christ's Hospital*, Blackie and Son.

ALLEN, E.H. and L.P. DEALTRY, (Eds) (n.d.) *The Preparatory Schoolboy and His Education*, Evans Bros.

ANDERSON, E. (Ed.) (1950) *Joy of Youth: Letters of Patrick Hore-Ruthven*, Peter Davies.

ANON. (1926) *Memorials of Lionel Helbert*, Humphrey Milford.

ANON. (1939) *Greenbank School, Liverpool*, Liverpool University Press.

ANON. (1940) *The Skipper — A Memoir of C.C. Lynam*, Oxford, Dragon School.

ANON. (1972) *A History of the Mall School 1872–1972*, printed privately.

ANON (1973) *A Short History of Bramcote School 1893–1973*, Scarborough.

ANSON, MAJ. GEN. SIR ARCHIBALD EDWARD (1920) *About Others and Myself*, John Murray.

ARIES, PHILIPPE (1979) *Centuries of Childhood*, Penguin Books.

ARNOLD, THOMAS (1858) Letters to *The Sheffield Courant* in *Arnold's Miscellaneous Works*, London.

BALFOUR, GRAHAM (1898) *The Educational Systems of Great Britain and Ireland*, Oxford.

BAMFORD, T.W. (1960) *Thomas Arnold*, Cresset Press.

BARING, MAURICE (1930) *The Puppet Show of Memory*, Heinemann.

BARNARD, H.C. (1970) *Were Those the Days?* Oxford, Pergamon.

BATES, MARJORY and HENDERSON JEAN M. (Eds) (1949) *Miss Gilpin and the Hall School*, Bannisdale Press.

BENSON, A.C. (1915) *Escape and Other Essays*, Smith, Elder and Co.

BENSON, A.C. (1924) *Memories and Friends*, John Murray.

BEST, G.F.A. (1964) *Temporal Pillars*, Cambridge University Press.

BEWSHER, JAMES, *et al.* (1963) *The Story of Colet Court*, Eastbourne, Strange the Printer.

BLAGDEN, CLAUDE MARTIN (1953) *Well Remembered*, Hodder and Stoughton.

BLYTH, W.A.L. (1965) *English Primary Education*, Vol. 2, Routledge and Kegan Paul.

B[OLTON], G. (1929) *Summer Fields Register, 1864–1929*, Oxford.

BOWRA, C.M. (1966) *Memories — 1896–1936*, Weidenfeld and Nicolson.

BOX, H. OLDFIELD, (Ed.) (1934) *The Preparatory Schools' Year Book*, Churchman.

BRIGGS, D.R. (1983) *The Millstone Race*, printed privately.

BRYANT, MARGARET E. (1969) 'Private education from the sixteenth century', in *Victoria County History — Middlesex*, Vol. 1.

BUSHELL, W.F. (1962) *School Memories*, Liverpool, Philip Son and Nephew.

BYRNE, L.S.R. and CHURCHILL, E.L. (1937) *Changing Eton*, Jonathan Cape.

CHADWICK, HUBERT (1962) *St Omer to Stoneyhurst*, Burns and Oates.

CHURCHILL, RANDOLPH S. (1966) *Winston S. Churchill*, Vol. 1, 1874–1900, Heinemann.

COKE, HON. HENRY J. (1905) *Tracks of a Rolling Stone*, Smith, Elder and Co.

COLLIS, MAURICE (1952) *The Journey Outward*, Faber and Faber.

CONNOLLY, CYRIL (1938) *Enemies of Promise*, Routledge and Kegan Paul.

COOPER, M.A.F. (1970) *Fonthill — 1970–150th Anniversary*, privately printed.

COTTERILL, C.C. (1885) *Suggested Reforms in Public Schools*, Edinburgh, Blackwood and Sons.

COULTON, G.G. (1945) *Fourscore Years*, Cambridge University Press.

COVERLEY, LEONARD (1971) *History of Chelmsford Hall*, Eastbourne, Sumfield & Day.

DANCY, J.C. (1963) *The Public Schools and the Future*, Faber and Faber.

DE CARTERET-BISSON, F.S. (1872) *Our Schools and Colleges*, Simpkin, Marshall and Co.

DEANE, ANTONY C. (1945) *Time Remembered*, Faber and Faber.

DOVER WILSON, J. (Ed.) (1928) *The Schools of England*, London, Sidgwick and Jackson.

DRURY-LOWE, P.G. (Ed.) (1964) *The Hall School Hampstead 1889–1964*, Monmouthshire, Starling Press.

DUKES, CLEMENT (1905) *Health at School*, Rivingtons.

DURLSTON, KENNETH (1926) *Preparatory School System*, Robert Holden and Co.

Eagle House 1829–1970, (1970) sesquicentenary history, Thame, Castle Printers.

EARLE, GRANVILLE (Ed.) (1932) *Bilton Grange Register 1873–1931*, 2nd. ed., Rugby.

FARRAR, F.W. (Ed.) (1867) *Essays on a Liberal Education*, Macmillan.

FRANKLAND, M.N.W. and FRANKLAND, S.J.C. (Eds) (1901) *Sketches from the Life of Edward Frankland, 1825–1899*, Spottiswoode and Co.

GASKELL, C.M. (Ed.) (1939) *An Eton Boy*, the letters of J.M. Gaskell from Eton and Oxford, 1829–1830, Constable and Co.

GATHORNE-HARDY, J. (1977) *The Public School Phenomenon, 597–1977*, Hodder and Stoughton.

GRANGE, R.M.D. (n.d.) *History of Rose Hill School*, Tunbridge Wells, Newson.

GRENFELL, A.G. (1921) *Custodibus Custos*, printed privately.

HALCOMB, R.J. (1935) *The Vital Years*, Winchester.

HAMILTON, LORD FREDERIC (1920) *The Days Before Yesterday*, Hodder and Stoughton.

HAMILTON, GENERAL SIR I. (1939) *When I Was a Boy*, Faber and Faber.

HANS, NICHOLAS (1951) *New Trends in Education in the Eighteenth Century*, Routledge and Kegan Paul.

HARE, AUGUSTUS, J.C. (1896) *The Story of My Life*, Vol. 1, George Allen.

HARRIS, STANLEY S. (1925) *The Master and His Boys*, Winchester, Warren and Son.

HARRISON, R.A. (1975) *How Was That, Sir?* Woodbridge, Baron Publishing.

HARTMAN, ROBERT (1964) *The Remainder Biscuit*, Andre Deutsch.

HEADLAM, MAURICE (1944) *Bishop and Friend, Nugent Hicks, Sixty-Fourth Bishop of Lincoln*, MacDonald and Co.

HILEY, R.W. (1899) *Memories of Half a Century*, Longmans, Green and Co.

HODGSON, C.P.B. (1965) *The First Eighty Years at Willington School*, printed privately.

HOLLIS, CHRISTOPHER (1974) *The Seven Ages*, Heinemann.

HONEY, J.R. DE S. (1977) *Tom Brown's Universe*, Millington.

IRVINE, A.L. (1958) *Sixty Years at School*, Winchester, Wykeham Press.

JAMES, M.R. (1926) *Eton and Kings*, Williams and Norgate.

JAMES, W.A. (1927) *An Account of Grammar and Song Schools*, Lincoln.

JAQUES, C.H. (1977) *A Dragon Century 1877–1977*, Blackwell.

JEBB, R. (1930) *The Proparatory School*, Sheed and Ward.

KENDALL, G. (1933) *A Headmaster Remembers*, V. Gollancz.

KINGSTON, W.H.G. (n.d.) *The Three Midshipmen*, Collins.

KITCHIN, G.W. (1857) *Prayers for the Use of Twyford School*.

LA TERRIÉRE, COL. B. DE SALES (1924) *Days That Are Gone*, Hutchinson.

LAMBERT, R. and MILLHAM, S. (1974) *The Hothouse Society*, Penguin Books.

LAWSON, W.R. (1908) *John Bull and His Schools*, Blackwood and Sons.

LEAKEY, J.H. (1951) *School Errant*, Queensgate Press.

LEWIS, CECIL DAY (1969) *The Buried Day*, Chatto and Windus.

LEWIS, MICHAEL (1965) *The Navy in Transition, 1814–1864*, Hodder and Stoughton.

LOCKER-LAMPSON, FREDERICK (1896) *My Confidences*, Smith, Elder and Co.

LORD, JOHN (1920) *Duty, Honour, Empire, the Life and Times of Colonel Richard Meinertzhagen*, Hutchinson.

LUSHINGTON, REV. F. DE W. (1898) *Sermons to Young Boys*, John Murray.

LYTTELTON, REV. THE HON. E. (1892) *Mothers and Sons*, Macmillan.

LYTTELTON, REV. THE HON. E. (1909) *Schoolboys and Schoolwork*, Longmans, Green and Co.

LYTTELTON, REV. THE HON. E. (1925) *Memories and Hopes*, John Murray.

MACK, E.C. and ARMYTAGE W.H.G. (1952) *Thomas Hughes, The Life of the Author of Tom Brown's Schooldays*, Ernest Benn.

MACKAIL, J.W. and WYNDHAM GUY (1925) *Life and Letters of George Wyndham*, Vol. 1, Hutchinson.

MACKENZIE, COMPTON (1963) *My Life and Times*, Octave 2, Chatto and Windus.

McLEAN, A.H.H. (1909) *The Law Concerning Secondary and Preparatory Schools*, Jordan and Sons.

MALAN, A.G. (Ed.) (1908) *Eagle House Register 1820–1908*, printed privately.

MARCUS, G.J. (1975) *Heart of Oak*, Oxford University Press.

MARSH, P.T. (1969) *The Victorian Church in Decline*, Routledge and Kegan Paul.

MARSHALL, A (1983) *Whimpering in the Rhododendrons*, Fontana.

MARTEN, C.H.K. (1938) *On the Teaching of History*, Blackwell.

MARTINEAU, H.D. (1975) *Half a Century of St Hugh's School, Woodhall Spa*, Horncastle, Cupit and Hindley.

MASTERS, PHILIP L. (1966) *Preparatory Schools Today: Some Facts and Inferences*, Adam and Charles Black.

MAXWELL, G. (1965) *The House of Eltig*, Longmans.

MAXWELL, RT HON. SIR HERBERT (1932) *Evening Memories*, Glasgow, Alexander Maclehose and Co.

MEINERTZHAGEN, R. (1964) *Diary of a Black Sheep*, Oliver and Boyd.

MELLY, GEORGE (1854) *School Experiences of a Fag at a Private and a Public School*, London.

MILNE, A.A. (1939) *It's Too Late Now*, Methuen.

MILNER-GULLAND, HARRY (1976) *School Story*, Guildford, Biddles.

MONROE, PAUL (Ed.) (1911–13) *Cyclopaedia of Education*, Vol. 5, New York, Macmillan.

MOZLEY, REV. T. (1885) *Reminiscences Chiefly of Towns, Villages and Schools*, Vol. 1, Longmans, Green and Co.

NEWSOME, DAVID (1961) *Godliness and Good Learning*, John Murray.

NICHOLSON, SYDNEY H. (1932) *Quires and Places Where They Sing*, Bell.

NORWOOD, SIR CYRIL (1929) *The English Tradition of Education*, John Murray.

NORWOOD, C. and HOPE, A.H. (1909) *The Higher Education of Boys in England*, Murray.

OLD RUGBOEAN, AN (n.d.) *Rugboeana*, Lichfield, The Johnson's Head.

OMAN, SIR CHARLES (1941) *Memories of Victorian Oxford*, Methuen.

ORWELL, S. and ANGUS I. (Eds) (1971) 'Such, such were the joys', from *The Collected Essays, Journalism and Letters of George Orwell, Vol. 4 In Front of Your Nose 1945–1950*, Penguin Books.

PATON J & J (1900) *Paton's List of Schools and Tutors 1900*, printed privately.

PAYN, JAMES (1884) *Some Literary Recollections*, Smith, Elder and Co.

PEARCE, E.H. (1901) *Annals of Christ's Hospital*, Methuen.

PEEL, EDWARD (1974) *Cheam School from 1645*, Thornhill Press.

PELLAT, T. (1936) *Boys in the Making*, Methuen.

PELLAT, T. (1904) *Public Schools and Public Opinion*, Longmans.

POUND, REV. WILLIAM (1866) *Remarks upon English Education, in Nineteenth Century (Educational Tract)*, Rivingtons.

PRITCHARD, FRANK C. (1939) 'The history and development of boys' preparatory schools in England', in USILL, H.V. (Ed.) (1939) *Year Book*, pp. 785–93.

Public Schools from Within (1906), essays by schoolmasters, Sampson, Low and Co.

PYCROFT, REV. J. (1843) *On School Education Designed to Assist Parents in Choosing and in Co-operating With Instructors for Their Sons*, Longman and Co.

RAGG, LONSDALE (1911) *A Memoir of Edward Charles Wickham*, Edward Arnold.

RANKILOR, HERBERT (1897) 'Suggestions on the preparation of young boys for public school life', pamphlet.

READER, W.J. (1966) *Professional Men — The Rise of the Professional Classes in Nineteenth Century England*, Weidenfeld and Nicolson.

RICHARDSON, M. (1968) *Little Victims*, Andre Deutsch.

ROBERTSON, F.L. and MacLACHLAN, N. (1903) *Routenburn Preparatory School Directory 1892–1903*, Glasgow, James Maclehose and Sons.

ROBERTSON, DORA H. (1969) *Sarum Close*, Firecrest.

RUTTON, W.L. (1906) *Temple Grove in East Sheen, Surrey*, Mitchell and Hughes.

SADLER, M.E. (Ed.) (1908) *Moral Instruction and Training in Schools*, Vol. 1, Longmans.

SANDERSON, I.C.M. (1978) *A History of Elstree School*, printed privately.

Schoolmasters Yearbook and Directory, (1904) Sonnenschein.

SEBRIGHT, ARTHUR (1922) *A Glance into the Past*, Eveleigh, Nash and Grayson.

SEWELL, J.S.N. (1928) *The Straight Left; Being Nine Talks to Boys about to Leave their Preparatory Schools*, SPCK.

SHAW, JEFFREY P. (1948) *A Schoolmaster's Apologia*, Whitby, Abbey Press.

SHELTON, H.S. (1932) *Thoughts of a Schoolmaster*, Hutchinson.

SIMPSON, J.H. (1936) *Sane Schooling*, Faber and Faber.

SIMPSON, J.H. (1954) *Schoolmaster's Harvest — Some Findings of Fifty Years 1894–1944*, Faber and Faber.

SITWELL, OSBERT (1946) *The Scarlet Tree*, Macmillan.

SOLOWAY, R.A. (1969) *Prelates and People — Ecclesiastical Social Thought in England 1783–1852*, Routledge and Kegan Paul.

SPILLANE, PAUL (1977) *St Andrew's School 1877–1977*, Southampton, Hobbis the Printers.

STANSKY, P. and ABRAHAMS, W. (1972) *The Unknown Orwell*, Constable.

STATHAM, E.P. (1904) *The Story of the 'Britannia'*, Cassell and Co.

STORR, F. (1899) *Life and Remains of Rev. R.H. Quick*, Cambridge University Press.

STRONG, L.A.G. (1961) *Green Memory*, Methuen.

THOMPSON, ERICA (1977) *Out of the Oak: The Story of Aysgarth School*, printed privately.

THOMPSON, F.M.L. (1963) *English Landed Society in the Nineteenth Century*, Routledge and Kegan Paul.

THOMPSON, P.D. (Ed.) (1939) *How to Become a Naval Officer*, Gieves.

THOMSON, REV. A.F. (1865) *The English Schoolroom or Thoughts on Private Tuition*, Sampson, Low, Son and Marston.

USBORNE, RICHARD (Ed.) (1964) *A Century of Summer Fields*, Methuen.

VAN ZELLER, HUBERT (1952) *Willingly to School*, Sheed and Ward.

VERNEY, RICHARD (1934) *The Passing Years*, Constable.

WARE, FABIAN (1900) *Educational Reform — The Task of the Board of Education*, Methuen.

WATSON, FOSTER (Ed.) (1921–2) *Encyclopaedia and Dictionary of Education*, Vol. 3, Sir I. Pitman and Sons.

WATTS, RICHARD (1977) *A History of Wolborough Hill School 1877–1977*, Southampton, Hobbis the Printers.

WENHAM, LESLIE P. (1958) *The History of Richmond School Yorkshire*, Arbroath.

WEST, GEOFFREY (1930) *H.G. Wells*, Gerald Howe Ltd.

WICKHAM, C.T. (Ed.) (1909) *The Story of Twyford School*, Winchester, Wykeham Press.

WILKINSON, SPENCER (Ed.) (n.d.) *The Nation's Need*, Archibald and Constable and Co.

WILSON, G.H. (1937) *Windlesham House School 1837–1937*, McCorquodale.

WOOD, GEORGE (1972) *A History of Denstone College Preparatory School 1902–1972*.

WOOTTON, PAUL (1970) *Eagle House 1820–1970* Thame, Castle Printers.

WORSLEY, T.C. (1967) *Flannelled Fool — A Slice of Life in the Thirties*, Alan Ross.

WRIDGWAY, NEVILLE (1980) *The Choristers of St George's Chapel*, Berkshire, Chas. Lyff and Co.

YOUNG, KENNETH (1963) *Arthur James Balfour*, Bell and Songs.

2   *Periodicals*

BENSON, A.C. (1912) 'Our gentlemen's schools again', in *The English Review*, October.

Blackwood Edinburgh Magazine (1894) 'The preparatory school', 155, March.

Blackwood Edinburgh Magazine (1897) 'The entry and training of naval officers', 162, December.

BRADLEY, GEORGE GRANVILLE (1884) 'My schooldays from 1834–1840', in *The Nineteenth Century*, 15, March.

BRERETON, CLOUDESLEY (1919) 'Educational reform — a bird's-eye view', in *The Nineteenth Century and After*, 81.

CURTIS, R.J.S. (1957) 'The future of independent schools', *Occasional Paper No. 3*, University of Sheffield, Institute of Education.

Educational Review (1899–1901) 1, 2, 3.

HOYLAND, GEOFFREY (1929) 'An experiment in preparatory school organization', in *The Journal of Education and School World*, April.

HUNTER, P.G. (1942) 'The preparatory and public school curriculum', in *The Journal of Education*, February.

INKERSLEY, ARTHUR (1893) 'An English preparatory school', in *Education*, November.

Journal of Education, The, December 1903, July 1919, September 1913, March 1931, June 1932.

KEGAN PAUL, C. (1883) 'Clergymen as headmasters', in *The Nineteenth Century*, September.

KING, H.C. (1926) 'Schools and universities of Great Britain — private and preparatory schools', in *The Journal of Education and School World*, April.

KING, HUGH C. (1932) 'The preparatory schools', in E. PERCY (Ed.) *Yearbook of Education 1932*, pp. 215–19.

LEINSTER-MACKAY, D.P. (1976) 'The dame school: A need for review', *British Journal of Educational Studies*, 24, 1, February.

LEINSTER-MACKAY, D.P. (1976) 'Out of the valley of the shadow of death via Cader Idris', in *Paedogogica Historica*, 16, 2, Gent.

LEINSTER-MACKAY, D.P. (1976) 'The evolution of 't'other schools': The development of nineteenth century private preparatory schools', *History of Education*, 5, 3, October.

LYONS, N. (1976) 'The clergy in education: Career structures in the 1830s',

Journal of Educational Administration and History, 8, 1, January.

LYTTELTON, EDWARD (1928) 'The nightmare of examinations', in *Quarterly Review,* 251, July.

LYTTELTON, EDWARD (1922) 'Feeding of schoolboys', *The Nineteenth Century,* March.

NORTON, LORD (1883) 'Middle class education', in *The Nineteenth Century,* 13, January–June.

NOWELL, JAMES (1955) 'The prospects of the independent schools', in *Quarterly Review,* 292, July.

PARKER, ERIC 'Private schools: Ancient and modern', in *Longman's Magazine,* 29, November 1896; April 1897.

Preparatory Schools Review (1895–1940, 1945–1983)

Private Schoolmaster, The (1880) 'The *Saturday Review* on "Private or Preparatory Schools"'.

Record, The (1898) Vol. 2, National Association for the Promotion of Technical and Secondary Education.

St James's Budget (1894) 'Aysgarth Preparatory School', 21 September.

St. Neots Magazine March 1934–March 1940 Nos. 1–7.

SANKEY, C. (1925) 'The evolution of the preparatory school', in *The Preparatory Schools Review,* June.

Saturday Review, The, 21 May 1864; 20 September 1873; 7 February 1880.

School Board Chronicle

SIMMONS, C. (1906) 'The preparatory day school of the future', in *Contemporary Review,* 90, September.

Times, The

Times Educational Supplement, The

WAUGH, ARTHUR (1930) 'A Victorian dame school', in *Fortnightly Review,* 127, January–June.

WELLDON, J.E.C. (1890) 'The educational system in public schools', in *Contemporary Review,* 57.

Wiltshire Gazette, The (1928) 'Reminiscences of a Wiltshire Vicar, 1814–1893', 7 June.

3   Official Publications

ASSOCIATION OF PUBLIC SCHOOL SCIENCE MASTERS, SUB-COMMITTEE REPORT (1905) *Nature Study in Preparatory Schools.*

BOARD OF EDUCATION (1900) *Special Reports on Educational Subjects,* Vol. 6.

BOARD OF EDUCATION (1913–14) *Report.*

BOARD OF EDUCATION (1920–1) *Preparatory Schools Listed As Efficient.*

BOARD OF EDUCATION (1932) *Report on Private Schools,* HMSO.

BRITISH PARLIAMENTARY PAPERS (1969) *Schools Inquiry Commission (Taunton) 1867–68,* Shannon, Irish University Press.

BRITISH PARLIAMENTARY PAPERS (1969) *Report of the Commissioners on the Revenues and Management of Certain Colleges and Schools (Clarendon)*

1864, Shannon, Irish University Press.

BRITISH PARLIAMENTARY PAPERS (1970) *Royal Commission on Secondary Education. Report of the Commissioners (Bryce) 1895*, Shannon, Irish University Press.

COLLIS, H.J.G. (1959) *Foundations*, IAPS Report.

CREWE, the Marquess of (1921) *The Classics in Education*, Report, HMSO.

HEADMASTERS' CONFERENCE, REPORTS, 1870–1872, 1890, 1895, 1907.

HILL, CRISPIN (n.d.) 'Natural Science', IAPS Pamphlet No. 20.

HMC/IAPS (1976) Joint Standing Committee Report, The Common Entrance Committee and the Curriculum Committee — a Definition of Responsibilities, November.

HMC/IAPS, Working Party on the Implicit Curriculum (1976) *Learning to Live*, report, Lymington, South Hants Printing Co.

HMC/IAPS, Working Party on the Continuity of the Curriculum (1972) *Progress Report and Recommendations to the Joint Standing Committee (Ellis)*.

INCORPORATED ASSOCIATION OF PREPARATORY SCHOOLS AND THE ASSOCIATION OF HEADMISTRESSES OF PREPARATORY SCHOOLS (1980) *Amalgamation Proposals for the Amalgamation of the Two Associations*, May.

INCORPORATED ASSOCIATION OF PREPARATORY SCHOOLS, Bulletin.

INCORPORATED ASSOCIATION OF PREPARATORY SCHOOLS, Census Returns, 1977, 1982.

INCORPORATED ASSOCIATION OF PREPARATORY SCHOOLS, (n.d.) *Choice — A Survey of the Opinions of Parents with Sons at IAPS Schools*.

INCORPORATED ASSOCIATION OF PREPARATORY SCHOOLS (1967) *Evidence Submitted to the Public Schools Commission*, January.

INCORPORATED ASSOCIATION OF PREPARATORY SCHOOLS (1973) *The Preparatory Years*, June.

INCORPORATED ASSOCIATION OF PREPARATORY SCHOOLS (1965) *Prospect: The Purposes and Practice of Teaching in Preparatory Schools*.

INCORPORATED ASSOCIATION OF PREPARATORY SCHOOLS Red Book 1977, 1980.

INCORPORATED ASSOCIATION OF PREPARATORY SCHOOLS (1975) 'The right start in a preparatory school', Document No. 10, September.

INDEPENDENT SCHOOLS INFORMATION SERVICE (1975) 'The Independent Schools Information Service and how it operates', Document No. 1, July.

WICKHAM, C.T. (1889) *Band of Purity — Advice to Boys*, Twyford School.

WILLIAMSON, I. (1961) Memorandum on the British Association Conference 29/30 September 1961 for the third Shell/IAPS conference on science in preparatory schools, 3 October.

4   *Theses*

BAMFORD, T.W. (1953) 'Sociological aspects of education in Rugby', MA thesis, University of London.

BARON, GEORGE (1952) 'The secondary schoolmaster 1895–1914', PhD thesis, University of London.

LEINSTER-MACKAY, D.P. (1972) 'The English private school 1830–1914 with special reference to the private preparatory school', 3 vols. PhD thesis, University of Durham.

PRITCHARD, FRANK, C. (1938) 'The history and development of boys' preparatory schools in England', MA thesis, University of London.

5   *School Magazines and Prospectuses*

AMESBURY SCHOOL, Hindhead, Surrey, Prospectus, n.d.

ARDEN HOUSE, Warwickshire, Prospectus, 1900.

ARNOLD LODGE SCHOOL, *The Arnoldian*, Centenary Year Edition, 1964.

AYSGARTH SCHOOL, Magazine, December 1908, August 1910.

Bilton Record 1939–45.

Carterian, The, 1900–17.

CHEAM SCHOOL, Berkshire, Prospectus, n.d.

EATON HOUSE, Aldeburgh, Suffolk, Prospectus, 1892.

MALVERN WELLS, Prospectus, Wells House, n.d.

MALVERN WELLS, *Wells House Magazine,* July 1903–July 1914.

MILLS, CANON, W.R., *Highfield School Magazine,* Vols. 13–14, 1922–3.

MOSTYN HOUSE SCHOOL, Parkgate, Cheshire, Prospectus, 1889; 1891; 1894; 1897, 1912.

OXFORD PREPARATORY SCHOOL, *The Draconian,* April 1889–August 1910.

Scaitcliffe Notes, December 1897; April, July, December 1898; July 1899; July, December 1900; December 1901; April, July, December 1902.

ST PIRAN'S YEARBOOK, n.d.

SUMMER FIELDS, magazine, April 1898; December 1903; April 1913.

SUNNINGDALE SCHOOL, Centenary Prospectus, 1974.

Swanbourne House School Magazine, Jubilee number, June 1970.

WILLINGTON SCHOOL, Magazine, 1965–6.

6   *Unpublished Sources*

ARDEN HOUSE, Report of Examiner, LIONEL F.K. HILL, MA, July 1882.

ARNOLD, THOMAS, Letter to Lord Denbigh, MS, 21 September 1829.

CHARTERHOUSE, Entry Book, 1914–24.

DUNCHURCH — WINTON HALL, History of, Anon., m.s., n.d.

ETON SCHOOL, Register of Admissions, 1792–1832.

FONTHILL SCHOOL, Admission Register (Scholars and Commoners), 1886–1926.

HAWTREYS, Wiltshire, Centenary History, typescript, n.d.

Incorporated Association of Preparatory Schools Minute Book, Vol. 3, Dec.

1938–1948.

MALAN, EDWARD, letter to prospective parent, m.s., 27 April 1885.

PEMBERTON, EDGAR, Early History of Arden House, m.s., 1903.

PLACE, G.W., History of Mostyn House, unpublished notes, n.d.

SPENCER, D.E.W., Amesbury School 1870–1970, typescript, n.d.

STUBBINGTON HOUSE HISTORY, typescript, n.d.

TREVELYAN, C.W., Memoirs of HERBERT BULL, m.s., 1970.

TWYFORD SCHOOL, Black Book, 1855–7, m.s.

TWYFORD SCHOOL, preparatory school science, diploma course, typescript, March 1970.

TWYFORD, register of names of young gentlemen … 1815–33.

WINCHESTER COLLEGE, Headmaster's Admissions Register, m.s., 1870–95.

WILLINGTON SCHOOL, Public School Admission Book, 1891–1914.

Appendix 1: Schools Founded in the Nineteenth Century

Note: With existing schools, where two dates are given the first refers to the original foundation, the second to when the school became a preparatory school. It is very likely that *many* more schools than those listed existed in the nineteenth century.

Existing Schools

Abberley Hall (c.1880), formerly Lindisfarne
Aldro (1898)
Allen House (1871), moved to purpose-designed school in Woking from Guildford
Amesbury House (1870)
Ardenhurst School, formerly Arden House (1869)
Ardvreck (1883)
Arnold Lodge (1864), a dame school 1859–64
Ashdown House (1886)
Aysgarth School (1877)

Beaudesert, Henley-in-Arden
Bedford Modern Junior School (1884)
Belmont School (1880)
Bilton Grange (1887)
Bishop's Court (1892)
Blue Coat School (1722/1956)

Bow School, Durham (1885)
Bramcote, Scarborough (1893)
Brunswick House (1866) cf. Stoke-Brunswick

Cargilfield (1873)
Chafyn Grove (1876)
Cheam School (1645/1855)
Cheltenham College J.S. (1892)
Claremont, St Leonard's (1880)
Colet Court, now St Paul's (1881)
Cordwalles, now St Piran's (early date)
Cottesmore School, W. Brighton (1894), now near Crawley

Dorset House, formerly Totteridge (early date)
Dover College Junior School (1893)
The Downs School, Wraxall (1894)
Dragon School (OPS) (1877)
Dulwich College Preparatory School, formerly Hillsborough (1885)

Dunchurch (1868) — Winton
 (1863), (amalg. 1940)
Durston House (1886)

Eagle House (1820)
Edinburgh House (1895)
The Elms, Colwall (1614/1867)
 (subsumed Seaford Court 1980)
Elstree School (refounded 1848)

Fonthill (1820)
Forest School J.S., Essex (? 1834)

Ghyll Royd (1889)
Glenhow, Saltburn (1870)
Glengorse, Eastbourne (merged
 with Hydneye)
The Grange, Crowborough,
 (? Gressons)

The Hall, Hampstead (1889),
 formerly Belsize J.S.
Hallfield School, formerly
 Edgbaston Preparatory School
 (1879)
Hawtrey's (1869), formerly Aldin
 House
Hazelwood, Limpsfield
Heath Mount School (1817/82)
Hendon Preparatory School (1873)
Highfield School, Liphook (1880)
Hoddesdon Grange (1854), now
 Newlands (1905)
Hollingbury Court (c1850)
Holme Grange School (1883)
Homefield School (1870)
Horris Hill (1888)

Ibstock Place (1894)

King Edward Junior School, Bath
 (1898)
Kingsland Grange (1899)
Kingswood House (1899)

Lambrook (1860)

The Leas, Hoylake (1898)
Llandaff Cathedral (1880)
Lockers Park (1874)
Ludgrove, New Barnet
Lyndhurst School (1895)

The Mall School (1872)
Malvern Link (1860)
Marlborough House (1874)
Marton Hall School (1889)
Milner Court, King's School
 Canterbury Junior School
 (1879)
Monkton Combe Junior School
 (1888)
Montpelier School (1885)
Moorlands School (1898)
Mostyn House School (1852)
Mount House School, Tavistock
 (1881)
Mowden Hall, Hatfield Peverel

Nevill Holt (1868)
New College School J.S., Oxford
 (1866)
Newlands House (1897)
Newlands, Seaford, formerly
 Hoddesdon Grange (1854)
Northcliffe, Nursling (formerly at
 Bognor) (1842)
Northaw (1881)

Oakley Hall, formerly Brandon
 House (1895–1905) and
 Pelham House (1905–17)
 (1895)
Old Buckenham Hall School,
 formerly South Lodge (1862)
Orley Farm School (1850)
Orwell Park, formerly Eaton House
 (1867)

Packwood Haugh (1893)
Parkside (1879)
Pinewood, Bourton (1875)

Port Regis (1881)
Pownall Hall (1895)

Quainton Hall School (1897)

Ripley Court (1893)
Rokeby (1877)
Rose Hill School (1832)
Rossall Junior School (1861)
The Ryleys (1877)

St Andrew's School, Eastbourne
(1877)
St Aubyn's, Rottingdean
St Bede's, Eastbourne (1895)
St Dunstan's, Burnham on Sea
(1898)
St Edmund's School (1874)
St Faith's (1884)
St George's, Windsor (1892)
St John's, Beaumont, Old Windsor
(1888)
St Lawrence College J.S. (1886)
St Michael's College, Tenbury
(1856)
St Michael's Otford Court,
Sevenoaks (1872)
St Neot's (1886)
St Paul's Cathedral Choir School
(1873)
St Peter's School, Exmouth (1885)
St Piran's, formerly Cordwalles
(c.1873/1919)
St Ronan's (1883)
Sandle Manor (1880)
Sandroyd School (1898)
Scaitcliffe (?)
Sevenoaks (1881)
Shrewsbury House (1865), moved to
Surbiton (1910)
Stoke House (1866), amalg. with
Brunswick House (1865), now
Stoke-Brunswick (1965)
Stoneygate School (1844), moved in
1857 from Leamington
Stubbington House (1841)

Summer Fields (1864)
Sunningdale School (1874)

Temple Grove (1810)
Terra Nova (1897)
Thone School (Taunton Junior
School) (1876)
Twyford School (1809)

University College School J.S.,
(1891)

Wellesley House School, Ramsgate
The Wells House, Malvern (1862)
Westbourne Preparatory School
(1885)
Westbrook Hay (1892)
West Downs (1897)
West House School, Birmingham
(1895)
Willington School (1885)
Winchester House School (1875)
Windlesham House (1837)
Wolborough Hill School (1877)
Woodcote House (1851)

Yarlet Hall (1873)
Yardley Court (1898)

Defunct Schools

Abbey School, Beckenham
The Abbey School, N. Berwick
Abbott Hall, Grange-over-Sands
Acreman House, Sherborne
Aldeburgh Lodge (1870–1937)
Alfred Place, S.W.
Arnold House, Hastings
Arthur House, Margate
Ascham School, Bournemouth
Ascham St Vincent's (1888–1939)
Ashburton House

Banstead Hall, Epsom
Rev. Barron's, Stanmore

Bayford School
The Beacon, Sevenoaks
Belmont, Brighton
Bengeo School (n.d.-1936),
    subsumed by Fonthill
Belvedere, Brighton
Bigshotte, Wokingham (n.d.-1977)
Blatchington Place, Seaford
Rev. Bloxam's, Rugby
Bowden House, Harrow
Bowood House, Leamington
Boxgrove, Guildford
Bradbourne Villas, Sevenoaks
Branksome, Bournemouth
Branksome, Godalming
Brockhurst (1893-1945)
Brook House, Dover
Broughton Hall (1847-1947)
Browning's, Everdon, moved to
    Thorpe Mandeville
Dr Burney's, Greenwich

Carberry School (1889-1939)
Carr's Exmouth
Castle Mount, Dorset
Charney Hall (1882)
The Chilterns, Tring
Clevedon (Cornish's)
Cleveland House School,
    Weymouth
Cliff House School (1884-1937)
Cliff House, Southbourne-on-Sea
Clifton, P.S. (Wilkinson's)
Clive House, Southport
Coldblow, Bexley
Colet House, Rhyl
Combe Field, Godalming
Connaught House, Weymouth
Cothill House, Abingdon
The Craig, Windermere (1899)
Crowthorne Towers, Berkshire
Croxton (1890)
Dr Curtis, Sunbury

Dane Court, Pyrford (1867)

Dr Dempster's, Brighton
The Dene (1870-1941)
Dent de Lion, Westgate-on-Sea
Devonshire House, S.E.
Doon House, Westgate
Durnford, Langton Maltravers

Eastfield House, Sussex
G. Eastman's Egerton, 13 Somerset
    Street, N.
Egerton House (1834-1941)
Elmhurst, South Croydon (1879)
Elmley Castle
Rev. Elwell's, Hammersmith
The Engadine, Torquay
Dr Everard's, Brighton
Evelyns, Uxbridge
Eversley, Southwold on Sea
Eversley, Winchfield

Fairfield House, Malvern
Farnborough School (n.d.-1939)
    (amalg. with Summer Fields)
Field House
Fir Lodge
Fordington Vicarage

Gaderbridge Park (1892)
Garfield House, Devonport
Miss Gilpin's (1898-1934)
Gisborne House, Watford
The Glebe House, Hunstanton
Glyngarth School (1862-1949)
The Grange, Eastbourne
The Grange (1873)
The Grange School, Stevenage
Greenbank (1890)
Gresson's School
Greyfriars, Brighton

Hailey School, Bournemouth
    (1886-1973)
The Hall, Hastings
Hamilton House, Lansdowne
Hardenwick (1898)

Harrow View, Ealing
Hartford House, Winchfield
Haseley Manor, Tetsworth
Hazelhurst, Frant, Tunbridge Wells
Heathermere, Haywards Heath
Heddon Court, Cockfosters
Henderson's
High Croft, Godalming
Hill-Brow, Meads, Eastbourne
Hill Brow, Northumberland
Hillbrow, Warwickshire
Hill House School, Wadhurst
　(? Wace's)
Hill Morton, Rugby (1867)
Hillside, Godalming (1871–1934)
Hillside, Reigate (1896)
Hillside, Brighton
Hillside, Swindon
Hillside, West Malvern
Hinwick House, Wellingborough
Hodder (1816)
Holbein House, SW
Holmby House, Bromley
Horton Hall, Northants
Dr Hooker's Rottingdean
Dr Horne's, Chiswick
Hurst Court (1862–1961)
Hurstleigh, Tunbridge Wells
Hussey's, Folkestone
Hythe

Inholmes, Cheltenham

Kent House School, Eastbourne
Kingsgate, Winchester
The Knoll (1892–1974)

Ladycross, R.C. (1894–1977)
Laleham (1819–1934)
110–112 Lansdowne Place, Hove
Dr Lee's, Brighton
The Lickey Hills School, Barnt
　Green
The Limes, Croydon
The Limes, Shrewsbury

Lindley Lodge, Nuneaton
Liscard Castle
Little Appley, I.O.W. (1899)
Lydgate House, Bury St Edmunds

Matfield Grange (amalg. with
　Hildershaw House 1941)
May Place, Malvern Wells
Maze Hill, St Leonard's
Merton House, Beckenham
Merton House, nr Brighton
Mickleover Manor (c.1864)
Middleton School, Bognor
Mistley Place (1860–1945)
Moorland House (1860–1970)
Mt Arlington
The Mount, Northallerton
The Mount Lodge, St Leonard's

Naish House
Newells (1886)
Dr Nicholas's, Ealing
Norfolk House (1896–1947)

Oakfield (1858)
Oakshade, Reigate
Oatlands (1874–1961)
Orleton School
Orme Square, Bayswater
Orwell House, Walton-cum-
　Felixstowe
Ovingdean Hall (n.d.–1943)

Park Hill, Lyndhurst
Park House, nr Tunbridge Wells
Park House, Reading
The Park School (1893–1939)
Parkfield, Haywards Heath
Peckham House, Folkestone
Pelham House, West Folkestone
Pembroke House (1883)
Pembroke Lodge (1886–1936)
Pencarwick, Exmouth
The Philberds
Pinewood, Farnborough

Portinscale, Keswick

Quebec House, St Leonard's-on-Sea

Rawson's, Seaforth
Remenham Place, Henley-on-
    Thames
Miss Roberts', Bath
Mr Roberts', Mitcham
Romanoff House (1832)
Rottingdean School (1890–1962)
Routenburn (1892)
Dr Ruddock's, Fulham

St Andrew's School, Tenby
St Andrew's, Southborough, Kent
St Anselm's, Bakewell
St Anthony's (1898–1945)
St Asaph's, Eastbourne
St Bernard's, Woking
St Cuthbert's, Gt Malvern
St Cyprian's, Eastbourne
St George's, Ascot
St Goar (1887)
St Ives, Clifton
St Peter's, Broadstairs
St Peter's Somerset (1882)
St Vincent's, Eastbourne
St Winifred's, Kemley
Saugeen School (1873)
The School, Aysgarth
Seabrook Lodge, Folkestone
Seafield House, Broughty Ferry
Seafield Park (1886)
Seaford Court, Malvern (1875)
Shirley House School, Blackheath
South Lodge, Lowestoft (1862)
Southcliffe, Filey
Southcliffe
South Hill Park School, Bromley
Southlea, Malvern
Southwood School, Devonport
Speldhurst Lodge, Tunbridge Wells
Spondon House School, Derbyshire
Stamford House School

Stone House (1881–1970)
Stoneleigh, Folkestone
Stratheden House, Blackheath
Streete Court School (1894–1949)
Suffield Park School, Cromer
Sunnyside, Godalming
Sunnymede, Slough
Sutherland House, Folkestone
Sywell House, Rhyl

Thring's (1886)
Tonbridge Castle, Tonbridge
Tormore School (1889)
Tor School House, East Molesey
The Tower, Dovercourt, Essex
Tyttenhanger Lodge (amalg. with St
    Bede's, Eastbourne)

Underhill's, 1 Warwick Road,
    Paddington
Upland House, Epsom
Upton School (1859)

Mrs Wallace's School, Brighton
Walton Lodge (1869)
Warden House, Upper Deal
Warren Hill, Eastbourne
Waynflete, Woodcote
Wellington House (1886–1970)
The Wergs, Tettenhall
Westfields (1887–95)
Weybridge School, Weybridge
Whitnash Rectory School
The Wick (? Thring's) and Parkfield,
    Haywards Heath (1886)
Wickham's, Worthing
Willeslie, South Kensington
Windermere House, Barnes
    Common
Wixenford (1855–1934)
Woodroughs School (1869)
Wynyard House, Watford

XIV School (1885–1977)

Yockleton Hall, Shrewsbury

Appendix 2: An Imperfect Genealogy of Dorset House School

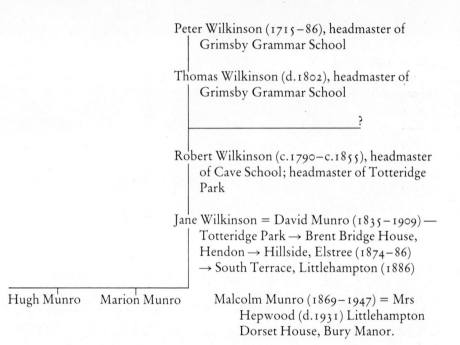

Peter Wilkinson (1715–86), headmaster of Grimsby Grammar School

Thomas Wilkinson (d.1802), headmaster of Grimsby Grammar School

?

Robert Wilkinson (c.1790–c.1855), headmaster of Cave School; headmaster of Totteridge Park

Jane Wilkinson = David Munro (1835–1909) — Totteridge Park → Brent Bridge House, Hendon → Hillside, Elstree (1874–86) → South Terrace, Littlehampton (1886)

Hugh Munro   Marion Munro

Malcolm Munro (1869–1947) = Mrs Hepwood (d.1931) Littlehampton Dorset House, Bury Manor.

Source: Compiled from extract from *The Old Dorset House Society News Letter*, September 1947.

Appendix 3: Closures and Amalgamations in the 1930s and 1940s

Many of these schools are listed in Appendix 1 or Appendix 4 as being ascertained nineteenth century or twentieth century schools.

* Amalgamations

Aldeburgh Lodge (1870–1937)
* Aldwich Grange (1905–41) with
 Hawtreys
Ascham St Vincent's (1888–1939)
Ashamptead
* Avondale with Braidlea (1941)

Banstead Hall
Barkston Preparatory
Bassets
Baswich House
* The Beacon (1941), with
 Swanbourne House
Beech Lawn
Bengeo School
Birchington House
Bowden House
Brightlands
* Brockhurst (1893–1945), with
 Broughton Hall (1847–1947)
Burstow

Cambridge House
Carberry School
Carlisle Preparatory School
Chartham Towers
Chartridge Hill (1919–41)

Cheadle House
Cherry Orchard
Cliff House School (1884–1937)
The Cliff School
* Colchester House (1945), with
 Blewett Manor
* Collington Rise School
Cordwalles (1949) Ballard-
 Cordwalles
Crowthorne Towers

The Daiglen School
Dane Court
The Dene
Devon House
Devonshire House
Didsbury Preparatory
Doon House
* Dunchurch with Winton
 (1863–1940)

Eastmans
Egerton House
Elleray
Ellerslie
Etonhurst

Appendices

Fairfield
* Farnborough, with Summer Fields
Field House
Field Place
Flete House
Fretherne House
Furzie Close

Gartin Place
Garfield
Gayton Hall
Gibbs School
Glyngarth School
The Grange, Cockfosters
The Grange, Matfield, with
        Hildersham House (1941)
The Grange, Stevenage
The Grange, Folkestone
The Grange, Hastings
The Grange, Ore
Grove Park

Haining Croft
The Hall
Harewood
Hawtrey House
Hazelhurst
Hazelwood School, Oxted
        (1927)
Heathfield
Hexham Preparatory
Hill Crest
Hillside (1871–1934)
Hilltop Court
Hollylea
Holmwood Park
Holyrood School
Horton School

Kent House
Killcott
Kingsmill
Kingwell Hall

Lake House

Laleham
Lancaster House
Lancing House
* Langley Place, with Yarlet Hall
        (1941)
Lea House
Leighton Park Junior School
Lexden House
Lingwood
* The Limes School, with Heath
        Mount School (1939)
Lime House
Lindley Lodge
Linton House
Little Abbey
Littlehampton
Lydgate House
Lynchmere
Lynfield

Magdalene Court
Meadowcroft
Mistley Place (1860–1945)
Moorhill
Moreton End School

Naish House
Norfolk House
Norman Court
Northdown Hill

Oaklands Court
The Old College
Old School House
Orleton
Orme School
Ovingdean Hall
Oxford House

Parkfield, Biggleswade
Parkfield, Haywards Heath
Pembroke Lodge (1886–1936)
Penryn School
Peterborough Lodge
Pinewood, Farnborough

334

* Pinewood School, Motcombe
    House
Port Regis, Broadstairs

Ravenscroft School (1941–6)
Rosslyn House

* St Andrew's (1933), with Hemel
    Hempstead
St Augustine's
St Christopher's
St Clare
St Cross
St Cuthbert's
* St Cyprian's, with Summer Fields
St Fillian's
St George's, Eastbourne
St George's Preparatory, Ascot
St Louis'
St Nicholas'
St Wilfrid's
Sandrock Hall
Saugeen
* Seabrook Lodge, subsumed by
    Fonthill
Seacroft School
Seafield
Seaford House
Shendish
Shortenills, with Boarzell (Little
    Abbey)
Singleton Hill
* Soberton Towers, with Arnold
    House
Somerville
Southdown School
South Kensington Preparatory
South Lodge, Enfield Chase

South Lodge, Lowestoft
Southlea
Stanmore Park
Stockton House
* Stratton Park, with Benington
    House
Streete Court
Summersdale Lodge
Sunnydown
Sydenham Hill
Tenterden Hall
Thring's
Tredennyke School
Trigge Preparatory

Upland House
Upton School

Vernon House

Warden House
Warren Hill
* Wavertree, with Stone House (1941)
Wayneflete House
The Junior School Wellington
Wellow Wood
The Wells School
Westbury Manor
West Hayes
Westwood School
Winton House
Wixenford
Woodhall
Woodlawn
Wood Norton
Woodroughs School
Wootton Court

Appendix 4: Preparatory Schools Founded in the Twentieth Century

Existing Schools

The Abbey School, Tewkesbury
The Abbey School (Junior School)
    Westgate-on-Sea (1919)
Aberdour School (1951)
Aldwickbury School (1949)
All Hallows (1943)
Alleyn Court
Ardingly College Junior School
    (1912)
Arnold House School, St John's
    Wood
Arnold Junior School, Blackpool
    (1970)
Ascham House, Newcastle upon
    Tyne (1920)
Ashbrooke House (1953)
Ashdown House
Ashfold, Handcross(1927)
    (including Abinger Hill and
    Akeley Wood)
Audley House, Chesterton
Aymestrey (1939)

Barfield (1947)
Barrow Hills School
Beachborough, Westbury (1910)
The Beacon School,
    Buckinghamshire (1934)

Becket's School
Bedales Junior School
Bedford School P.S.
Beech Hall, Macclesfield (1925)
Beech Hill
Beechwood Park, St Albans (c.1900)
    incorporating Shirley House
    and Heath Brow Schools
Beeston Hall (1948)
Belhaven Hill
Belmont School, Dorking
Belmont, The Mill Hill Junior
    (1912)
Bembridge P.S.
Betteshanger School (1933) (amalg.
    with Tormore (1980)
Bickley Park (1918)
Birchfield, Albrighton (1935)
Birkdale Preparatory School (1905)
Bishop's Stortford College P.S.
Boundary Oak School, Farnham
    (1921)
Braidlea
Brambletye
Bramcote, Gamston
Brentwood Preparatory School
    (1951)
Brightlands, Newnham-on-Severn
    (1908)
Brighton College Junior School

(1919)
Broadwater Manor House (1930)
Brockhurst, Newbury (1947)
Brocksford Hall (1945)
Bromsgrove Junior School (1951)
Brook House, Bray
Bryanston Junior School
Buckfast Abbey School (1967)
Buckland House (and Upcott
    House)
Burys Court School (1954)

Caldicott, Farnham Royal (1904)
Castle Court, Corfe Mullen (1954)
Caterham School Preparatory
    School (1934)
The Cathedral School, Exeter
The Cathedral School, Lincoln
    (1961)
The Cathedral School, Salisbury
Catteral Hall, Giggleswick
Chelmsford Hall (1920)
Cheltenham College Junior School
Chigwell Junior School
Chinthurst, Tadworth
The Chorister, Durham
Christ Church Cathedral School
    (1941)
Claires Court, Maidenhead (1960)
Claremont Fan Court
Claremont (1935)
Clayesmore Preparatory School
    (1947)
Clevedon House, Ben Rhydding
Clifton College Preparatory School
    (1927)
Colston's Preparatory School
Copthorne, (1902), offshoot of
    Twyford
Coursehorn (1949), offshoot of
    DCPS
Coventry Preparatory School,
    'Swallows' (1920)
Cranleigh Junior School (1913)
Cranmore School

Crosfields School, Reading (1940)
Cumnor House School (1931)
Cumnor House, Purley (1941)
Cundall Manor

Danes Hill, Oxshott (1954)
Davenies School, Beaconsfield
    (1941)
Dean Close Junior School (1946)
Denmead School, Middlesex
Denstone College Preparatory
    School (Smallwood Manor
    1902)
The Downs School, Colwall (1900)
Downsend (1918)
Downside, Purley (1920)
Duke of Kent School, Ewhurst
Dumpton School, Wimborne (1907)
Dunhurst, Petersfield
Durlston Court, Swanage (1903)

Earnseat School (1900–1979)
Edenhurst, Staffs (1961)
Edgarley Hall, Street
Edgeborough, Frensham (1906)
Edge Grove, Aldenham (1936)
Edinburgh House
Edington School, Bridgewater
    (1974)
Emscote (1947)
Eversfield Preparatory School,
    Solihull
Exeter Preparatory School

Farleigh House, Basingstoke
Felsted Junior School (1933)
Feltonfleet, Cobham (1903)
Fernden (1907)
Fettes Junior School
Forest Grange School
Forres (1910)
Framlingham College Junior School
    (1953)
Friars School, Ashford (1949)

Gayhurst School, Gerrards Cross
Gilling Castle (1929)
Glenhow Preparatory School
Grace Dieu Manor House (1933)
The Grange, Matfield (amalg. with
    Hildersham 1941)
Great Ballard (amalg. with
    Cordwalles 1949)
Great Houghton (1955)
Great Walstead (1925)
Grosvenor House, Harrogate (1907)
Grosvenor School, Nottingham
    (1940)

Haileybury Junior School, formerly
    Clewer Manor (1922)
Hall Grove (1957)
Handcross Park
Haslemere (1954)
Hawford Lodge (1955)
The Hawthorns, Bletchingley (1926)
Hazlegrove House
Heath Brow (amalg. with Shirley
    House 1981)
Heather Bank (1951)
Heatherdown, Ascot
Hendon P.S.
Highgate Junior School (1951)
Hilden Grange, Tonbridge
Hill House, Doncaster
The Hill School, Westerham (1950)
Hillstone, Malvern
Holme Grange School, Wokingham
    (1945)
Holmewood House, Lexden (1922)
Holmewood House, Tunbridge
    Wells (1945)
Holmwood, Formby (1900)
Holmwood Park, Wimborne, (1937)
Hordle House, Milford-on-Sea
Hurworth House School,
    Darlington (1946)
Hutton Park (1961)

Ipswich Preparatory School

Josca's Preparatory School, Frilford
    Heath (1956)

Keble, P.S., Winchmore Hill (1929)
Kent College Junior School (Vernon
    Holme)
King Edward Junior School, Bath
King's College P.S. (Taunton 1939)
King's College School, Cambridge
    (Choir School in 1878)
King's College Junior School,
    Wimbledon (1912)
King's House School (1947)
Kingsmead, Hoylake
King's School, Ely, The Junior
    School (1957)
King's School, The Junior School,
    Rochester (1916)
Kingshott (1930)
Kingswood House, Epsom

Lanesborough Preparatory
Lawrence House, St Anne's on Sea
Lockinver House School (1953)
Long Close School (1947)
Lyndhurst House School,
    Hampstead

Maidwell Hall (1911)
Malsis Preparatory School (1920)
The Manor House, Ashby-de-la
    Zouche
Marsh Court (1953)
Milbourne Lodge (1934)
Millfield J.S. (1945)
Moffats School, Bewdley, (1941)
Monkton Combe J.S.
Moor Allerton (1914)
Moor Park School R.C. (1964)
Moreton Hall
Moulsford (1966)
Mowden School, Hove.

The New Beacon, Sevenoaks (1943)
Newcastle upon Tyne P.S (1920)

Newlands, Newcastle upon Tyne
(c.1900)
Normansal, Seaford (1929)
Northbourne Park (Betteshanger
and Tormore, 1980)
Northwood Preparatory ('Terry's')
(1910)
Nottingham High School P.S. (1905)
Nower Lodge School (1962),
successor to Charlton House
School 1922–39.

Oakham Junior House
Oakmount School, Southampton
(1908)
Oakwood School, Chichester (1912)
The Old Malthouse, Swanage (1906)
The Old Hall, Wellington
Oratory Preparatory School,
Reading R.C. (1925)
Oratory, Bournemouth (1913)

Papplewick (1947)
The Park School, Bath (1957)
Pennthorpe, Rudgewick (1939)
Perrott Hill (1946)
The Pilgrim's School (1934)
Plymouth College J.S. (1951)
Port Regis, Bryanston Junior School
(1945)
Portsmouth Lower School
Prebendal School, Chichester
(1497/1931)
Prestfelde (1929) (on Woodard
Foundation since 1949)
Prior's Court (Junior School for
Kingswood)
Prior Park School (? 1946)
The Priory School, Banstead, (1954)
Pyrland Hall (1954)

Ramillies Hall (1936)
Ranby House (Worksop
Preparatory School) (1948)

Ravenswood School, Tiverton
(1922)
Red House (1902), formerly
Carteret House
Reigate St Mary's
Repton P.S. (1940)
Rose Hill School,
Wotton-under-Edge
Rydal Preparatory School
Ryde Junior School

St Andrew's, Horsell (1951)
St Andrew's, Pangbourne (1936)
St Anthony's, Hampstead (1954)
St Aubyn's School, Tiverton (1928)
St Aubyn's School, Woodford
Green (c.1941)
St Bede's Wolseley Bridge, Staffs
(1945)
St Chad's Cathedral School (1943)
St Crispin's, Leics. (1945)
St David's Preparatory,
Huddersfield (1947)
St Edmund's Junior School
St Edward's, Reading (1953)
St Erbyn's School, Penzance
St George's Preparatory School,
Jersey (1924)
St Hugh's Faringdon (1906)
St Hugh's, Woodall Spa (1925)
St John's College School,
Cambridge (refounded 1955;
Byron House School amalg.
with it in 1973)
St John's-on-the-Hill, Chepstow
St John's School, Northwood (1920)
St John's Preparatory School, Stoke
on Trent
St John's, Beaumont, Old Windsor
(Preparatory for Stonyhurst)
St John's, Sidmouth
St Martin's, Nawton R.C. (1946)
St Martin's, Northwood
St Mary's Hall, Stonyhurst (R.C.)
Seaford

St Michael's, Tawstock Court,
    Barnstaple (1920)
St Peter's, Seaford
St Petroc's (1912)
St Pius X Preparatory, Preston
St Richard's, Bredenbury R.C.
St Wilfrid's, Seaford
Scarborough College Preparatory
    School
Sevenoaks Preparatory (1921)
Sherborne Preparatory School
Skippers Hill Manor Preparatory
    (1945)
Solefield Preparatory (1949)
Sompting Abbots, Lancing
Spratton Hall (1951)
Stamford Junior School
Stancliffe Hall
The Stroud School, Romsey (1926)
Sussex House (1952)
Sutherland House, now Woodcote
    (1905–1931)
Swanbourne House (1920) (amalg.
    with The Beacon)

Taunton Junior School (1951)
Taverham Hall (? 1920)
Terrington Hall (1936)
Thorpe House, Gerrards Cross
    (? 1939)
Tockington Manor (1947)
Tonstall School (1910)
Tower House, East Sheen (1931)
Town Close House Preparatory
    (1932)
Treliske School (1934)
Tormore School (1933) (amalg.
    with Betteshanger 1980 Cf.
    Northbourne Park)

Upcott House (merged with
    Buckland House)

Victoria College Preparatory (1922)
Vinehall, Sussex (1938)

Walhampton, Lymington (1948)
Wallop (1900)
Warminster School Junior School
Waterside, Bishops Stortford (1921)
Wellingborough J.S. (1941)
Wellington Junior School (1943)
Wells Cathedral Junior School (St
    Andrew's) (1948)
Westbourne House, Chichester
    (1949)
Westerleigh (1907)
West Hill Park (1920)
Westminster Abbey Choir School
    (1947)
Westminster Cathedral Choir
    School (1901)
Westminster Under School (1943)
Widford Lodge, Chelmsford (1935)
Winchester House, Sevenoaks
    (1938)
Winterfold House, Chaddesley
    Corbett
Witham Hall, Lincs. (1959)
Woburn Hill, Weybridge (1955)
Woodleigh School, Malton
Wootonley House (1952)
Wycliffe College Junior (1928)

Yateley Manor, Camberley (1947)
York House, Herts (1910)
York Minster Song School (1903—
    refounded)

Defunct Schools

Abinger Hill (1934)
Akeley Wood (1947)
Alderwasley Hall, Matlock (closed
    1974)
The American School (1953)
Ascham, Eastbourne (closed 1977)
Ashampstead
Avisford (closed in 1973)

Avondale, Bristol

Banstead Hall
Barnes Lodge (1954)
Bassets
Beachborough Park
Beaconsfield (1947)
The Beacon School, Crowborough
The Beacon School, Teignmouth
Beaufort Lodge
Beaumont House (1905–70)
Beech Lawn
Belmont School, Clayton, Wickham
    (1902)
Belmont House School, Blackheath
    (1939)
Bickley Hall
Birchfield, Tettenhall (1943)
Boarzell (1916) (amalg. with
    Shortenills; closed in 1974)
Braeside, West Kirby
Bramcote Hall (1939)
Bramdean
Bramshott Chase (1949)
Brandon House, Cheltenham
Branksome-Hilders (1945)
Brightland, Dulwich Common
Broadlands (1945)
Burstow, Horley

Caldicott School, Hitchin
Cambridge House, Margate
Canterbury House (1954)
Carlisle Preparatory School
Carn Brea (closed in 1973)
Charney Hall (closed in 1972)
Chartham Towers (1936)
Chartridge Hill (1910)
Cheadle House
Chelsea Preparatory School
Cherry Orchard, Old Charlton
Chesterton
Cleeve Court, Lower Wick,
    Worcester
The Cliff School, Shanklin, I.O.W.

Cliftonville School (1949)
35 Clivedon Place, Eaton Square,
    London
Colchester House, Clifton
Collington Rise School
Connaught House, Weymouth
Corchester (closed in 1975)
Cressbrook School (closed in 1976)

The Daiglen School, Essex (1939)
Dane Court (1911)
Desmoor School (1947)
Devon House, W11
Didsbury Preparatory School (1922)
Dolphin School (1947)

Earleywood
Eastacre (1939–70)
Eastbourne College Preparatory
    School (1947)
Eastmans, Burnham-on-Sea (1941)
Eaton House School, SW1 (1937)
Eddington House, Herne Bay
    (1941)
Elleray, Wallasey
Ellerslie, Barnstaple
Ellingham Hall Preparatory School
Emsworth House
Etonhurst, Weston-super-Mare

Falconbury
Fan Court (1936)
Feltonfleet, Folkestone
Field House, Birmingham
Field Place, Hampshire
Flete House, Westgate-on-Sea
Forton House (1954)
Fretherne House, Welwyn Garden
    City
Frilsham House (1949)
Furzedown (1949)
Furzie Close, Barton-on-Sea (1914)

Garfield, Langton Maltravers
Garth Place, Bexhill-on-Sea

The Gate House School, Kingston Hill (1903)
Gayton Hall, Ross (1943)
Gibbs School, SW1 (1939)
Gorse Cliffe, Bournemouth (1943)
Gove Court
The Grange, Crowborough
Greenways School
Grenham House (known as Bay School 1901–11)
Gresham's Junior School
Grove Park, NW9
Gunnersbury, Chiswick

Haining Croft, Hexham (1939)
Hampton House
The Hall, Sydenham
The Hall, Cheshurst
Harcourt (1954)
Harewood (closed in 1970)
Hawtrey House, Ruislip (1936)
Heather Bank (1951)
Heathfield, nr Halifax (1954)
Heathfield, Kent (1914)
Heathfield, Rishworth, Staffs (closed in 1974)
Hildersham House
Hillcrest
Hill Crest, Swanage
Hill Crest, Frinton-on-Sea
Hill Place, Stow-on-the-Wold (1945)
Hill Place School, Maidstone (1941–1973)
Hilltop Court, Seaford
Hoe Place
Holm Leigh
Holyrood, Bognor
Huyton Hill (1926)
Hydneye House

Kent House
Kestrel's (1951)
Killcott, Godalming
King Henry VIII Junior School

Kingsfield School (1939–70)
King's Mead, Seaford
Kingsmill, (R.C.) Cromer
Kingwell Hall, Bath

Lake House, Bexhill-on-Sea
Lancaster House, W3 (1936)
Lancing House, Lowestoft
Langley Junior School
Langley Place, St Leonard's
The Lawn School, St Austell (1941)
Lea House School (1945)
Leeson (1949)
Leighton Park Junior School (1940)
Lexden House, Eastbourne (1901)
Lime House School (1937)
Lindfield
Lingwood, Cobham (1933)
Linton House, W11, Lingwood, Cobham (1933)
Lisvane School (1941)
Little Abbey (closed in 1951)
Little Abbey, Bucks (1947)
Little Abbey, Liss, Hants. (closed in 1974)
Little Hampden Manor
Littlehampton Preparatory School (1947)
Lydgate, Hunstanton
Lympne Place, Hythe (closed 1975)
Lynchmere, Eastbourne
Lynfield, Hunstanton (1939)

Magdalene Court, Broadstairs
Manor House School, Horsham (closed in 1970)
Mattersey Hall (1951)
Meadowcroft, Windermere
Melbreck (closed in 1973)
Merrion House School, nr Battle (1951)
Mickleover Manor (1949)
Millmead, Shrewsbury
Moorhill, Leek
Moorland House (1970)

Moreton End School, Harpenden
(1941)
Mount Pleasant (1907)

New Place (1957)
Norfolk House (1943)
Norman Court, Herts
Normandale Preparatory
Northcliffe House (1931)
Northfield House (1941)
Norwood, Exeter (closed in 1975)

Oaklands Court, Broadstairs
Oakwood House, Winchester
(1954)
The Old College, Windermere
The Old Ride, Branksome Park
Old School House, Holt
Oxford House, St Anne's-on-Sea

Parkfield, Sefton Park (1927)
Parkfield, Bedford
Park House, Devon
Park School, Henleaze
Peterborough Lodge, NW2
Pilgrims, Westerham (1931)
Pinewood, nr Shrivenham (1947)
Pinewood, Melchet Court, Romsey
(1943)
Pinewood, Motcombe House,
Dorset (1939)
Prestonville School (1936)
Purton Stoke School (1942)

Ravenscroft, Bath (1931)
Rickerby House, Carlisle (1939)
Rosslyn House, Felixstowe
Royal Masonic Junior (1954–70)
Rushmoor
Rutland House, Hillingdon (closed
1970)

St Andrew's Church Hill House
(1937)
St Anselm's, Croydon (1902)

St Aubyn's, Rottingdean
St Augustine's, Eastbourne
St Bede's, Hornsea, Yorks
St Benet's School, (1945)
St Chad's Prestatyn, Wales (closed
in 1975)
St Christopher's School,
Kingswood, Surrey
St Christopher's, Nr Bath
St Clare, Walmer
St Cross, Surrey
St Dunstan's School, West Worthing
St Edmund's Ipswich (closed 1975)
St Edmund's House (1941)
St Edward's, Broadstairs
St Felix (1930)
St Fillans, Cheshire (1912)
St George's, Broadstairs
St George's, Folkestone
St Joseph's Preparatory, R.C.,
Ipswich (1937)
St Louis, Banbury, (1945)
St Martin's, Walton-on-Thames
(closed in 1974)
St Michael's (1939)
St Michael's, East Horsley (1954)
St Nicholas, Bassett, Southampton
(1941)
St Nicholas, Yeovil
St Nicholas, Ridley Hall (1949)
St Ninian School (1953)
St Olave's, Ripon
St Peter's Court, Sussex
St Peter's Court, Broadstairs
St Peter's, Sheringham
St Philip's, SW7, R.C. (1949)
St Wilfrid's, Hawkhurst

The Sanctuary (1951)
Sandrock Hall, Hastings
Seabrook Lodge, Hythe
Seacroft, Skegness
Seaford Court
Seascale School
Selwyn House (1916–77)

Shardlow Hall (1911)
Sharrow Preparatory (1937)
Shendish, Herts. (1936)
Shortenills, Bucks.
Singleton Hill School, Manchester
(1924)
Soberton Towers, Hants
Somerville, Cheshire
The Southbourne Preparatory
Southdown School, Seaford
Southey Hall, Leatherhead
South Kensington Preparatory
School, SW7
South Lodge Preparatory School,
Herts (1937)
South Lodge, Middlesex
Springfield Park
Spyway (closed in 1976)
Staddles, Andover (closed in 1970)
Stanley House, Edgbaston
Stirling Court
Stockton House, Fleet (1935)
Stouts Hill (1939)
Stratton Park, Bletchley
Summersdale Lodge, Chichester
Sunninghill, Dorchester (1939)
Sunnydown, Hogs Back
Sutton Place (1951)
Sydenham Hill School

Tenterden Hall, Hendon

Tredennyke, Worcs.
'Trigge', Wimborne

Upland House, Crawley

Vanbrugh Castle School
Vernon House, NW6

Wadham House
Wagner's (1903)
Wavertree Horley
The Welkin (1949)
Wellbury Park
The Wells Court (1949)
Westbury House, Petersfield (1907)
Westbury Manor, Northants (1936)
West Hayes, Winchester
Westwood School, Bath (1933)
Whilton Lodge, Daventry (1951)
Whitchurch House, Oxford (1947)
Winchester House, Meads,
Eastbourne
Winchester Lodge, Torquay
Winterdyne, Southport
Wisborough Lodge (1947)
Wood Norton, nr Evesham
Woolpit, Cranleigh (1951)
Worth Preparatory (1947)
Wotton Court, Kent (1952)
Wychwood, Bournemouth (1931)
Wynyard Ascot (1951)

Appendix 5: Chairmen of IAPS (Taken from IAPS 'Red Book')

1892	A.S. Tabor, Cheam (Inaugural Meeting)
1892	Rev. J.H. Edgar, Temple Grove, East Sheen
1893	E.D. Mansfield, Lambrook
1894	Rev. C. Darnell, Cargilfield, Edinburgh
1895	E.D. Mansfield, Lambrook
1896	Rev. J.H. Wilkinson, Wayneflete, Woodcote, Oxon
1897	E.P. Arnold, Wixenford, Wokingham
1898	G. Gidley Robinson, Hillside, Godalming
1899	Rev. H. Bull, Wellington House, Westgate-on-Sea
1900	F. Ritchie, The Beacon, Sevenoaks
1901	F. Hollins, The Grange, Eastbourne
1902	Rev. C. Black, The Elms, Colwall, Malvern
1903	E.D. Mansfield, Lambrook
1904	Rev. C.T. Wickham, Twyford School, Winchester
1905	H. Strahan, Seabrook Lodge, Hythe
1906	Rev. Vernon Royle, Stanmore Park, Middlesex
1907	E.H. Parry, Stoke House, Stoke Poges
1908	C.C. Lynam, The Dragon School, Oxford
1909	J.S. Norman, The New Beacon, Sevenoaks
1910	Rev. H. Bull, Wellington House, Westgate-on-Sea
1911	Rev. Vernon Royle, Stanmore Park, Middlesex
1912	H. Wilkinson, 10 Orme Square, London, W.
1913	P. Christopherson, Lockers Park, Hemel Hempstead
1914	J.S. Norman, The New Beacon, Sevenoaks
1915	H.C. King, The Downs School, Bristol
1916	A.J. Richardson, St Peter's Court, Broadstairs
1917	Rev. E.L. Browne, St Andrew's Eastbourne
1918	H.F. Stallard, Heddon Court, Cockfosters
1919	J.S. Norman, The New Beacon, Sevenoaks
1920	E.G.G. North, The School, Farnborough
1921	C.C. Lynam, The Dragon School, Oxford

1922	Rev. E.L. Browne, St Andrew's, Eastbourne
1923	Rev. E.L. Browne, St Andrew's, Eastbourne
1924	S.S. Harris, St Ronan's Worthing
1925	B. Rendall, Copthorne School, Sussex
1926	A.E. Lynam, The Dragon School, Oxford
1927	T.W. Holme, Lockers Park, Hemel Hempstead
1928	E.G.H. North, The School, Farnborough
1929	A.S. Grant, Hillside, Reigate
1930	O.H. Wagner, 90 Queen's Gate, London
1931	R.G. Thornton, Hill Brow, Meads, Eastbourne
1932	J.L. Stow, Horris Hill, Newbury
1933	Rev. P.C. Underhill, Wellington House, Westgate
1934	J.E. Maitland, Banstead Hall, Banstead, Surrey
1935	R.G. Thornton, Hill Brow, Meads, Eastbourne
1936	F.E. Chappell, Beachborough, Newington, Kent
1937	G. Ashton, Abberley Hall, Worcester
1938	W.P. Singleton, The Elms, Colwall, Malvern
1939	H.F. Pooley, Dane Court, Pyrford
1940	P. Knox-Shaw, St Peter's, Seaford.
1941	J.H.R. Lynam, The Dragon School, Oxford
1942	J.H.R. Lynam, The Dragon School, Oxford
1943	P. Knox-Shaw, St Peter's, Seaford
1944	O.E.P. Wyatt, Maidwell Hall, Northampton
1945	T.C. Elliott, Fan Court, Longcross, Chertsey
1946	G. Ashton, Abberley Hall, Worcester
1947	J.W. Woodroffe, St Martin's Northwood
1948	O.E.P. Wyatt, Maidwell Hall, Northampton
1949	K.B. Tindall, West Downs, Winchester
1950	J. Boyce, Wellesley House, Broadstairs
1951	J. Boyce, Wellesley House, Broadstairs
1952	C.B. Mitchell, Edgeborough, Frensham
1953	R.A. Harrison, Marlborough House, Hawkhurst
1954	L.H.A. Hankey, Clifton College Preparatory School
1955	C.B. Mitchell, Edgeborough, Frensham
1956	R.R. Killick, Clifton Hall, Newbridge, Midlothian
1957	R.J.S. Curtis, Hurst Court, Ore, Hastings
1958	L.H.A. Hankey, Clifton College Preparatory School
1959	H.L.G. Collis, St Paul's Junior School, Colet Court, London, W6
1960	H.A.C. Evans, Swanbourne House, Bletchley, Bucks.
1961	G.M. Singleton, The Elms, Colwall, Malvern, Worcs.
1962	L.H.A. Hankey, Clifton College Preparatory School
1963	Rev. R.G. Wickham, Twyford School, Winchester
1964	Rev. R.G. Wickham, Twyford School, Winchester
1965	J.H. Dodd, Downside School, Purley
1966	J.W. Hornby, Bramcote, Scarborough

1967   J.R.G. Higgs, Brentwood Preparatory School
1968   J.H. Dodd, Downside School, Purley
1969   W.L.V. Caldwell, Belhaven Hill, Dunbar
1970   R.A. Cooper, The Hall School, Hampstead
1971   J.W. Hornby, Clifton College Preparatory School
1972   J.D. Sewell, Old Buckenham Hall School, Ipswich
1973   A.H. Mould, St John's College School, Cambridge
1974   W.P.C. Davies, Cheltenham College Junior School
1975   J.R.G. Higgs, Beechwood Park School
1976   M. Timpson, Bedford Lower School
1977   H.E.P. Woodcock, Dulwich College Preparatory School, London
1978   J.W. Hornby, Clifton College Preparatory School
1979   R.A. Stillman, Crosfields
1980   T.H.B. Bowles, Bramcote
1981   G.H. Mathewson, Clifton Hall
1982   H.E.P. Woodcock, Dulwich College Preparatory School, London
1983   A.H. Mould, St John's College School, Cambridge
1984   J.D. Clark, Malsis School, Cross Hills

Appendix 6:   Secretaries of IAPS (Taken from IAPS 'Red Book')

1895–1898	Rev. H. Bull
1898–1901	C.C. Cotterill
1901–1917	F. Ritchie
1917–1918	J. Ritchie
1919–1937	H.C. King
1937–1957	Rev. P.C. Underhill
1958–1963	L.P. Dealtry
1963–1967	R.A. Harrison
1968–1976	L.H.A. Hankey, OBE
1976–1982	J.H. Dodd
1982–1983	J.W. Hornby
1983–1984	J.H. Dodd (acting Secretary)
1984–	M. Coates

Appendix 7: Presidents and Vice-Presidents of IAPS (Taken from IAPS 'Red Book')

Presidents

1920–1925	The Rt Hon. J.F.P. Rawlinson, KC
1926–1943	Sir A.A. Somerville
1944–1954	The Rt Hon. The Lord Brooke of Cumnor
1955–1957	Angus Maude, Esq., MP
1958–1965	Sir Wilfred Anson, MBE, MC
1965–1970	The Rt Hon. The Lord Pearson, CBE
1970–1974	The Rt Hon. The Lord Boyle of Handsworth
1974–1979	The Rt Hon. John Davies, MBE, MP
1980–	The Rt Hon. Peter Brooke, MP

Vice-Presidents

1961–1963	Rev. P.C. Underhill, OBE
1963	L.P. Dealtry
1967–	R.J.S. Curtis, OBE
1969–1970	P. Knox-Shaw
1971–1980	R.A. Harrison
1976–	Rev. R.G. Wickham
1976–	L.H.A. Hankey, OBE
1982–	J.H. Dodd

Appendix 8: Editors of the *PSR*

1895–1900	C.C. Lynam
1901–1906	Frank Ritchie
1906–1923	G. Gidley Robinson
1923–1929	Boswell King
1929–1937	Bernard Rendall
1937–1940	Lord Wrenbury
1940–1945	[No publication]
1945–1946	Robert Allan
1946	Mr Wallace
1946–1947	Robert Allan
1947–1956	L.P. Dealtry
1956–1970	Pat Knox-Shaw
1971–present	W.L.V. Caldwell

Appendix 9: Cheltenham College Scholarship Examination

May, 1879.

Seniors

1. Give the meaning of the following names: Nottingham, Washington, Brockhurst, Wednesbury, Thoresby, Exeter, Winchester, Sheffield, Cambridge.

2. Give a list of Shakspeare's chief dramatic works; and analyse the plot of one tragedy and one comedy.

3. What is the connection of the words *guard* and *ward*?

4. Who were the chief writers of the reign of Queen Anne? Mention the most celebrated of their works.

5. State what you know of Doctor Johnson; criticise his style, and estimate his position in English Literature.

6. Name the authors of the following works: Essay on Man, Hudibras, Rasselas, The New Timon, She Stoops to Conquer, Every Man in his Humour, Atalanta in Calydon. In Memoriam, Christmas Eve, Novum Organon, Tom Jones.

7. Give some account of the Canterbury Tales.

8. 'Call him up who left half told the story of Cambuscan bold.' Explain this allusion.

Analyse the metre in which that story is told.

Index

Tizard, Sir Henry, 94, 101
Tockington Manor, 341
Tomlinson, L., 218
Tomson, R.S., 8
Tonbridge, 6–7, 111, 112, 113, 115, 184,
  229, 261
Tonbridge Castle, 330
Tonstall School, 235, 341
Tooting, 57
Tor School House, 330
Tormore School, 99, 330, 341
Tory Government
  see Conservative Government
Totteridge Park, 28, 78, 88, 106, 325, 331
  see also Dorset House
Totteridge Park, 331
Tower, The, 330
Tower House, 245, 341
Towle, E., 87
Town Close House, 245, 341
Toynbee, A., 162
Toynbee, P., 162
trade unions, 1, 216
Trafalgar (battle of), 64
Tredennyke School, 335, 345
Treliske, 245, 341
Trench, R.C., 46
Trevelyan, C., 54, 141
Trevelyan, C.W., 204
Trevelyan, G.M., 51, 141
Trevelyan, P.C.W., 179
Trevelyan, R., 141
Trevor, G., 164
Trevor, Miss G., 101
Trevor, M., 164
Trevor-Roper, H., 164
Trigge Preparatory School, 335, 345
Trollope, A., 21, 39, 49, 97
Tropp, A., 219
Trott, Rev. T., 86
Truro, 245
Tuck, Rev. J., 80
Tudhoe Academy, 12
Tudor House, 118
Tudor period, 12
Tunbridge Wells, 38, 56, 106, 113
Turner, Major Gen. Sir Alfred E., 39, 49
Twickenham, 35, 58, 114, 139, 268
Twyford, 4, 11–12, 14, 19, 20, 23, 24–5,
  30–1, 32, 40–8, 57, 59, 106, 109, 113,
  116, 123–4, 129, 130, 135, 136, 147, 177,
  178, 183, 185, 192, 193, 281, 283, 285,
  287, 289, 290, 295, 297, 327
Twyford Vicarage, 30

Tyler, Miss, 94
typhoid, 125
Tyrwhitt-Wilson, Sir Gerald, 156, 193
Tyttenhanger Lodge School, 97, 330
  see also St Bede's

Uckfield, 135, 265
Underhill, Rev. P.C., 244, 256, 257, 258,
  269, 348, 351, 353
Underhill's, 330
Union of Sovier Socialist Republics,
  309–10
unions
  see teachers' unions; trade unions
United Kingdom, *passim*
United Nations Covenant on Economic,
  Social and Cultural Rights, 301–2
United States of America, 265, 274, 308,
  309, 311
universities, 2, 3, 13, 14, 15, 16, 18, 40, 42,
  74, 76, 88, 146–9, 230, 308
University Appointments Board, 286
University College School, 112, 168, 169
University College School Junior School,
  327
Upcott, Dr, 186, 188
Upcott House, 297, 341
Upland House, 330, 335, 345
Upper Deal, 99
Uppingham School, 1, 6, 98, 112, 114, 115,
  134, 154, 188, 200, 229, 288
Upton School, 330, 335
Upward, E., 216
Upward, J.M., 216
Usborne, R., 163, 220, 274
ushers, 59, 106, 133

Vachell, H.A., 32
Vaganova (Kirov) Ballet School, 310
Value Added Tax (VAT), 296–8
Van Straubenzee, W., 303
Vanbrugh Castle School, 345
Vanquisher (*HMS*), 268
Vassar-Smith family, 108
Vaughan, C.J., 33, 60, 153
Vecqueray, J.W.J., 118, 172
Verney, R.G., 200, 205
Vernon House, 335, 345
Verulam, Lord, 150
Vesey Hon. I., 80
Vezey, P.H., 230, 279
Vickers, R., 108, 117, 198
Victoria, Queen, 37, 46, 65, 71, 78, 135,
  143, 145, 150, 161

Wilson, Rev. H.J., 82
Wilson, Canon J.M., 161
Wilson, Rev. J.W., 136, 160
Wilson, Mrs K.T., 253
Wimbledon, 43, 96, 114, 135, 158
Winchester, 65, 80, 93, 107, 124, 139, 161, 171, 201, 223
Winchester College, 31, 58
Winchester House School, 245, 327, 341, 345
Winchester Lodge, 345
Winchester School, xiv, 5, 46, 89, 105, 109, 110, 112, 113, 114, 115, 116, 118, 139, 144, 181, 186, 264, 269, 287, 327
Windermere House, 68, 171, 330
Windlesham, 25–6
Windlesham House, 23, 29–30, 32, 34, 40–8, 56, 59, 62, 100, 106, 109, 116, 138–9, 140–1, 161, 177, 199, 200, 251, 259, 265, 294, 303, 304, 327
Windsor, 87, 145, 153
Windsor Barracks, 197
'Wings for Victory Week', 268
Winnie the Pooh, 157
Winterdyne, 345
Winterfold House, 341
Winnington-Ingram, A.F., 110
Winton, 325, 333
    see also Dunchurch
Winton, Rev. A.J. de, 177, 198
Winton House School, 57–8, 200, 267, 335
Wirral, 106, 122
Wisborough Lodge, 345
Wiseman, J., 301
    see also Peacock and Wiseman
Witham Hall, 341
Wixenford School, 141, 154, 164, 178, 208, 246, 330, 335
Woburn Hill, 341
Woburn Sands, 114, 127, 297
Wodehouse, P.G., 129
Woking, 245
Wokingham, 144, 154, 297
Wolborough Hill School, 114, 196, 265, 327
Wolf, Mr, 140
Wolfenden, J.F., 256
women
    and AHPS, 251–3, 255
    and preparatory schools, xv, 15, 25, 91–101, 140–1, 158, 233, 266, 279
    as principals of schools, 251–3, 255
    status of, 134

see also dame schools
Wood, Mr, 28
Wood, Rev. J., 87
Wood, M. and A., 162
Wood Norton, 335, 345
Woodard, N., 6
Woodard Schools, 6, 164
Woodcock, H.E.P., 258, 295, 349
Woodcote, 178
Woodcote House School, 106–7, 265, 327
Woodcote School, 23–4, 25–6
Woodhall, 335
Woodhall Spa, 234, 265, 277, 278
Woodhouse, Rev. F., 82
Woodlawn, 335
Woodleigh School, 341
Woodroffe, J.W., 348
Woodroughs School, 330, 335
Woolf, L., 162
Woolhampton, 118, 263
Woolpit, 345
Woolwich, 66
Wooton, P., 50
Wootonley House, 341
Wootton Court, 335
Worcester, 94
Worcester College, 209
Worcestershire
    dame schools in, 92
    principals in, 84–6
Wordsworth, C., 95
Wordsworth, J., 95
Wordsworth, W., 88
World War, First, 64, 65, 69, 175, 176, 199, 208, 216, 228, 233–4, 245, 248, 261, 281
World War, Second, 65, 198, 209, 213, 230, 246, 257–9, 261–75, 277, 294, 304
Worshipful Company of Grocers, 25, 31
Worsley, Rev., 34
Worsley, T.C., 234, 248
Worth Preparatory, 345
Worthing, 176, 193, 245
Worthington, Mrs, 57
Wotton Court, 345
Wragg, Miss, 98
Wratislaw, W.F., 6, 7, 34
Wrenbury, Lord, 255, 355
Wright, A.R.D., 289
Wright, T., 49
Wyatt, O.E.P., 171, 256, 257, 258, 269, 271, 272, 303, 348, 345
Wycliffe College Junior School, 234, 341